Virtual Selves, Real Persons

How do we know and understand who we really are as human beings? The concept of 'the self' is central to many strands of psychology and philosophy. This book tackles the problem of how to define persons and selves and discusses the ways in which different disciplines, such as biology, sociology and philosophy, have dealt with this topic. Richard S. Hallam examines the notion that the idea of the self as some sort of entity is a human construction and, in effect, a virtual reality. At the same time, this virtual self is intimately related to the reality of ourselves as biological organisms. Aiming to integrate a constructionist understanding of self with the universalising assumptions that are needed in natural science approaches, this text is unique in its attempt to create a dialogue across academic disciplines, while retaining a consistent perspective on the problem of relating nature to culture.

Richard S. Hallam is Visiting Professor of Psychology at the University of Greenwich. His career has combined teaching, research and professional practice in clinical psychology, and he is the author of *Counselling for Anxiety Problems* (1992) and *Anxiety: Psychological Perspectives on Panic and Agoraphobia* (1985).

Virtual Selves, Real Persons

A Dialogue across Disciplines

Richard S. Hallam

CAMBRIDGE
UNIVERSITY PRESS

CAMBRIDGE UNIVERSITY PRESS
Cambridge, New York, Melbourne, Madrid, Cape Town, Singapore, São Paulo, Delhi

Cambridge University Press
The Edinburgh Building, Cambridge CB2 8RU, UK

Published in the United States of America by Cambridge University Press, New York

www.cambridge.org
Information on this title: www.cambridge.org/9780521509893

First published 2009

Printed in the United Kingdom at the University Press, Cambridge

A catalogue record for this publication is available from the British Library

Library of Congress Cataloguing in Publication data
Hallam, Richard S.
    Virtual selves, real persons : a dialogue across disciplines / Richard S. Hallam.
        p.   cm.
    ISBN 978-0-521-50989-3 (hardback)   1. Self.   I. Title.
    [DNLM: 1. Self Concept.   2. Self Psychology. BF 697 H182v 2009]
    BF697.H2347 2009
    126–dc22
                                                              2009009883

ISBN 978-0-521-50989-3 hardback

Contents

Acknowledgements

I am grateful to everyone who commented, or promised to comment, on sections of the manuscript including Mike Bender, Sophie Hallam, Chris Lee and Clare Penney. A special thanks to Mary Boyle, Roger Marsden, Kieron O'Connor and Graham Richards who all helped me to raise my game. Finally, I would like to pay tribute to Ted Sarbin who was an inspiration to so many.

Part I

A constructionist framework for person and self

For I tried to expose the falsity or uncertainty of the propositions I was examining by clear and certain arguments [...] and I never encountered any proposition so doubtful that I could not draw from it some quite certain conclusion, if only the conclusion that it contained nothing certain.

Réne Descartes, *The Philosophical Writings of Descartes*
(Cambridge University Press 1985)

1   The main themes: virtual selves, mind–body dualism and natural science

There is nothing more intriguing than one's own 'self'. Yet there is also nothing more opaque than the process of reflecting on self. It is a familiar mental activity, sometimes involving great effort. But whether this effort produces results is uncertain. Long deliberation may be followed by an impulse to act that flies in the face of one's own good counsel. Despite doubts of this nature, most people who reflect on the matter have a strong desire to be in charge of themselves, however difficult the task and uncertain the outcome. Self, in western society, has become a central idea. It is the focus of an endless number of popular and academic books. Since the seventeenth century, it has become attached as a prefix to an increasing number of words, such as self-esteem. In sum, self is central to our beliefs, and in this important area of our life we do not want to be led – by authority, dogma, or false prophets. It is a journey we take alone whether or not we find ourselves surrendering control to others. It is widely supposed that we have to find ourselves.

The theme running through this book is that our common-sense idea of self as some sort of entity is a human construction, in effect, a virtual reality. This perspective is by no means original. Berrios and Marková (2003: 9) interpret St Augustine (354–430) as meaning by self 'a metaphorical or virtual space within which theological models of responsibility, guilt and sin could be played out'. Over the centuries, however, belief in the existence of the self as an entity has become firmly entrenched, and it is an integral part of our view of the cosmos. The point of stressing that self is a human construction is to suggest that, as an idea, it is not inevitable. I will view it as a feature of the historical and cultural circumstances in which we live. As such, it is closely related to concepts of the person. However, I will also be arguing for the biological reality of persons and the need to reconcile scientific with folk perspectives.

This topic is such a slippery one conceptually that I will try to be clear and consistent in my use of terms. I will refer to our intimate knowledge of self as the 'sense-of-self'. This is what we feel and know from the inside, so to speak, as expressed through a common language. It was captured pretty well by William James (1842–1910) as the sum total of what a person identifies with or calls 'mine'. In other words, it is anything felt to be a part of one's self, whether 'in the mind' or extended into the environment, like one's home or one's job. A sense-of-self pre-supposes a power to choose, a continuity of memory, an identification by age and sex, etc.

The sense-of-self becomes slippery as soon as we ask what it is self refers to, and, if it is supposed to be an entity, how that entity relates to biological processes or social and linguistic practices. Self is such a centrally import-ant idea that it inevitably finds expression at many levels in both the nat-ural and social sciences. In the next few paragraphs I will sketch out a 'position statement' and elaborate upon it in the rest of the book.

First of all, my own assumption that self is a virtual entity refers to the fact that we have to construct it by analogy with other entities of a public nature. It has an 'as if' existence in much the same way that 'the mind' has been treated as if it were a telephone switchboard or a computer. Self as a virtual entity is not something we immediately com-prehend simply by looking into ourselves and introspecting its nature. As I argue in Chapters 11 and 12, a sense-of-self and its associated beliefs is part of a cultural legacy, learned in infancy, and a product of a long process of human social evolution. This does not mean that a vir-tual self is fictional or illusory. I argue that the reality in which we live our lives cannot be described only in literal terms; it needs analogical, metaphorical and virtual crutches to render it intelligible, explicable and shareable.

Of course, people refer to each other literally, as individual persons, usually with a name or identification tag. In fact, we are known in this minimal way by governmental authorities. In addition, it is common to imagine a figurative analogue of a person inside us – a kind of little person 'in our mind' that we consult about our (its) opinions and deci-sions. In Chapter 8, I discuss how this modern understanding of self developed out of earlier concepts of soul and spirit. In Chapter 12, I speculate about the role of analogical reasoning in the evolution of self-reference from hominids to *Homo sapiens*.

The systematic study of persons and selves by philosophers and scientists clarifies, deepens or goes entirely beyond the common-sense view. Within the human and social sciences, persons and selves have been conceived both as natural organisms and as human agents reflex-ively studying themselves. One of the themes I explore is the conflict between these two perspectives and also the more general point that any learned reflection on the nature of persons has the potential to change our common-sense view of them. In other words, as self-interpreting animals, groping with virtual realities, we are likely to be attracted to metaphors and explanations supplied by science and speculative thought in general. Following Freud, we analyse slips of the tongue for hidden impulses. And now, with neuroscience as powerful as it is, we imagine that our low moods are caused by depletions of brain chemicals. The influence between common sense and learned reflection is two-way because the former is also the jumping-off point for the latter.

Although it is usual to think of persons as more substantial or real than selves, the criteria for being a person are also a product of local historical and cultural circumstances and therefore, in part, conventional. A person is a kind of hybrid entity, a biological human being who comes to be perceived by others and who perceives her or himself in ways that are shaped by the society in which they live. In view of the obvious biological constraints on becoming a person, and also logical arguments for the necessity of the empirical reality of persons (Strawson 1959), I will treat the concept of person as more fundamental than a concept of self. Discussion of the relationship between biological human beings, persons and selves can be traced back principally to the philosopher John Locke (1632–1704). He set in train a set of intellectual puzzles that still stir up obstinate disagreements today, and this book can be seen as a continuation of these debates.

Part I of the book develops a constructionist position on person and self. The essential idea of construction is that human beings, through their joint activity, constitute their reality in a particular form. By joint activity, I mean what they are doing together and how they communicate about what they are doing. I do not assume that people are necessarily aware of this process. Adopting a natural attitude, reality is simply taken 'at face value' for that social group. Of course, the way ordinary folk construe persons and selves differs from the way natural scientists conceive of human beings. I will examine these differences, including the way persons and selves have been understood as entities (their ontological status) within different schools of thought in social science.

Some critics of constructionism, such as Malcolm Williams (1999: 85), have taken it to imply that everything we perceive is somehow an artefact of social practices. He asserts that one of the tasks of science is to distinguish between what is 'real' and what is constructed as 'real'. I agree that scientists produce theoretical explanations about 'real' forces that exist independently of us, such as gravity, and no one assumes, I think, that people themselves construct the force of gravity. However, I take it that our conception of gravity is constructed by practising scientists. An assumption I make throughout this book is that there is a unified and independent physical reality. So, in arguing that self has been constructed as a virtual entity, I am not suggesting that it is unrelated to natural reality; I only argue that it is not related as directly to natural reality as 'gravity' appears to be. This is true of many constructed entities, including many early attempts to understand the world naturalistically. I am advocating that we should study the beliefs and social practices associated with talk about selves and relate them to natural processes.

Constructionists have been relatively uninterested in natural science except to study science as a social activity. They have explored where ideas about human nature come from, how they are justified and how they relate to a culture's social practices. This book goes further in seeking a productive dialogue between constructionists and natural scientists with respect to persons and selves. I will adopt the view of science (*naturalism*) put forward by Roy Bhaskar (1979: 9) in which scientific activity is construed as a search for the (universal and *unobserved*) structures, generative mechanisms and laws that can account for events *observed*, often in contrived experimental situations. Bhaskar put forward this conception to replace the idea that causal laws can be reduced to regularities in sequences of experienced events (1979: 15).

Bhaskar notes that two schools of thought have dominated the scene within the social sciences. In the first, the search for empirical regularities amounts to a registration of systematic co-variation between discrete events. An example would be, say, the relationship between patterns of migration and expectations of economic benefit. The second school emphasises the interpretation of unique events rather than the formation of general laws. In one version of interpretation, people's acts are assumed to reflect the mental state of human agents in their cultural and historical context. For instance, in the example given above, it would advocate interviewing migrants to discover their unique reasons for migrating (see Benton and Craib 2001, for Bhaskar's views on social science). I will now expand on these various points in relation to person and self, and also on Bhaskar's *critical realist* view of social science as a complement to constructionism.

If, as I suggested earlier, people employ analogy to interpret the world and their own activities, it is likely that their conceptions will differ considerably from models produced by natural science. Moreover, there is no reason to suppose that common sense can be modelled on science, especially as the former is likely to be much more concerned with persuasion and justification than with prediction. However, 'our common sense', can be explored both naturalistically – what natural mechanisms are implicated in the way we think as we do – and also interpretively.

Interpretation enlarges upon common sense by reflecting in a systematic and disciplined way on what people say and do, paying attention to an interpretation's completeness, exhaustiveness and consistency (Seale 1999). Any attempt to reconcile biological and social sciences would have to be compatible with the results of interpretation, but a more systematic description of 'common sense' does not necessarily provide a basis for reconciling the various sciences. For instance, interpretivists cannot easily depart from the assumption that people 'really' have minds or exercise autonomous agency, assumptions that could be questioned from a natural perspective. The relationship between common sense and natural science is an enduring problem that I attempt to tackle throughout the book. One solution within the philosophy of science has been to reject the possibility of integrating concepts of natural causation with the results of interpretation. I will now briefly turn to consider the views of those philosophers who have taken this stance.

One way to distinguish interpretive from scientific explanation is to see it as involving reasons rather than causes. It is clear that the sort of criteria for describing a person's act as governed by reason differ from the conventions that natural scientists follow in describing events in a causal explanation. One obvious difference concerns standards of description. Everyday interpretations include all kinds of value judgements and unexamined assumptions; by contrast, scientists attempt to eliminate any 'excess meaning' that is not essential to defining a phenomenon according to their theoretical assumptions. Ordinary folk tend not to spell out their taken-for-granted assumptions. For a discipline such as psychology, there exists the obvious problem of separating terms that belong legitimately to a natural, causal mode of explanation from the terms of everyday reasoning, such as intentions and goals.

Another difference concerns the meaning of 'rule-governed' behaviour. Thomas Leahey (2003: 126–143) represents it as a contrast between *natural rules* (or laws) which have to be obeyed and *constitutive rules* which are similar to the rules of a game, whether implicit or explicit, which have to be enforced. The rules governing reasons are of a constitutive type, and, obviously enough, the rules that any culture happens to uphold can be, and often are, disobeyed. These rules regulate how we ought to behave rather than how we do in fact behave. In the case of constitutive rules, something is true or false by definition. The concept of truth and error built into norms and conventions means that it is simply incorrect to call Bill by the name of Fred if that is not his name. Likewise, 2 + 2 cannot make 5 if certain conventions are followed. In the case of natural law, error is probabilistic and associated with the match between theoretical prediction and empirical observation. It is believed that nature is lawful, but, at the same time, it is assumed that our methods of measurement and theoretical predictions are associated with a margin of error.

I intend to avoid setting up causes and reasons as incompatible, that is, producing explanations that could not, in principle, be reconciled, but I will leave it to the final chapter to discuss this problem in detail. I will also argue against a *naive* reduction of constitutive rules or 'norms' to 'natural laws' while recognising the need to show how the two could be related. A key question seems to be whether the formation and maintenance of social norms can be made compatible with an explanation in terms of universal, natural processes. I assume that this question can be answered affirmatively but I also suggest that in whatever way natural mechanisms are involved in installing a normative influence over human affairs, the causal processes implicated in their installation are not necessarily as interesting as the causal consequences of the existence of the norms themselves.

For example, once a child has learned to repeat the two-times table correctly, the natural capacity to learn this skill, on which the educational process relies, ceases to hold much interest. The ability to reason about numbers and apply numerical concepts to practical tasks is the significant outcome, and these abilities and their consequences are involved in higher-level social processes that, in my view, can also be studied naturalistically. I suggest that the fact that rules in mathematics have been given a conventional form is not incompatible with a naturalistic account of their evolutionary development or current maintenance by social processes.

There is little doubt that social conventions have had far-reaching implications, especially in logic, mathematics and science. The norms and practices of science have led to a theoretical understanding of many aspects of human behaviour. But in areas where the number of variables to consider is inordinately large, their historical influence untraceable, and we lack any credible natural theory to relate them together, the attempt to make predictions from an understanding of universal natural processes would be futile. Society is an open system in which 'mechanisms coexist and interact with one another in contingent ways' (Benton and Craib 2001: 129). Consequently, the social sciences cannot rely wholly on explaining through natural mechanisms but must utilise a knowledge of regularities derived from a variety of sources – a practical knowledge of culture and language, an imaginative projection into unfamiliar situations, manuals and rule books, etc. I assume that knowledge of constitutive rules is essentially a form of practical knowledge which is compatible with natural causation even though, like the weather, it is neither feasible nor possible to explain in fine detail. Of course, constitutive rules often take for granted a tacit understanding of natural processes that conforms closely (or depends upon) natural-science explanations.

While I clearly endorse the constructionist emphasis on regularities constituted within social practices, this book will also examine the limitations of this perspective. One of my targets for criticism is the idea that processes or entities theorised in terms of natural causes exist at a 'lower level' than norms, intentions, acts, etc., theorised about at a 'higher' cultural or personal level. This orientation to the cause–reason issue has been very clearly stated by Elmer Sprague (1999) who draws heavily on the later writings of Ludwig Wittgenstein (1889–1951). Wittgenstein contributed a central notion to constructionist thinking which is that the meaning of words and sentences can be discovered in how they are used in practical activities such as giving orders or describing events (Sprague 1999: 37–66). The main message is that speech is intertwined with action and conforms to a game-like structure in which persons have agreed the rules, implicit or explicit, for correct use. These various 'language games' as Wittgenstein called them are, in turn, linked to forms of social life.

Forms of life undergo change, and, consequently, language games may fall out of use and new ones may come into existence. The rules for the game are said to be expressed in a person's behaviour and are cited as 'reasons' if a person is called upon to explain their action, e.g., 'Why did you call him Bill? Because that's his name.' As Sprague (1999: 88) sums it up: 'Wittgenstein contrasts citing a reason to explain what persons are doing with finding a cause for a change in a physical object', and in so doing, Sprague maintains, Wittgenstein 'rescues persons from the omnicompetence of physics'. As well as denying that natural (physical) processes could provide an adequate explanation for human activities as we ordinarily describe them, Sprague also argues strongly against the view that a person's reasons for acting are some kind of 'mental' thing. Sprague dubs his own position as 'personism' to contrast it with 'mindism'.

Personism is a succinct description of Sprague's position, and it refers to a level of explanation grounded in the attributes of persons. This distinguishes it from the sub-personal level that refers to parts of a person such as activities in the brain or so-called mental mechanisms. Personists usually subsume interpersonal relationships within personism, but I will make out a case for saying that they constitute a level of causation that deserves consideration in its own right. I am going to use the term 'supra-personal' to refer to explanations grounded in the causal consequences of relationships between persons. My aim in this book is to avoid slipping into 'mindism' (as Sprague calls it), and I will reinterpret anything to do with 'the mental' in terms of sub-personal, personal and supra-personal levels of explanation.

Sprague himself reinterprets a person's so-called mental powers as their disposition to behave in certain ways. He uses arguments of Gilbert Ryle (1900–76) that I discuss at greater length in Chapter 2. For Sprague, reference to the mind and its mental states is just 'a way of talking' that should be understood correctly as reference to the dispositions, capacities, abilities and acts of *persons*, not minds. Persons are considered to be the agents of their acts. According to personism, it is not necessary to explain acts by mental acts of will; the person acts, period. Persons don't act in isolation, of course, and their reasons for acting often only make sense in the context of their social practices. They follow social conventions, as noted earlier.

Although I will be taking up many of the arguments for personism, the latter is usually presented in a way that cannot be reconciled with naturalism. Personists assume that a person's acts are explicable only in terms of the local norms and concepts that apply to persons (intentions, reasons, etc.) and not by natural causes. For Sprague, mechanisms and processes in the mind/brain can only explain things at a sub-personal level. As Sprague (1999: 88) puts it, 'Wittgenstein makes persons their own kind of thing, unlike any other kind of thing […] The doings of persons are not to be explained by causes, even by internal, hidden causes.' On the one hand, in favour of personism, it does seem to make sense from a natural-science perspective to treat the whole organism as a functional unit. People and many animals recognise each other as whole individuals and direct their acts towards them as whole units. Similarly, an organism's health is often best viewed as a state of the whole organism, even though health is not an entirely personal matter. On the other hand, if a person's status as a person is, in part, assigned by other persons, a person is not entirely 'their own kind of thing' (Sprague 1999: 88). A person is not *sui generis* a person. Persons do not pronounce themselves persons until they have learned to do so.

Moreover, persons do not explain everything they do in person-level concepts. For instance, we simply take it for granted that we can naturally produce the sounds that make up words, and occasionally we note that a natural process, like a cold, can produce a croaky voice. We cannot help sounding croaky, not that we have a reason for producing a croaky voice. This admittedly trivial example illustrates how rule-governed and 'naturally caused' behaviour are combined in common sense. Theorists influenced by Wittgenstein such as Jeff Coulter (1983) tend to offer a stark choice between behavioural events (movements, reflexes, etc.) and actions which are 'logically irreducible to "behavioural events" per se' (1983: 98). Although he rightly rejects any attempt to reduce actions to sub-personal mechanisms, Coulter still advocates a search for 'orderliness' in the phenomena of action and interaction, treated as a level in its own right (1983: 164). He advocates studying 'naturally occurring human activities' in order to generate 'theorems and principles' (Coulter 1983: 164). This seems to imply that natural enquiry is compatible with a study of constitutive rules.

As noted above, I will use the term 'supra-personal' to refer to the natural causal effect of one human being on another as a whole unit (or those effects as realised systemically in groups of human beings). The supra-personal level seems to be needed in order to give a satisfactory account of the acquisition of concepts of person and self in the human infant. It is also required if we are to explain the fact that our primate ancestors acquired the ability to communicate in such a way that normatively controlled behaviour became a daily reality. From a natural-science perspective, it is difficult to see how a person-level explanation could provide a resource for its own generation because a person is not a natural kind. Unless we assume that persons just appear, their origin needs to be explained naturalistically.

Matthew Ratcliffe (2006: 222) argues that we don't understand each other, person to person, from a third-person spectator stance, and, therefore, the project of naturalism can never provide an exhaustive explanation of human life. He points out that we appreciate each other as persons in certain direct 'second person' ways. But this direct phenomenological appreciation seems to be true of any relationship to nature; I take it that the object of natural science is to explain, not to replace, phenomena.

Of course, many resources for generating the personal level could be said to reside, sub-personally, within a person's body. However, what makes the personal level distinctive is the variety of ways in which personhood is related to collective social actions and conventions. For example, the concept of punishment is closely tied to personhood. People who are not considered to be 'fully persons', such as individuals who do not understand what they are doing, may not be punished when other fully functioning persons are. That the personal is intrinsically related to the supra-personal seems to be implied by Wittgensteinian arguments.

If supra-personal interactions are, from a natural perspective, biologically mediated, the supra-personal level of explanation does not supplant the personal, more than the personal and sub-personal are necessarily opposed to one another or hierarchically related. Of course, a supra-personal mechanism can only operate when one human being can identify a characteristic of another human being to which it can respond. It may be for this reason that we 'naturally' see others in terms of their unique attributes. As I see it, the mistake, from a supra-personal point of view, would be to see those characteristics as emanating purely from the person. A typical example would be the belief that a person's ability to control their own behaviour is an intrinsic expression of the power of their will. Equally narrow is the assumption that personal control is the product of a sub-personal 'executive' mechanism in the mind/brain. A target for criticism in this book is any attempt to reduce all explanations to one level. I discuss the relationship between levels and the concept of 'emergent' properties in the final chapter.

I am not suggesting that the direct causal effect of one human being on another is the only way in which social norms are mediated. In addition, we have to consider logical processes underlying rules, other reasoning processes and, no doubt, many other influences. It is self-evident that human acts are influenced by reasoning that has developed within circumscribed historical and cultural circumstances. It is largely on these grounds that constructionists have objected to some attempts by natural scientists to apply their methodology to describe and explain what constructionists consider to be cultural phenomena. In what follows, I will adhere to the idea of a unified science and monism (i.e. that there are no fundamental divisions in nature and that it is possible to develop a unified explanation) and reject the Wittgensteinian assumption that social norms and conventions are immune from naturalistic investigation.

It is in the sphere of moral reasoning that objections to naturalism have principally arisen. Philosophers such as Charles Taylor (1989) do not believe that our moral response to situations, such as a sense that human life is always to be respected, can be reduced to natural responses like a gut reaction to smells (Taylor 1989: 6). For him, there is a separate 'ontology of the human', meaning that there is a framework of human life that pre-exists any response we might make. In other words, we have to presuppose moral criteria concerning 'the good' against which our human responses can be judged. The dignity and respect we accord to each other cannot be compared, he thinks, with the natural response of one baboon to another that underpins their social hierarchy (1989: 15). He says that humans are concerned about self and identity in ways with which baboons could never be concerned. Presumably, a baboon does not have a concept of a baboon *qua* baboon and therefore cannot conceive of what is good for baboons in general rather than what is good for it, individually, when being, say, dominant or submissive. According to Taylor, concepts of person and self are intricately tied to the sphere of moral reasoning.

It is difficult to fault Taylor's arguments on this point. As far as we know, the great apes do not adopt arbitrary conventions for the naming of individual animals or share moral standards, even though they do recognise and evaluate each other. Taylor sets up an opposition between nature and culture that is very difficult to bridge. As he states: 'No argument can take someone from a neutral stance towards the world, either adopted from the demands of "science" or fallen into as a consequence of pathology, to insight into moral ontology' (Taylor 1989: 8). However, granted that moral reasoning is dependent on language, other social institutions and an intellectual tradition, learned 'gut responses' of a kind do, nevertheless, seem to be required for the moral approval or disapproval handed out by one person to another or, indeed, for an assent to moral arguments in the first place. It is necessary to love logic to be persuaded by reasons, moral or otherwise. Taylor (1989: 56) argues both that 'good and right are not part of the natural world as studied by natural science' and that they are 'as real, objective, and non-relative as any other part of the natural world'. However, he does not explain how the ontology of human nature and the ontology of morality intersect. In my view, the complexity of natural mechanisms at the personal and supra-personal levels would have to match the subtlety and variety of behaviour at these levels. It is only on a Newtonian billiard-ball view of causation that natural explanations at the personal level seem inconceivable. Moreover, there is no need to accept a hierarchical view of natural causation that reduces all higher-order mechanisms to simpler processes that act in a 'blind' fashion.

Rom Harré (1997a, 2005) is another philosopher who directly tackles the problem of relating reasons and causes. He conceives of psychology as a hybrid science that respects molecular, organismic and personist (discursive) modes of explanation. His own solution in creating the hybrid is to place the person 'at the apex of an ontological tree'. At the personal level, human acts are interpreted with reference to norms and standards that underpin judgements of correctness or success, such as meeting goals or completing tasks successfully. According to Harré, natural science is not invoked at this level because norms belong to cultural and historical forms of social life. Natural processes and entities come lower down on the ontological tree.

Harré employs a task/tool metaphor to represent this relationship, the tools consisting of the brain and bodily mechanisms (reserved for natural science) while tasks are constituted at the cultural level

(1998: 44). I consider this proposal critically in the final chapter, along with some other solutions to the problem. At this point, I will simply reiterate my belief that it is possible to integrate the sub-personal, personal and supra-personal levels of explanation without considering that they form a hierarchy governed 'from the top'. For instance, past cultural arrangements (at the supra-personal level) may have shaped biological evolution to the extent that culture has determined the present (natural/physical) distribution (and perhaps composition) of human genetic material (at the sub-personal level) that now exerts its influence 'from below'.

Acceptance of naturalism encourages the idea that the capacity of groups of people to act together to create their own unique norms is also compatible with strong cross-cultural similarities. However, it may simply be unproductive to attempt to comprehend cultural patterns in terms of universal processes even if, in principle, the differences between cultures could be reconciled within a unified natural perspective on the world. Many events relevant to the formation of culture may represent contingent historical circumstances of no universal significance. In like manner, many natural scientists are not that interested in phenomena in their unique configuration.

For example, a geologist may possess some general principles for explaining the folds and fissures in a rock formation, but it may not be possible to explain the configuration fully or precisely. This may not matter if it holds little scientific interest. As human beings, we are certainly likely to be interested in our own unique circumstances but in many cases this interest revolves around events that, similarly, have little significance in the larger picture (e.g., who has married who, which musical group has achieved fame, etc.). Other human achievements, such as an alphabet, which also possesses unique and arbitrary characteristics, clearly have far greater importance in the development of a culture. But, viewed naturalistically, an alphabet only has to possess certain features possessed by all possible alphabets in order to suit it for its particular purpose.

Artefacts like an alphabet appear to be innovations that allow a culture to bootstrap its way to further technical advances. A codification of forms of reasoning must also have contributed to the development of new cultural norms that people themselves played a part in constructing. If a culture's concepts and rules for reasoning can be discerned, interpretation is probably the surest and quickest means of understanding what a particular human group might be up to. Nevertheless, I will assume that this methodological approach need not be seen as incompatible with an attempt to look for generalisations about humankind of a universal nature (see especially Chapter 3).

One common-sense folk belief is the idea that each person has a mind and a self. This idea has been so influential in science that I will now introduce some of its implications and return to this theme throughout the book.

Mindism

Although, in my view, personism has certain limitations, this book will advance personist arguments against mindism. Mindism derives from the seventeenth-century philosophy of mind–body dualism, which has had a major impact on subsequent natural-science conceptions of human behaviour. I consider this legacy in more detail in Chapter 8. Sprague notes that René Descartes (1596–1650), the chief proponent of dualism, had somewhat similar philosophical purposes to Wittgenstein. The purpose was to protect persons from a purely natural conception of their existence. Descartes took the mind or soul to consist of an immaterial substance, interacting with, but quite unlike, the material substance of the body acting through mechanical processes. Animals could be explained on purely physical and mechanical principles, but human beings possessed a mind that allowed them to act according to reasons. Mechanistic explanation was presumably perceived as a threat to the dignity of human beings and the supposed need to preserve a special place for them outside the natural world. For Descartes, the mind or soul was uniquely human. And for some people today, certain theories in natural science, such as human evolution, are still seen as a threat to religious belief.

Some early philosophers of nature rejected dualism, seeking an explanation for everything, including the mind, within a unified science. Sprague argues that in response to dualism, a person's powers came to be explained by means of sub-personal mechanisms in the brain. This response to dualism is still much in evidence, and in Chapter 9 I discuss how mind and self have been handled by cognitive science and neuroscience. The problem of other minds, inherited from dualism, has also fixed the terms of the principal philosophical conception of common sense, often referred to as 'folk psychology' (Andrews 2008). Sprague characterises mindism as the conception that mind is an entity private to its owner, that it contains other entities (ideas, representations, etc.), that it is a thing that is self-moving (working on its own) and that the contents of the mind define personal identity, i.e. that the sameness of a person is constituted by the continuity and connectedness of that person's mental contents over time. Mindism leads to a very different conception of the person than Sprague's own personist view.

Descartes's concept of mind as an immaterial substance has largely given way to a view that sees mind in mechanical terms, either by identifying it with brain activity or by setting it up as a functional system of mental states. Besides revealing their dualist origins, these conceptions reduce mental phenomena to processes or mechanisms in a stand-alone brain or mind. This book is deeply critical of the project of mechanising the mind in a way that perpetuates dualism and downplays or ignores a supra-personal level of natural causation. In my view, a constructionist has no reason to be opposed to a sub-personal level of explanation or, indeed, to naturalism. My discussions in Part II of contemporary theory and research in neuroscience, child development and human social evolution, as it applies to self, are critical of the way this is done, not of the aims of natural science.

As things stand at the moment in the philosophy of the human sciences, even the personal level of explanation has not been widely accepted as a level in its own right. As Sprague remarks, personism 'is hardly at the center of the philosophy of mind today, but it seems to me worthwhile to try to put it there' (1999: 10). In a similar plaintive, and sometimes exasperated, tone, Bennett and Hacker (2003) strive to advance a Wittgensteinian philosophical foundation for neuroscience. Their book has generated vigorous attacks from other philosophers of science (see Chapter 9). There is a real sense, in reading current literature, that the battle of ideas surrounding the question of mind is once more generating considerable heat.

One of my aims is to critically appraise natural-science conceptions of self that are grounded in mindism. To a large extent, my criticisms follow the personist agenda of Wittgenstein and Ryle and also later writers in this tradition, such as Rom Harré (1998). It follows from a rejection of mindism that self is not a mental thing: i.e. it is not an idea made of mental stuff. Personists follow Ryle in arguing that to think of mind as an entity is to commit a category mistake – that whatever the mental is, it does not fall into the same category as things like brains or boulders. If we accept this argument, mind, like self, is a virtual reality – for Ryle it was 'the ghost in the machine'. He went on to redescribe mental terms in the language of actions and dispositions (see Chapter 2). Strangely, some cognitive neuroscientists who accept Ryle's arguments still assert that 'such a ghost may be governed by scientific principles', and they blithely proceed to define mind as an object for science (Dror and Thomas 2005: 285). 'The mind' refuses to lie down in virtually all discussions of alternative forms of discourse. Even a textual theorist like Jens Brockmeier (2005: 440) who acknowledges that both Jacques Derrida (1930–2004) and Mikhail Bakhtin (1895–1975) 'repudiate the idea of a substantial, autonomous, and exclusively mental or spiritual mind', goes on in the next sentence to refer to 'the dialogical principle as a model of the mind'.

Some of the difficulties in setting up mind (and, by inclusion, self) as a scientific object have been pointed out by Christina Erneling (2005: 247–50). She notes that even when cognitive scientists or neuroscientists reject a dualist ontology of body stuff and mind stuff, 'they all embrace another Cartesian assumption, that of atomism, in the sense of claiming that all basic mental or cognitive entities count as individual states of mind stuff and, as such, are states of particular brains that belong to particular persons' (Erneling 2005: 249).

To restate her general argument differently, one mind, if it is the activity of one brain, can only be one part of the natural world. But, according to mindism, there are many minds in the world. However, we have no way of marking the boundaries of minds in nature – our brains might clash under unfortunate circumstances but my mind does not literally bump into yours. In other words, if the mind is a product of the brain and each mind is only one subsystem in nature, it becomes difficult to see how these subsystems are to be linked up in a comprehensive natural-science picture of the world.

A constructionist must of course tackle, first, the undeniable fact that people experience themselves as having minds and selves and, second, connect this belief to an account of natural reality. Broadly speaking, these are questions that this book addresses. And even more broadly speaking, the answer to the first question is that persons refer to virtual realities such as mind and self because these ideas have proved pragmatically useful in human communication and social practices. And in response to the second question, it is suggested that persons are real (they have material bodies), and they also express real skills and capacities, producing material effects on the world and on each other. Consequently, whatever any reference to mental events and processes achieves (clearly it has uses), a natural-science perspective on this linguistic and social activity would have to comprise more than generalisations about single brains.

My own constructionist stance does not eliminate mind and self as folk ideas that contribute to an experienced reality. It reinterprets them and relates them to linguistic and social practices more closely tied to empirical observations. Like most scientific accounts, it leaves something out. In this sense it is no different from, say, a scientific account of ice, water and steam that reduces them to forms of H_2O. A constructionist does not eliminate a sense-of-self or the belief that one is a self any more than an understanding of H_2O changes our experience of ice, water and steam. In Chapter 5, I will argue that the manner in which phenomena present themselves to us has also provided us with a source of data from which to draw theoretical conclusions about person and self. The tradition of reflecting on experience – phenomenology – has produced a rich set of ideas that, in my opinion, are compatible with constructionism.

The broader picture

I do not want to say that a general acceptance of the constructionist thesis that self is a virtual reality would have no effect on a sense-of-self as commonly understood. In fact, this is just what one would expect if we are self-interpreting creatures. This leads me to consider, in broader perspective, the implications of the views expressed in this book. First of all, if self is a virtual reality and intrinsically temporal and malleable, we cannot afford to say, nor is it possible to say, that we have produced a final scientific analysis of the subject. This should hardly be a concern given the huge amount of literature published on the subject in recent years.

This book also claims that there is a need for integrative and cross-disciplinary thinking. Under the influence of academic specialisation, the subject of self has fragmented into narrower and deeper channels. Although there are good arguments for breaking down complex topics and studying them in depth, the result has been a body of literature that is difficult to digest in the round. Some academics have delved so deeply that they have left many of us behind. In the view of Raymond Martin (a professor of philosophy) and John Barresi (a professor of psychology), few philosophers of personal identity know much about related developments in contemporary psychology, and vice versa (Martin and Barresi 2000: 175–6). Indeed, they wonder whether even a philosopher could keep up with current debates about whether persons are three-dimensional or four-dimensional beings. Martin and Barresi conclude there is nothing to be done about fragmentation except to stop worrying about it.

I take the contrary view that cross-disciplinary dialogues are essential as a counterweight to over-specialisation. There are dangers in a narrowness of perspective – a failure to think outside the box of assumptions that tend to be made by each discipline. Specialisation has yielded huge dividends, but there is still a lack of agreement over fundamental questions. Most social scientists accept that there are universal features of human nature but they cannot agree on what they are. In the biological sciences, some experts in human evolution hold diametrically opposed views on such centrally important topics as the origins of language. Many would find it hard to draw a firm line between the innate cognitive abilities of humans and the great apes. Neuroscientists and psychologists are often deeply divided over their definitions of self. Some of these divisions may be related to rival interpretations of the empirical evidence but a good many are probably founded in different philosophical assumptions. Cross-disciplinary exchange may at least help to highlight what these are.

However reasonable this might seem, the suggestion risks contravening the rules of academic etiquette. Unlike thinkers of the Renaissance who turned their mind to any subject under the sun, modern academics are protective of their corner of knowledge and resent any 'amateur' who tries to muscle in. And between themselves, academics exercise extreme caution. A historian who is an expert on the seventeenth century might preface a question to an expert on the eighteenth century with the phrase, 'Of course, I know absolutely nothing about the subject, but I wonder if it might have occurred to you that ...'

A few brave scientists have ventured to suggest that one way to deal with a multiplicity of views is to take an interdisciplinary approach. Merlin Donald (2004) believes that the human mind is far too complicated for any single field to master and that it is only by comparing the findings of different disciplines (biological and social) that one can hopefully converge on simple and parsimonious solutions. While welcoming these sentiments, even Donald's objectives may seem too narrow. Philosophers may wonder what he means by the mind, and cultural historians may wonder if their interest in self can be called theoretical. There is also the problem of reconciling first-person phenomenological approaches to self with third-person observations of scientists and linguists. In my own attempt to develop a cross-disciplinary dialogue, I am well aware that I might seem to jump between conceptual frameworks with disrespectful abandon. However, I do not see an alternative.

Adopting the view that self is a virtual reality does not mean that we have to stop believing in selves. An emphasis on the game-like structure of human life only points us in the direction of understanding the rules; it does not assert that the game is not worth playing. As well as emphasising the cultural and creative aspects of self, this book argues that it is possible to view the constructive process naturalistically. It is not as if we can ignore natural science because self is not a natural entity. We can legitimately ask the 'how' of self as well as the 'what' and 'why'. For instance, how do we actually manage the feat of conceiving of ourselves? This is a perfectly reasonable question for a specialist in human social evolution or child development, but it may seem more out of place in the social sciences. Sociologists are usually more interested in relating a belief in self to political institutions and mechanisms of social control (e.g., Rose 1998) rather than with how persons and selves are constructed through psychological processes. Historians, too, have subjected concepts of personhood and selfhood to deep analysis, but they are less concerned with how persons and selves are produced than they are with acts that have actually been performed or texts that have been written.

However ancient the idea of self as a virtual reality, it does not seem to have been taken seriously to heart. Our sense of the reality of self may be so strong that it leads us into believing that it is really mirrored by a force, principle, process or entity that can be studied 'in itself'. Although this conviction is strong, it has to be admitted that there are many terms for the loss of this reality (depersonalisation, alienation, etc.) and a rich literary tradition of lost souls, stolen souls, zombies and empty selves. My argument is not that constructions exist only 'in the mind' as if a virtual reality is unrelated to things more substantial. Self is not the only virtual reality we take for granted. Many other social realities are potentially empty, like paper money, but they acquire the status of reality through the operation of political institutions, social practices and their associated systems of reciprocal obligations, promises and rewards. Virtual selves are also embroiled in a mucky reality, so perhaps even natural scientists and social realists might learn to embrace them.

2 Conceptualising self

In this chapter, I discuss various approaches to defining self and contrast them with the view that a virtual self is constructed in a dialogue between persons. It is worth noting that all analyses of person and self draw upon an intuitive grasp of what a person is and what it means to express a self. These are everyday, not theoretical, notions. However, the taken-for-granted meaning of what it is to be a person with a sense-of-self is not transparent, and these phenomena show considerable variation across history and culture. Philosophers and psychologists who explore and clarify concepts of person and self aim for generality, but they also have to recognise the idiosyncratic local form these concepts take. I also confront this difficulty and offer a general conceptual framework in Chapter 3. My present focus, however, is on approaching the problem of definition within different theoretical orientations.

From a familiar starting point and a customary grammar of self-reference, analysis branches out in different directions. Philosophical analysis distinguishes between the ontology and epistemology of self. Ontology is concerned with the mode of existence of persons and selves; for instance, do persons exist independently of the ideas that people have about them, and, if so, what is that mode of existence? What do we have to presuppose about persons and selves for them to have the properties and capacities that they are seen, actually, to possess? Do persons have 'minds' that innately organise things so that they appear to them as objects in space and time? If so, what is the mode of existence of a mind? In contrast with ontology, epistemology is concerned with how we know we are persons and selves and what kind of knowledge that is. For example, one aim is to map out the conventional and legitimate application of these concepts (in their everyday sense) and another is to consider how criteria for personhood and selfhood can be specified in such a way that persons and selves are assured of both continuity and change over time. The answers to ontological and epistemological questions are usually closely intertwined.

Some constructionist thinkers have taken the sceptical position that person and self are simply constructs that humans happen to have developed to understand who and what they are; there is nothing essential or substantial about selves, and self is a linguistic invention that floats free from any universal features of human life. If we were to take this suggestion seriously, a concept of self would only make sense in the culture that employed the term, and there would be nothing of a general nature that could be said about it. Although I have claimed that the entity the concept of self refers to is a virtual reality and therefore not something we can literally observe (i.e. it is a reification that we cannot sensibly make inferences about *as* an entity), I reject the constructionist position I have just outlined. I hope to argue that there is something we can say generically about all possible persons and selves. If we were to treat self as an idea that a group of humans at some stage in their history happened to favour, it would be of interest only to historians.

Nevertheless, it could reasonably be argued that we can only really understand what it is like to be a self in a particular culture by being thoroughly immersed in that culture's form of life. If so, it would be hard to say exactly what the term means or how self is related to social reality. A person so immersed might be ignorant about many of the presuppositions he or she holds about that reality. The term 'self' might be used routinely without that person ever getting to know what it is 'in itself'. To talk intelligibly about self might amount to little more than listing a set of attributes compatible with the conventional concepts and linguistic resources that are available. This kind of reflection on self might not reveal anything new or interesting. However, as David Jopling points out, there are traditions that view the search for knowledge about self as an enlightening quest (2000: 1–29). In seeking to discover who we are, we may become extremely sceptical and question the assumptions that underpin our conventional understanding. I endorse the view that thinking about self is a never-ending reflection, so that its meaning can never be finally pinned down. Nevertheless, I do not think that this need inhibit an exploration of how most people are routinely made into (and, to some degree, make themselves into) conventional persons and selves.

The idea that selves are 'made' might be thought to raise unnecessary mysteries – are not people intrinsically self-making? In a partly trivial sense it must be true that a statement such as 'I don't feel my self today' presupposes a person that feels that way. At a deeper level, people are expected to put some effort into becoming a 'well-fashioned self'. I regard the latter assumption as one that most modern people naturally make, and that it is the expression of an ideological position. I will label this orientation to self-making as 'autocentric' because it places person or self in the position of an originating centre. Stated in broad-brush terms, in the recent history of the West, it replaced a theocentric view that saw God as the centre and origin of the universe. Some of the social-science literature on self reflects this autocentric ideology. For instance, Augusto Blasi (2004: 21) says that the 'The ideal goal (of the subjective self) is autonomy, individuality, and an identity rooted in a hierarchy of commitments.'

Blasi is describing what people themselves say. Perhaps the ideal goal should be this, but the aims of social science extend beyond just describing what people believe or do. People do 'exercise their will', 'make moral choices', and 'plan their future', on their own, but these autocentric descriptions are often stated in such a way that makes it difficult to integrate them with the idea that persons are made in other ways, such as being instructed by God or controlled passively by natural processes that make things happen automatically. There is clearly a problem in reconciling these fundamentally different ways of understanding human beings.

In any event, the recent surge of academic interest in self is likely to be due to its ideological significance. Since the Middle Ages, autonomous self-making has become increasingly important, and the rational independent thinker has been highly valued. It is not my intention in this book to add to the literature on western individualism. Instead, I suggest it is probably unwise to valorise autonomous self-making until we understand how we are made naturally and heteronomously. My focus is on how ordinary people routinely acquire a concept of, and sense of, self and how scientists and others have theorised about this process.

A problem that faces natural scientists is how to produce an account of phenomena like consciousness, will and intention, while still giving people a human face. Some aspects of being human, like digestion, can be treated as complex natural phenomena and reduced to their constituent processes, with the result that the whole is seen, unobjectionably, as a sum of the parts. The brain can also be studied as a self-contained organ of the body. Another option is to assume that the brain is a complex dynamic system that demonstrates emergent properties when its constituent elements or sub-systems interact (see Chapter 13). Extending this notion, human beings have been regarded as sub-systems within a larger social system, whose emergent properties could account for our distinctly personal attributes. Whether this kind of explanation diminishes human beings is open to debate but any natural-science theory is likely to conflict with autocentric assumptions.

An account of self that replaces or eliminates everyday terms by introducing new technical definitions is likely to be seen as reductionist in an anti-human sense. I will argue that naturalistic explanations need not be viewed as anti-human. For instance, knowledge of neurological disorders does not remove medicine from the sphere of morality, and attempts to understand social mechanisms, such as Karl Marx's analysis of capitalism, could be interpreted as advancing human emancipation (Benton and Craib 2001: 135). I am therefore unapologetic that the integration of constructionist and biological thinking that I seek will be seen as reductionist. However, I will certainly criticise some attempts to define persons and selves reductively, especially when the aim is to eliminate personal and supra-personal levels of explanation. The framework I attempt to develop is best described as *ecocentric* in the sense that it attempts to integrate biological and cultural aspects of humans within their natural ecology. The person or self is no longer the lynchpin of all explanation.

What I have to say might therefore be viewed as deconstructive – an attempt to take the shine off a self-serving and overblown image of what we, as autocentric selves, think of as our natural powers. The book's project could be seen in this way because I highlight internal contradictions in natural-science thinking and place ideas about self in a historical context. Whether intended or not, certain biological and mentalist theories often seem to bolster up ideological positions. However, if any of the findings of science grounded in naturalism contribute to the persuasiveness of deconstructive arguments, this seems to me to be a fair exchange.

Defining self

There is enough literature on the subject of 'the self' to fill several libraries but little agreement on how to define it. One author claims that the self was invented in the 1760s (Lyons 1978). Almost as soon as people talked about the self as a familiar notion, philosophers argued that it was a fiction or just a convenient label for all the experiences a person could report. This scepticism no longer alarms us, which is not to say that we now have a clear definition of self. If we are unhappy or agonising about the future, we do not automatically lay these problems at the door of 'the self'. It is our life as persons that we are talking about, not our self. Yet if we ask who is at the centre of our life and who decides what happens, the answer may still be given as 'the self'. As Blasi (2004: 7) discovered in his interviews with both religious and secular Americans, many people do 'distinguish a core part of themselves, frequently identified with those values and ideals to which one is deeply committed; are concerned with protecting this core identity from potentially corrupting influences, and try to actualise it'.

It is a person who does all this, and, as I have mentioned before, I will treat 'person' as a foundational concept. There is a double meaning in the way we are able to refer in the same breath to self and concept of self. Blasi adopts a definition of self that he extracts from Søren Kierkegaard (1813–55) and Michel Foucault (1926–84). Blasi agrees with Foucault that it is 'a relationship a person establishes with oneself' (Blasi 2004: 6). In Blasi's definition, 'person' and 'oneself' presumably refer to the same entity. A person relates to their own factual experience and behaviour in a similar way to relating to anything else. A person is an object for themself and exercises personal powers to grasp that object. But who is relating to whom or what?

One source of ambiguity lies in the fact that it is persons who act, not selves. But persons may explain how they act by referring to their own attributes – their idea of some inner core or the kind of person they think they are. At the beginning of his memoirs, Henri Beyle (Stendhal) wrote, in 1835, 'What kind of man am I? […] Have I a notable mind? Truly I do not know. Besides as things fall out from day to day, I rarely think of these basic questions, and then my judgements change with my mood, my judgements are only a rough estimate' (Beyle 1949: 1–2).

Stendhal is sceptical that his self-analysis is worth much, but he is still motivated to proceed with his memoirs. Self-analysis is a circular or reflexive process. A person is both the knowledge-seeker and the thing known about. She or he may know enough to have some idea about what they don't know and can set up a situation (like writing their memoirs) to find out more. A person's concept of who they are may change as a result. I conclude that the only way to avoid confusion about this circular process is to make a firm distinction between a concept of the person (as a knower or doer *qua* human organism) and a concept of self (as some means of comprehending who or what one is, including the fact that one is a person). As it is a human organism that is engaged in knowing, concepts of personhood and selfhood are not merely forms of knowledge: they also relate to the actions and experiences of that organism. In other words, knowledge is made known through being an organism that knows. In my view, most of us live our real lives as virtual selves.

I assume that people, as biological organisms, live out their relationship to the world and postulate a self, to be understood as an object of knowledge. This object is almost certainly going to be just one element in a much larger network of presuppositions and beliefs that serve to make sense of the world (Taylor 1989: 27–30). The concept of a person, in so far as a person is conceptual, is also interpretable within a wider semantic and social system of relationships. Consequently, we find that concepts of both person and self vary between societies and across historical periods. However, I will take it as universally true that human beings each have a singular and unique body and that it is ultimately the human organism that is the actor and knowledge-seeker. On this basis, I infer that persons, as hybrid material and conceptual entities, have logical and empirical priority over selves. I will elaborate on this point later.

The inherent ambiguity of the meaning of self, as both knower and known, can be illustrated by examining how it is frequently defined in books on the subject. Typically, authors define it as an umbrella term and do not bring out its existential nature. For instance, Jerrold Siegel, at the beginning of his grand survey of intellectual ideas about self since the seventeenth century, takes the common meaning of self to be 'the particular being any person is' (2005: 3). He goes on to say that the basis of selfhood has been sought within three dimensions: the bodily, the relational and the reflective. The bodily dimension is physical, corporeal existence; the relational is our social and cultural interaction; and the reflective is our propensity to reflect on the other dimensions as well as on conscious awareness itself. On this level, 'the self is an active agent of its own realisation' (Siegel 2005: 6–7). Siegel further subdivides accounts of self as one-dimensional or multidimensional and favours the latter view of self 'as taking shape at the intersection of multiple coordinates' (2005: 7).

This way of talking about self makes it into a single noun (both person and self), and it also serves as a term that includes anything that can be meaningfully said on the subject. But it is simply confusing to refer to self globally (to include all possible meanings) and to refer to it as a single thing, as if it refers to something we can sensibly talk about. Instead, it seems preferable to distinguish 'oneself' (the human animal, typically given to us in the shape of a unique person) and 'one's self', which for lay people is a product of their reflection and interpretation. In this way, we can avoid the circularity of Siegel's statement that self is the active agent of its own realisation. The meaning of this statement slides between oneself and one's self. Put differently, only persons can reflect as active agents. A person's interpretation of their own active powers is not a power of agency in itself.

Moreover, Siegel's suggestion that self can be defined as an 'intersection of coordinates' (2005: 7) does not make it clear whether the coordinates are conceptual dimensions or whether the various aspects of self are literally coordinated. Self, as an interpretation, is not coordinated with the body or with social relations but with a set of ideas and assumptions about, or interpretations of, the body, its behaviour and its social relations. A person cannot help but be a body that acts and be in relation with others, and so the relationship between self and a person's body and social relationships is one of constitution or production, not coordination.

In another book that aims to define self, Anthony Elliot, a sociologist, refers to the following terms in his introductory chapter: individual, person, identity, personal identity, collective identity, personal experience, selfhood, the self, individual self, self-identity, the subject, multiple selves, concepts of the self, inner worlds, and psyche (Elliot 2001). Although his aim is to differentiate different concepts (2001: 15), the author says that the terminological differences are not especially significant because they all concern the 'subjectivity of the individual' and that he will not trace their 'nuances' (2001: 9–10). How then, can he continue to refer to 'the self' as if its meaning were self-evident? Elliot also asserts that a key characteristic of the self is that it is personally created and interpersonally constructed, and that it survives and adapts to changes in the social world (2001: 5). But the self cannot be both a construction (a product) and that which reconstructs itself (a producer). To use the same term to refer to producer and produced is confusing.

Reflection and interpretation imply awareness of something on which to reflect, whether this object is real or imaginary. I will now go on to consider various understandings of what kind of object of knowledge the self is. Not all societies apparently demonstrate a need for a self as object. In Baining society in Papua New Guinea (Fajans 1985), people have social roles that alter from one social context to another. Personal descriptions amount to judgements that persons have conformed to these roles, and there is a general term for all deviations from the social norm. There seems to be little curiosity in explaining idiosyncrasies or personal motives. The deviant person is not expressing an individual personality but is usually regarded as being shameful or, in extreme cases, as having been invaded by a ghost or spirit.

The observations of anthropologists certainly make us aware of the dangers of generalising from the perspective of theorists who hold strong cultural assumptions of their own. However, I will take it that all social groups require persons (however they are locally defined) as material human beings. It may not be inevitable that societies need selves, depending on how self is defined, although doing without an idea of self is hardly an option in western societies – at least for anyone who wants to be regarded as sane.

My task of defining self theoretically will be made easier if I give a brief sketch of the intellectual context in which current theories have developed.

The nineteenth-century legacy of mind

At the beginning of the twentieth century, the human sciences were operating within a worldview inherited from Christianity and western philosophy that typically divided up existence into material things and mental things. This worldview was either implicitly adopted in the human sciences or provoked movements that opposed it. As regards human beings, the traditional view set body against mind, the latter being seen as made up of mental faculties and mental states. Sigmund Freud (1856–1939), one of the most influential theorists of the period, can be firmly placed in this tradition. Recognising that the conscious mind was full of anomalies and could not be taken at face value, he proposed an 'unconscious mind', another set of mental processes to which a person had limited, if any, access. His concept of the ego, which roughly translates as the everyday self, was also a mental structure, one that mediated between instinctual desires and external reality. Freud was not alone, of course, in making mind the focus of self-understanding.

It was unfortunate for the future of the human sciences that academics in Freud's day were carving out territories and building barriers between them. Psychology was split off from the study of society (sociology) and the study of humankind in general (anthropology). The biological sciences such as physiology and neuroscience, although linked to psychology, also went their own way. The result today is that we have many different specialists all tending to sound like salesmen for their own discipline. For example, as Joseph LeDoux, the celebrated neuroscientist, has phrased it, 'You are your synapses' (2002). Or as Ian Burkitt, a sociologist, says, 'There is no division between the individual and the social' (1991: 212). Or as psychobiologist, Henry Plotkin states: 'Culture is *in* minds and brains' (2002: 113). The challenge of remaking connections between the subject matter and methods of the various human sciences has been left largely to philosophers, acknowledged specialists in conceptual analysis.

In spite of these distracting rivalries, the various disciplines, in their different ways, joined in a great escape from the straitjacket of mind and its mental contents. The twentieth century saw innumerable movements pitting themselves against mind–body dualism and using a different starting point for theory. The most significant of these movements chose behaviour, conscious experience, language or social structure. What they have in common is a shift away from the properties of the so-called mind. As I mentioned in Chapter 1, the dualistic legacy of mind and body lives on, in part because it is installed in our vocabulary and simply presents itself as common sense. And being consistent with common sense, it has been easy to recast 'the mind' as what the brain does. This is the position taken by many cognitive scientists and neuroscientists.

Constructionism

The constructionist movement of the late twentieth century has many intellectual precursors, most of which come from philosophy or the study of language. The novelty of constructionism resides mainly in taking some ancient philosophical concerns out of the academic arena and emphasising the social origins of a person's sense of (and conceptualisation of) reality. It stresses the way our everyday sense of reality is shaped by human communication, language and social practices which are tied to a certain way of life.

Most theorists accept the meaningfulness of a distinction between a natural (or literal) reality and the ways in which that reality is conceptualised, tacitly or explicitly. The idea that we can grasp reality naively without imposing a humanly constructed frame of reference is no longer credible; consequently, we have to assume that there may be more than one viable theoretical interpretation of the same reality. Our need for questioning the fixed nature of reality becomes obvious in the case of social realities. Exposure to the huge variety of forms of social life around the globe makes it increasingly difficult to distinguish between universal and relative truths. And although most of us retain a distinction between what is real and 'fictional', the boundaries are drawn differently in different parts of the world.

As already noted, social constructionists have examined how the ideas through which we apprehend reality originate in, and are maintained by, social practices embedded in a historical tradition. This perspective can be applied also to scientific constructs, and so the word 'social' before construction is redundant. Scientists form their own communities of knowledge generation with agreed ways of arguing about the evidence, and so, to this extent, scientific constructs are also social. Some critics of constructionism have taken it to mean the implantation of a mental filter that distorts reality. This is a misunderstanding, and I will regard all 'versions' of reality as constructed and treat the question of what is distorted or undistorted, real or illusory, as a separate issue (see Chapter 13).

The main targets for constructionist analysis have been everyday and professional concepts, such as 'sex' or 'selfishness', which are often taken to reflect some fixed and universal characteristic of human beings.

The aim is to show how these concepts are tied to broader features of social life in which they perform certain functions and, therefore, that the form they take need not be regarded as inevitable. The aim of the analysis is to comment critically on traditional interpretations rather than to claim a more objective truth; rejoinders are invited in a spirit of openness. The analysis aims to modify rather than replace what, until then, had been taken for granted.

As Ian Hacking (1999) points out, constructionist analyses can be graded according to the strength of the underlying message. Some analyses simply describe a historical process, some are reminders that an idea has arisen out of an almost accidental combination of circumstances, and other analyses have an unmasking, reforming or revolutionary intent. The aim of the present analysis is primarily descriptive although a description is never neutral. The present book might be viewed as unmasking the givenness of a sense-of-self, either to destroy it or, more positively, to strengthen those aspects we wish to retain and to reform the aspects of which we might disapprove. However, my aim is not primarily ethical or political; rather, it is to get a clearer idea of how selves are constructed in the first place, including the role of sub-personal processes.

There are several species of constructionist thinking but they all focus on how human societies 'make' and reproduce themselves. For this reason, they are mainly concerned with the effects of different social arrangements, linguistic practices and historical influences. They are rather silent (or completely silent) on what is assumed to be universal. The more purely linguistic approach to construction sees language as a system of signs and emphasises the open-ended possibilities of language. It therefore implies that there is potential for an almost infinite variety of meanings and social arrangements. For followers of this approach, the social reality of a community is constituted by a system of interrelated meanings, each community possessing its own reality.

This approach to construction seems to grant language far too much autonomy and its relativism generates significant problems (Nightingale and Cromby 1999). I will follow those authors who argue that construction is constrained by some universal features of human beings and their material conditions of existence, and therefore I will view language as only semi-autonomous. In Rom Harré's words: 'The conditions for developing a language rich enough to construct local diversity are universal' (1998: 18). These conditions, according to Harré, include a repertoire of innately determined behaviour patterns. Like him, I aim to incorporate human biology into our understanding of persons and selves. This approach differs from that of writers who can

find no foundations for a constructed reality beyond the social and linguistic practices of a particular society. For this camp, there is no truth
that is not relative to some specific cultural context (e.g., Gergen 1988).
In effect, this means that: 'There is no universal, trans-historical self,
only local selves' (Cushman 1990).

Before attempting to reconcile constructionist insights with universal
constraints, I will examine some definitions of self that can be traced
back to the influence of mind–body dualism and Christianity. It is
these definitions that, in my opinion, hinder the kind of integration I
am seeking.

Self as consciousness

Blasi (2004: 8) centres what he calls a 'basic self' in 'what is experienced
immediately but nonfocally in the very process of acting, every time
there is intentional action'. In other words, people as agents sense that
they are controlling the action as something that belongs to them. This
is not a representation of self as such, more an experience that is associated with intended acts but not with passive movements. Blasi (2004:
8–9) believes that the experience is non-cognitive, primitive and fundamental, and quite unlike the perception of external objects and persons.
It is 'to be present to oneself in the process of acting' (Blasi 2004: 8–9).

This is a good description of what it feels like to be a western self but
it does not provide a basis for a usable definition. A scientist might ask
what it is that allows us to feel this way – or not feel like a basic self, as
sometimes happens (Sass 1997). One interpretation of Blasi's sense-
of-self is dualistic in the ontological sense. It would suppose that this
consciousness of self exists in a mental realm that does not obey natural
causal laws. It would not be a biological phenomenon, and our felt sense
of controlling our own behaviour could not be explained naturalistically. With a few exceptions (e.g., Popper and Eccles 1977) natural scientists are monists and consider 'mind' as part of the natural world. Most
natural scientists also endorse a belief in the self of humanism – that
what a person consciously thinks about is important in its own right in
the control of behaviour – and still hold (as I would) to monism.

William James, in his *Principles of Psychology* (1890), led the way in
providing a strong precedent for theorising about self as an aspect of
conscious thought (see Scheibe 1998). James's 'I' is a non-empirical,
non-substantial, theoretical concept that has the function of 'providing
a sense and conviction of continuity over time for the entire stream of
self' (Scheibe 1998: 29). James's theorising is embedded in a dualism
of material reality versus thoughts about it belonging to a thinker. His

way of phrasing the issue is as follows: 'each human mind' is said to take an interest in the self (James 1890: 289, quoted by Scheibe 1998: 28). From a naturalistic perspective, only animals or persons take an interest and so it is difficult to see any value in James's mindist approach. Nevertheless, there are recent exponents of similar views.

Jonathan Shear (1999) outlines a 'pure consciousness theory of self' which does not, according to him, have any ontological implications. He defines self in phenomenal terms as a pure quality-less awareness, an experience that he considers to have been identified universally. He claims that there is evidence that it correlates with states of the brain, from which I infer, to the contrary, that the experience *does* have ontological implications. Pure consciousness has been reported chiefly by people who meditate and by mystics, and so it can hardly be put forward, as Shear does, as an unnoticed background to all of a person's experience. Moreover, if each person has this experience separately, consciousness must be divisible and boundaried, and this seems incompatible with it being quality-less. Such an empty self seems empty of meaning.

Arthur Deikman (1999) also identifies 'I' with pure awareness. He seems to equate awareness with being conscious rather than unconscious, a difference that must apply as much to primates as humans. It is therefore unclear whether his statement 'I am sure that I exist because my core "I" is awareness itself' (1999: 424) would apply also to an ape. 'I' is a pronoun, part of a language, and so the best explication of its meaning is likely to be linguistic (see below). His notion that 'I' is an observer of experience that is never observed leaves quite opaque what 'I' refers to or how 'I' would be used in this sense in everyday discourse.

Primates do, of course, demonstrate awareness of themselves as an object in space, and Robert Mitchell (1994) attributes this ability largely to an animal's capacity to match visual information (what it or another animal looks like) with kinaesthetic information (what it feels like to do something). This matching is bidirectional and so the animal might, say, respond mimetically when viewing another animal as if it was in the same situation as that animal. He also cites evidence that chimpanzees appear to recognise that other animals perceive and evaluate them. Mitchell highlights the importance of a non-linguistic sense-of-self and an intuited sense of what others are doing and feeling. He also goes on to speculate that self-reflective self-awareness in humans stems from the ability to imagine oneself as an object and to create oneself as an audience that evaluates the image (Mitchell 1994: 97). However, without denying the role of consciousness and imagery in a sense-of-self, it is difficult to see how self-referential awareness could develop without a shared symbolic means of indicating that self and other (I and You) belong, in the abstract sense, to the category of persons (see Chapters 11 and 12).

Some natural scientists have combined a belief that consciousness is a brain process with the idea that to be conscious is to know (or feel) that one is a self. If this were true, the causes of the self would be discoverable in the brain. Ordinarily, we do not seek to relate our conscious experience to the brain unless we have a headache or need to consult a neurologist. We managed as a species for aeons of time without knowing anything much about the function of the brain. We now know that the brain is necessary for persons to have selves but this doesn't tell us what a self is.

Nevertheless, it has been proposed that if it were possible to cream off the activities of the brain that correspond to being conscious, these activities could be put forward as a causal explanation for consciousness and self. Antti Revonsuo (2005: 303) suggests that we just need to identify a micro-level of neurobiological organisation that 'directly mirrors the structure, organisation, and contents of the phenomenal level'. I reject this suggestion on the basis that conscious experience only appears against a backdrop of processes that lie outside our awareness (see Chapter 5). Some of these processes presumably take place in the brain as a whole, and others relate to our connections with other people in cultural contexts. An approach that seeks the immediate neural antecedents and correlates of a 'basic self' would be like equating the whole of an iceberg with the tip that appears above the waterline.

In any case, the hypothesis of an identity between 'mind' and brain has not yet provided a credible explanation of self. We know from volunteers connected up to various measuring devices that self-reported experience is correlated with events in the brain. But even if a difference were to be found in the neural correlates of, let us say, an intended and an unintended act, this would only account for one neural antecedent in a chain of causal events (see Chapter 10).

Marcel Kinsbourne (2005: 152–5) proposes (purely speculatively it seems) that there are neural correlates of the distinction between being aware and self-aware. The brain of a person who is self-aware is said to be in more than one brain state at the same time without the states collapsing into one dominant state. Kinsbourne is an identity monist so, for him, a conscious experience 'does nothing'; it is 'the result of a brain state' not its cause and, in fact, 'consciousness is always a step behind the action' (2005: 154).

The idea being proposed here is that the neural network of the brain 'has subjective access to some of its own states' (Kinsbourne 2005: 150).

Apart from a difficulty understanding what this statement could possibly mean, it seems to imply a form of ontological dualism. All that a mind/brain identity theorist can really claim is that being conscious of something is nothing more nor less than the brain state with which it is said to be identical. If this brain state controls behaviour, so does the conscious experience with which it is identical. If conscious experience occurs later than the events that are supposed to be identical with it, this version of identity monism doesn't work on present physical assumptions.

Self as knowledge

Another avenue into the problem of definition is to consider self as an item of knowledge. The key question is: What is it that the knowledge is about? If we consider the human organism as our object of knowledge, it is not unreasonable to suppose that a scientist can aim for an increasingly accurate representation of parts of the body and how they function. However, the same cannot easily be said of self. If self is a virtual reality, as I claim, it does not make sense to seek to represent it accurately, that is, in order to mirror an actual or 'real' self. For example, if instead of selves, we were to investigate elves, it would make no sense to try to obtain an increasingly accurate specification of a real elf. Presumably, we could more or less accurately describe what most people think an elf is, any experiences they may have had of elves, how they talk about elves, and what functions elves serve in the social practices of people who believe in them. A constructionist exploration of self as an as-if entity could be conducted along similar lines. Self would not then be an item of knowledge – it would figuratively represent some kind of shared but largely unexamined understanding that explains a person's place in the world, related to what a person does, thinks or feels. In this case, the concept of self would function rather like a concept of an elf; we would not have to suppose that self was a form of knowledge about a discoverable entity.

However, reference to a virtual self must bear some relationship to our knowledge of reality. But unlike the human body, which is tangible and open to direct and indirect observation, the reality to which I assume self relates – rule-governed forms of talk, material social practices, possible ways of acting, etc. – is so complex and multilayered, and so unlike any entity that could be compared to the body, that we have to suppose that people conceive of it symbolically in ways that simplify or manage that reality. One suggestion is that self functions like a scientific concept in a theory of reality (Epstein 1973).

In other words, it is assumed that there is a knowable reality and self is a theoretical term in a person's attempt to comprehend that reality. In this case, self could be compared with a scientific concept such as 'a force', 'an organising principle' or a 'mechanism'. We would be comparing a person's search for self-understanding with a scientist's search for an adequate description of reality.

This analogy is inadequate if there is a reflexive relationship between the phenomenon of self and attempts to pin it down scientifically. Any naturalistic account would have to do justice to this reflexive characteristic. Although I consider it possible to study self generically (see Chapter 3), this does not imply that there is an independent entity about which more and more could be discovered. If a scientific conception of the western self changes, so, at the same time, does social reality. A generic concept of self might provide a *framework* for comparing the selves of ancient Egyptians and modern selves but this would cast light only on the adequacy of the framework rather than tell us more about Egyptian selves.

A second plank in Epstein's proposal is that the concept of self is an element in 'folk theory' that functions much like a scientific theory. I examine this much-discussed idea in Chapter 9 but I will reject the view that people adopt scientific methods when they seek self-understanding or that infants have to develop a 'theory-of-mind' (see Chapter 11).

A person's knowledge of themselves is unlikely to be based only on conceptual distinctions or analogical reasoning. A person, like any organism, presumably learns their way around the world on the basis of what can be done with the body. And the body provides sensory feedback that is unique to that organism. In this sense, a person's self-knowledge is singular and we can refer to their concept of their own self as what it feels like for them to be this entity with its unique memories, relationships and projects. This is not equivalent to saying that they understand the conventional uses of self as a shared symbol. Consequently, a person may report what it feels like to be a self without this experience corresponding closely to what most people take to be the normal way of feeling like a self. For example, a person might believe that their thoughts have been inserted into their head by means of a device implanted by aliens. This does not match a conventional view of reality, social or physical. The unfortunate person has not used 'self' as conventionally understood but we do not deny that they are stating a true fact about what they feel or believe.

Given the diversity of self-experience, we cannot safely conclude that a sense-of-self, as conventionally understood in western society, is the only way in which reality can be experienced. And the fact that we share a common understanding may say little about the particular natural and social conditions that give rise to anyone's sensed reality of a self. We can only say of any person's knowledge of their 'self' that it accords or does not accord with social reality as generally understood. In order to pursue naturalism, I assume that there is something of a universal nature that can be said about the way particular selves are formed, and I explore attempts in this direction in Part II. However, we cannot expect to obtain a precise understanding of one person's sense-of-self from a naturalistic standpoint any more than we would expect a biologist to account for all differences between 'identical' members of the same species.

Given that there are norms governing the use of self-related terms, people's conceptions of their own attributes might sometimes be described as inaccurate, e.g., they have an overinflated idea of their abilities or underestimate their true worth. However, these are normative judgements and not claims to the existence of natural criteria that could really decide the matter without dispute. We might use 'true' or 'false' to characterise a person's beliefs about themselves, especially if the claims were empirically verifiable, such as their age, but the only thing we can say factually about norms is whether a particular society happens to demonstrate them in a certain form.

When cognitive scientists conceptualise a person's acquisition of an idea such as self, they usually understand it as a process of forming a representation or schema that is located within a person's brain or mind. The cognitive structure is seen as an entity that mediates a person's own thinking and their transactions with the social world. Hazel Markus has defined self-schemata as 'cognitive generalisations about the self derived from past experience, that organize and guide the processing of self-related information contained in the individual's social experience' (1977; quoted by Jopling 1997: 251). There are two aspects worth noting about this conceptualisation. The first is the metaphor of containment: representations are contained in brains/minds, and information is 'contained' in social experience. The person forms representations as if they were an independent information processor. The second is the idea that the representation mirrors 'information' that exists independently 'out there' in the social world or 'in here' in private experience.

In Markus's definition, it would appear that 'the self' is both a cognitive entity and some 'thing', out there that can be generalised about – but what precisely is that? Is her definition any more informative than saying that elf schemata are generalisations about elves that guide the processing of elf-related information? Clearly, Markus means more than this, and the ambiguity of her statement rests on using self both as a cognitive structure and as a person (self) who generates information to be processed. Cognitive research on self-schemata has drawn attention to similarities between the way people process information associated with their unique concept of themselves and information associated with anything else, including other persons or even elves. However, it is not clear from this research how self-schemata relate to all the other presuppositions we hold about the world, many of them unheeded or inaccessible to awareness. People interpret self in relation to things that are 'not self' – other people, alien powers, concepts of how the body works, etc. The processing of 'self-related information' potentially covers such a massive domain that, in this research context, we are likely to take it superficially to mean information that refers to a common-sense notion of personal acts, personalities or 'selves'. The methods used in research on self-schemata are usually based on lists of adjectives or responses to questions in an interview. These techniques underline the narrowness with which self is conceptualised. As Markus (1986: 966) notes in relation to a study of delinquents, helping them to develop a system of positive self-relevant thoughts might involve creating a broader context for 'specific positive possibilities'. This hints at social interventions and a policy context in which it might be possible to influence the way in which delinquents talk about themselves. Her acknowledgement of the social context may explain why Markus has now moved her theoretical position in a constructionist direction (Markus and Kitayama 2002).

However, this new position still leaves the relationship between knowledge and other processes (individual or social) poorly defined. Markus and Kitayama (2002) refer to models of human agency which are inscribed in, *inter alia,* 'modes of being', material practices, cultural affordances, historical constructions and social structures. They are no longer 'properties or dispositions of people', and, in fact, 'they are typically invisible to those that engage or enact them' (2002: 6). But if, as these authors state, they are really concerned with the 'mutual constitution of culture and psyche' (2002: 6) we need a theory to relate attributes of the individual to social and cultural processes.

According to Ulric Neisser (1997), our concept of self is what we bring to mind when we think about ourselves – in other words, a mental representation of who we are and how we act in the world. He says that this self-concept is something we evaluate, defend, glorify or seek to improve. However, this representational view of the self-concept does not seem to capture what we do when we express our 'self'. For instance, we do not attempt to convince others of the accuracy of our own representations. We seek to express the kind of self we want to present, not necessarily drawing on our knowledge of the person we *really* think we are. We dispute with others about the way we are represented but not on the basis of the accuracy of our own representation (which, in fact, we might want to conceal).

It is true that we might have to defend the adequacy of our knowledge and may privately question whether our self-concept should be revised, but it doesn't make sense to glorify an item of knowledge. Neisser suggests that his own knowledge of himself is likely to be 'more elaborate and detailed' (1997: 3) than his reader's but this may be irrelevant in many social contexts in which Neisser expresses who he is. He goes on to remark that self-concepts never do full justice to the self, and he describes neuroses as failures of self-understanding. But some neuroses could be seen, with equal justification, as the result of adhering too closely to a strategy of honestly and faithfully expressing an accurate representation (as one sees it) of oneself.

Neisser seems to argue that a good self-concept has two possible meanings: first, good in the sense of adequate or faithful knowledge, and second, good in the sense that one believes (not always accurately, of course) that one is a good person. For instance, he acknowledges that we have a concept of how we would like our 'real self' to behave and that our 'ideal self' shapes our real self. However, it is unnecessarily confusing to state that 'the boundary between the self and the self-concept is difficult to fix with certainty' (Neisser 1997: 4). This is a relationship that needs conceptual analysis, and, although its reflexive nature is certainly complex, we can make some statements with confidence. For instance, we may reflect on our prior self-reflections, but it is a person who does this, not an inner self who is self-reflecting.

John Kihlstrom and his colleagues also define the self as a person's mental representation of their personality, including physical characteristics and autobiographical knowledge about past events (Kihlstrom et al. 1997). They also claim that the self-concept is accessible to introspective awareness by which they seem to mean that people can report what they think they are like. In that sense, we all have access to our concepts. But if it is meant that we have access to a mental representation (e.g., in Neisser's sense of a mental image of self, in the same way that we have an image of the house that we inhabit), it seems odd to say that this is access to a concept. We assume that concepts shape our perceptions (and our images) but we do not perceive our concepts. In any case, these authors argue that 'the self also represents the sociocultural matrix in which the person lives as well as his or her internal attributes' (Kihlstrom et al. 1997: 155). It is not clear whether this representation is a form of knowledge or a perceived/imagined sense of what it is like for a unique individual to inhabit their social environment.

Kihlstrom and his colleagues reject certain understandings of what a self-concept is, for instance, that it is the proper set of 'an entire class of objects whose features are singly necessary and jointly sufficient to identify an object as an instance of a category' (1997: 159). They must be correct in this because there is an element of choice in saying what is me or not me, and the features may belong to a future, unrealised person, making the features of the set indeterminate. And if the self is defined as a unique combination of traits, this would define a concept in which the self is the only member. These authors also find unsatisfactory various versions of the idea of self as a prototype. As they say, 'if the self is a prototype, what is the self a prototype of?' (1997: 161). In any case, they argue that the mental representation of the self is unlikely to be monolithic but consist, instead, of 'a large set of context-specific selves' (Kihlstrom et al. 1997: 162). They speculate that these could be groupings of concrete exemplars of person-in-context, with or without the addition of an abstract prototype. The authors conclude that people's categorisations of their own attributes are unlikely to be on the basis of a similarity between the features of the object to be categorised. They suggest instead that it is guided by explicit or implicit theories that explain the relations amongst objects, their features and the categories to which the objects belong.

Although I will argue against the 'folk theory' view of a person's common-sense understanding of the world, a constructionist would accept that the concept of self is embedded in wider assumptions and social practices. But persons do not work out a folk theory 'on their own'. The dialogical approach I will now consider argues that self is constituted when persons act jointly with others.

Self as a dialogical reality

As a way of introducing a dialogical perspective, I will discuss Jerome Bruner's ideas on the process of self-construction and then a chapter written by John Shotter in honour of Bruner's contribution to psychology (Shotter 2001). Bruner's (1997) views on self seem to represent a halfway house between a cognitive and a dialogical position. Shotter considers that Bruner is caught between two methodological approaches, one that interprets a person's actions in terms of their reasons for acting and another that examines the natural causes of behaviour.

In his 1997 chapter, Bruner concisely draws up the main terms of any debate on self: the need to reconcile intersubjective communicability with individual distinctness, the need to consider the phylogenesis and ontogenesis of self-development, the necessity of recognising the possibility of change in self while maintaining its sameness and, finally, comprehending the transaction between inner knowledge and public/ cultural conceptions of self. The signs of selfhood, he says, are evident in our own acts and the acts of others, and he goes on to list them. At this point, Bruner resists any discussion of the 'reality' of self: 'such ontological issues need not concern us now' (1997: 148). It is necessary to dig further into his text to extract his ontological commitments.

Bruner refers to a self-system – a system that processes cues about selfhood and produces the experience of self as an output. He notes that the function of cultural adaptation is served by 'mutual self-systems' and that we are governed by the rule that 'other minds operate as ours do' (1997: 151). He therefore seems to be committed to mindism and cognitive structures. The capacity to produce selves would appear to be situated in a person's mind or brain. He does not want to say that self-constructions are guided by internal schemata, preferring to view the process as the exercise of a meta-cognitive skill (1997: 159). But when persons produce their accounts of self, he does acknowledge that 'Most of the time we help each other in the process of dialogue' (1997: 156). In this and other writing (e.g., *Acts of Meaning,* Bruner 1990), he points the way to a transactional or dialogical theoretical perspective.

Like Bruner, Shotter (2001) wants to describe in close detail the dialogue that takes place between people and not merely in terms of words exchanged. The signs and gestures which are used in these situations typically draw upon meanings that are shared because they have acquired a conventional significance. A word, considered in isolation, has an open-ended meaning. Its precise meaning does not get fixed until it is employed as part of an exchange in a specific situation. An analogy could be drawn between a word and a tool (such as a hammer) that has a range of potential and conventional uses, only one of which is actualised when, say, a nail is struck. A person using a hammer (at least, on an inanimate object) is engaging in a monological act. In dialogical acts, more than one actor is implied and each calls forth responses from the other, anticipating the other and predicting the likely effect of what is said or done. Shotter points out that the precise outcome is indeterminate because there is a degree of openendedness in the uses to which any conventional tool can be put.

Shotter remarks that it was only with the advent of audio and video recording that it became possible to repeatedly view or listen to a transaction and describe it in detail. Sticking closely to Wittgenstein's account of meaning and intention, Shotter advocates studying dialogical transactions descriptively, discovering the regularities within those descriptions, rather than imposing either a paradigm of stated intentions (supposedly existing in each actor's mind) or a paradigm that belongs to natural science (e.g., viewing acts merely as responses in a chain of causal reactions). Shotter, in unison with Bruner wearing his 1990 hat, adds that jointly performed meanings 'are only intelligible as variations within the already existing, ongoing background flow of activity constitutive of our current forms of life' (2001: 173).

Applying a dialogical perspective to persons and selves, we are led to suppose that reference to self involves the performance by more than one actor (typically real persons) of an exchange that utilises the conventional resources from which the term 'self' is drawn. One unintended effect of this performance is to preserve the resources in the culture. It is assumed that there is a rule-governed, game-like structure to this performance. In addition to conserving the rules, the performance leaves room for new meanings to emerge because the meaning of a conventional sign is not fixed – there is room for variation around modal (dictionary-type) definitions. Shotter underscores Wittgenstein's insistence that the co-creation of meaning is not a natural process like digestion or even like a 'mental process' (see also Williams 1985). Shotter says that what Wittgenstein objected to was the grammar of process. For him, 'Meaning moves whereas a process stands still' (Wittgenstein 1980, para. 237; quoted by Shotter 2001: 174). In effect, a natural process, like the chemical reactions inside a cell, is conceived as 'dead'.

While I endorse a dialogical conception of self and say more about it in Chapter 7, I will distance myself from Wittgenstein's separation of reasons and causes and the idea that nature is 'dead'. I will adopt the idea that there is a universal potential for 'selfhood' that arises within natural and social conditions. As Jopling expresses it, 'Human selfhood is a problem to which there is a range of flexible and adaptive solutions' (1997: 265). Human beings, who possess a limited range of biological capacities, everywhere confront an environment that affords a limited set of responses to it. Life can be seen as a set of predicaments that may be solved in different ways. Humans, with their capacity for language and their considerable intellectual powers, have greater opportunity to vary their solutions than the great apes. Nevertheless, the existential situation they confront is not totally dissimilar.

Jopling sees human beings as forging identities within the constraints imposed by the singleness of their embodied nature, their prolonged infancy, an awareness of the destruction of the organism at death and their use of speech for communication in the service of a shared identity and cooperation. At the heart of this conception lie the constraints imposed by existence as a singular organism, but acting, perceiving and self-perceiving agents are also located in particular physical and social environments which are equally essential for existence. In this sense, Jopling's conception of selfhood is not person-centred but eco-centric. The introduction of a concept of selfhood amounts to a refusal to specify self but it does attempt to specify the conditions (biological, social, logical) that constrain the concept of self that any group of human beings might happen to come up with. However, the notion of selfhood leaves undefined the relationship between organisms, persons and selves, and this is an issue that needs to be addressed first.

Persons and selves

Not everything a person thinks or does is reflected in their sense-of-self; that is, not everything I do expresses me, even if it is connected with my body. I may trip over, I may be coerced into something, or I may try something out as an experiment. In retrospect, I may judge which of my experiences express my idea of who I am and which are accidental or passively undergone. Over a longer stretch of time, I might look back and evaluate 'what I thought I was doing' at a particular point in time and think about 'what I am now aiming for'. For contemporary persons, the theme of self has a strong temporal aspect because it encompasses what has happened and what is likely to happen.

In the process I have just alluded to – a person evaluating their 'self' – it is not being proposed that there is actually any 'thing', a self, that is making decisions on a person's behalf or making plans for their future. It seems preferable to maintain that these powers emanate from the person. A person may think that they have generally acted in a consist-ent fashion and that what has been experienced is more or less intelli-gible, but it seems clear to me that there is nothing within a person, like a self, that can command a person to exercise their powers. This does not mean that to reflect on experience serves no useful purpose. People often act on the basis of reflection, but it cannot be claimed that there is any automatic translation of the results of reflection into good inten-tions or into any action at all. Our reasons for acting or failing to act on our reflections are often mysterious.

When a person reflects, a circular, reflexive process seems to be at work. A person's concept of self influences their behaviour, and the consequences that may result from this, in turn, shape their idea of self. If self is understood as a mediating idea, it falls on persons as bio-logical and social entities to be the source of self-expression and self-interpretation in conjunction, of course, with other persons. I maintain that self as a mediating idea should not be regarded as the originator of itself. This amounts to saying that 'person' is a foundational concept and that persons, in their capacity as human organisms, originate the circle of reflection.

Taking the person as agent is at odds with a prevalent notion that self reveals itself to itself by reflection. This notion follows from the idea that self is a mental object that is self-illuminating – all we have to do is introspect to find it. Gilbert Ryle (1900–76), in his classic text *The Concept of Mind* (1949: 159) traces this form of self-understanding to the philosopher John Locke who borrowed the newly discovered properties of light and applied them to mental light (consciousness), which could illuminate the mental world. One could then literally see oneself as in a mirror (reflexion, in Locke's terms).

Ryle's formulation conflicts with an intuitive sense that it is not 'person' but 'self' that makes decisions, acts and so forth. I may weigh up what is in my own best interest and feel that it is my 'self' that is doing this. However, this interpretation of what is going on involves a sleight of hand because, as noted earlier, self is used in two senses: as a person who thinks and as a vehicle of thought for the entity that this person produces when the future is entertained. It is the person who is the ultimate actor in this scenario. As a person, I consider my own interests in order to place them in accord with the theme of the self that runs through my life. I may suppose that a self (a kind of virtual person) is doing all this, but, according to the framework I am putting forward, the powers of the self are entirely contingent on the person (as a hybrid biological/conceptual entity), their social network and the wider cultural context. The social context must be introduced because human beings, in strict isolation, are unlikely to be the source of anything. Of course, making 'person' a foundational theoretical concept does not imply that it is the only foundation for constructing a universe that includes self.

In daily life, we often think of the self as making up our mind for us. The request to 'Go away and think about it' could be taken to mean a process of self-consultation as if there were an inner person who really knew what was going on. Ryle counters this interpretation by asserting that mind is not like an organ of the body that does things for us. He says we should follow the example set by novelists for whom only persons do things or undergo things (Ryle 1949: 168). Ryle argues that in self-understanding a person discovers their own mental attributes (motives, character, etc.) in the same way that they discover anyone else's. We draw conclusions from what is said and match it up with other evidence, interpreting gestures, mannerisms and so forth. In his words, 'we eavesdrop on our own voiced utterances and our own silent monologues' (Ryle 1949: 184). It is a person doing this, and, consequently, it is a person who catches themself in retrospection. Persons catch themselves thinking, but they cannot catch themselves catching themselves thinking.

Persons refer to their own utterances by using the word 'I', and so it is tempting to make I into a name for something, such as 'the I'. Ryle says that this is a mistake. 'I' is an indexical term, like 'this' or 'now', which can only be understood in a particular context where 'this' indicates a particular 'this', and where 'now' is a particular moment. Similarly, 'I' expresses the point of view of the particular speaker who utters it in a defined context of reference, allowing others to identify the location of the speaker. I, of course, may behave differently at different times and so 'I' may convey different characteristics while being expressions of the same literal person. This means that in the very same sentence, the first-person pronoun may have different senses but emanate from the same person. For instance, in the same sentence, a person might refer to what they are doing and comment on the fact that they are doing it (e.g., 'What an idiot I look to myself when I wear this hat').

Ryle believes that any performance can be subjected to higher-order appraisal about it (e.g., a further commenting thought) but only in retrospect; self-commentary is condemned to 'eternal penultimacy' (Ryle 1949: 195–8). This means that 'I' is systematically elusive. I might decide to think about my annual vacation, but the one thing I cannot prepare myself for is precisely the next thought I am going to think. So anyone who is concerned about the problem of the self 'fails to catch more than the flying coat-tails of that which he is pursuing. His quarry was the hunter' (Ryle 1949: 198). This does not stop a human tendency to fill in the inevitable gap in understanding. This is where people may turn to analogical thinking. Typically, self is thought of as a figurative person (homunculus) inside the (literal) person. This 'as if' or virtual self only becomes substantial if we interpret the analogy literally.

So, even though we might attribute our powers to mental states or to internal causes 'in the mind' like 'one's willpower' or a virtual self, Ryle would argue that this is a category mistake that involves categorising dispositions as things. Shaun Nichols (2008) interprets Ryle as saying that a term like 'desire' (and also presumably 'self') refers to a publicly observable phenomenon. However, Ryle need not be interpreted as meaning that we do not privately experience a phenomenon of desire (or a sense-of-self). Ryle's point is that we know this, and others know it, because desires and selves are expressed publicly not because they are nothing more than publicly observable behavioural dispositions. For example, we can imagine ghosts in machines even if ghosts do not exist.

Stephen Stich and Nichols (2002) also object to Ryle's analysis on the grounds that it is circular. The argument is that any public observation is theory-laden and so it would follow that a theoretical concept, like, say, an intention, is needed in order to categorise a behaviour as an expression of a disposition to intend. If this were really the case, an infant could never learn the concept of intending from public expressions of behaviour without already possessing the concept, presumably innately. This is an implausible account of concept learning. Moreover, even if the infant has to be able to make some other conceptual distinctions before acquiring a concept of intending, there is no reason to assume that these have anything to do with the western folk theory of mind.

To grant that self is not substantial opens up several possible ways of thinking about the nature of its existence. Ryle disputes a definition of self as a thinking being. He does not deny that persons think. It is also the case that besides having thoughts, people have a felt sense of themselves as being a body located in time and space (part of a sense-of-self) and also as existing in a moral order. The moral dimension – that persons are considered responsible for their acts – introduces a level of analysis that has been considered to go beyond the natural order. However, nobody would deny that being a moral agent is unconnected with the fact that a person has a material body: to have a moral sense does not remove people from their participation in a natural reality. And a virtual self is not immaterial inasmuch as self is communicated through gestures, words and images. In this sense, self is no more illusory than the economy or democracy.

Of course, some theorists have argued that self *is* illusory, and the sense in which this is true needs to be unpacked (see Chapter 13). The general position I take is that persons, not selves, are held accountable for their acts. Rom Harré (1997a; 1998) has used the word 'illusory' in connection with self, but only within a philosophical context.

Harré's account of persons and selves can be seen as a development of the ideas of Ryle and Wittgenstein. He uses Wittgenstein's concept of a grammar to elucidate the entities, relations, processes, etc., that the human sciences lay out as their subject matter. By a grammar, he means the normative rules that govern what can be legitimately said about the subject matter from the point of view of that grammar. For instance, he talks of psychology adopting a dual or hybrid grammar of causal mechanisms and a grammar of persons and their intended acts. While arguing that a grammar of persons is the appropriate language for psychology, Harré also stresses the fact that persons are doubly constituted as material and conceptual beings. So, applying his ideas to the expression 'I have to find out who I am', this would translate out as 'I (as a biological individual and public person) am engaged in finding out about my self (my idea about who I am, privately or as a public person).'

According to Harré, whatever 'I' assert is understood as being expressed from a position within several personal arrays, primarily the location (or imagined location) of the speaker's body in space and time but also arrays in the local moral and social order (1997a: 186–7). As with Ryle, Harré takes 'I' to be an indexical expression, not an entity, although when I refer to myself as a public speaker, I am certainly referring to an entity. It is on these grounds that Harré has referred to self as a grammatical fiction – a fiction or illusion created by the sense that 'I' actually refers to some 'thing' rather than being a means of referring to what I (as a particular speaker) am doing, saying, perceiving or thinking in a particular time and place.

Making the person into the ultimate actor avoids potential confusion but still leaves some conceptual puzzles. If persons are doubly constituted as biological and conceptual, we have to consider the social origins of the concept of a person and the biological properties of persons that enable them to act. There is also the complication of explaining how, in rare cases, several persons apparently inhabit the same body. Despite this anomaly, I suggest that societies that lacked a concept of publicly identifiable singular human beings (if any such society could exist) could not develop an explicit concept of self. I assume that animals and pre-linguistic infants tacitly experience the world from the standpoint of their own body in space and time, but I will argue that *explicit* concepts of person and self have had to develop over the course of human social evolution and have to be acquired routinely in infancy by all of us.

In line with Ryle and Harré, I will regard the contemporary western notion of being a self as a figurative extension of the concept of person. Rather than talking about 'the self', I will refer simply to 'self'. Selves are attributes of persons, but how do persons get to know they have selves? And if persons are first and foremost biological human beings, how do human beings get to know they are persons? The modern western self is presumably not the only way in which persons can figuratively or otherwise conceive of who they are. The word 'self', with the connotation of an entity within the person (as distinct from herself, himself, etc.) came into general use in the eighteenth century. As a figure of speech, we may regard self as fictional, but, in so far as we understand each other as selves, and presuppose that selves belong to real persons, selves are as real to us as any other taken-for-granted cultural presupposition.

A concept of self is embedded in an experienced sense-of-self, a conscious awareness of our bodies and our surroundings, which is something I assume that we share with many species of animal. However, to reflect that we are aware in this way I consider to be uniquely human.

Universal constraints on person and self

As there are clearly very many different local/historical ideas about persons and selves, I will use 'Person' and 'Self' with the initial letter capitalised to indicate generic concepts. When not capitalised, persons and selves refer to specific expressions of the generic concept in a particular culture. Person and Self (capitalised) are theoretical terms that refer to the general empirical, linguistic and logical conditions that have to be presupposed by any specific concept of person and self (lower case). Specific senses of person and self refer to the historical forms in which persons have identified each other over a long cultural tradition, as part of their social and material way of life.

Language provides resources for person reference (personal pronouns, personal characteristics, models for self-expression, etc.), and these resources are used in social contexts in which persons collaborate together and address one another. The infant is addressed as a named individual and later acquires a more sophisticated understanding of person-related terms, including an idea of self. Personal attributes encapsulate moral judgements, and self-expression is subjected to social surveillance and evaluation.

If the ability to think about oneself involves expressing thoughts in words, humans need to possess a body, an intact brain and the organs of speech. Embodiment therefore has a central place in any analysis of Person and Self. Embodiment must be essential for a sense-of-self, whether we are talking about animals or humans. With respect to an explicit reference to self, it is difficult to imagine how we could ascribe self-conscious thinking to beings that could not make abstract distinctions and manipulate symbols to express them. This suggests that any generic framework for Person and Self has to account for the way particular persons and selves are referred to linguistically, even though persons and selves are not constituted solely through language. Language use implies communicating humans who recognise each other as persons. Given the empirical and foundational role of persons, there is a need to explain how one human being recognises another as being a member of the class of Persons.

According to the philosopher Peter Strawson (1919–2006), the concept of Person is logically primitive: it cannot be analysed into necessary and sufficient conditions of a logical kind (1959). For Strawson, the fact that persons are living bodies existing amongst other material things, laid out in space and time, is logically tied up with the possession of a unique personal identity. The idea of a disembodied person is incoherent unless we are extending the meaning of person figuratively. Raziel Abelson (1977) explains why, according to Strawson, a person cannot be defined as a mind plus a body. He says that the possession of a mind presupposes that its owner is a person, and, therefore, it cannot serve as one of the elements in a composite definition of person. Abelson argues that person status is recognised independently of behavioural criteria alone so that an extremely clever simulation of human behaviour by a machine would not be enough to ascribe personhood to it. 'Person' is more like the concept 'good', a judgement that we may make of other human beings on the basis that they are human beings (and not machines, etc.).

However, the fact that we can also assign psychological and moral predicates to 'gods, angels and Martians' (Abelson 1977: 87) implies that person is a status that can be assigned independently of biological classification. Abelson (1977: 86–7) states that 'Human spans the fact-value gap through its dual use, being limited in reference to *Homo sapiens* at the same time that it conveys more than biological taxonomy, as in "He's only human".' Abelson argues that 'Person' has a more open-ended reference than 'Human', as noted above, but he would presumably still assert that living bodies are needed for the concept to arise in the first place.

Abelson (1977: 92–3) points out that the way we use 'self' (except as a reflexive pronoun) is quite different to the way we use 'person' and that to confuse the two is a philosophical error. For instance, he says that Sartre's idea of self as a project implies that self is not an object of inspection because it only exists by virtue of a project that is not yet fulfilled. Self has an *as if* existence in so far as we do have reasons for acting on the basis that it will exist and as if, in one sense, it already exists (see also Josephs 1998).

If personhood is assigned by way of a judgement, an analysis of the way we use the concept can be viewed as an unfolding of our own cultural practices, and these reveal a patchwork of related meanings. As another philosopher, Amélie Rorty, puts it, 'there is no such thing as "the" concept of a person' (1988: 31). She describes a variety of functions of the concept, each conceptual dimension bearing its exemplar and opposite, such as freeman versus slave, citizen versus alien, the saved versus the damned, the rational versus the deranged. Having pointed out this conceptual variety, she concludes that the dimensions cannot plausibly be combined into a single concept (Rorty 1988: 42).

Nonetheless, I would argue that reference to our fellow creatures presupposes some natural conditions of existence that have to be in place before humans are in a position to use any concept of Person. These conditions are not a definition of the concept of Person but logical and empirical conditions for having any such concept at all. Philosophers are interested in meaning rather than empirical matters, and Rorty rightly rejects the possibility of defining Person as a synthesis of several conditions, believing that this would only be a parody of a characterisation in which the conditions do not cohere. She proposes the following (my summary) only to reject them: a unit of agency having a conception of its identity and what is important to it, interacting with others in a common world, reflexively sensitive to the context of its activity, critically reflective and inventing its own storyline. Rorty notes that it is not clear whether these conditions are conjunctive or nested or even consistent with each other.

As far as it goes though, Rorty has pinpointed some of the essential empirical circumstances in which Persons can be talked about (assuming language has evolved). It is difficult to imagine any human capable of self-reference who was not an agent in the sense of making some choices, who was not aware of itself as a distinct object amongst a similar class of objects (other humans) and who was not capable of evaluating its own behaviour and that of others. Whether or not it would invent a personal storyline or reflect on it to any degree could be debated but it would, by default, produce a storyline for any other human who cared to read it. None of these conditions are entirely absent in the higher primates – as we would expect if self/other reference is relatively recent in evolutionary terms and has grown out of capacities shared with other animals.

I will use the term 'Person' as a generic description of all the possible ways in which human beings may refer to each other as unique public individuals. As noted earlier, the English personal pronoun 'I' indexes the speaker as a publicly identifiable person and is not an entity whose characteristics I describe when I refer to myself. I express myself through the use of I rather than describe myself, which are logically distinct kinds of utterance. If I wanted to describe my characteristics, I might even turn to a third-person grammar. And when describing myself in the first person, I might say 'I am X' but then change my mind: 'No I am not really that.' Clearly, the way 'I' is used here (indicating an expression of the particular speaker concerned) does not change from one moment to the next but the description of me does. A reference to a continuously identifiable speaker whose description may change is a logical consequence of using the grammar of personal pronouns.

The etymological derivation of the word 'person' is from the Latin *persona,* for mask. The donning of a mask presupposes a material being who dons it. Masks are worn by persons, not by other masks, and so we may assume that 'person' originally referred to some status that actual human beings occupied. Local definitions of person normally include moral, legal and political criteria. These change historically, and, to illustrate the point, Rorty notes that women and slaves in Roman society were not persons who could originate lawsuits; they needed a representative to act on their behalf (1988: 85). The concept person has historical origins, but I wish to extend it as a generic concept for all societies with language. As applied to hunting and gathering societies, it is anachronistic but serves well enough. Persons are there usually defined not as separate persons but as members of a collective (clan, tribe, family, etc.) that may assume responsibility for the actions of each of its members. Nevertheless, unique identities must be present in some form. Strictly speaking, person implies a publicly identified individual who is, in Rorty's words, 'a unified center of choice and action, the unit of legal and theological responsibility' (1988: 85). The idea of individual legal rights may be absent in some societies but it seems likely that certain rights, such as the right to a share of food, are assigned to individual members of the group and publicly acknowledged.

The difficulty encountered in being more precise about the concept Person resides in the fact that human beings ascribe Personhood to each other. The origins of the concept must have something to do with the mutual recognition by one human being that they share their humanity with another. This reciprocal relationship in fact allows for great variation in precise criteria, hence the difficulty of establishing necessary and sufficient conditions. In some societies, the word for being a member of the group is the same as the word for being human (e.g., Read 1955). Outsiders are not, in some sense, seen as being members of the human race. In western societies, one's fellow humans are usually assumed to have rights and obligations, and so this becomes part of the concept of a person.

It is evidently too restrictive to claim that human beings only came to recognise individual uniqueness with the advent of a linguistic term for personhood. Non-linguistic animals and pre-linguistic infants also go about their business to satisfy their needs; they have an individual body-based perspective. They also recognise other individual animals or humans. Before the developing infant can refer to itself through language, it must have acquired some pre-linguistic capacities such as the ability to make distinctions of an abstract nature that are not yet put into words. I will take up this point later, but, for the moment, I will focus on the capacity of a human being to reflect that it is a being that experiences things from a unique viewpoint, and this, I suggest, requires language.

This capacity implies that an explicit awareness of, and reference to, personhood is only possible for members of a community who use a shared system of signs, such as a common language. Language communities have to adhere to certain conventions as agreed criteria for the meaning of words and have a general desire to tell the truth to each other. They have to be motivated to communicate with each other and form relationships. All of this might sound rather obvious, but these issues are inevitably raised when adult humans are compared with higher primates and pre-linguistic infants. In any event, I assume that the generic Person and Self emerge out of other cognitive abilities and forms of social life shared with other animals.

The process of reciprocal naming (i.e. the naming of one person by another) has been called 'interpellation' by the Marxist philosopher Louis Althusser (1918–90). In his view, persons are constituted symbolically and exist naturally 'in ideology'. He assumes that the daily rituals of recognition are practised without even thinking about them (Althusser 1969). He points out that we respond to this calling because we already know who we are; we already exist 'in ideology'. He notes that the process is more subtle than it first appears because we may not wish to acknowledge the manner of our calling. That is, we may believe ourselves to exist outside ideology.

Althusser uses the example of Christianity to illustrate his thesis. The whole corpus of texts, rituals and sacraments in effect address an individual and call them into existence as a particular kind of person, with given origins, given powers and given obligations (assuming, of course, that they respond to this calling). In this example, typical of ideology in general according to Althusser, the person is called by an Other Subject, i.e. God. He writes this other subject with a capital S to distinguish it from ordinary subjects. In the Scriptures, God is defined as the absolute subject ('I am that I am') and humans are declared as created in the image of God. In being called as subjects, they subject themselves to God, and Subject and subject mutually recognise one another. The subject is ambiguously positioned as '(1) a free subjectivity, a centre of initiatives, author of and responsible for its actions; (2) a subjected being who submits to a higher authority, and is therefore stripped of all freedom except that of freely accepting his submission' (Althusser 1969: 56).

Stuart Hall (2000: 21) cites a criticism of Althusser that there is a contradiction in his theory: it seems that the subject has to be constituted as a subject before it can recognise itself as a subject (Hirst 1979). However, if persons are doubly constituted, the human organism is already a biological subject that learns how to *become* a social subject; human babies learn this routinely (see Chapter 11). Hall offers similar counter-arguments to Hirst's criticism.

In Althusser's theory, reciprocal naming is extended beyond literal persons by introducing figurative persons, such as God. The recent history of personhood has created complex layers of interpellation, climaxing in the ultimate injunction to call oneself into existence: to be one's own person and to form one's life in one's own image. However, this kind of interpellation can still be viewed as dependent on an abstract Other subject, although the nature of the Other is far more opaque.

I proposed earlier that people may conceive of a self by analogy with a person. But figurative persons (homunculi) are only one possible means by which people comprehend their existence. I will therefore introduce another abstract concept, a generic Self, that includes all of the possible ways in which people might comprehend their own existence. The generic Self is likely to refer to the persistence of personal attributes through time and to relationships with other people or other entities, such as gods or animals. As it is persons who refer in this way, all instance of the generic Self are attributes of the person. The *concept* of a person is also an attribute of a person *qua* human being, but persons, in the way I have defined them, are necessarily jointly constituted with a material body. Of course, some of the entities with which persons are understood to be related are person-like. There are mythical figures, gods and stock characters that are imaginatively conceived as embodied. I intend to include all these person-like entities that lack an actual body under the generic Self in order to emphasise their non-material status. For example, spirits of the ancestors, internalised mother-figures and the like are easier to handle theoretically if they are lumped together as analogical or figurative means by which persons (embodied) communicate with other people (embodied) and with the natural world.

This is not to deny that some of these 'imaginary persons' are believed to really exist. When this is the case, imaginary persons are often assumed to have powers comparable to embodied persons and are perceived as the agents of their acts. One of the most significant expressions of agency is speech. Selves are spoken of and are therefore essentially without agency. Imaginary persons may be understood as conversing with mere mortals, but I will view the agencies involved in this relationship as the product of real persons, whatever the local conception might be. Western persons have talked about themselves in a variety of ways, and in earlier centuries (but not exclusively then) this has included souls and spirits. Viewed historically, apart from 'myself' (as a public person), there does not seem to have been an entity 'the self' that obviously emerges as an identifiable common thread. I will therefore treat the contemporary western self as one expression of the generic Self.

One implication of treating the generic Self in this way is the need to expand the context of interpretation for any reference to local selves. The cultural context includes all the various beliefs, norms and social practices that concern persons. Given that these are often taken for granted, their presence may be hidden and unarticulated. For instance, when explicit reference is made to a notion of self, there will also be a tacit context of assumptions that frame or ground the expression of the consciously articulated idea. This greatly complicates an integration of constructionist and biological perspectives, but it seems unavoidable. The need to see beyond the surface structure of talk or text is, of course, an inevitable feature of interpretation.

The acquisition of reference to persons or selves

If reference to person and self is a symbolic achievement, it is necessary to theorise about its acquisition in childhood and in human social evolution (see Chapters 11 and 12). Having dispensed with the idea that a conscious subject knows that they are the originator of that consciousness, we have to ask how a sense-of-self with its unique point of view is acquired.

An ability to reflect on oneself as an object in the world presupposes a capacity to make abstract distinctions and at least, in part, express them symbolically. A language of self-reference must have precursors, and so it seems reasonable to suppose that self-referential thought develops in a series of steps, with one stage being logically and empirically dependent on previous stages. These stages must be discernible in the development of any child. The modern child, as distinct from our earliest ancestors, is born into a world of adults that already possess a sophisticated set of terms for self-reference. This must represent a huge advantage that makes the process of developing into a self-conscious human being something that seems completely natural and inevitable.

A watershed in the acquisition of thoughts that refer to the person who is having them occurs when a child is able to refer to individual speakers, including themself, as the person who speaks. This means learning how to use a set of concepts that imply identity and personal possession: I, me, mine, you, yours, theirs, etc. Pronouns index speakers and actors rather than naming people, and they need not imply anything about inner selves or private access to a mind.

Some theorists disagree with this linguistic approach on the grounds that there is some thing to which 'I' refers. Usually this thing is the mind or one of its states. They assume that pre-linguistic infants instinctively know the contents of their own minds and then infer that other people have minds similar to their own on the basis that others seem to be human beings like themselves. On the contrary, I will be suggesting that an infant needs to assimilate certain conceptual tools from culture in order to acquire the feat of thinking about itself. These tools are largely mediated through language, passed on from one generation to the next (see Chapter 11).

Language does not, of course, arise suddenly in infants without intellectual antecedents and exposure to carers who address them through the spoken word. Before a child can identify persons as speakers (including itself), it needs to be able to differentiate itself as a separate entity from the world and also be able to identify objects (like speakers) that have a continuing and independent existence. The child also needs the abstract concept of a person, as well as the means to pick out exemplars of the concept, so that it can recognise them as the same person from one occasion to the next. For a pre-linguistic infant, this is initially a purely behavioural competence that later becomes a linguistic competence.

According to José Bermúdez (1998) it would be paradoxical to suppose that a capacity to think self-referential thoughts ('I' thoughts) rested entirely on a mastery of the correct use of personal pronouns. This leads to a logical circularity: that mastery of the first person would have to be in place before it could be acquired. He argues that a pre-linguistic infant needs a prior unarticulated sense of itself as a centre of experience in order to be able to master the necessary pronominal distinctions. And, as he points out, there is substantial evidence that infants are provided with and can utilise information about their location in space and learn to coordinate their reactions with those of their caregivers. Infants as living organisms perceive the world from a precise location, at a point from which they act; infants already possess a primitive point of view, as must many other animals. All of these philosophical points are readily granted but the capacity I will be focusing on in this book is the capacity to reflect that one is a being that experiences things from a unique viewpoint, and this, I suggest, requires language.

In the next chapter, I elaborate on the generic Person and Self and introduce some further ways of characterising them.

3   Generic persons and selves

As already explained in Chapter 2, I regard generic concepts of Person and Self (capitalised) as theoretical abstractions in a framework for interpreting local concepts of person and self across time and culture. They are not constructs in a psychological theory that explain how an individual functions. They are more like foundation conditions for a theory within social science that can be applied cross-culturally. This is a challenging task but if it were not possible to develop a framework of this kind, we would be condemned to viewing every concept of person and self in relative terms. This would make it impossible to identify, appraise and compare persons and selves historically or cross-culturally.

Theorists take different attitudes to the inevitable cultural relativity of their own theories. Psychologists usually proceed as if their constructs have universal application. Cultural psychologists focus on cultural differences but they may still assume that these represent variations of universal processes. Anthropologists, working at a meeting place of cultures, cannot avoid being aware that constructs are relative. They distance themselves from the universalist bias of psychology, and those who adopt a universal framework are in a minority (e.g., Spiro 1993). Constructionists, almost by definition, are little concerned with constructs that overarch different social or cultural locations. From their perspective, concepts such as mind, mental state or behavioural response are already problematic because they prejudge the terms in which arguments about persons and selves are couched.

Philosophers are in the unusual position of studying arguments often written centuries or millennia earlier yet still translating them into a form that can be questioned for its validity and logical coherence. Their natural bias is universalist. But for those philosophers who believe that contemporary scientific evidence has implications for the nature of the issues in question, a reliance on ordinary language and a form of rationality that stretches across time has come into question. Some philosophers have bracketed off the way ordinary people make sense of reality and described it as 'folk psychology' (Dennett 1991).

Folk concepts then need to be interpreted in terms of the preferred universal philosophical language (idealist, materialist, neuroscientific, or whatever it happens to be). A philosophy that distances itself from folk psychology is therefore another potential source from which to construct a universal framework.

Cross-cultural descriptions

A comparison of the way selves are understood in different cultures necessarily demands a set of concepts that can be applied in different situations (Harris 1989). The work of Markus and Kitayama (2002), mentioned in Chapter 2, required them to search for a definition of agency 'with relatively few culture-specific philosophical commitments' (2002: 17). They adopt one that does not commit them to saying that the source of agency resides solely in the individual, such as a person's intentions. They refer to social processes shaping individual action and to cultural models as frameworks 'that hold intended worlds together' (2002: 20). These authors do not expand on the ontological status of the processes and social relationships that achieve this effect, but their theoretical difficulties are understandable.

Cross-cultural studies of folk constructs have often failed to make a clear distinction between person and self and have made sweeping claims. In a review of many such studies, Hope Landrine (1992) distinguishes between the *indexical* and the *referential* self, the latter said to be typical of western society. She conceives of the western self as a mental entity that is unique, singular, boundaried and a centre of awareness, emotion and judgement. It is represented as 'existing free of any and all contexts' (Landrine 1992: 403) and also as a moral agent that is free to do as it wishes. Landrine thinks that this representation is especially typical of white, male, middle-class Americans, and she believes that it is unknown among most Asians, Native Americans, Black Americans and, indeed, among most White American women! The *indexical* self is viewed as the principal alternative representation. This self is indexed by the contextual features of social interactions in diverse situations. It is not an entity to which one can refer in isolation. In an often-cited quotation from the writings of the anthropologist, Clifford Geertz, the western conception of the person (the referential self) has been portrayed as 'a rather peculiar idea within the context of world cultures' (1983: 59).

Geertz and Landrine put their finger on some important observations, but, as Melford Spiro (1993) convincingly shows, the conceptual distinctions and methods from which their conclusions are drawn are seriously inadequate to the task.

Spiro points to a need for clarity in relation to the following concepts:

1. a person, who is constituted biologically and culturally;
2. cultural conceptions of the person;
3. cultural conceptions of an entity like ego or soul within the person;
4. a person's own construal of this inner entity in relation to their experience;
5. a configuration of traits (personality) that are considered to be uniquely characteristic of each person;
6. each person's awareness that they are separate and different from other persons;
7. a person's own representation, conscious or unconscious, of their own attributes as they are known to the person themself.

Spiro's analysis helps to clarify cross-cultural differences, for example, in the degree to which there is collective ownership of a benefit or harm that befalls any one individual. For instance, in one culture a person might perceive an insult to a member of their family as something for which the family is collectively responsible whereas this would not be true in another culture. Drawing on his own research, Spiro also points out that one cannot assume that 'cultural conceptions of the person are isomorphic with the actor's conception of the self' (1993: 117). In other words, a person's sense-of-self might be experienced and conceptualised in ways that depart significantly from the way they are construed culturally. Furthermore, Spiro says that allegiance may be given to a folk psychological model of self, viewed as an ideal, but not an ideal that is necessarily followed.

Spiro sees things from a universal standpoint, and this belongs to a now unfashionable anthropological tradition that can be traced back to, amongst others, Marcel Mauss (1872–1950) and A. Irving Hallowell (1892–1974). I will now examine some views within this tradition to see how they might contribute to the development of a generic framework.

Universal dimensions of person and self

Mauss (1985) takes both a universal and historical stand in his celebrated essay on the notions of person and self. He distinguishes *personage* ('role'), *personne* ('person') and *moi* ('self'), reminding us that self (at the time of writing) was only about 150 years old. He notes that it is 'an echo of the Declaration of the Rights of Man' (1985: 22). Mauss does not doubt that human beings have always had a sense of their own existence as separate beings and, through language, have used personal pronouns (or their equivalent) to locate themselves in space and time. His essay is about person and self as cultural conceptions.

Mauss produces anthropological and historical evidence that human beings are everywhere assigned statuses or names in rituals that often involve masks. The assigned status links the individual to social groups, ranks and roles within the group, or to the spirits of ancestors. He notes that in ancient Rome the right to names was protected, and usurpers or frauds were challenged under the law. Roman citizens were entitled to a civil *persona*. Slaves were excluded from the right to a *persona*, as they did not own their own bodies, nor did they have ancestors, family names or personal belongings. Patrician families sometimes made a wax mask, moulded from the face of an ancestor, kept in the wings of the *aula* of the house.

Mauss maintains that out of the ancient and broader ritualistic assignment of roles, person eventually became a legal status, associated with certain rights. The etymology of the word person in Greek and Latin is 'mask'; the equivalent in Chinese culture is 'face'. Mauss argues that in recent history, the meaning of person acquired new additions such as 'character' (e.g., the masks of tragedy and comedy) and personality. It was also 'extended into the individual, with his nature laid bare and every mask torn away' (1985: 18). Mauss says that moral conscience was added to the juridical meaning from around 200 BC, especially under the influence of Stoic philosophers. The great significance of Christianity was its recognition that everyone, slaves included, could be admitted to the status of a distinct moral being with a soul. Mauss observes that the category of person/self has continued to develop in the past two millennia to encompass the horizons of consciousness and self-knowledge. I discuss aspects of this development in Chapter 8.

Mauss does not make his universalist assumptions crystal clear, although they can be inferred. In 1954, Hallowell took up this task explicitly by delineating some universal dimensions of Self so that he could apply them to his own anthropological research (Hallowell 1967). He wanted a framework that could be applied to the 'insider views' of the members of all societies without imposing a universal and objective 'outsider's view'. The problem is to understand how we can meet these seemingly incompatible demands.

Hallowell's framework assumes that Persons come to be aware of themselves as objects amongst a world of objects (other Persons and things) and that the nature of this object becomes an object of self-reflection. Persons may reflect on themselves as a Person but more commonly as a Self. In general terms, Self is reflected upon as an element in a cosmology that has metaphysical and moral dimensions. Persons are also aware of their own conduct as Selves, evaluate them with reference to local standards and, to some degree, have volitional control over what they do. Their folk cosmology describes the nature and attributes of things, including invisible symbolic entities of personal relevance, and how these things are causally related, spatially and temporally. Persons reflect that they are singular objects, and this implies some degree of sameness and continuity of Self through time, often including past lives and afterlives.

Building on Hallowell's frame of reference, Paul Heelas and Andrew Lock (1981) attempt to classify the entities that make up a society's conception of the entities in their world, including persons and selves. They propose that entities can be classified as either intrinsic or extrinsic to the conceiver (1981: 29). They do not assume that the boundary of the conceiver is the human body. Self, in their model, is conceptually bounded, and the boundary may take different forms. This Self is, in turn, either in control of what happens or under the control of other entities or forces. Their third feature of Self is that it exists in time.

Heelas and Lock's proposal runs up against a number of difficulties when we equate Self with the conceiver. The problem is to know how to conceive of the conceiver. If the intention is to develop a generic framework and relate it to biological science, problems arise if the conceiver is taken to be any local conception of agency, such as the spirit of an ancestor. To be consistent with human biology, it is more reasonable to ground the capacity to acquire knowledge and to control events in the organism. The theoretical position I took in the previous chapter is that only persons, as human organisms, can control others and events. Persons may represent their agency as a species of Self, but a representation is not an agent, even though in certain local contexts people may view the matter quite differently. I have argued that only persons, jointly constituted with the body, have a material effect on the world and so their conception of themselves as a self that is controlling, or being controlled, is just that: a conception that their self has certain attributes. My conceptual framework is not intended to homogenise local constructs but to show how local differences can arise. The framework makes assumptions about control that may differ from certain folk conceptions about control, but I assume that that is an inevitable feature of any abstract scheme of this nature.

I also argued in Chapter 2 that a person who claims that it was their 'self' that controlled something, or willed something, can only give this as an 'after-the-fact' interpretation. I suggest that for people to construe their own attributes in one way or another is to interpret what they, as persons, have already thought, said or done, including the intentions to respond that they find themselves expressing. If a person's intentions regularly have their expected consequences, they may well retrospectively conceive of themself as an effective agentive self. Other actions may be conceived as unintended or as produced in other ways altogether. The question of how to set boundaries around the agent, as Person conceives it, is obviously a very complex one, and I will now discuss it further.

Boundaries of person and self from a universal standpoint

It is very difficult to escape metaphors of space and containment when talking about human beings (Lakoff 1997; Reddy 1993). If persons have material bodies, this should not really surprise us. The boundary of our physical body and its movements in physical space and time correspond reasonably closely with our experience of our own body. There are exceptions, of course, such as phantom limbs, out-of-body experiences and neurological syndromes of an ignored felt sense of the body. Their rarity and peculiarity only underline the normal case. But Person as a material entity is ultimately only a temporary spatial arrangement of matter whose self-organising structural integrity is dependent on continual transactions with matter outside the body. In this light, the body, as a natural entity, is only one possible way of construing a boundary in the physical world.

I have already suggested that the material integrity of a singular body is a precondition for the fact that human beings call each other into existence as Persons. It is not surprising that we should strongly identify Person with the experienced body and Self as contained inside it. This way of viewing matters suits wider constructions of reality. For example, in criminal prosecutions, a person may produce a satisfactory alibi by proving that they were not physically present at the scene of the crime. A perpetrator has to be 'in' their body. But a figurative entity like self *literally* inside an actual body makes no more sense in material terms than a pain experienced 'inside' a phantom limb. In other words, the container metaphor, modelled on the human body, does not explain, in a causal sense, how phenomena present themselves to us, although it may be a good approximation and serve useful social functions.

When it comes to person and self as linguistic constructs related to social and legal practices, it is rather more difficult to be clear about boundaries. One problem is that shared meaning depends on norms (i.e. conventions that cannot be violated without loss of meaning) while at the same time they require repeated confirmation of that meaning in the face of inevitable violations (errors, occasions for correction, etc.).

If construing someone as having Person status is dependent on social norms, Person cannot be reduced to fixed capacities, skills, abilities, etc., as if these were like a bird's capacity to build a nest or Robinson Crusoe's capacity to build a hut on his desert island. If Robinson Crusoe forgets his identity, another person is needed to confirm who he is, just as a person suffering Alzheimer's disease may need to be continually reminded about the where, what and why of their existence. If Person attributes are constituted dialogically, they do not exist 'within' any participant to the dialogue. A person may retain the disposition to express themself *as* a person, and, in that sense, the potential to be a person resides within a person's body. Robinson Crusoe may remember who he is all his life. However, this disposition loses its significance – there is no one else to share it with – and I assume that it would not have arisen in the first place unless he had originally lived amongst other people.

The dialogical and normative perspective on Person/Self therefore raises significant problems in drawing boundaries. The mere repetition of a skill does not capture what we mean by being a person or self. This can be illustrated by one version of the idea of 'self as narrative' (see Chapter 7). The ability to enact a story repeatedly, in the same manner, would quickly lead to the judgement that the person was 'self-obsessed', 'narcissistic' or simply 'a bore'. The social exchange would have the quality of 'Nice day. Yes, isn't it?' Personhood and selfhood seem to demand recognition of the open-ended nature of dialogue (or of a narrative). This is a social effect created between people, and it does not pre-exist the dialogue except as a potential to engage in non-repetitive interactions. If anyone's 'self' has to be confirmed or constituted in dialogue, it is insufficient to say that a person's boundary is simply coterminous with their body.

It is certainly difficult to capture in words what this process of constituting entities through social interaction consists of. Marková (2000: 114) talks about 'examining the interdependence of the individual and society as a dynamic ontological unit' and she points to the importance of 'social representations'. However, it is still difficult to fathom what it is that exists and how it relates to human beings as ontologically independent organisms.

Shotter (1997) understands semiotic signs (i.e. signs in a system of conventional meanings) as being contained within communities rather than within persons. Because dialogue is split up into units with gaps in the speech flow, Shotter thinks that these gaps reinforce the metaphor of boundaries even though a dialogue has to be understood as a whole (i.e. as a two-sided act). The gaps in speech are moments of indeterminacy in which persons shape each other's acts. The gap is not really (or not only) a physical boundary between persons. For instance, it is largely within *metaphorical* space that people are intrusive or nosy.

The sense that our self is inside us may derive from the fact that our thoughts are private and 'in our heads'. One constructionist view is that private thoughts are a form of internalised dialogue. Child psychologists influenced by Lev Vygotsky (1896–1934) argue that infants learn the meaning of utterances when conversing with adults and that private thoughts are a later developmental stage arising out of the internalisation of spoken words (Vygotsky 1962; see also Chapter 11). Adult speech is passed on and 'into' the child. The experience of an internal world is then reinforced when the child has unspoken thoughts in private. Private thoughts can be original, with surprising twists, as is true in the case of public dialogue. However, most people probably believe that their thoughts are more original than they really are, neglecting to consider them as responses to previous utterances, written or spoken, by other persons.

My purpose in raising these various perspectives on the boundaries of person and self is to illustrate the complexity of the issue and to suggest that, from the point of view of natural causation, boundaries are selected for theoretical reasons. When considered as folk concepts, boundaries are chosen for pragmatic reasons and typically employ metaphor. Before proposing my own conceptual framework for the generic Person and Self, I will outline what I consider to be some problems with a mindist perspective on boundaries and also criticise certain dialogical accounts of person/self that seem to misrepresent the issues.

A mindist understanding of the folk model of person/self

Mindists may or may not draw a distinction between self and mind, but, if they do, self has a boundary within mind. A person is usually conceived as a body 'plus their mind'. I have chosen to discuss Bertram Malle's interpretation of folk concepts because it is tightly argued and very clearly presented (2004). He presupposes that folk concepts are organised into a 'theory' – a network of concepts such as agent, belief, reason, desire, etc., which in turn are related to cultural assumptions about the nature of society and persons. Malle (2004: 32) takes the concept of mind as foundational for the 'folk theory'; it is not an assumption, he says, that any person can break. It is not clear whether Malle means that people who adopt the theory necessarily believe this (how could it be otherwise?) or whether he, Malle, could not conceive of people having a folk theory that does not invoke the concept of mind. He says that people may vary in their ability to represent 'mental states' but he considers that, by necessity, they engage in this activity. His ambition is to construct a scientific theory-of-mind (a folk-conceptual theory) that accounts for a folk theory-of-mind. This is put forward as a genuine (presumably universal) scientific theory but it still focuses on modes of explanation (e.g., beliefs and reasons) and psychological mechanisms that determine 'choices among explanatory tools' (Malle 2004: 236). By implication, it is a theory of how an individual functions personally or sub-personally. His statement that the 'exact cognitive process of constructing explanations' remains an open issue seems to confirm this (Malle 2004: 236).

Malle assumes that everyday folk might not accurately represent other people's mental states, or even their own mental states, but he does think it reasonable to expect a correspondence between folk concepts and a natural science (theory-of-mind) concept of reality. A problem that Malle acknowledges is that folk theory helps to constitute a large part of the reality that surrounds us, and this means that any correspondence between the two could be the consequence of a self-fulfilling prophecy. This seems to me to be a fatal flaw for if we presuppose that we have to begin with a theory-of-mind, we cannot interrogate the natural processes that lead people to suppose that they *have* a 'mind'.

Malle (2004: 34) is clear that folk concepts do not have the same characteristics as scientific concepts. He compares the former to a set of Kantian categories through which people grasp social reality. Malle's own theory-of-mind treats mental states as perceptual objects that are the product of cognitive processes. For instance, these processes are said to select, categorise and retrieve sensory and memory information. This theory is therefore quite unlike a set of Kantian categories. The stand-alone brain is said to possess the innate capacity to process incoming information and produce mental states.

The principal social aspect of his theory is that people act to produce mental states in others in order to influence their intentions. Malle conceives of the activity of explaining behaviour as a social tool to manage interactions (2004: 219). If that really is one of its main purposes, it would seem likely that the ascription of mental states is learned in social interaction where it could be equated with learning, instrumentally, how the tool is operated. However, Malle presents the acquisition of a folk theory (in child development and in human social evolution) as a form of learning about the natural world. He notes that babies learn in the first three months to distinguish human motion from random non-biological movements and, later on, to attend to objects jointly with another person. He describes this activity as 'a meeting of minds' (2004: 43) but it is not clear why mind enters the equation at this point. Joint attention can also be observed in primates (see Chapter 12) but we might not want to assume that this signifies a meeting of minds.

Malle also considers agency, but he does not really show how we get from agency as naturally observed to a folk concept of agency. He says that by eighteen months, children can infer the goal or intention of an initiated action and can then execute the intention themselves. However, he does not believe that the child has acquired '*genuinely* mentalistic concepts' which finally emerge only later on in development (2004: 44). At this later stage (beginning around three years), the child can reliably use mental state terms for description and explanation. He assumes that the child at first just 'copies reality' and then, later, is able to represent reality. One implication of this claim seems to be that copying reality allows an infant to experiment and get results by trial and error. Malle describes the child's acquisition of a folk theory-of-mind as a 'watershed'. Are we meant to infer from this that the child is finally able to put in place the last jigsaw piece in a rather complex folk theory? Or is this a cognitive achievement (beyond the reach of any animal) to really figure out how nature (including other people's behaviour and mind) actually works? Malle presumably means the latter because he goes on to speak of human evolution and the selective advantages that favoured the emerging capacity to represent 'mind' (2004: 48).

The former interpretation of the watershed is, in my view, also viable. This would mean that the ability to 'represent minds' is an accomplishment that relates to just one possible set of folk concepts amongst others. We are not forced to assume that there are minds containing mental states unless we live among people who construe reality in that fashion. I am not implying that there are societies in which people do not think – only that there may be societies in which explanatory accounts do not include the concept of a mind. Malle claims that intentionality becomes 'mentalized' (2004: 46) which rather suggests that human organisms can understand intentionality without necessarily conceiving of it as the product of a mind. On the one hand, he refers to the advantages of a capacity to represent the mind as if it was a universal natural phenomenon but, on the other hand, he believes that there must have been a precursor to an evolved mind that was 'primitive enough to operate without mental state concepts or inferences' (2004: 51).

The precursors are listed as imitation, empathy, directedness to a goal, parsing of the behavioural stream and joint attention. He points out that language is a crucial element but rather than explain what 'mentalising' is, he just takes mind to be the next step in evolution. For instance, he does not think that apes are mind-readers because they do not recognise that 'the mind' is the underlying source of observed behaviour. From my perspective, the idea that people acquire a folk theory-of-mind because they really have a mind is itself a piece of the self-same folk psychology.

If we are to dispense with mind, and a 'self' contained within it, it is obviously incumbent on a theorist to produce an alternative way of viewing the matter. I will now return to a dialogical conception of boundaries, as described earlier, and try to locate this approach within my proposal for a generic framework.

Boundaries of person and self within dialogical models

The complexity of the issues I am addressing is illustrated by certain misrepresentations of the dialogical perspective. As I see it, dialogue needs to be conceptualised at the supra-personal level, although it is persons who engage in dialogue. If persons are jointly constituted, materially and conceptually, they also belong to a world of physical objects. However, any explanation of the behaviour of persons that is confined to processes within their bodies should be classified, in my view, as a sub-personal explanation.

Even a strong advocate of a dialogical view of self such as Hubert Hermans (2001) falls under the spell of the spatial metaphor of intersecting circles in which, in my terms, levels of explanation are confounded. He argues that 'the' self is composed of internal positions (various 'voices') and external positions (like 'my children') that are felt to be part of the environment. But if we think of positioning (see Chapter 7) as a supra-personal process, it is important to distinguish between *actual* embodied children from my *addressing (positioning) a child* as mine, rather than, say, my neighbour's. A dialogue is not between dialogical positions as entities but between persons (or figuratively extended persons) positing (positioning) other persons or things as entities.

Hermans describes the circles as 'highly permeable, suggesting open boundaries not only between the internal and external domains of the self but also between the self and the outside world' (2001: 253). In my view, talk about permeability (which implies a boundary of some sort) must be expressed very carefully, especially when the 'outside world' is introduced. The view that human beings are doubly constituted as material and conceptual means that voices are both material (e.g., patterns of sound emitted by a body) and semiotic (e.g., signalling assumptions about the speaker and addressee). An inherent risk when interpreting the meaning of what is said is to confuse an actual state of affairs with something else that is being communicated. Self is mistakenly placed literally in space when it is only symbolically in space. It is legitimate to speak of persons in space (as bodies), but self in space is figurative. A person's boundaries are only permeable in the sense that the kind of person or self they are taken to be is open to repositioning by others.

Gerrit Glas (2004) clarifies the ontological issues when he distinguishes the person as an entity with a unique identity from self as a reflexive structure that is constituted in relation to values and commitments shared with others. Glas argues that the fact that a person remains the same (as a numerically unique body) or demonstrates qualitative sameness across time does not necessarily distinguish a person from any other kind of thing. Glas also makes the point that the reflexivity of persons is not limited to conscious self-reflection. Thinking of oneself as engaged in a narrative is not just a means of self-description but may entail experimentation with possible ways of living in the world. There is a temptation to reify self as an entity that is somehow possessed by or contained within persons. However, if self is a dialogical construction, it is confusing to think of it as having literal boundaries. Actual persons, material practices and cultural resources place limits on the construction of selves, but these limits are constraints on possible selves rather than literal boundaries on self.

Alexandra Michel and Stanton Wortham (2002) criticise a view of self-construction that sees it as the act of a person who defines their self in terms of a storyline, repeatedly making these definitions salient in their social interactions in order to establish a preferred identity. This characterisation of self-construction would indeed amount to a narrow and monological conception of self-construction. It could be made minimally dialogical if a person's preferred definition is at least reciprocated and complemented by others.

In order to go beyond their own narrow conception of self-construction, Michel and Wortham suggest that people identify with their 'lived experience' and 'then search for appropriate texts' (2002: 627). They compare this process with the position of a novelist who makes use of the storylines of different characters. They argue that a person can clear away all their preferred identifications and act spontaneously, allowing the structural dynamics of the situation to take over. 'In such instances, situations organize themselves' (2002: 633). In my view, these authors have abandoned a dialogical theory and have reinstated the autocentric self of humanism, free to 'relinquish the compulsion to supply particular types of texts' (2002: 638). They relocate the boundaries of self within lived experience but have gone on to reify the latter as a self-organising system obeying unspecified principles.

Before proceeding to further discussion of boundaries, it is worth considering contemporary western folk models in a little more depth.

Boundaries of person and self in contemporary folk models

It is understandable that a child develops attributes that it comes to see as personal (as 'really' its alone). A child's responsibility for its own actions is exactly the construal that the parent attempts to impart, even though it is generally acknowledged that the child appropriates the concept of personal responsibility through a process of education and training. In conceptualising itself as the person it has become, the boundaries of the child's attributes become increasingly complex and inextricably linked with other elaborations of the language of personhood and selfhood.

Shared and unshared thought is one such boundary. Although I can choose not to express my thoughts, they are normally understood by others, when heard or read, without having to decode what is in the privacy of my own mind. The meaning of words is shared and so we are not dealing here with an input/output device, as if everything that is spoken has to be decoded like semaphore. The privacy of unspoken thought is a normal fact of personal relationships but it is not the privacy of a bank vault. The meaning of anyone's private experience involves some degree of public negotiation but not mental divining. *My* experiences (whether perceived to be public or private) are clearly not *your* experiences, but this is a function of the fact that we are numerically two separate bodies but, as speakers, we are not necessarily qualitatively different in terms of our understanding of a concept.

I can also form another boundary within my experience, namely inner (deep) 'Me's and outer (superficial) 'Me's. Again, the boundary implied here has nothing to do with physical space but more to do with the strength of my commitments and my strategic concerns. How it feels qualitatively to be more or less like my 'true self' is a first-person point of view. It is often as a result of feeling personally uncomfortable that people seek therapy, and a disturbed sense-of-self is commonly acknowledged to be a consequence of abnormal forms of care in childhood. Schools of psychotherapy have had to invent systems for classifying the subtleties of self-experience, and these systems are often designed to reflect individual variation in the way the child has appropriated and responded to the positions it has occupied in the family (often by rejecting and countering these positions). Therapy for the adult is frequently about the way a person recycles these appropriations in their personal relationships.

For example, 'enmeshment' is the clinical judgement that an adult is unable to distinguish between the self they were trained to be (let's say, by a parent for whom the child was a mere accessory to their own personality) and the adult self they have become. The adult views their sense-of-self as problematic, often when the adult feels that they lack autonomy but does not know why. The adult remains 'enmeshed' with their original caregiver's definition of it. The process has traditionally been conceptualised by psychologists in spatial terms, for instance, as an internalisation of the adult's positioning of the child's self (introjection) and as a later sending outwards (projection) when this appropriation is recycled. None of this is confusing unless taken literally.

A generic framework for person and self

I have argued that material embodiment is a necessary precondition for the concept Person but that Self is only indirectly dependent (through analogy) on embodiment. The concept Person can be figuratively extended into imaginary persons such as gods and cartoon characters, which means that the Person–Self distinction is blurred. In other words, disembodied imaginary persons often seem to serve the same sorts of purpose (in folk explanation and personal accounting) as selves. I conceive of both the generic Person and generic Self as products of a reflexive process. Human organisms do not have to reflect consciously that they are Persons but they find themselves constituted as such when they are members of a social group, that is, self-reflection is only one form of human reflexivity.

Attributes of the Person are likely to be to be heavily constrained by relatively fixed features of embodiment such as sex and age and also by accidents of birth. The latter are likely to include the power and status of the parents. A useful framework for thinking about Person is the model of social identity put forward by Theodore Sarbin and Karl Scheibe (1983). This model has three dimensions: *status, involvement* and *value*. A status is defined as an abstraction that sums up the expectations held by members of the relevant society. *Role* is defined by what a person does to fulfil their occupancy of their status. Some statuses are ascribed, that is granted, such as that of citizen, whereas others are achieved by dint of effort, such as that of teacher. The distinction between granted and achieved status is not absolute, and there is likely to be a continuum of choice. As Sarbin and Scheibe point out, achieved statuses are normally a joint product of choosing and being chosen.

The involvement dimension describes the extent to which a person is involved in enacting the roles associated with their status. A theorist has a choice of possible criteria for involvement such as time and effort expended, the degree to which a person is 'playing the part' or, at the other extreme, expressing a kind of mystical union or 'possession'. Sarbin and Scheibe suggest that the closer a status is to being granted, the less potential there is for differential involvement. A status like sex is usually assigned from birth, and although a person may not reflect that they are 'involved' in being a woman or a man, they enact gendered roles most of the time without, *necessarily*, expending effort on doing so. Sarbin and Scheibe describe 'person' as the ultimate ascribed or granted role.

A person's enactment of a role that fulfils their status on the dimension granted/achieved does not, therefore, always correlate closely with their position on a dimension of involvement. This presumably applies even to the ultimate role of person. Persons may be described (or describe themselves) as filling a non-person role, such as nonentity, brute or beast, and do this with greater or lesser involvement, especially if that person is also considered to be deranged.

Sarbin and Scheibe suggest that 'self' is related to the amount of involvement in enacted roles. When involvement is low (such as when a person is asked to chair a committee meeting), role and self are clearly differentiated. Sarbin and Scheibe are using the concept of self here to mark out a more permanent and unquestioned sense of identity. I have defined the concept Self in a quite different way but I will retain some of the elements of Sarbin and Scheibe's model.

The third dimension, that of value, is also viewed by Sarbin and Scheibe to lie at right angles to the other two. For instance, a status can be highly valued (e.g., university professor) but a person may be relatively uninvolved in performing the roles expected and value their enactment of them negatively. The status of mother, granted on producing children, may or may not receive positive evaluation, although a lack of involvement in fulfilling the necessary expectations often calls forth a strong negative evaluation. (The relationship between the dimensions depends, of course, on who is doing the valuing).

In the framework I develop (see Chapter 4), I intend to expand on the dimension of involvement and introduce a new dimension of fragmentation. Person and Self are both social categories but Person alone is jointly constituted with a material body. Self is a subset of Person attributes, essentially the *optional* ones (analogous to attained status) while Person is defined, prototypically, by its *non-optional* attributes (analogous to ascribed status). Accordingly, the generic Self can be defined as an aspect of the generic Person, a means of referring to things that are less essential to persons than, say, their body. For example, a person in our culture might conceive of self as a referential self (an entity), which is only one form that self could, in theory, take. In defining the generic Self in terms of optional attributes of Person, I mean optionally available, i.e. normatively regulated but not normatively enforced for all members of the group. Actual persons may or may not construe themselves as being able to exercise choice over optional Person attributes. For example, they might view their choice of occupation as fixed for them, even though they could in principle change it.

Of course, the general compass of agency – and what actual human beings have the *natural* potential to control – must heavily constrain what is optionally ascribable to Persons as agents. Actual persons, like mythical pigs, might attempt to fly but I am concerned here with natural assumptions about human beings and their ability to fly unaided. I will assume that the *capacity* for choice is a non-optional attribute of Person – a capacity that is continuous with the natural ability of animals to vary their behaviour according to circumstances. This does not imply that one attribute of Person is unconstrained choice. However, I will still maintain (see also Chapter 10) that the *form* the folk construct of human agency actually takes is, to a large degree, optional, and therefore likely to vary considerably across social groups. In other words, a folk construction of agency (and self generally) need not correspond with the way agency is theorised about in natural, causal terms.

Given that Person, unlike Self, is necessarily embodied, other natural constraints are likely to determine its non-optional attributes. However, features of the local culture could also determine which attributes are non-optional if they are essential criteria for personhood. But it is embodied persons that conceive of themselves jointly as persons and selves, and this is a biological stipulation. As noted earlier, scientific conceptions of 'conceiving' as a natural process may bear little relationship to a person's conception of conceiving from a folk standpoint. For instance, a 'belief-desire' concept of human intentionality may turn out to be quite inappropriate as a scientific model of interpersonal understanding (Bermúdez 2003).

Four ways of theorising generically about person/self

I will now consider how my assertions about the generic Person and Self could be applied to a local culture. There are at least four kinds of question to consider: semantic, pragmatic, scientific and ontological.

(1) The first question is semantic: what is it that constitutes the standard ways in which self and self-expression are used to mean something in an everyday context? What folk entities are presupposed? (2) The second is to ask how reference to self functions in human affairs. To what pragmatic uses is it put?

Questions of meaning and use can be answered from a first- or third-person perspective. In the first person, I know what it feels like to be my self, and I hold beliefs about the functions that I perform (e.g., smiling at someone or writing a letter to a friend). I also know that I can intend some actions and not others. From a third-person standpoint, the meaning that I attribute to my own actions could be interpreted differently by someone else. I might claim that I am smiling at my boss but someone else might say that I am just currying favour in order to get promoted. The intended purposes of acts are open to dispute within the limits of what counts as a reasonable explanation within the culture.

(3) A different type of third-person account employs scientific concepts to explain the uses to which self-expression is put. My colleague, trained in animal behaviour, might say that I am not smiling at my boss but expressing a submissive posture that maintains my ranking in the office hierarchy. A scientific enquiry could also be made into the empirical correlates of (folk) self-expression. For instance, it may be of interest to know what neurological, hormonal or behavioural events are occurring when I express my 'self' or when someone else hails 'me' from across the street.

(4) A final question is the ontological, and so far I have dealt with it in terms of Harré's notion of a double constitution (1998). Person and Self as categorial descriptions of human beings are not *things,* although the existence of particular persons and selves may be regarded as being dependent on conceptual and other powers of material human beings. The functional aspect of these powers can also be viewed from a double perspective. Thus, the capacity to make conceptual distinctions is a power of an individual human being but the functions of concepts that mediate personal interaction are not literally 'possessed' by any individual person. I have referred to those functions that are constituted by relationships between persons as the supra-personal level of description and explanation. These functions can, in turn, be described either in material terms as patterns of observable events amongst a group of persons or as elements in a system of shared meanings. As already noted, it is difficult to find a way to describe the ontological status of a dialogical entity like a functional relationship between persons.

Further implications and distinctions

Folk concepts of person and self are not always clearly distinguished, but persons are more closely associated with embodiment. For example, the statement 'She no longer seems the same person' is sometimes intended as a stronger version of 'She no longer seems her normal self'. The former suggests a permanent alteration in a person's physical appearance while the latter indicates a temporary alteration in behaviour or mood. It could be argued that disembodied persons are a counter-example to the proposal that persons are necessarily materially embodied. I have regarded a disembodied person as a figurative extension of the natural condition of embodiment and therefore best included as a variant of Self. I consider the special case of multiple personalities expressed by a singular body in the next chapter.

I assume that non-optional person attributes are related to material constraints as well as to arbitrary cultural constructions. Within a critical realist perspective, it is maintained that while categories of human thought are constructed, they are constrained by the independent nature of material reality. In Ian Hacking's words, people are 'made up' but they are not made up regardless of other physical and social realities (1995). Hacking examines the conditions that led to the creation of the category 'multiple personality' around 1875. Hacking argues that categories like 'homosexual' were also made up but, in this case, a social group was created that subsequently autonomously modified its own self-definition, the term 'homosexual' now largely being replaced by the designation 'gay'.

We can see in the latter example how being a gay person has both optional and non-optional aspects. A person may say that they were 'born gay', having no choice to be otherwise. However, some people might claim to be attracted to partners of both sexes. Being gay may be publicly constructed (and personally perceived) as being either optional or non-optional. It may define someone as a person or feel like an optional self.

Being a person is simply non-optional for any paid-up member of a human community. Some human beings may be regarded as non-persons, but this is just a way of excluding them from the community. The body has a material reality that dictates a unique perspective on the world. For instance, my line of sight on an object will be different to yours. The statement that 'I see something' is likely to be taken by a hearer as a truthful statement that says something about my unique perspective. My appearance and what else is known about me (gender, age, name, etc.) intrinsically tie me to a particular public person who is assumed to inhabit the same body from day to day. This singularity is generally expressed by the personal pronoun or, in some languages, by the inflexion of a verb. Embodiment implies singularity (Harré 1998). Nevertheless, a person can choose to present themself in an endless number of ways and quite legitimately employ the personal pronoun 'I' for each of them.

To illustrate the latter point, I can give the example of a person who is receiving therapy because they have been physically abused as a child and are now experiencing intrusive memories of the abuse. Therapeutic dialogues can be arranged between voices that represent the client's feelings towards the abuser in which the client is instructed to use the first-person present tense to express them (Young et al. 2003). A dialogue might take place between (1) the client speaking as the abused child; (2) the client responding in the guise of the abuser; (3) the client injecting their adult perspective into what the abused child is saying; and (4) the client expressing an evaluative commentary on the dialogue they have just observed themselves producing. In each voice, 'I' indexes the same speaker (there is only one client), but it is common to find that each enactment is experienced differently, with each 'self' adopting a different tone of voice, set of beliefs or body posture.

The singularity of the embodied voice does not dictate every assumption we make about it as a speaker. Moreover, when the use of 'I' is transposed into a different context, we usually retain a tacit understanding of the singular embodied person who expresses it. Actors on stage may personify real characters, but we know that the character is embodied in a real actor. A person reading out a letter from a friend, written in the first person, knows that any listener will take 'I' to be referring to the friend. These conventions can be transgressed in cartoon animation, but even a cartoon character, atomised out of existence, has to be reconstituted ('re-embodied') to continue the story.

Speakers may possess attributes of which they are unaware. These attributes are possessed by the person (as viewed publicly) although they cannot be claimed as part of that person's concept of person or self. When expressed, they are, in one sense at least, involuntary. The fascination with mirror reflections can be explained by the way that they give a glimpse into one's external, and normally unseen, personal attributes. The danger of misinterpreting the mirror image is highlighted in the myth of Narcissus. When mirrors first became cheap enough to be widely available in the Middle Ages, stories circulated (perhaps like modern urban myths) of the peasant's wife who, on receiving the mirror, does not recognise herself as the 'tramp' standing next to her husband. He, in turn, sees himself as his wife's new lover and fights ensue (Melchior-Bonnet 2002).

Attributes of the person are not usually contested as dramatically as this but the same sort of thing happens routinely in a minor way, e.g., 'Is this tie really me?' The real me is the one we consider to be non-optional, i.e. how we take ourselves to be publicly perceived or the person we cannot help revealing or expressing.

Some doubts about personal attributes are much more significant. For example, a newly bereaved person might hear the voice of their departed loved one as a public voice. The phenomenon of hearing voices, often associated with madness, may lead a person to question their sanity. Insanity is usually understood to be a non-optional affliction, leading understandably to great anxiety. Even a person's sense of their bodily being, normally a non-optional and taken-for-granted attribute, can come into question when disturbed by illness or accident. A recently amputated limb may be experienced as a phantom extension of the body that continues to have its own sensations and original functions. Here there is a conflict between a prior limb responding as if under voluntary control and a current 'absent limb' that cannot function in the real world.

Harré (1998) has referred to selves as 'evanescent', 'fictions', or 'illusions', but this is to highlight a contrast with material embodiment. It should not be taken to imply anything about the felt reality of different selves. When self first came to prominence as an everyday concept in the eighteenth century, philosophical opinion was divided as to whether it referred to something fictional or real (see Chapter 8). Philosophers did not set out to determine how people experienced the world but they did question how it should be understood. Harré rightly places great importance on Person as a foundational concept but this does not mean that it cannot be extended for legal purposes, so that corporations are treated as persons, or stretched in other ways such as assigning moral responsibility to animals.

The attributes of persons as unique speakers are bound to be shaped by their physical bodies, their gender, their moral and legal status within a social group and all the other publicly identifiable features, inherited or assigned, that lead one to say they are the 'same person' of a certain type. The body changes between birth and death but we still acknowledge its continuity even though this continuity may not be directly sensed. We are still guilty of crimes committed in our youth whether or not we feel like the person who committed them. Parts of the body can be removed or replaced without damaging this identity too much. Some individuals have even managed to simulate their own death and re-emerge with a new public identity. Spies play a deadly game with their public identity.

However, in these latter examples, the person can be 'unmasked' to reveal a unique body and, under normal circumstances, we cannot play with our public identity without getting into serious trouble. It is not advisable to have a second spouse unknown to the first in another part of the world or to simulate being a policeman without the necessary credentials. In order to be taken seriously as a member of society we need to speak from a particular body that is assumed to have had a credible public history that can be placed in the established social order.

From an awareness of how we are perceived by others, and how we want to be seen by them, we get the idea of public standing, of honour and shame, of acting above or below our station, of acting the part of another, of deceiving others about who we are and so on. Some of our (in principle) optional personal attributes may be taken so much for granted that they are never questioned and certainly do not appear to be chosen. For instance, a person's grumpiness, their weight or their mode of dress might be seen as fixed or inborn. However, considered as 'optional in principle', we can see that many of our personal attributes are not publicly enforced or generally regarded as unchangeable.

Although being identified as a speaker or actor is non-optional, the same personal pronouns are used in both Person and Self senses. This means that we sometimes have to distinguish between ourselves as embodied, public persons (e.g., 'I do not want to be included') and 'I/me' as representing an optional self (e.g., 'Don't include me in your despicable opinions'). In the latter case, 'include' is used figuratively, not to designate a spatial location for my body. Selves are not identifiable public speakers even though they are often thing-like or person-like. I may refer to them as Its or Mes but they do not normally act as persons act. I say 'I drank the cup of coffee', not that one of my selves drank it unless that self is clearly embodied (e.g., as an actor, I am playing a part).

A person might make it clear that there are different selves associated with different social roles or moods as when they say 'I am announcing this with my political hat on' or 'Don't pay any attention to me, I'm in a bad mood.' This implies an overlap between person and self in so far as optional selves are being expressed by actual speakers whose moods or political status could be perceived as non-optional and part of their public identity. The way that society regards multiple personality as pathological illustrates the point that, in general, society requires only one credible mouthpiece per body. The latitude granted to this mouthpiece to speak differently at different times is likely to depend on cultural conventions and special contexts for doing so.

A person may feel that the person they are taken to be does not match their sense-of-self. A man or woman may feel trapped in a body of the opposite sex and seek a surgical transformation of its appearance. Disturbance of a person's sense-of-self does not normally reach the proportions of a rejection of the body, and it is usually a temporary phenomenon. By contrast, a person's body cannot be radically altered without changing the sense of whom we are referring to. By entering into a sex-change operation, a person necessarily attempts a total change in dress, habits and mannerisms. He or she is exercising a choice but on the basis of what is perceived as an 'incorrect' gender assignment, their 'real' gender being non-negotiable and therefore not simply one of their optional selves.

Expanding the category of the generic Self

Selves can be expressed as imaginary voices, often by mimicking stock characters for ironic purposes. Incipient selves may crystallise over time into figurative entities that we can name (such as 'Mr Comedian'), but it is clear that there is only one speaker.

In order to do justice to the enormous range of optional person-related attributes, I will treat the generic Self as including reference to entities such as soul, mind, inner self, spirit, persona, self-image, self-concept, the real me, etc. These entities may not always be considered to be internal to the boundary of self as conceived locally. They are related through a network of semantic associations to other entities such as gods or spirits that are *not* conventionally understood to be attributes of persons or selves. But concepts that pertain to Person or Self cannot be understood without their contrast terms, and personal description is peppered with presuppositions about other entities that are quite clearly understood to be impersonal or non-personal.

Volition is one example. It has traditionally been regarded as a God-given capacity for free will and, more recently, as a mental faculty. These notions still influence personality description. People may think of themselves as having a strong or a weak will, as if this was an entity rather than a disposition to act in certain ways. Concepts of will straddle the boundary between the personal and non-personal. 'My own free will' is clearly mine but 'this craving for cigarettes has a will of its own' locates my craving as subject to external forces.

In sum, our self appears to us as a phenomenon only against a largely invisible background of other assumptions about the nature of reality. The local, historical self is just one of a number of potential expressions of the generic Self, on a par with entities like 'the will', 'the voice of the

Devil' or 'internalised parent figures'. It is, of course, the speaker who refers to these entities, but the speaker is an embodied Person, not 'a self' or 'the self'. In the next chapter I consider the anomaly of more than one personality apparently occupying one body. This anomaly contradicts the generic concept of person I have so far put forward, and it needs to be reconciled with this account.

4   Multiplicity within singularity

In this chapter I consider the anomaly of multiple personality – the existence of certain rare individuals who present themselves in the form of several credible persons that separately fulfil the criteria for personhood. I then go on to view this phenomenon as an extreme instance of the sort of fragmentation of personal identity and self-identity that is quite commonplace and perfectly acceptable. I also attempt to conceptualise fragmentation in relation to the dimension of involvement introduced in the last chapter. I illustrate this kind of conceptual analysis by applying it to some textual examples.

Rom Harré is well aware that his understanding of the preconditions for personhood is potentially challenged by the existence of persons who, as a singular body, express several public identities. In his words, 'multiplicity of the embodied person marks a sharp break with the human form of life' (Harré 1998: 152). Normally, we occupy only one standpoint from which to perceive and act, made manifest in the use of a first-person grammar. Harré argues that use of the first person, indexing the spatio-temporal location of the embodied person, is a transcultural and robust feature of all discourses. He regards the existence of multiple persons in one body as an example of the pathological use of grammar, at least for English speakers, although it might not be pathological in an absolute sense because grammars are said to be culturally diverse (Harré 1998: 189).

Persons only rarely express multiple public identities in the strong sense of acting as if they were separate persons. By a strong sense, I mean that a person is not just playing a part like a stage actor. Multiple identities are like 'sub-persons' who each possess a different public persona and sense-of-self that may be expressed with the same candidness and integrity as anyone else one might happen to meet. Each 'person' might appear in different circumstances or sometimes they alternate in the same situation. They may perceive their age and gender differently, dress differently and express different needs and interests. Each sub-person normally employs the grammar of separate persons, using 'I' to express itself and 'her, he, it, they, etc.', to refer to their other sub-persons, as if they were separate embodied beings. Each one may struggle for the executive control of action, and one might even wish to kill another. The extent to which sub-persons are aware of each other, or reciprocally aware, is variable (Braude 1995). In some cases, it is as if one sub-person has direct access to another's thoughts but, in other cases, a sub-person's thoughts can only be inferred from their behaviour. This strong sense of multiple identity is certainly more extreme than common forms of fragmentation in which 'I' choose to present myself differently at different times but it does not seem to differ in a fundamental way.

In order to defend the trans-cultural robustness of a first-person grammar, Harré would presumably have to argue that each sub-person's existence as a credible public individual is dependent on a singular spatio-temporal location for that sub-person *at the time it is expressed*, otherwise meaningful communication with others would cease. Harré states (1998: 149) that: 'it is logically impossible for someone to be at the same time human and have more than one Self 1' (i.e. meaning an indexical self). However, to the extent that Self 1 is also a conceptual attribute of Person, it is not clear why this should be so, unless he means that it is logically impossible to express more than one Self 1 at the moment of its expression, for example, as different subjects of the same sentence.

Stephen Braude (1995), another philosopher, also argues that it is normal to have only one centre of self-consciousness and that a person usually refers to successive experiences as 'mine' even when they are uncharacteristic or anomalous. But, in his view, the indexicality of experience from an embodied standpoint only comes about if the person believes the experience to be their own. In the case of animals and pre-linguistic infants, he uses the term 'autobiographical experience', by which he seems to mean experiencing something as one's own but not being in a position (conceptually speaking) to believe it is one's own.

For adults too, he claims that an experience such as intense fear might be so absorbing of our attention that it cannot be claimed as our own until after the event. Braude therefore considers indexicality to be dependent on having a worldview in which to locate experience. For example, he suggests that in automatic writing a person's hand movements may be indexical (I recognise them as mine) but the thoughts expressed by the writing are non-autobiographical (they appear to be someone else's thoughts). He also considers phenomena like depersonalisation to be indexical (I know it's my experience) but non-autobiographical because it doesn't feel like me.

According to Braude, a child who has not yet mastered a first-person grammar has experiences on which they tacitly act, but the experiences are not indexical. According to the logic of Braude's argument, a pre-linguistic child could have experiences that were non-autobiographical on the basis of what they felt like. However, it is not clear what might be meant by a child having a non-autobiographical experience if they have not yet acquired a worldview in which they are capable of indexing their own experiences.

Harré follows Strawson in arguing that it is only as a persisting material being that a person can be identified and reidentified by others (1998: 156). Persons are basic particulars. After all, even sub-persons seem to make the assumption that other sub-persons are singularly embodied. Braude, on the other hand, argues that no concept of a person is inherently privileged (1995: 208). Although he thinks that we would not normally regard the husband of someone with a multiple personality to be a bigamist (his wife being a unitary person), he raises a hypothetical example that might cause us to doubt this assumption.

His thought experiment concerns two sub-persons, each having distinctive personalities and physical appearances and alternately living in two different cities. One could then imagine a man marrying both, actually believing himself to be a bigamist. Even though this man is unlikely to face legal prosecution, it could be argued, claims Braude, that he still deserves condemnation. His point is that the existence of sub-persons is a real phenomenon and potentially raises moral issues. Nevertheless, he is at one with Harré in saying that a personal unity is needed to explain some of the central features of multiple personal identity. These are the fact that sub-persons usually possess interlocking abilities and memories and the observation that the emergence of the different identities can often be interpreted as a functional adaptation to life events such as trauma. And, of course, therapy often introduces a merging and integration of the sub-persons into a unitary sense-of-self.

Multiple personal identity is a rare phenomenon, but, nevertheless, I think it is one that can be accommodated within the generic framework I have already outlined by pointing out that personhood is jointly constituted by embodiment and social categorisation. The construction of the social category, contingent on social processes, is subject to variation. I will view multiple identity as an extreme manifestation of a dimension of fragmentation. I will now turn to more familiar and less extreme variations in the construction of persons and selves. One example is the category of 'personage' that seems to fall between person and self.

The ambiguous status of personages

The potential to confuse 'myself' (Person) with 'my self' (Self) introduces considerable uncertainty into any reading of speech or text. 'I' and 'Me' may be used in contexts where either person or self is implied. In the English that has been spoken for hundreds of years, 'himself', 'yourself' and 'myself' usually mean the public person who talks or acts. The pronouns 'itself' and 'themselves' may be used to indicate the speech, acts or passive bodily movements of particular persons or things. For instance, a person might say that 'it' (i.e. my arm) feels numb, emphasising the thing-like nature of a numb arm. When a public person acts intentionally, this normally implies voluntary control over the body's means of expression. Where this control is lacking, public acts may be referred to impersonally in the third person. For example, an author describing a highway robbery might write, 'His arms shot up' (i.e. in effect, passively by themselves) rather than 'He put up his hands.' A speaker's claim to possess their public body and the acts it performs is a matter of degree.

The possibility of using a third-person grammar when talking about oneself, or about relationships with entities outside oneself, adds considerably to the complexity of interpretation. External entities can assume a variety of figurative forms, and a person's own utterances might also be perceived as external, such as voices from another world. I will refer to figurative persons as personages. Personage corresponds roughly to Rorty's notions of character and figure (1988: 78–98).

Personages are assumed to exist as actual persons or are regarded *as if* they existed publicly or in another world. Authors mostly write about personages as if they are actual public persons (like gods) or use them as symbols to represent a class of persons. I will regard personage as belonging to the generic Self even though, in a folk sense, they are thought of as embodied or simply considered to be special persons. We do not refer to 'my' personage unless it is a poetic creation, and, even in this case, it is invented as a public figure not as part of self. 'My' God also implies a relationship with a personage that is not oneself. Nevertheless, from my perspective, personages are optional.

To complicate matters further, personages can be referred to allegorically, in which case they can express Self indirectly. For example, when a writer such as Francesco Petrarca (1304–74) describes a conversation with the figure of St Augustine, we can be fairly confident that he is using a literary figure to express a debate he is having with himself (Petrarca 1992). Rorty (1988: 84) argues that allegorical figures introduced the germ of what would later become a distinction between the inner and the outer person: 'An individual's perspective on his model, his idealized real figure, is originally externally presented, but it becomes internalized, becomes the internal model of self representation.'

In the contemporary world, the word 'self' can be attached to virtually anything connected with ourselves, even our own belief in our self, our 'self-belief', but we do not now approve of persons who refer too readily to personages (apart from God) that influence or control their lives. The unity and integrity of the person are valued, and actions that seem to lie outside a person's control are often viewed as pathological. Guardian angels and guiding lights are about as far as most people are willing to go, and these are rather watered-down entities compared to muses or devils. Our major concern seems to be with controlling our own destiny. Voices from another world are decidedly unpredictable entities, and we fear their influence upon us.

However, when reading a novel, our imagination is let loose, and we enter into a relationship with the characters depicted there. The way a writer sets up this relationship relies upon the deliberate employment of grammatical devices. The techniques an author employs to position a character in a novel, or a reader of the novel, has become an important area in literary studies. David Lodge (2003) describes developments from the eighteenth century onwards, in which authors experimented with variations on the simple first-person (I thought...) and third-person (She thought...). For instance, the author's own voice in the first person was introduced as an omniscient observer of what was going in the minds of the protagonists or, in another technique, an exchange of letters was employed to represent each character's state of mind, the reader now being placed in the position of interpreting the characters' motives.

According to Lodge, the 'Silence and privacy of the reading experience afforded by books mimicked the silent privacy of individual consciousness' (2003: 40). Turning this around, we could claim, with justification, that a private and individual consciousness was created by reading. The ability to read silently was apparently a very rare skill in the ancient world (Benediktson 2006). The ease with which first and third person can be tinkered with, or substituted, suggests that public speech and private thought are continuous. The literary style that Lodge calls 'free indirect' began to appear at the end of the eighteenth century, in which the author describes a character's lived experience in the third person. In free indirect style, the narrative discourse moves freely back and forth between the author's voice and the character's voice. So, in the line 'She tried to be sad, so as not to be angry', it is as if the author is inside the mind of the protagonist. In an earlier period, such sentiments might have been expressed in the first person: '"I tried to be sad so as not to feel angry," she said.'

A textual illustration of singular personhood

A text may refer to conversations or events in such a way that they can be seen to relate to singular persons whose public identity is immediately recognisable. Reference may also be made to singular personages. This excerpt from a poem by the London poet Thomas Hood (1799–1845) illustrates what I mean. (A copper is a heating vessel, in this case used in the wash-house, and Mrs Brown was trying to get the fire going beneath it by throwing in some gunpowder):

'Lawk, Mrs. Brown!' says I, and stares, 'that quantum is unproper, I'm sartin sure it can't not take a pound to sky a copper; You'll powder both our heads off, so I tells you, with its puff.' But she only dried her fingers, and she takes a pinch of snuff. Well, when the pinch is over – 'Teach your grandmother to suck a powder-horn,' says she – well says I, 'I wish you luck'. (Hood 1900)

This is a conversation between clearly identified speakers whose social standing is that of servants. There is no reference (at least in this excerpt) to inner selves or to entities that govern the mind. The phrase 'Teach your grandmother to suck a powder-horn' is presumably Hood's adaptation of the saying 'Teach your grandmother to suck eggs.' A grandmother is a type of public person, a personage, of whom we have certain expectations, associated with the wisdom of age. There is an exchange of opinions about what sort of person each is and comments on what they are doing. Luck is invoked ironically because the speaker clearly thinks the consequences of using gunpowder are avoidable. The pause in the conversation as Mrs Brown dries her hands and completes her snuff-taking makes it clear that Mrs Brown is top dog in the wash-house. The reference to grandmothers is Mrs Brown's riposte to a criticism, not an explanation of a state of mind or a motivation for replying in this manner.

Both protagonists are certainly aware of what the other might be thinking about her but they do not appear to be taking up positions as a self-reflective voice. It is by no means clear how they would respond to being interrogated about the kind of self they were trying to express. Perhaps the question would be met with a Cockney expletive. We do not learn that Mrs Brown's attempts to get the fire lit under the copper is the expression of her simmering unconscious resentment of her Master or that she is expressing an incipient working-class self rebelling against the conditions of the time. (This is not to say that Tom Hood, as author, did not intend to raise the political consciousness of his readers but in this poem, the reader is positioned as an eavesdropper on a scene.)

Reflection on one's own attributes begins to depart from singular personhood. In fact, one could characterise any reference to a self as marking the beginning of a departure from conceiving of the actor/speaker as participating 'with' the world and 'at one' with it, rather in the way a young child can be seen as totally engrossed in play. Adults sometimes prize this kind of singular connection to the world, a sense of complete involvement in an activity that can also be observed in the way a craftsman relates to their materials. When a person describes this state, they might say that 'I lost myself...', or turn to words such as 'bewitching' and 'beguiling' in which there seems to be a suspension of judgement and total capture of our senses. Singular personhood is combined with unreflective absorption in an activity. In the excerpt from the poem by Tom Hood, two people appear to be singularly involved in a conversation. They reflect on each other, as persons but not on the kind of self they are expressing.

Departures from singularity

Singular personhood and singular involvement with the world can be altered principally in two ways. The first is an explicit awareness that we are acting in the world and are separate from it. This is a symbolised boundary between self and other, forms of which I discussed in Chapter 3. So, departing from singular unreflective absorption in activity, we have the development of multiple perspectives within a unified field of awareness. I will assume that holding multiple perspectives need not imply anything about the degree of involvement in each perspective.

When the field of awareness is no longer unified, multiple perspective amounts to fragmentation into more or less separable sub-persons, selves or 'forces' that take control, however temporarily, of a person's awareness and actions. An implication of fragmentation is multiple agency (or causation) in addition to multiple perspective. In a simple and unremarkable sense, fragmentation is an almost co-conscious experience of prevarication – 'acting with two minds' or simply 'acting inconsistently'. In a more extreme form, there may be an almost complete compartmentalisation of identity and agency, as described above in the section on multiple personality. A singular personal identity is the normal condition, but it is quite common for some other force or 'personality' to take temporary control of behaviour. For instance, apparently voluntary acts may subsequently be disowned as inexplicable.

The second kind of departure from singular unreflective absorption is emotional or intellectual detachment from oneself as an actor. With detachment, it is the quality of experience that changes, not the perspective on experience or the themes of the projects in which the person is engaged. At one end of this dimension, we might have passionate, unreflective absorption in one project. At the other end, there might be a sense of mechanical or robotic execution of acts, either unreflectively, as in a driving skill, or reflectively, as in 'going through the motions'. Detachment can also take the form of a diminished sense of ownership or responsibility for action, without the implication that another source of agency has taken over, as in fragmentation.

I will now consider the dimensions of fragmentation and involvement in more detail.

Multiple perspectives and fragmentation

As noted above, it is typical for multiple perspectives to coexist within a person's unified field of awareness. Engaging in a dialogue seems to entail appreciating the position of the other, and so multiplicity of perspective is a normal and necessary state of affairs. However, knowing how another might act is not the same as being controlled by another's agency. As we move away from the 'normal' situation, a wide variety of inconvenient experiences or disowned acts may be deposited into other categories and attributed to external forces or fragmented into different agencies. However, before a unitary sense of agency is lost, multiple perspectives may be endorsed as expressing different 'Me's, each of which may be expressed with varying amounts of involvement.

The strength with which fragmented perspectives are endorsed may depend on presuppositions about other people and the world (e.g., 'Am I being fooled here?' or 'Is this a mirage or an oasis?'). The language of self-expression is altered to represent the strength with which persons allow themselves, or feel themselves, to be endorsing and owning up to a perspective, or keeping another in reserve. Even actions that appear to be initiated by me can be construed in a variety of ways. There is an element of choice in claiming that what my body does is part of me and under my control. If a vase is broken and someone says 'Own up, that was not the cat', I have a choice in taking responsibility. I may have broken it by accident, or deliberately, or had nothing to do with the broken vase (except putting it down where the cat could knock it over).

Even if I remember that I had an impulse to break the vase deliberately, I can wonder, a moment later, why that impulse came over me. I might attribute the action to my genes, the stars, my upbringing, and so forth. In other words, it is possible to impersonalise the cause of an act and attribute it elsewhere. 'My mind's all over the place, "it" isn't working.' My mind becomes an 'it' when it suits me. These departures from a person or self that feels that it owns its own forms of expression are minor examples of what I have called fragmentation. Fragmentation multiplies the sources of agency, and there are ample resources in the language, and in social accounting, to place the motive or cause of an action elsewhere.

By contrast, multiplicity of perspective only implies that the singular person takes up, *figuratively speaking*, more than one spatio-temporal viewpoint. The viewpoint might represent a physical or a social position. Multiplicity in dialogue can be represented as a conversation between the voices of different selves. Colloquially, it is often expressed in this manner, e.g., 'I told myself to be sensible, but sometimes, you know, you can't help yourself.' As pointed out by Mühlhäusler and Harré (1993), multiple voices can be comprehended within the same pronoun. In their example, 'Sir, I'm late' (Voice 1), 'Cos, I took my time' (Voice 2), the public speaker is the same but the implicit context of speech (polite schoolboy self, rebel self) are different.

Multiplicity of perspective is commonplace and unremarkable. However, when competing voices are really at odds with each other, a person might feel split, and a voice can sound like a mental intrusion, even though it is still owned as part of a self sensed as unitary (Hallam and O'Connor 2002). A mental intrusion has not quite reached the point of being a fragmented agent. In a more extreme form, a person might hear voices encouraging or criticising them, as if they are the voices of another person in the public world. In fact, when first heard, the person might search to find the source of the voice, only later realising that it is 'in the head' (Leudar and Thomas 2000). As noted earlier, agency or causation (depending on the nature of the entity) may also be attributed to impersonal forces, commonly understood to be natural, like an illness, or supernatural, in the case of God or the Devil.

Fragmentation does not necessarily imply intellectual or emotional detachment from the separate centres of agency – human-like agents can act with conviction and unreflective absorption, and impersonal forces can 'take one over'. For those rare persons expressing multiple identities, there is usually no unifying viewpoint that enables the person to switch voluntarily from one sub-person to another. However, under most circumstances, fragmentation and degree of involvement are combined in any social performance, and especially in stage acting. Actors exercise and monitor their skill of personification (i.e. they remain detached from, or uninvolved in, their performance), while at the same time retaining a capacity for sufficient involvement to allow a fictional person to take possession, an 'agent' who may, of course, demonstrate great passion. Involvement in a part can never amount to total absorption (i.e. there is only partial involvement in the fragmented agent) otherwise the clash of swords on stage could become fatal. The actor is sufficiently detached from the swordfight to know that they are acting and can disengage at the end of the performance.

The sense of having a flexible and well-disciplined set of selves is not always maintained of course. An actor may have to research a character and identify to the point of 'living' it. They may not be able to shake it off after the performance. Even cool characters are apt to lose their cool. The phrase 'blind passion' points to the absence of an accompanying observing voice that checks and monitors the consequences of action. The totally absorbed self is, in a sense, blind to the possibility of acting otherwise, and the customary self that is normally in charge is blind to what is going on. I do not conceive of this state of affairs as one self repressing another but, rather, as the outcome of a competitive struggle for agency (see Chapter 10) in which there is no all-seeing judge to call the tune.

Involvement in separate perspectives/centres of agency

Theodore Sarbin develops his ideas about involvement in social roles when he explores the relationship between narration, reality, imagination, belief and knowledge (1998). He does not want to reify these terms and views them instead as actions that serve human purposes. To imagine something is, for him, an action that a person performs when they construct a narrative – a sequence of actions in which self and others are involved. Developmentally, this begins as a child's participation in the scripts of another person and then progresses into 'let's pretend' role-taking and finally into a muted 'as if' performing, or imagining, of roles. Sarbin argues that believing is a highly involving and highly valued form of imagining. He says that to describe something as real is just 'employed as a term to convince one's self or another that the credibility assigned to an imagining is warranted' (1998: 24). He argues that 'believing requires no test, only high degrees of organismic involvement' (1998: 28). Knowledge, by contrast, is belief that has passed some other pragmatic test of acceptability as truth.

Sarbin defines the dimension of involvement by adjectives that apply to actions: force, vigour, passion, ecstasy, etc. I will use the term more broadly to include (1) unquestioned frames of reference from which one cannot extract oneself and (2) responsibility or ownership. Frames of reference may be implied by grammatical forms. Of course, an *unquestioned* involvement may be defended with extreme vigour if it turns out to be questioned. To assert that social class does (or does not) exist in the United Kingdom could easily turn into a fistfight, whereas people ordinarily do not give much thought to the matter.

The most involving form of *linguistic* self-expression uses the pronoun 'I'. 'I know' has more force than 'you know?' or 'we know', which have more force than 'one knows'. Similarly, responsibility for an act can be dispersed amongst a group of anonymous others or impersonal forces by judicious choice of pronoun (e.g., 'we felt obliged', 'it happened this way'). Choice of pronoun is used in many languages to encode personal and social distance, for example, when a person of status is referred to in the third person or second-person plural (Mühlhäusler and Harré 1993). One's (!) relationship with oneself can employ similar tactics, even if one's own thoughts are not couched in grammatically precise forms.

Language plays a vital role in engendering involvement or detachment in a person's projects. It is only necessary to compare a poem and a scientific paper to get a sense of how an author can use words to create passionate ownership or, conversely, disinterested detachment. Degree of involvement also applies to a person's activities. As Sarbin suggests, a person may need a set of imagined narrative possibilities in which they are sufficiently involved in order to be persuaded of the reality of their self at all. To have a sense of oneself as a project carried forward through time requires a leap of faith. We generate imagined possibilities that range from the highly probable to the highly improbable. Amongst the most probable, so deeply involving that to question them risks madness, are beliefs that we will wake up the next day as the same person, that we will not suffer a loss of memory for our past history, that we do not, for some reason, unaccountably stop being vegetarian and acquire a love for meat. These are the kinds of personal attribute that are believed in with utter conviction. They are articles of faith that only philosophers or novelists seriously put into question (e.g., as in Franz Kafka's story *Metamorphosis*).

A sudden loss of faith in a familiar perspective on reality may contribute to the phenomenon of depersonalisation (not feeling one's normal self) or derealisation (feeling that the world around one is unreal, as if seen through a pane of glass) both of them well described in Sartre's novel *Nausea*. People may feel as if their familiar self has been removed to be replaced by a robot that is being observed in a detached way by another self (Davison 1964). It is difficult to say whether this phenomenon represents a loss of involvement or a fragmentation of agency (or both). Reference to a sense of alienation from a lost or 'real' self seems to have become commonplace in the modern period. Its equivalent in earlier times seems to have had a distinctly religious quality and included states of the soul, such as *accidie* (Harré 1986).

A textual illustration of singularity, fragmentation and involvement

In order to illustrate how the above dimensions of the generic framework for Person and Self can be applied to the analysis of dialogue in social interactions or to text, I will analyse a short extract from a piece of medieval writing. The alien quality of the text allows us to shift more easily from familiar assumptions. For example, in the medieval period, a person could become possessed or inspired by spiritual entities, good or evil, that were perceived as guiding or controlling influences. This mode of self-expression has not disappeared, of course. One difficulty encountered when interpreting a historical text is to decide how much a person is unreflectively absorbed in their personal presentation or is deliberately choosing a form of self-expression (that is, whether a person is uninvolved to the degree that they are aware of the possibility of holding contrasting positions). This is a perennial problem, even in the contemporary world, when it is not always possible to read the degree of ownership for a belief or action from a person's declarations.

Another difficulty is to discern whether a writer is being literal or is adopting a conventional 'as if' style when referring to spiritual entities or personages as literal. Medieval persons frequently experienced themselves as being in 'virtual' relationships with gods, spirits and magical forces, and it is probably safe to assume that this simply represented an unreflective absorption in their reality.

In the text I have selected, the Abbess, Hildegard of Bingen (1098–1179), defends herself against criticism of the attire worn by her nuns, and represents the nuns' relationship to God (the text is translated from Latin):

Thus through the permission granted her and the revelation of the mystic inspiration of the finger of God, it is appropriate for a virgin to wear a white vestment, the lucent symbol of her betrothal to Christ, considering that her mind is made one with the interwoven whole, and keeping in mind the One to whom she is joined, as it is written: 'Having his name and the name of his Father, written on their foreheads' [Rev. 14: 1] and also 'These follow the Lamb whithersoever he goeth' [Rev. 14: 4]. (Cited in Maddocks 2001: 82)

There is both identity with God and distance from God within this description. On the one hand, a marriage symbolises a relationship, but one does not marry oneself. A personage is the recipient of these affections. On the other hand, the nun's mind is one with the 'interwoven whole'. We may take the latter to mean a shared religious discourse, seen as handed down by God, but metaphorically shared with him, as a 'discourse of marriage' would be in an actual marriage. So on both counts, the 'marriage' and the religious discourse are, in an important sense, external to the nun as a public individual.

The criticism that Hildegard was exposed to derived from the suspicion that impulses originating *within* some other aspect of her person could explain the abbess's choice of dress for her nuns. The charge was that, 'They say that on feast days your virgins stand in the church with unbound hair when singing the psalms and that as part of their dress they wear white, silk veils so long, they touch the floor […]' (Cited in Maddocks 2001: 81).

The implied vice here is, presumably, vanity or pride, and a vice is viewed as the responsibility of the person concerned and therefore within the compass of free will (barring the Devil's trickery). Hildegard defends herself by falling back on her social position as abbess ('through the permission granted her') and her reputation as a mystic ('the revelation of the mystic inspiration of the finger of God'). Of course, it would require a great deal more textual analysis to interpret the basis of Hildegard's deliberations more precisely, if that is possible at all. For instance, we do not know how she represented to herself her choice of dress for her nuns during the services on feast days or whether what she thought privately differed from her public response.

The virtual marriages to which our contemporaries commit are more likely to be enjoined with a political party, a cultural identity or simply a football team. However, these social entities to which a person is externally related (or, to put it differently, internally identified) remain much less clearly symbolised in modern western society. In the case of some football fans, we may suppose there is complete identity of self with the favoured team. The fan suffers the team's defeats personally. For other fans, there may be some intermediate degree of involvement or even complete detachment.

In principle, the white-painted faces of football fans can be seen as symbolically equivalent to the long white veils of virgin nuns. One cannot, of course, compare a relationship with a football team to a relationship with God, although some fans might disagree. The distinctive features of a relationship with God are its all-embracing moral justification, the subtlety of its articulation and the formality of its rituals. Modern individuals, by and large, lack the capacity to spell out their commitments so comprehensively, or have so many competing commitments that each one is hedged in by conditions. Even so, it seems possible to apply the same generic framework in both situations. The medieval person, like the modern individual, had not only actual relationships (with kinsman, as bondsman, etc.) but also relationships with a panoply of spiritual beings and forces of an external nature (often mediated through another person such as a priest).

Relationships for us are more likely to be perceived as personal commitments and therefore seen as internal, thereby engendering relationships with parts of our own self (e.g., a self-evaluation). Changing oneself is seen as 'self-help' – the making of resolutions and plans that are undertakings to be truthful (with oneself), determined (for oneself), etc. For a medieval person, the acts undertaken to quell, calm and regulate one's relationships with public persons or spiritual entities were more likely to take the form of appeasements, penances, confessions, bonds, pledges, vows, propitiations, atonements, self-flagellation, pilgrimage, fastings, purgings, indulgences or the magic arts. Even the agents of religion, or of sorcery, acquired their power by virtue of external forces.

In brief, the medieval person was externally related to capricious powers. This must account for the profound importance of signs and omens in this period. It is interesting to speculate how these powers came to be referred to as supernatural, a word that first entered the lexicon of written English in the early sixteenth century. C. S. Lewis (1960) traces the Greek and Latin roots of 'nature', from meaning the 'being of all things' to the nature of individual kinds of being. In Christianity, mankind had a fallen nature, and Nature was also distinct from God, as it was God's creation. Mankind had to be refashioned by divine grace from its inherent nature. To act supernaturally was to arise above inherent nature, and this quality may have been attributed to the beings (including ghosts and spirits) that made this possible. Lewis believes that 'supernatural' was a learned term that entered into common speech to refer to an emotion elicited by ghosts, spirits and the like. However, another interpretation is that spiritual entities rose above nature (became supernatural) in a new sense when a belief in Nature as the *primary* reality was firmly established. William Shakespeare, in *As You Like It*, Act II, Scene 3 (1601) wrote: 'They say miracles are past; and we have our philosophical persons, to make modern and familiar, things supernatural and causeless.' This suggests that a reduced involvement in an unreflected spiritual contact with the world permitted relationships with new powers residing in the person or in Nature.

I have made considerable use of analogical thought processes in my development of a generic framework. At the core is a person singularly involved in acting in a concrete situation with other persons or things. By analogy, this person's spatio-temporal perspective can be elaborated into 'as if' perspectives – themself as the same person at other times or places or 'as if' they were another person with a different perspective. A person develops multiple perspectives, some of which, deriving from actual conversations, are internally and dialogically related. In so far as perspectives lack any internal coherence, the person is fragmented. An as-if perspective may be reified into a real entity, that is, a personage or, reflexively attributed to oneself as an entity within one's own person. For example, I have suggested that self is an 'internal' analogue person who is assigned powers that are similar to those of a public person.

Even though I have taken real persons interacting with other real persons as the theoretical foundation of my generic framework, this outlook is not necessarily anthropocentric. Relationships with important personages (gods, spirits, etc.) may take precedence over 'real' person-related interests. Neither is this account anthropomorphic. I have not suggested that human characteristics are projected onto the natural world and then reflexively reappropriated back into our own 'human nature'. This view of the process is mistaken on several counts. First, I suggest that infants learn to comprehend their powers and personal characteristics by publicly expressing (not projecting) them, largely under the control of environmental events. The child later internalises them, with the effect that they become 'personal' and within its own control (see Chapter 11). Second, I assume that infants learn from adults how to describe their personal characteristics; adults will pass on whatever the local folk cosmology happens to be. In other words, the child cannot project human characteristics until it has first introjected them. In contemporary times, the predominant perspective is autocentric and so events are quite likely to be interpreted in a self-referent way.

Third, and most important, it is by no means certain that ancestral humans projected their personal characteristics onto the world. In Chapter 12, I provide an account of the social evolution of self-reference based on the writings of Graham Richards (1989). He suggests that the earliest languages may have contained terms that did not distinguish animate from inanimate things. For instance, he supposes that there might have been a concept of 'coming into being' that referred to childbirth, the new moon, the dawn, etc. It need not be assumed that the root metaphor here is a feature of human beings, namely childbirth. Any talk of the 'birth' of the new moon would be anthropomorphic only if the analogy first arose by drawing a similarity with human childbirth. Richards believes that a physiomorphic process was more likely to be central to the evolution of terms descriptive of personal powers and attributes. Human characteristics may have been understood by analogy with public world events, such as the coming into being of moons, dawns, plants, etc. Physiomorphism is a concept first coined by the anthropologist Claude Lévi-Strauss, and it essentially reverses the anthropomorphic argument (Richards 1989: 6). In Richards' example, it is as likely that a baby 'dawned' as a new moon was 'born'. This is an oversimplification, but I develop the idea further in Chapter 12.

5   Sense-of-self:
the first-person perspective

I have so far referred to first-person experience as a sense-of-self. Philosophers have asked how we get to know this reality. It is not sufficient to say that we just know it intuitively and immediately – or at least a constructionist is not content with that answer. I will first spend a few paragraphs introducing Wittgenstein's 'private language argument' and then go on to discuss some views of self that have been put forward by phenomenologists.

On the face of it, my sense-of-self rests on the fact that my experiences are private to me and are not accessible to anyone else. This is most evident in the case of pain. Although you and I understand the word 'pain' in the same way, my understanding of it, when I am actually experiencing pain, is different from yours, as you can only empathise with me rather than experience my pain yourself. We talk about a first-person perspective on events and contrast it with a third-person perspective that can be had by anyone in possession of their normal senses. So, for instance, we assume that a person who is blind or deaf does not have experiences that a sighted or hearing person has. Extending this idea to a sense-of-self, it could be concluded that only I know what it is like to have my experiences. However, although there is a sense in which this must be true, it does not justify the further claim that the only way we know we are a particular self is by examining the quality of our own experiences, as if knowing I am a self is equivalent to knowing I am feeling pain or seeing red. A constructionist disputes the claim that a sense-of-self is solely derived from access to private experience or that the latter is sufficient to possess a sense-of-self.

The seminal arguments against the position were put forward by Wittgenstein (see Bennett and Hacker 2003: 97, Harré 1998: 39–44). Stated very briefly, Wittgenstein argued that we learn the meaning of a term by having others point to, say, a red object and say 'That is red.' The object pointed at serves as a standard for the correct application of the word. Learning the concept 'red' presents no problem for a sighted person who is not colour-blind. The object pointed at is a public object and perceived by means of the same sensory mechanism in different people. However, when an experience is intrinsically private to the person who experiences it, there is no equivalent public object to serve as a standard. A sensation of pain cannot be pointed out to a child. There is no internal template against which a pain can be compared, equivalent to the external template against which the colour red can be compared. A child might compare two pains on different days and judge them to be similar, but there is no way for the child to verify this or for an adult to confirm it.

How is it, then, that an infant learns to apply a concept like pain correctly? Children do learn to refer to 'the same pain they had yesterday' and also refer to other people's pains. The concept, pain, is the same in both contexts and has the same publicly shared meaning. Wittgenstein proposed that the experience of pain is accompanied by behaviour, like screaming or groaning, which form part of its natural expression. This is a public act to which adults can attend and can use to teach the child to express its pain in more sophisticated ways, such as, 'there is a pain' or 'it hurts'. Other people also express this kind of public pain behaviour and so the child learns descriptive criteria for pain as well as learning to correctly label its own expressions of pain. In a similar way, a child learns how to get its wants attended to by public expressions of behaviour that an adult interprets (and labels for the child) as 'wanting'. These arguments maintain that psychological concepts are learned on the basis of both first-person experience and natural expressions and on observations of public behaviour. Consequently, the third-person publicly available aspect is essential and just as much part of the meaning of a concept as the privately felt aspect. Put differently, the act of smiling is as much part of the meaning of friendliness as whatever the smiling person might be feeling at the time. Or, in the more complex case of believing something, to hold a belief is not simply to be in possession of a private mental state that corresponds to the belief. Rather, it is to act in accordance with the publicly accepted criteria for what it is for anyone to hold that particular belief. People who state beliefs are expected to behave in a certain way, and, if they don't, we rightly object that: 'It would appear that they obviously don't believe what they say.'

The Wittgensteinian approach to meaning can also be applied to a child's acquisition of the concept of self (see Chapter 11). The pre-linguistic infant has a bodily point of view for perception and action, perceives itself as an entity that is separate from the world and has a burgeoning sense of being a temporally extended being. It can be taught to name itself and others as public persons and to use personal pronouns to index speakers, including itself. However, for the pre-linguistic infant, there is no entity, like a self, to which attention could be drawn. But, as with pain, there are shared contexts and public behaviours for learning a variety of personally relevant concepts, such as being angry, which are expressed 'naturally' and also experienced privately. This does not imply that a child's expression of, say, anger implies an awareness of a *self* that is angry. I maintain that 'self-reflection' only comes into being when there is an awareness that one's singular set of experiences belong to the public person one knows oneself to be. It is not an additional perception of these experiences by an invisible observer but an extension of the possibilities for learning about a phenomenon (one's experiences and one's behaviour) that have already been exercised in other situations and are available to others as well. Self-reflection is clearly not a once-and-for-all realisation. As a child gets older, it can reflect on the fact that it reflects, and self-reflection is limited only by the meaningfulness of the questions that can be brought to bear on an issue.

Awareness and sense-of-self

The chief implication of all the above is that talk about experience entails publicly shared criteria and that the meaning of psychological terms cannot be reduced to access to certain kinds of private experience. I can 'see' that another person is angry without having to deduce from external signs what a person is feeling privately. This view contrasts with the one derived from mind–body dualism. A mental state is assumed to reveal what it is through the quality of what it feels like to have it or be in it. We are said to be able to perceive the mental state or introspect it. Dualists assume that experiences are contained 'in the mind'. If we want to find out more about an experience, it is assumed that we can do so by focusing our mind on what it feels like to have it.

Linguistic philosophers have countered this dualist perspective by close analysis of the way mental concepts are actually used by non-philosophers. For instance, evidence that a person is conscious is primarily behavioural. The criteria for deciding whether a person is asleep, unconscious or in a coma are based on responses they make to stimuli (Bennett and Hacker 2003: 244). These authors argue that being conscious is simply a precondition for any experience; 'That one is conscious is not a piece of information which one might lack and acquire by having access to it by some means or other' (Bennett and Hacker 2003: 247). They also point out that being conscious of something can take a variety of forms, so there is no one thing, 'consciousness', that requires scientific investigation. A person may become conscious of being jealous, but it is not as if a mental state of jealousy can be divorced from the person experiencing it and reduced to a particular kind of qualitative feeling. In fact, it might be the case that a person could be correctly described as jealous before they became aware of the fact.

Of course, attending to something and becoming conscious of it have important psychological consequences. I share the view of many scientists that to become conscious of something is to be exhibiting a biological phenomenon and that it is one that we share with animals. But it seems a mistake to treat consciousness as a noun except in the sense of 'being in a state of consciousness' rather than being asleep. However, if a state of consciousness is a valid description of a unique organism, then it seems legitimate to refer to *its* consciousness of something. Consequently, we might suppose that any one of that organism's experiences possesses a pre-reflective sense of 'mineness' for that organism (see Gallagher 2005: 105). On these grounds, any perception is personal to the perceiver. For example, my perception of a red table might possess some experiential evidence of being mine, just as your experience will be of yours. Before accepting this argument too readily, it is necessary to distinguish two senses of a 'sense-of-self', one tacit, the other explicit.

It certainly follows from the fact that sensations and perceptions have a reference point in a perceiving organism moving around in space, that experience should be structured according to that organism's unique trajectory and sensory capacities. Shaun Gallagher refers to an implicit 'body schema' that he defines as a system of sensory-motor capacities that function without awareness or the necessity of perceptual monitoring (2005). In addition, our own body supplies sensations to which we may attend periodically. For instance, the human visual field includes the tip of the nose, and other sensory features, that provide spatial coordinates. Some writers have therefore identified 'self' with a perceptual 'body image' (Revonsuo 2005). Jeffrey Gray (2004: 264) states that 'the very manner in which the brain creates conscious experience entails that point of view and the perceived world are two sides of the same coin.' He suggests that there is no additional mystery about how or why there is an observing self.

There seems no reason to doubt that there is a tacit sense-of-self grounded in the body. However, to be aware of the fact that one's experiences are referenced to one's own body does seem to suggest further mysteries to be solved. Gray goes on to remark that the objects we perceive have personal meaning and that they may be placed in a personal temporal order. He thinks that autobiographical memory (see Chapter 11) comes closest to the everyday meaning of self but this introduces levels of complexity that go far beyond body schemas and body images, important though these are. Gray and Revonsuo seem to imply that the brain creates conscious experience and that experience is somehow inside the brain where the self can observe it. From a constructionist perspective, these views are misleading.

The belief that there is no need to distinguish between a body-centred field of awareness and self-reflective awareness may derive from the mistaken assumption that conscious experience is always an experience of one's *self* experiencing something. This belief is probably connected to an overly simple interpretation of Descartes's philosophical argument that one can infer one's own existence from the fact that one is normally aware of one's own experience (see Chapter 8). This argument can be pursued (if one wants to) without claiming that experience is *always* accompanied by an awareness that it is oneself that is experiencing it. A distinction can be made between reflective and pre-reflective awareness, one that Descartes himself made and a distinction later elaborated upon by philosophers in the phenomenological tradition (see below). The supposed existence of a self that observes its own experiences was further reinforced by the writings of John Locke, who argued that self was an object of introspection, each person having their own unique self that was, in essence, an empirical psychological phenomenon (Bennett and Hacker 2003: 325).

Conceptualising unconscious causes of a sense-of-self

What does seem plain in nearly all writings on a person's awareness of being a self is that the *content* of experience (what one is conscious of) can only be understood theoretically in relation to a concept of something that is not-conscious or is just hinted at – events, processes, discourses, automatic habits, etc. This is often called simply 'the unconscious'. In a pre-scientific era, the causes of behaviour were located in a variety of unseen forces, such as the work of the Devil. It was, perhaps, always obvious to human beings that the sources of experience are not wholly transparent. It seems that a variety of explanations are put forward to introduce coherence and consistency. We may laugh at something hilariously and then wonder why we found it so funny. We often do not know why we want something or why we make the choices we do. We may answer these questions by invoking a concept of something unseen, unheard and unfelt. A belief in these unconscious forces may then partly determine what we *can* see, hear and feel.

One implication of taking an unconscious realm seriously is that it makes us sceptical of any certainties derived from immediate perception or reason. We might begin to question whether our sense of self-determination, freedom or creativity is really 'ours' or whether we possess these attributes thanks to processes or events whose real significance eludes us or about which we are systematically misled in our usual mode of awareness.

There are at least three kinds of unconscious explanation. In the first, the explanation may have nothing whatsoever to do with experience except explain it more or less well in a causal manner. For instance, processes in the retina and brain may account quite well for the colour of an after-image. In the second type of explanation, the unconscious is understood in terms that are very close to the way we think our conscious mind works, such as motives or desires that we would recognise if they were consciously attended to. Let's assume, for example, that I quickly realise why the joke that amused me so much touched on a sensitive spot. The third kind of explanation falls between the other two because it's plausibly related to how human beings behave and think but it's not directly modelled on everyday understanding. The unconscious may be compared to computer software, to a language, to hidden assumptions, etc. The theory that self is a virtual reality is of this type – the sense of being a self appears to us only against an unconscious background of social, linguistic and historical practices that are not obviously or necessarily related to self as we experience it.

The humanistic self and its freedom

The unconscious influences on our sense-of-self have been variously conceived as a realm of determination that may completely remove our apparent freedom (fatalism or determinism), as a panoply of forces that we have to fight or repress (such as enticements of the Devil and urges of the id) or as a realm that we can co-opt or channel to enhance our freedom (such as a creative urge). The modern view of human beings as having potentially unlimited choice depends on a first-person sense-of-self with an (unseen) capacity for choice, virtually a *sine qua non* of the autocentric western concept of the individual since the rise of humanism. Human beings experience their freedom (or oppression) by being thrown into situations in which they are consciously aware of having to make choices or, conversely, are prevented from making a choice. The modern person typically comprehends their acts in terms of a self that chooses responsibly and consciously directs life in terms of an ideal. How all this comes about remains largely mysterious.

In the past 300 years, the humanistic self has been subjected to assaults from theories that have sought to unseat, decentre or eradicate it. A socially constructed self also departs significantly from the self of humanism. However, if we regard the idea of self as constructed, and as related to political ideals, some of the theoretical assaults on self can be seen as a political challenge rather than a knock-down argument that threatens to destroy the idea completely. Unless the idea of self doesn't work any more, or people feel that they cannot command their destiny to some degree, there is no need to deny the meaningfulness of a sense-of-self. It would be more useful to ask how selves are constructed and what might threaten to undermine the reality of self. There is nothing about a construction per se that should cause us to deride it.

It would be more undermining, in my opinion, to ignore the fact that selves are made and therefore that they are largely the product of social and political circumstances. In the philosophy of Jean-Paul Sartre (1905–80), the individual is invited to believe that they are, in principle, absolutely free. Theoretical freedoms can weigh on us with the heaviness of a gravestone unless the individual is given a means to transcend the bad choices and oppressive life circumstances that have already taken their toll. Sartre would not disagree with this, recognising that an individual acts from a determinate life situation, often not of their own choosing. Sartre's stance on freedom at least gives us some grounds for guidance by a belief that any choice is, in theory, possible; after all, we are not then allowed to get off the hook by pleading that we have been determined by this, that or the other. Unless we believed that we were, in principle, free to act, perhaps any initiative to change would be defeated before it was begun. Sartre did not put forward his philosophy in this pragmatic vein, and he would reject the argument that believing we are free to choose is compatible with naturalism. But if it is accepted that a belief in freedom is a political idea, the social pressure to exercise it need not be interpreted solely as a heavy responsibility on the individual. Absence of free choice in any given person could be subjected to empirical investigation and remaking. I will leave further consideration of agency to Chapter 10 and now consider some phenomenological reflections on self.

Phenomenological approaches to self

Acknowledging a first-person aspect to experience does not justify a belief that there is a royal road to explaining self from this perspective. Phenomenologists have worked long and hard at reflecting on the content and structure of conscious experience, and they can hardly be said to have reached unanimous conclusions. First-person experience is just another avenue for interpretation or theorisation about self.

It is possible to reflect on how experience presents itself to me either naturally or when I suspend my natural assumptions and take a naive attitude. A distinction can also be made between what presents itself to me immanently in an immediate and concrete way and what I perceive transcendentally, that is, as an object of perception that transcends immanent experience because it links the latter into themes. Thus, I might perceive a shape that looks like a chair and then perceive it is a chair, or a particular chair I am familiar with from previous experiences. In all three cases, I am looking at the 'same' patch of colour, thematically interpreted in different ways. Phenomenological theories take us beyond what I perceive, or think I know, when describing my own experience, to what must necessarily be inferred if conscious experience is to present itself in the way that it does. For instance, it may be necessary to presuppose facts about embodiment, the role of others, time perception, history and language.

It is a commonplace that people routinely describe their experiences and may report them as individual mental states or as a stream of consciousness. Many thinkers have assumed that there is a process called reflection which entails a further conceptualisation of a particular experience. And it seems to be the case (see Chapter 11) that infants go through a process of placing their experience into a temporal framework, enabling them to talk about past and future experiences. Prior to this stage, the infant may be living in a perpetual present, unable to reflect that it is having experiences at all.

Opinions differ on how self-reflection develops and what it is but I will make the assumption that humans (and many animals) can be conscious of something without the experiencing organism knowing that it is 'conscious' or that its experience is temporal. Animals and humans can learn, and implement what they have learnt, without needing to be conscious that they are learning, i.e. they do not need to remember the process of learning. Without this assumption, it would make no sense to argue that children learn to be self-reflective. The distinction between pre-reflective and reflective awareness is a central one for phenomenologists.

Phenomenological and existential conceptions of self

The influence of phenomenology on modern movements within social science has been profound but to some degree indirect. The original sources (mostly in German or French) use unfamiliar and sometimes off-putting terms. The ideas of thinkers like Edmund Husserl (1859–1938), Martin Heidegger (1889–1976) and Maurice Merleau-Ponty (1908–61)

have been taken up and reworked by others. In Continental phenomenology, experience is studied *as* experience and so everything comes into
question, including things appearing as objects. By contrast, philosophy conducted within the Anglo-Saxon tradition has tended to accept,
'naively', the reality of things as they appear and has also been more
attracted to pragmatic definitions of truth (i.e. truth as what is useful or 'works'). These differences are revealed in conceptions of the
unconscious. Freud's unconscious (although Freud was a native of the
Continent) seems very much like a real place containing real biological
forces. By contrast, phenomenological reference to a pre-ontological
realm of being (i.e. one that precedes what is known to exist) introduces
us to a world of abstract thought. The aim, however, is the same – to
explain how things appear to us as particular experiences.

A convenient metaphor for understanding how things appear is structure or structuring. Freud's model of the mind is structural and consists
of three layers arranged vertically – hence the term 'depth psychology'.
This leads naturally to the idea of unconscious structuring principles.
The metaphor of structure can also be applied *horizontally* to consciousness. According to Husserl, experience appears to us as significant
wholes – it is structured horizontally rather than being a random flux
of sensations. So, for example, when we gaze at the ambiguous drawing
of the young woman and the witch, our perception alternates sequen-
tially between one and the other, and these are, in a sense, adjacent
(horizontal) possibilities. According to Husserl, experience also appears
to us as temporal in the sense of appearing and disappearing, and always
in the process of becoming something. This view of structure is different
from the notion of, say, a memory buried (vertically) in a deeper structure and having to be unearthed or exerting its influence from below.

By focusing on experience *as* experience, we can put to one side the
question of who is doing the experiencing, almost as if the source of conscious experience is independent of any particular subject of experience.
But philosophers have generally shied away from the idea that experience
could exist in some anonymous form and have argued for an abstract subject of experience. Immanuel Kant (1724–1804) assumed that a person's
conscious experience is logically predicated on a rational moral agent
that in some sense exists outside nature (see Jopling 2000: 87–9).

It would be easy to identify the subject of experience with an
actual human being but this leaves unanswered a number of important questions. First, as flagged up earlier, does conscious awareness
necessarily imply self-awareness? Is a minimal sense-of-self part of any
experience, given that it is the experience of a particular organism and
not just any organism? Most phenomenologists assume that awareness

can take pre-reflective and reflective forms. Second, does the involvement of a subject of experience at a pre-reflective level imply anything about the structuring of the pre-reflective experience? Is this experience temporally ordered or chunked in a way that implies a unity? Or is it a changing flux of experience responding passively to bodily or environmental events? Third, is there any theoretical advantage in assuming that there is a minimal sense-of-self if this accompanies every single experience as a necessary precondition of experience? This assumption amounts to saying experience is not anonymous. However, it is not clear what follows theoretically from this assumption.

Before taking up these issues as seen from a contemporary perspective, I will briefly lay out some views expressed by Sartre and Merleau-Ponty. Sartre, in 1936, addressed the issues directly and so his paper is a useful starting point for discussion (1992).

Sartre's self

On one interpretation, all experience is integrated as 'my' experience because object implies subject. This leads us to question how 'self' comes to exist as an object of consciousness. The phrase 'I perceive myself' contains two terms, an apprehending I and an object apprehended. However, Sartre, in 1936, denied that to be conscious of an object need imply a proprietor who owns that experience (i.e. in the sense of an 'I' that is 'added' to the experience of an object). He says that objects are not contained *in* consciousness: objects exist *for* consciousness. Sartre does not deny that there is a felt me, a sense-of-self, but he says that this is an *object* of consciousness that exists within the field of awareness. This is the self that Descartes sensed when he turned his thoughts inwards. Sartre goes on to theorise about the nature of a self that only exists as an object for a reflecting consciousness.

Sartre takes the step of describing the reflecting mode of consciousness as grounded in a pre-reflective awareness that is pre-personal and non-positional. For example, I might reflect on the dinner I am eating, and, while doing so, I am aware of the objects around me, such as the size of the portions, the taste of the olives. I might even entertain an image of myself as an object at the table, but this would be a retrospective reflection. At any one moment, I am not aware of myself as an object in the process of reflecting. In other words, reflecting does not catch itself in the act of reflecting – it is pre-personal. Pre-reflection and reflection are not separate structures but more like moments in an unfolding process.

Sartre realises that his arguments raise further questions about the unity of consciousness: does this reflect the Kantian preconditions of a conscious subject or is it a feature of self as an object of consciousness? Sartre theorises self (ego in his terms) as a virtual object, a poetic creation, of a reflecting mode of conscious being. There is nothing indubitable about this self because it is an abstract unification of a temporal series of reflected acts that can always be revised (in its content) by further reflection. It is not to be confused with the body (the 'psychophysical me', in Sartre's terms) although in reflecting, self is reflected in the acts of the body, as in the example of myself having dinner.

For Sartre, there is always the possibility of self-deception, which, once realised, may prompt a person to revise their view of self, but this does not imply that there is a 'true me'. The unity of self is an abstraction, but not hypothetical. It is a real creation, not an 'as if' or 'perhaps I have' a self notion. This created self may present itself as a surprise (e.g., can I really be so hateful?), and there are, of course, anomalous experiences of self. However, Sartre argues that self as an object of reflection is shared by others too, because it exists in the world as an object for others. I do not live in a solipsistic world, and Sartre says that 'My "I", in effect, is no more certain for consciousness than the I of other men. It is only more intimate' (1992: 104).

Self as a thematic object created by the subject is not the source of the agent's spontaneity although it may appear to be so. Self is only 'a virtual locus of unity' and 'we are sorcerers for ourselves each time we view our me' (1992: 81–2). In Sartre's view, pre-reflective consciousness is spontaneous, pre-personal and 'monstrously free' (1992: 100). This is not to say that pre-reflective consciousness belongs to no one, only that it does not yet belong to someone until reflected upon – it is pre-personal. Sartre wonders if the function of the ego (self) is to mask from conscious awareness its very spontaneity, as if this spontaneity constitutes self as a false representation of itself. Sartre also questions whether such fundamental distinctions as those that are made between the 'possible and the real', 'the willed and the undergone' are self-deceptions (1992: 101) or, expressed in a different terminology, virtual realities (see Chapter 10).

Sartre's views at this time were a mix of ontological and epistemological assertions. They form part of an analysis of the human existential situation, not a scientific theory. Human beings are by the nature of their existence free, reminiscent of Jean-Jacques Rousseau's (1712–78) remark that 'Man is born free, but everywhere he is in chains.' Sartre does not deny that persons are born into a determinate world in which they see themselves as historical selves. He thinks that the virtual self they imagine themselves to be masks their true nature which is to be engaged in a project of shaping themselves into a self that fulfils their lifetime project and for which they are totally responsible in every act. Self as an object of a reflecting consciousness can be revised if a person comes to realise that it is the product of earlier choices it has made unknowingly. The unawareness of these choices is not like an unconscious determination in the Freudian sense. Choices are responses to historically determinate situations and so they are meaningfully related to a person's life project (even if such choices are made 'in bad faith' and fail to face up to the necessity of that project).

Sartre does not think that the agent for a person's life project is determined by a person's history, however oppressive it might be. There is always the possibility, in each new act, of shaping the life that is dealt to one. It seems that this agent also belongs to a creative, pre-personal mode of being, not to the self one imagines oneself to be who is, to all intents and purposes, unaware of its own true purpose. In revising an old self, a person may be confronted with the existential anxiety of having to make a new one, in a sense, 'out of nothing' (Cannon 2003).

Some of Sartre's views come close to the idea that self is constructed, though for Sartre it seems to be an entirely personal process. People find themselves in historically determined situations but this does not prevent them from making autonomous choices. It is not clear why he believes that a person's lifetime project has to be singular. His views seem to imply that we have to think of agency (like self) in a double aspect. A person acts spontaneously, as it were, and yet in reflecting, it posits a virtual idea of itself as an agent. According to Sartre, the meaning we give to an act as willed or passive may be a mystification of a reflecting mode of consciousness, a denial of our real freedom to act. If that is so, when I reflect on choosing deliberately, I may only be passively compliant with a normatively held assumption that my act is willed. In other words, it is possible to view willing as a discursive construction or 'believed in imagining' (Kirsch 1998).

Merleau-Ponty on self and language

To be a conscious self has traditionally been equated, at least since Descartes, with a self that knows its own existence, essentially by announcing it in words. Merleau-Ponty discusses Descartes's 'I think therefore I am' and comes to a different conclusion (1966: 369–409). He points out that there would have been no speech and no ideas if there had not been 'mankind with phonatory or articulatory organs, and a respiratory apparatus' (1966: 390–1). He presents the problem as follows: 'how I can be the constituting agent of my thought in general [...] without ever being that agent of my particular thoughts, since I never see them come into being [...], but merely know myself through them' (1966: 400). According to Merleau-Ponty, the meaning of Descartes's statement only allows one to grasp one's thought and existence verbally, and the words themselves, taken out of context, already presuppose a timeless subject. The words 'promote their own oblivion'; they are only 'a minimal setting of some invisible operation' (1966: 401).

Merleau-Ponty goes on to assert that signs and meanings only appear in the first place as part of an expressive act in a determinate situation. They were part of a problem that Descartes happened to pose to himself and Descartes had to exist before he could pose the question. Similarly, for the developing child, words acquire significance by functioning pragmatically in situations in which they can be understood. Merleau-Ponty compares words to tools, a way of grasping the world and creating meaning: 'the presence of oneself to oneself is anterior to any philosophy' (1966: 403).

As for Sartre, Merleau-Ponty argues that awareness of self presupposes a hidden horizon of existence – a world before a person becomes aware of having thoughts. Language has a special status because it is lived *as* experience and, at the same time, it constitutes a person's mode of *knowing* that self exists. We see ourselves as employing language to construct past and future selves, but verbal thoughts are also the medium of self in debate with itself. Language is therefore key in allowing a person to be present to themself as self. Having done so, a person can think reflexively about themself. A person is born at a point in history and therefore inherits the sedimented meanings of words, that is, the significance they have already acquired in multiple social and institutional contexts. For Merleau-Ponty, then, we cannot theorise about self without also theorising about language and history.

Sartre and Merleau-Ponty have different conceptions of the subject as an experiencer and as an agent of action. Sartre retains the idea of an underlying, rational and unitary agent, but this subject only captures itself in its own reflections. Merleau-Ponty, like Martin Heidegger, understands conscious experience to be structured by the whole human being's 'being-in-the world' instead of two entities, human being and world, in a relation of the former representing the latter. There remains a subject/object pole to all experience, but self is not a proprietor of its experiences. Self is, in fact, one of the *objects* of experience (as with Sartre). The having of a conscious experience presupposes a context in which 'objects' show up and make sense. What counts as a human being and as reality depends on a shared, social, understanding that precedes both. Merleau-Ponty emphasises the tacit involvement of the body in all perceptions of the world whereas Heidegger stresses the social world as the background context.

Hubert Dreyfus (1989) contrasts the idea of self as being-in-the-world with self as a proprietor of experience – a self that represents the world and has intentions towards it. This was the view held implicitly by Freud. Freud learned from his work with hypnotism that not all objects are accessible to consciousness. This led to a view of *unconscious* intentions that are not accessible to consciousness but are nevertheless directed towards objects. Psychoanalysis became an unfolding of the unconscious sources of a person's overt symptoms, tracing them back to instinctual impulses or repressed memories of specific events. This is consistent with a view of the 'normal self' as a proprietor of its conscious experiences, albeit a self that may not always know what intentions it may harbour unconsciously.

By contrast, for Merleau-Ponty, there is always an invisible horizon that underlies what is consciously perceived. Dreyfus gives Merleau-Ponty's own illustration of this horizon when he compares it to the illumination of a room that makes directedness towards objects possible but is not itself an object to which the eye can be directed. This is a different conception of an unconscious. On this analysis, there is no two-way engagement between conscious and unconscious, as in Freud, because 'a person's way of relating to objects in the world becomes part of the context on the basis of which all objects are encountered' (Dreyfus 1989: 42). This is not repression but blindness. For Merleau-Ponty, something in a person's life might become *emblematic* of that blindness, forcing the horizon to become noticed as a *difficulty*, but the person is blind to the horizon against which the emblem shows up.

When we compare this way of viewing matters to the humanist self of the Renaissance, we can see that the autocentric self in charge of the world has been knocked off its perch – it has been de-centred though not eliminated. Dreyfus calls the conceptualisation of the centred self that masters the world by representing it (part of a mind that confronts the world as a knower) the *epistemological* conception. He calls the second conceptualisation *ontological* because it understands self as a mode of being-in-the-world, not as the font of its own knowledge of itself. To adopt Merleau-Ponty's terminology, the sense-of-self by which we know ourselves is emblematic of an invisible context that allows it to be encountered as such. The normal self of well-acculturated individuals is not necessarily emblematic of a difficulty but anomalies of self-experience, as well as other psychological abnormalities, might well reveal the hidden horizon against which the normal self shows up.

Henri Ey (1900–77), a Catalan psychiatrist greatly influenced by phenomenology and existentialism, agrees that self is, in his own words, virtual being. Although he sees the trajectory of self as containing 'an infinity of virtualities' (Ey 1978: 281), he also views self as transcending the body from which it has emerged 'by unfolding itself in a system of relations' (1978: 283), essentially a symbolic, linguistic system of relations, which lead it to become a body in time – a historical body. Ey then notes a paradox in the humanistic idea of a personalised self, i.e. self as master or proprietor of itself. This self-definition is a product of historical circumstances. The ontological conception of self as being-in-the-world would have to assert that any historical definition of self is transcended as an inevitable consequence of what it means for human beings to exist. In this case, the autocentric, proprietorial self will eventually be replaced by another self-conception.

Self and self-awareness: a contemporary view

Phenomenological approaches to self-awareness are still very much alive. In a recent book on subjectivity and selfhood, Dan Zahavi accepts the fundamental distinction between pre-reflective and reflective awareness and acknowledges Sartre's point that the two modes of self-awareness must share an affinity and structural similarity, otherwise it would not be possible to explain how the one could give rise to the other (Zahavi 2005: 92). Zahavi points out that it is difficult to capture what this affinity consists of. The act of reflecting is an element in a temporal process, and it would seem that the reflecting awareness is always opaque to itself until it is, in turn, reflected upon. In other words, the act of reflecting cannot grasp itself as an object of awareness. The writings of several phenomenologists therefore lead one to conclude that there is an 'unthematic and anonymous spot in the life of the subject' (2005: 92).

Zahavi argues that this blind spot is not, presumably, pre-reflective awareness which is generally assumed to be a form of first-person awareness and therefore not opaque to experience, nor anonymous. If so, it is only the act of reflecting that remains opaque. Reflecting could be compared to the act of remembering that is not present to us in addition to the memory recalled. The distinctive feature of reflective awareness is that the experience is thematised – it is an experience of an object or abstract idea, and, in some sense, a human construction. Pre-reflective awareness is usually portrayed as a vague background of awareness or even, by some theorists, as unconscious. For the latter school of theorists, higher-order mental processes are needed to allow us to be conscious at all.

Zahavi questions whether pre-reflective awareness can be said to be structured and temporal or whether reflection achieves this effect. If there is an affinity between pre-reflective and reflective awareness, they must share certain characteristics, and, if there is a continuum of thematisation, they may even merge into one another. Reflective awareness need not imply a co-present consciousness of self if a thematised self is just one object of reflection amongst others. For instance, the subject/object pole may remain implicit during abstract thought and may not be brought to attention as *my* thought until I reflect that it is *me* that is having the thought. Another aspect of reflection is its association with a process of bringing something pre-reflective into the focus of attention, thereby rendering it more vivid.

It is instructive to give one of Sartre's examples to provide a concrete illustration of all these points. Zahavi (2005: 94) describes it as follows (my summary). Sartre poses the situation of sitting up late at night writing a book. You have been reading most of the day and so your eyes are hurting. Sartre suggests that the pain in your eyes is not at first an object of reflection. It simply influences the way you perceive the world. You become restless and have difficulty focusing on the page. The pain is not reflected on as an object of perception but it still influences your interaction with the world and colours the total feeling state of your body. Then, in reflecting on these feelings, the pain as an object is transformed. Different isolated twinges of pain are perceived as part of one and the same suffering. It is also seen as being owned by you. It is now the pain of a somebody (you) who may even be manifesting the first signs of a disease. Others can diagnose this pain as well, and so you may begin to adopt this third-person perspective as if it was the experience of someone else.

Zahavi points out that Sartre's interpretation of perceiving oneself from the perspective of another is to understand it as a form of alienation – I am then perceived as having characteristics I have not chosen. One exists for others rather than for oneself. Zahavi notes that 'self-alteration is something inherent to reflection' (2005: 96). Pre-reflective experience constrains reflection, but reflection may well involve a loss as well as a gain. Reflection involves a stepping back from experience, and this enables critical reasoning. At the same time, experience that is not lived spontaneously may become arid or fragmented.

Zahavi believes that we cannot do without the concept of a minimal or core self that has first-person access to its own experience (2005: 106). This is not assumed to be a first-person givenness (mineness) that one is explicitly aware of. Zahavi notes that Sartre later rejected his own idea that pre-reflective consciousness is pre-personal, arguing that an ego or self as an object for consciousness can only arise out of a pre-reflective awareness that is self-given or self-referential (2005: 115). This minimal sense of what it is like for somebody to experience something must also inhere in the perception of public objects that are available to others as well. Accordingly, there is no pure third-person perspective even though, for everyday purposes, we can ignore this and say 'Pass the salt' without bothering with the fact that the salt cellar appears differently to me and to somebody else. Perspective becomes an issue only if it is relevant (e.g., my fellow diner cannot see the salt cellar) and then this self-referential aspect of experience may become the focus of attention.

Zahavi rejects the potential criticism that a minimal sense of mineness is trivial because it belongs to all experience. A minimal sense-of-self counters the idea that experience could be anonymous. The mineness of experience does not constitute self as an object and so it could be viewed as complementing any theory that supposes self to be constructed. It would, however, conflict with the idea that self is *merely* a construction, meaning that particular persons are irrelevant to a configuration of social/linguistic symbols and practices. The minimal sense-of-self, contingent on embodiment, contributes to the constitution of self.

6   Self in historical explanation

Having outlined a generic framework for person and self, I now discuss
how the concept of self has entered into the thinking of some philosophers
of history. One area of interest has been the way ideas and practices associated with persons and selves change over time. This chapter prepares
the ground for the next that considers self to be a narrative or discursive construction and therefore inherently historical. Historical analysis,
like cross-cultural comparison, seems to need at least a few universal
assumptions to get a contextual analysis onto first base. The oppositions
between reason versus cause, culture versus nature, etc., are certainly
alive in historical explanation, but their presence is often muted. As an
arts discipline, history has concerned itself mainly with phases of history
and the impact of ideas in general and has not thoroughly assimilated the
natural or social sciences into its own modes of explanation.

Michel Foucault has been a major influence in the last quarter of the
twentieth century (e.g., Foucault 1984). He worked on historical material in his treatment of topics such as madness, sexuality and punishment, in part to illuminate the meaning of present-day social categories
such as 'mankind' and 'self'. Foucault's analyses are radical because of
the way he located self in history. In common with some other theorists,
Foucault 'de-centres' the self (see Giddens 1979). People are demoted
from their position as the central actor or instigator of social change
and become much more passive figures: they become instruments of
change served up in a historically determined form. People are passive
in the sense that the origins of the categories with which they think are
dispersed amongst impersonal processes – frameworks or paradigms
for thinking, relationships of power and the technologies that get drawn
in to solve social problems. The person is conceived more as instrument
than instrumental. This calls into question an assumption often made
by historians that there is a shared humanity that makes it possible to
empathise with the thought of a past era. In other words, assumptions
are made about a common human nature although they may not be
spelled out explicitly.

Discussing Foucault's contribution, Hayden White (1978) divides his fellow historians into 'refamiliarisers' and 'defamiliarisers'. The former suppose that 'a vaguely conceived "human nature" must be capable of recognizing something of itself in the residues of such thought and action appearing as artifacts in the historical record' (White 1978: 256). The other camp attempts to 'render the familiar strange' (1978: 256), which has the effect of isolating the contemporary thinker from the historical actor. This kind of historian has to decode the ways in which the surface structure of thought conceals the reality of the world. Nevertheless, the historian has to play a double game in order to be attuned to (familiar with) the unfamiliar so that its strangeness manages to be conveyed. White places Foucault in this camp.

Foucault himself says that: 'All my analyses are against the idea of universal necessities in human existence' (quoted in Martin 1988: 11), but this makes his own ability to interpret the inner dynamics or figurative forms that permeate a body of historical material rather mysterious. Any use of historical material seems to presuppose the possibility of translation. For instance, it implies an ability to recognise the relevance of archaic figures of speech such as 'money-changer' or 'night-watchman'. In my view, a universalising framework is needed for historical analysis, which is not to prescribe what these universal concepts should be.

Foucault's methods seem to reflect a shift in social science towards what I have called an ecocentric perspective. Foucault interprets a person's reflection on themself as a set of practical techniques that constitute self in a historical form. These techniques are placed on a level with technologies that relate to the production of things, of signs and of power (Martin 1998: 16–49). Of course, Foucault's analyses of texts from the classical period apply a kind of intellectual detachment that was not available, presumably, to the theocentric and autocentric historical players themselves (see below).

The idea of de-centring the self is fundamental to the textual methods outlined in the next chapter. I will therefore use this chapter to contrast two different ways of assimilating self into historical explanation, the autocentric and ecocentric. After outlining the former approach, I will discuss the ecocentric view that people can be 'positioned' as selves by the linguistic categories, stories and ways of reasoning available to them. I will also introduce some key terms, used by Foucault, such as 'discourse'. Approaches to defining self that employ concepts of positioning and narrative leave behind the autocentric assumption that people's self-reflections are transparently a product of their own activity. They are, instead, the product of a total way of life: its language, historical traditions and material practices. It is for this reason that positioned and narrated selves are inherently historical in character. I will highlight Foucault's method rather than his extensive writings on self. I will also attempt to connect the material aspects of social practices (i.e. the non-discursive realm of human life) with arguments about naturalism presented in earlier chapters.

Autocentric (mindist) history

It is worth being reminded of prototypic autocentric attitudes as expressed in Pico della Mirandola's (1463–94) famous 'Oration on the Dignity of Man' (1960). This helps us to see how they are carried through as pervasive assumptions across the sciences and the arts: 'You, with no limit or no bound, may choose for yourself the limits and bounds of your nature. We have placed you at the world's centre so that you may survey everything else in the world.'

The centrality of a person's mind, which surveys and marks out the limits, defines this perspective. A twentieth-century example in historical explanation is Robin G. Collingwood's 1936 essay 'Human Nature and Human History' (1961a). Collingwood (1889–1943) was a philosopher who set out his case in a particularly clear and forthright manner. What is remarkable about his essay, and also his book *The Idea of History* ([1946] 1961b) is his junking of the idea that history is about the course of human events 'viewed from the outside'. It is not for him about battles, monarchs and statutes. He views history, and for that matter psychology as well, as an extension in time of the process a person might go through in recalling what they had thought about in the previous five minutes. This process involves putting thoughts into some kind of order, critically examining them, or simply trying to interpret what they mean. Thinking historically is seen as a form of self-reflective reasoning which must be able to conjure up 'from the inside' how people thought in earlier times. If it proves impossible to recreate the thought of the past, then whatever happened is dead history, as dead as any indecipherable ancient script.

This view does not exclude an examination of human events, observed and described, nor the artefacts and technologies of a period of history. All of the circumstances surrounding an act can help to interpret the thought that is assumed to motivate it, just as they would be useful in understanding the thinking that might lie behind a nation's decision to go to war in the present century. What Collingwood wanted to counter was history conceived as a natural science, building up general laws from patterns of historical events. However, it seems to me that in *both* his own position and the one he was criticising, historical events are assumed to be the outcome of the acts of people who are motivated by their beliefs, reasons and desires.

In Collingwood's view, doing history is a species of interpretation rather than fitting an actual event into an empirical generalisation in order to classify and explain it (1961b: 215). He does not mean to imply that the historian must reproduce exactly the *same* thought as the original thought because understanding is an active process that involves critical reflection. For this reason, reaching out to a past mentality can only ever be conducted from a present perspective. Past thoughts cannot be preserved in aspic. They were past occurrences, it is true, but, in another sense, Collingwood argues that history is timeless. In so far as past thoughts are rethought in the present, they do not belong in time. All history is living history and, therefore, if alive, it is permanently alive. This is a refreshing perspective that highlights the importance of a historian's empathic reliving of a historical context, but Collingwood puts all his money on mental processes and can hardly think of a role for natural science.

He doesn't entirely dismiss the possibility that knowledge of a universal human nature might have a bearing on understanding human mentalities, but his sharp separation of nature and culture now appears naive. For instance, he suggests there is an irrational part of the mind, governed by blind forces and activities within us, which is not part of history. These forces are, for example, appetites and feelings that supposedly feed and support the mind while it goes on with its more important task of creative and rational self-conscious reflection. But his general position is clear: 'the processes of events which constitute the world of nature are altogether different in kind from the processes of thought which constitute the world of history' (Collingwood 1961b: 217).

Collingwood extended the notion of knowing another person's thoughts to knowing the mentality of a period or, as he put it, 'the corporate mind', but then added, 'whatever, exactly, that phrase means' (1961b: 219). Each person is the heir to a history and must absorb it from others. He also implies that as a society acquires greater knowledge of different ways of thinking (across time and across cultures) it becomes better able to appreciate, with greater detachment, the thought of its own age. For instance, he argues that eighteenth-century writers simply mistook the conditions of their own age as a permanent and unchanging law of nature. They also assumed that the human species was a special creation with unalterable characteristics. Collingwood's advice on doing history is therefore more subtle than it looks at first sight because it acknowledges an understanding of the conditions in which past thoughts were produced.

Collingwood's idea of the 'the corporate mind' was developed into what a later school of French historians called 'mentalities' or 'collective representations'. The French school, reviewed and discussed by Michel Vovelle (1990), dealt with subjects such as happiness, the family and death by taking the long view over many centuries. Upon examination, the approach is not as attractive as it first appears. Like Collingwood, these historians carry over outdated philosophies of mind. The mentality of a period is thought of as a collective consciousness (or as an unconscious collective representation) that has a semi-autonomous existence. This is a rather vague sort of entity as Vovelle admits (1990: 5). If it is not merely a theme in the mind of the historian, it must be a schema in the minds of individuals, helping them to make sense of the world. It is collective in the two senses that, first, it derives from how people talk about the topic in question in an agreed manner, and, second, that it is shared by a large number of people. (See Potter and Wetherell 1987: 138–57, for a critique of the concept of collective representation).

Viewed 'from the inside', a group representation seems to be an extension of the idea that individual minds represent the world, in the sense that it simply aggregates a large number of individual minds. For instance, a Victorian mentality could be defined by the sum of the individual expressions of people living in the Victorian period. But on this basis, we have no criteria for deciding whether the Victorian mentality pre-existed or outlived this period. It is rather pointless to try to average out how Victorians talked about the self and call this the Victorian self. This group representation would have homogenised a very complex phenomenon into a phoney group consensus. What seems to be needed is some way of analysing how a person in one period refers to self so that we can begin to distinguish it from how a person in another period refers to self. There will, of course, be commonalities in a certain period but, in addition, the historian has to identify principles to establish what is different or novel.

What is it, exactly, that unifies a mentality, and how can its interconnected elements be related to each other? Vovelle says that mentalities have to be related back to the material conditions in which people lived – 'the objective conditions of human life' (1990: 12). The mentality is thought of as a kind of mental mediation between people and their 'real human life' (Vovelle 1990: 11). However, it is not easy to find a language for talking about 'real life' (e.g., political, economic and social structures) that is independent of a mentality. Nevertheless, the French school makes a good case for the 'inertial force of mental structures' (Vovelle 1990: 8). In other words, so it is argued, the traces of earlier historical contexts remain as fragments of ways of thinking in times when they have less relevance (or no relevance) to real life. It seems undeniable that language and other social practices change rather slowly, and perhaps too slowly to deal with new and urgent circumstances.

However, a historical explanation that takes the human mind as its chief starting point appears to handicap itself from the outset. This is not, of course, an objection to historical descriptions that employ the concepts available to historical players themselves. Moreover, the concept of 'collective representation', which has had a long life since its coining by the founding father of French sociology, Émile Durkheim (1858–1917), has been developed in a direction that takes it away from individual minds (e.g., see Marková 2003 and Chapter 13).

Ecocentric historical theory

Ecocentric theory does not place person or self at the fulcrum of a set of influences or forces. The person is de-centred, and personal attributes are not given a privileged place in the analysis. Thus, a person's intentions are not excluded from the analysis, but they are included on a par with other elements in a network of influences identified by the theorist. Mindist theory essentially terminates with individual minds reacting to 'real life'. By contrast, in an approach like Foucault's, people's categories of thought and the objects and technologies they use are conceived as the product of an interplay between the linguistic, symbolic and meaning-creating aspects of human life (usually referred to as the discursive realm) and the actual observable and material social practices that people engage in (usually referred to as the non-discursive realm). Neither is given priority in the sense that a material social practice might generate categories of thought or vice versa. Each realm conditions the other and so they are not truly independent.

Foucault argues that the same stricture applies to categories of event regarded as natural. 'The natural' is not set up as an a-priori category independent of the practical concerns of people (and scientists) who obviously find a use for it in describing and explaining what they are doing. This idea is not inconsistent with the position of naturalism outlined in Chapter 1. Thus, the assumption that there is such a thing as 'human nature' that exists independently of any actual person can be seen as a product of the social circumstances in which the notion is entertained. It may have truth value (i.e. within the context of a naturalistic theory) even though no human being stripped down to their basic human nature has ever existed.

In an ecocentric perspective, individual persons are removed from the centre of the analysis because they are seen as the joint product of their communicative and material practices, that is, as jointly produced by their discursive and non-discursive activities. The concept of discourse in Foucauldian and related approaches is not limited to written or spoken words because many other cultural artefacts are viewed as partaking in a broader system of cultural signs. People are understood as the witting and unwitting agents of influence on each other; they transmit culture, enforce and submit to practices, and, through the competition of ideas in discourse, determine who is silenced and who passes on a legacy to history. Even as witting agents, they are as much products as producers of influence. For instance, when discussing power, Foucault aligns it with knowledge; power is not employed in the traditional sense of superior force or authority. Individual selves are caught up in a web of established meanings that impels their conduct as participants in the currents of history. In this sense, people exercise power unwittingly through exercising their knowledge.

The concept of discourse has been employed differently by different theorists. I will briefly outline Foucault's concept (see Kendall and Wickham 1999). Discourse emphasises the systematic ordering of social life as if it was governed by rules, and this ordering applies both to 'statements' expressed through language and to the forms of material social practices. Discourse, in the abstract, denotes meaning ordered by a system of signs, linguistic or otherwise. In the singular, a discourse refers to a subset of statements with a definable boundary or, in Foucauldian terms, as a particular network of elements.

The forms of discourse analysis described in the next chapter set to one side the fact that people's utterances refer to their mental intentions. This approach is clearly compatible with Ryle's analysis of the mind discussed in Chapter 2; for Ryle, there is no invisible mental act that precedes each expressed thought or act. It differs from Ryle in placing attention on 'social acts', not on acts performed singly by persons because they possess a disposition to express them. 'Discursive objects' are understood to be constructed by interacting persons, the linguistic resources they draw upon and their shared practices. However, as in Ryle's personism, a discourse operates without each participant necessarily thinking about how they contribute to it.

A particular discursive object is created or manufactured in a defined context, taking account of what is written, spoken, done or meant to be done, within the local arrangement of 'apparatuses' and institutional practices. So, for instance, we can think of the intelligence quotient (IQ) as being a discursive object created by test procedures carried out for institutional purposes (Danziger 1997: 66). It generates a new vocabulary such as 'intellectual potential' and 'borderline low intelligence'. People are understood to be 'positioned' when they occupy the categories created through the discourse – and people routinely position each other when they employ the forms of talk appropriate to the context, occupy its physical space and make use of the techniques/apparatuses it affords.

The practice of intelligence testing was a response to a problem arising out of mass public schooling and the need to sift and sort pupils. 'They were employed to assess capacity for scholastic achievement, not "zeal" or hard work, which teachers could quite easily assess for themselves' (Danziger 1997: 67). This practice illustrates one of Foucault's key concepts – 'problematisation'. His idea is that historical transformations in thought and practice arise out of questions asked and solutions found in response to practical problems. Foucault applies this approach to many historical themes, including self (see the introduction to Paul Rabinow and Nikolas Rose, *The Essential Foucault,* 2003). Foucault does not write history or do history in the traditional sense. In relation to self, he analyses techniques of self-care in the classical period, beginning with the 'problem' of training citizens in the principles of social and personal conduct appropriate to the Greek city-state. Although western categories of self and human nature are likely to have had a far more ancient origin than this, there are no extant written materials to research them. In Chapter 12, I draw on theories of human social evolution to speculate about practices that might have been related to self-reference in pre-history.

The interplay of discourses

A definition of a discourse as a domain of related statements (e.g., Parker 1992) usually acknowledges that some of the statements specify relationships with other discourses and help to establish the borders between them. Furthermore, the rules that regulate what is sayable within a discourse are not assumed to close it off to all possibility of innovation. That kind of closure is only found in the rules of a game like chess. A discourse may include statements that can be interpreted as a defence against competitor discourses. A discourse may evolve as it meets resistance. It may contain contradictions within itself that must be 'covered up'. As noted earlier, the way a discourse is perpetuated is coordinated with material practices. A discourse, defined in these general terms, does not have a fixed point of reference in entities or processes. There is obviously a vagueness to all of this but this quality does nevertheless serve an important function in loosening up our thinking about a subject like self.

As I see it, one of the tasks of this book is to make a connection between discourses of nature and culture, and we could ask in what way the concept of discourse facilitates an attempt to reconnect them. The stance of critical realism is to include the 'natural' as a constraint on what can be discursively produced. In this case, the non-discursive realm (e.g., the hypothesis of a human nature) is a set of constraints constructed by philosophers and scientists. The non-discursive realm could also refer to the conditions of possibility for discourse itself. Nature could be viewed as a constraint rather than as a separate onto-logical reality that cannot be reconciled with mental or social phenom-ena. Clearly, discourses of nature and culture came into existence for historical reasons, and we can imagine a period in which their differen-tiation would have been meaningless.

The separate discourses of nature and culture have certainly had a profound effect on the way research is conducted in the human sciences. One example is the domain of human life in which people are regarded as mad. In the nineteenth century, different professional groups com-peted through moral and scientific argument for the right to label mad-ness in their own way and to act as custodians for mad people (Boyle 2002). Medical hospitalisation was justified on the basis of nervous dys-function – a discourse of nature. In present circumstances, for a variety of reasons, the voices of professional groups offering different solutions and definitions, drawing on discourses of empathy and re-education, now hold greater sway. Both discourses supply persuasive arguments and each phenomenon is probably best analysed on a case-by-case basis (see Chapter 13).

Discursive analysis of persons and selves

The discursive approach has been applied to whole historical epochs and also to social exchanges in small corners of obscure cultural practices. The category 'person' is applicable to all forms of analysis in the sense that discourse presupposes actors or speakers. Analysis may focus on spontaneous conversation, interviews or archival documents. In some forms of analysis the emphasis is placed on rhetorical strategies that perform a function like avoiding (or laying) blame, or simply describ-ing events (Edwards and Potter 1992). Speakers are said to draw upon 'resources' that may include linguistic categories for persons and social roles, as well as grammatical devices that serve to personalise or imper-sonalise a course of events. This means that 'sub-agents' (aspects of the

speaker) or 'collectives' (groups of speakers) might constitute the puta-
tive actors (Edwards and Potter 1992: 170).

The form of discursive analysis I discuss in the next chapter is aimed
at a somewhat broader socio-historical level. At this level, social positioning and self-accounting cuts across many specific contexts of use.
In positioning theory (Harré and van Langenhove 1999), the subjects
of a discourse (persons, speakers, etc.) are identified by the vocabulary,
grammar and rhetorical strategies they employ. Narrative analysis, a
different form of discourse analysis, goes beyond an identification of
kinds of persons and the nature of their interactions, and focuses more
on the storylike structure of what actors are doing together. For the nar-
rativist school, 'story' is the guiding metaphor, and it has a somewhat
broader conception of language as a resource, drawing upon shared
meanings embodied in sayings, stories and myths.

Narrativists conceive of a person's identity or self as an element in
a story, for instance, as a protagonist of a particular kind who follows
a certain plot structure when enacting their life. A protagonist may
view themselves as the storyteller who also plays a part in the story or,
alternatively, a person's identity is interpreted as being constructed
(unwittingly) *as if* they were a storyteller. In contrast to an emphasis
on narrative, positioning theory is more concerned with the features of
conversations and texts that enable persons and selves to be identified
in the first place, as entities around which stories could be told.

7   Self as historically positioned and narrated

In this chapter, I will compare two types of discursive analysis, 'positioning theory' and 'narrative analysis', that attempt to show how reference to person and self is manifested in conversation, writing and other social practices. I have selected these approaches because they are prominent, popular and influential.

Positioning theory attempts to show how the subjects of a discourse (persons, speakers, etc.) are constituted by the vocabulary, grammar and rhetorical strategies that speakers employ in their dealings with each other in various social contexts. Narrative analysis focuses more on the storylike structure of what actors are doing together, and, within this approach, a person's identity or self has also been understood as an element in a story – as a protagonist of a particular kind whose self-interpretation can be equated with the sort of plot they are enacting. In one version of the theory, a person is viewed as the storyteller who also plays a part in the story and, in another, a person's identity is interpreted as being constructed (unwittingly) *as if* they were a storyteller.

Before embarking upon a detailed discussion, I would like to set the scene by commenting on two well-known early theorists of self and identity, William James (1842–1910) and George H. Mead (1863–1931). Their ideas have been so influential that it is difficult to discuss a discursive approach to persons without first considering their contribution. A discussion of their ideas also highlights how a discursive approach differs from theirs. Moreover, their writings have been analysed by Hubert Hermans and Harry Kempen in connection with their own theory of the dialogical self (Hermans and Kempen 1993). Their commentary on James and Mead helps to bring out differences that also exist within constructionist views.

William James

William James's 1892 discussion of self (1961) is rather confusing because he refers to 'the I' and 'the Me' as nouns while maintaining that it is an 'ineradicable dictum of common sense' that I and Me are identical. He describes them as two 'discriminable aspects' of self (1961: 43). However, it is not clear whether it is James, the psychological theorist, who is doing the discriminating or the person of common sense. He vacillates between one position and the other. He argues that self is 'partly knower' and 'partly known' and expands on this conception. The self as known is the empirical Me in his terms, and self as knower is that aspect of self that recognises something as mine.

The 'knower' and the 'known' are philosophical concepts rather than common sense, and James incorporates them into his essentially psychological theory of self. Self as known is said to include the material body, the bodily self and one's family, but only in so far as one recognises them as 'mine'. He acknowledges that religious ascetics might disown their bodies as 'prisons of clay' (1961: 44) rejecting their inclusion in a sense-of-self. He points out that the death of a family member might lead to a loss of the known Me, but he can only mean by this a part of a person's life that is felt to be mine. For James, the known Me is a *conceptual* aspect of self, and this interpretation is supported by his Hierarchy of the Mes which ranges from the bodily to the spiritual.

Who, then, is the knower in James's theory? At one point, he states that 'In the judgement "I am the same," etc., the "I" was taken broadly as the concrete person' but he quickly goes on to suggest that 'we take it narrowly as the Thinker' (James 1961: 69). From this point on, his theory is thoroughly mentalistic, reflecting the dualism of his period. In brief, the knower is the stream of mental states that are unified by the fact that the 'I' of one mental state appropriates the 'Mes' of previous mental states. The unity is a kind of common memory or representation; the mental states are functionally related but it is up to the judgement of any I to reject previous Mes as no longer recognisable as Mine, thereby allowing for the possibility of change over time.

Hermans and Kempen (1993) believe that James has met objections to mind–body dualism by relating the I to the material Me. However, on my interpretation, James has only succeeded in relating thought with thought. Moreover, he does not account for the mental power of the thinker to recognise some conscious states as an acceptable continuation of self and others as not. James makes 'the I' into a noun, easing the identification of I with the person but, in reality, I, in his theory, is a knower or thinker, an abstraction, not a real entity that thinks. James seems to place agency within the mind rather than the person. Dan McAdams, a recent exponent of Jamesian ideas, makes I into a verb 'selfing' but continues to refer to it as a noun when he says that 'the Me may be viewed as the self that the I narrates' (McAdams 1996). On the one hand, 'selfing' seems to introduce a vicious circularity and, on the other, 'the I' remains a mysterious entity. McAdams implicitly retains a concept of the real person when he says, for instance, that introverts self themselves differently than extroverts (McAdams 1996: 303).

James's ideas continue the autocentric humanist tradition of the person (actually, the person's mind) as the entity that constructs self, acting as if alone. This way of thinking is incompatible with a de-centred locus for construction. However, even within a de-centred perspective, there remains a tension between the person as capable of making an independent contribution to the constructive process and the person as a passive receiver of social influences. I will pick up this point in other chapters.

George H. Mead

Mead also refers to *the* I and *the* Me as phases of *the* self. A child acquires a self when it imports social attitudes – a child learns to respond to itself as if it were, say, in the role of its mother speaking to it. Self clearly arises in what Mead calls an individual organism or body. Self is a thematic organisation of experience into 'the experience of the self' (Mead 1962: 135), and our body is presented to us as an *experience* of the body. Self is therefore experienced as a subject (a knower) that also knows itself as an object of knowledge. In just the same way that Gilbert Ryle views the matter, Mead's knower or doer 'does not get into the limelight' (1962: 174). The 'I' is only known retrospectively as a 'Me'. Human beings are said to differ from lower animals in the respect that humans can experience themselves as an object rather than just merely experience. Mead says that in order to become human, the individual 'should thus take an objective, impersonal attitude toward himself' (1962: 138).

There is a risk that Mead's words could be misconstrued here. The human organism, as an animal, cannot be enjoined to do anything to become human. Mead assumes that it is persons who do things – they are the active agents – but they do not experience themselves as agents until they have conceptualised themselves as agents. For James, the agent is a thinker, but James does not explain how persons become thinkers. For Mead, human beings only come to experience themselves as a 'self with agency' by internalising this conception as it is transmitted to them (i.e. during childhood) by society at large. Persons come to know themselves as agents in the course of responding to others. Eventually they respond to their own internalised conceptions of self, as they have been earlier played out in social interaction. A person's concept of who they are is therefore ultimately derived from others. At the same time, a person never knows in advance how they will respond to a situation. The uncertainty associated with the I's response to the Me 'gives a sense of freedom, of initiative' (Mead 1962: 177).

Mead seems to regard a conceptualised Me as a complex stimulus to which the human organism responds automatically. This does not mean that the response is unintelligent, although it may be impulsive. The response may take the form of an intention to respond in a particular way (e.g., to be rational), but this is simply a complex response to a complex stimulus. In declaring an intention, a person is not reflexively aware that this is what they are doing – they can only construe themselves as being an active and intending agent in *retrospect,* though the retrospective interval in this context might be measured in milliseconds. Mead accepts that we feel as though there is an observer of consciousness, a subject responsible for conduct, but he rejects the idea that the self 'is an entity that could conceivably exist by itself' (1962: 164). The so-called reflective self is responding to prior conduct, and these reflections are already objectified Mes and temporally in the past.

Mead's theory is compatible with the idea of a person being positioned (as a certain kind of subject) by their use of language. Although he talks of *the* I, we can interpret what he says as a way of explaining a common-sense (but, in my view, theoretically mistaken) notion that I is some sort of mental entity, an initiator of acts. In positioning theory, the originator of acts is the speaker or doer (the substantive person), and personal pronouns can be understood as a means of indicating to others who is speaking, acting or expressing an intention: Who wants ice-cream? Me. The pronoun I is also employed to indicate the characteristics of the speaker, as in, 'I like ice-cream.' This is a means of specifying the *attributes* of a person, not an entity within, or separate from, that person.

Hermans and Kempen (1993) argue that Mead's I is always historical, and, therefore, being reduced to a memory, it is incapable of intentional and purposive behaviour; it is not an original author with its own view of the world. However, Mead talks of 'the I' as a response, and, therefore, it does seem to be the response of an implicit actor (a person) – it is just that it cannot know itself except as a historical I. The theoretical problem of its historical nature can be overcome by assuming that persons (as real human beings) are capable of conceptualising what happens to them in milliseconds. There should be no objection from a causal point of view that retrospective conceptions lag behind the action. The person as author can still be original – it is just that recognising an act as original is something that occurs after the act. As Mead says with regard to a scientist solving a problem: 'What he is going to do he does not know, nor does anybody else' (1962: 177).

In less creative contexts, a person will have learned from experience what is likely to happen. So, an anticipation of the way others will respond to me can act as a stimulus for my present response to them. Dialogue can be future-oriented at the same time as being controlled by retrospective appraisals. Mead states that a person 'not only hears himself but responds to himself, talks and replies to himself as truly as the other person replies to him' (1962: 139). Mead is keen to point out that this sequence of events should not be portrayed as a monologue, as in the case of a dog hearing itself barking, and another dog growling, which could be construed as an automatic sequence of stimuli and responses (1962: 162). Mead can be interpreted as saying that human beings, unlike dogs, can conceptualise the other as capable of expressing a range of responses and know that by varying the response they emit, they can control how the other will behave. His language of stimuli and responses is somewhat dated, but Mead stresses the mediating role of linguistic symbols as stimuli that both speakers understand in the same way. Mead provides a general causal account of how speech can control behaviour rather than giving a detailed account of conversational practices. For him, the common meaning of the symbol allows the child to internalise the attitude of others and to anticipate, rather than simply react to, the other.

It has to be admitted that Mead occasionally slips into referring to the human individual as 'the I'. When he says that the 'I' gives a sense of freedom and initiative, he should only be arguing for an element of novelty in a person's response. Mead locates the source of much of human behaviour, and therefore its spontaneity, in the biological properties of the human organism, and views the given sensuous reality as a biological characteristic. What he denies is that consciousness of a self existing in time is given innately. The social order is a both a logical and biological precondition for the appearance of selves (Mead 1962: 222).

Having prepared the ground by describing what the newer discursive perspective can be seen as replacing, I will now go on to give an account of positioning theory and narrative analysis. It seems that neither perspective offers much opportunity for a theoretical integration with a biological approach to human beings but nor are they incompatible with naturalism.

Positioning theory

It is important to emphasise that discursive (textual) analysis always assumes a *context* for any particular interaction or sample of writing or conversation. The context includes features of the environment as well as human gestures and other social signs. The context helps to make clear what is being communicated and what is relevant to the communication. For instance, when buying a railway ticket, the context includes the station, a sign, a counter, etc., and what is said is usually strictly limited. But even in this situation, contextual boundaries are flexible, as might be the case if the ticket office clerk shows interest in the traveller's reasons for wanting to reach a particular destination. The terms of reference might be reset, allowing the transaction to expand. Thus, discursive analysis deals with sets of related meanings each with a tacit but open boundary. If the context changes, the elements and their relationship also change. In the case of a written text, there is an implied context for the author (e.g., who they are writing for) and a different context for a reader of the text.

In the method of analysis proposed by Parker (1992), speakers are said to draw upon a variety of different 'discourses', each one thought of as a set of statements that cohere as a means of constituting a particular theme or topic. The types of person participating are implied by the terms employed and mode of address, and these, in turn, specify certain rights of response or delimit what can or cannot be spoken about. A given text (conversation, document, etc.) is assumed to contain several discourses, each of which is systematically articulated with related discourses. A discourse operates in the context of social institutions and social practices and, by so doing, serves to support and reproduce them, together with the power relationships that they entail. Certain discourses, such as ones relating to gender, would be found in a very wide range of contexts.

An example may help to illustrate this type of analysis. The interviewees were some people given a diagnosis of psychosis, and they were asked what they thought about their experience of receiving psychological therapy in their clinical setting (Messari and Hallam 2003). Analysis of the transcribed interviews identified several themes common to most participants. These themes were interpretations placed on what was said and do not directly represent the way interviewees structured their replies. Given that the interviewer was a psychologist and the interviews took place in a hospital or clinic, the overall medical context must have constrained what was said and how it was said. Indeed, as might have been expected, participants sometimes construed meeting a therapist as a means of cooperating with the medical establishment, thereby facilitating their discharge. Other statements were interpreted as participants' identification with being 'ill' and in need of medical treatment. At other times, the way participants talked about their experiences implied they were in touch with real events that others simply did not believe or understand; in this case, they were not 'ill'. Psychological therapy was understood primarily in three ways: first, as a healing process alleviating distress; second as a useful educational or exploratory learning experience; and third, as a respectful friendship between equals. Most participants expressed all of the discursive themes, often switching between them, and sometimes, within the space of a few moments, expressed the contradictory ideas that they were ill and not ill. At one moment they saw themselves as a patient, at another as giving friendly assistance to a person (a therapist) who took an interest in them. One overriding feature of the interview transcripts was the variety of discursive themes, and another was the fact that the themes could be interpreted as interrelated reactions to a medical context.

There is, of course, a considerable difference between analysing an interview transcript and a piece of writing. A conversation often takes place in more open-ended circumstances, and speakers and hearers are usually in face-to-face dialogue. By contrast, an author of a written text only has a notion of the readers they are addressing although this can be made more or less explicit in the text. The social context is generally less influential in reading and writing than in conversation. Although an author may be writing for a particular audience, the reader has considerable choice over how to relate to the author and the characters portrayed. The life of the characters can be interpreted in the broader context of the reader's tacit relationship with the author. Of course, *within* a text an author may be quite specific about who is being addressed by whom. The author's characters address each other and jointly construct their dialogue. Autobiography is a special kind of text because the author is writing about themself. Even so, the author has some idea of the audience they are addressing and what kind of self is being presented.

The spoken or written word is often quite explicit about the kind of person or self it refers to. A speaker's identity is normally assumed to be singular although the speaker might use several 'voices' to achieve different effects. In any situation we need to know who is addressing who, their salient social attributes, and the nature of their relationship. All this is indicated by the content of the discourse (e.g., specific names, general denotations), grammatical constructions (especially the use of pronouns), non-verbal signs (e.g., gestures), style (e.g., parody) and the total environmental context (e.g., seating arrangement). For example, talk of 'my boss' in a work context clearly implies a kind of person and a defined relationship to the speaker. Different grammatical constructions produce different intended meanings and implied contexts

of discourse, as illustrated by the following: What do you think of...
my boss, your boss, 'the boss' or bosses? 'The boss' implies a similar
relationship to both speakers, but 'bosses' extends the boundary to anyone's experience of any kind of boss.

A personal pronoun like 'my' indicates a relationship with the speaker,
but the noun to which it is attached further specifies moral obligations
and power differentials. For instance, the implied status relationship
would be different for 'my Lord' and 'my son'. A letter written to the
former might be signed off 'your humble and obedient servant', but this
is very unlikely for the latter. The form of words indicates relationships
of power, moral status, implied rights, mutual obligations and so forth.
Rather than develop these ideas in a general way, I will focus on one
influential approach to discourse analysis: Rom Harré's theory of subject positioning.

Harré's positioning theory

The positioning theory of Harré and his colleagues (Harré and van
Langenhove 1992, 1999) has been influenced by the work of Lev
Vygotsky, the later Wittgenstein, Peter Strawson and John Austin
(Howie and Peters 1996). Harré is keen to stress that conversation
is embedded in culture – a social and moral order – but is also conducted by material persons within material practices. Harré employs
Wittgenstein's distinction between descriptive and expressive uses of
words in order to make the point that in using a personal pronoun like
'I', a person is not referring to themself as if referring to, or describing,
an object. This kind of descriptive reference would be open to error,
but the pronoun 'I' is used 'to express oneself as a singular, responsible
being' (Harré 1998: 40). A person's use of the pronoun might be insincere but not mistaken in the sense that I could mistake another person
for someone I know. For Harré, the first-person form of self-expression
is simply part of the frame of the human form of life. The grammatical
I is not a device for referring to a subject for whom properties and states
could be ascribed but is a means of indexing the embodied speaker.

Speakers possess the power to express themselves and are known by
others through the skills (linguistic and otherwise) that they employ.
For example, in searching for the right expression of a thought, a person has the *power* to reformulate it but the reformulated thought does
not exist before it is expressed. All that exists prior to the thought is an
already poorly expressed thought or a hunch that there is something
else worth expressing. As for Mead and Ryle, the knower is known in
retrospect. Harré understands the agent of an act to be a person. It is

important to maintain the distinction between powers of expression and conduct that is actually expressed (acts, thoughts, etc.), otherwise positioning theory could be interpreted as reducing personhood to *knowledge* of social and grammatical rules. However, this would ignore the fact that knowledge requires a *knower* as a being that knows.

Harré (2002) argues that there is more to human powers than what anyone currently brings into being. In fact, we may not realise all the possibilities inherent in those powers of which we are aware. In this respect, the being of a person is a hidden potential, unknown until it is expressed in discourse and practice. Persons follow social rules, wittingly or unwittingly, and constitute themselves as a kind of person or self in so doing. However, as agents with the *power* to follow rules, they cannot be defined only by the rules that they follow.

According to Harré, the grammatical 'I' in expressions, like 'Why didn't I see, etc.', indexes a singular person who perceives things from a particular standpoint – the spatio-temporal location of their unique body. When using a first-person grammar, Harré assumes that people take responsibility for what they say and the consequences of saying it. This is the default interpretation, and, in order to repudiate it, people have to appeal to constraints they cannot escape. They might also pass on doubt about the veracity of their statement, e.g., 'I think I can see it.' The singularity of selfhood is immanent in first-person expressions, the expressions of a material person, and so Harré is not reducing personhood to mere avowals of thought and feeling. Charles Taylor (1988) makes a similar point when he argues that the criteria for valid knowledge, such as the rules of the grammar that pertain to persons and selves, should not be confused with a person's lived experience. We may construct (position) persons and selves through discourse, but we do not thereby eliminate their reality.

It is tempting to suppose that there is 'a self behind the self' that directs self-expression, but this idea should be rejected if it is understood as an agent distinct from the person. Nevertheless, there is a strong tendency to regard self as the 'director of operations'. We see this tendency at work in literary interpretation as well. When C. S. Lewis explains allegory, he writes, 'If you are hesitating between an angry retort and a soft answer, you can express your state of mind by inventing a person called *Ira* with a torch and letting her contend with another person called *Patientia*' (quoted in Heelas and Locke 1981: 42).

What we are led to entertain here is the picture of a self deciding how it is going to express its own state of mind. This is a distinctly modern conception. It is the idea of a 'hidden observer' lurking in the background, always able to catch itself in the act of reflecting. If there is no such observer, then when we reflect we are already enacting another self and 'taking a position'.

The Cartesian and Lockean idea of self as an observer of its own mental states is that of an all-seeing, position-less position. A less exalted view of our power to reflect is suggested by retrospective musings – as in, 'Why didn't I see what was coming' or 'If only I had realised my limitations.' This suggests that the absence of self-reflection is the absence of an identifiable perspective, not the absence of a hidden observer who is temporarily asleep. Retrospective reflections are inspired by a new perspective from which to view self and therefore position it as a certain kind of self. There is no reason to suppose, as Lewis did, that to write in allegory necessarily presupposes a deliberate choice; it may simply be the way an author expresses themself.

Reflexive positioning: self as a presumptive reality

Raya Jones (1997) points out that positioning theory could be accused of reducing self to the fleeting and random ways in which persons are positioned by discourse, and she emphasises the role of *reflexive* positioning, at least in modern western culture. Jones compares reflexive positioning to Ryle's idea of second-order operations performed on first-order acts. This move can also be described as second-order positioning (Harré and van Langenhove 1992: 396–7). Reflexivity points to a construct of self that goes beyond a singular standpoint expressed in the course of material practices and a body-centred experience of the world. We don't just position each other moment to moment but *presume* the existence of higher-order selves. Theoretically speaking, it is reasonable to assume that there are repeating types of positioning across and within persons, on account of the fact that positioning depends on customary usage, including consistent ways of addressing individuals (e.g., by name, social-security number). Harré argues that a person's life is a story 'which I tell myself and which is forever being updated and revised' (1998: 138). Moreover, common biological predispositions to behave must generate assumptions about how persons are to be described (and do behave) in certain contexts.

In reflexive positioning, a person presupposes a higher-order construct of self that is logically related to other constructs. The reflexive self is something that we can reason about. Jones says that this dimension is 'entered most readily in momentary lapses of collaborative sense-making, moments in which a person becomes aware of more than one construction of "me", and must take a stand, take a position' (1997: 469). A person becomes aware of how they are being positioned and may intervene to generate a rhetorical redescription. It is not clear that we have to go beyond discursive analysis to theorise a reflexive self, as Jones suggests, but it is certainly true that the reflexive self has become a familiar object of everyday thought and a topic for scientific investigation.

As we have seen, the idea of an interior and agentive self is a central pillar of western thought, and it may be conceived as an entity that generates a person's allegiance and commitment. A person might act and judge *on behalf* of this self. It is not unusual for people to challenge their positioning by others ('Don't take me for…') or they might reflect later on what has been said. They try to account for the fact they were taken to be 'so-and-so' and reconstrue it within a private dialogue. In part, persons may acquire their own rules for reflexive self-positioning, based on their unique life experiences.

People also give an account of themselves when reporting their activities, and, within a certain degree of latitude, this account has to provide a consistent view of who they are. Their biography is generally known. They may, in addition, write autobiographically. When doing so, people generally stress their responsibility for things that have happened, their unique point of view on them, or their evaluation and description of episodes in their life. Harré and van Langenhove (1999: 60–73) point out differences between oral and literate cultures in biographical story-telling. Oral stories are less fixed in form because it is not possible to make reference back to a written standard; the context of telling is variable because the demands of the audience change.

Harré and van Langenhove note that oral autobiographical telling can take different forms. It may index what has happened to the speaker (e.g., 'She said to *me*, you can't do that') or index an imagined or assumed self, as if this self is a character in a drama. The former emphasises the spatio-temporal positioning of the speaker and their moral commitment to the act of narrating, while the latter does not. In other words, in the latter case, a story is told that you (the reader or listener) can take to *represent* me. A person's written autobiography is likely to be taken as definitive or final; the author cannot revise it in the telling, according to audience response. Modern autobiography amounts to creating the fiction that there is a 'real life' to be written, a story to be told in terms of goals, plots and causal links. The autobiographer can be compared to a historian who has to research the facts and interpret 'the evidence' of a life.

Harré and van Langenhove argue that the narrative of a self should not confuse self as 'the kind of person I think I am' with self as the unitary person to whom those events happen. Persons position each other in conversation, out of which the telling of stories emerges. In autobiography, the story is a rhetorical redescription of previous episodes, usually giving them greater coherence than they actually possessed. A person who engages in self-examination may derive a theory about 'who they are'. It may be assumed, as a tenet of the theory, that there is a personal unity about which a theory can be told. Theory-building of this kind can be interpreted as an assimilation of scientific practices. Indeed, some forms of psychological therapy encourage their clients to model their self-examination on those of scientific observation (e.g., Kelly 1955).

The reality of selves

Harré sometimes writes as if persons are real but selves are illusory. Could we therefore argue that when persons speak as though their self really exists as a substantive entity, they are using grammar incorrectly? This question has been debated by constructionists (Coulter 1999; Potter and Edwards 2003). Jeff Coulter argues that what is at issue is the appropriate use of grammar in a philosophical sense. In an *everyday* sense, people construct grammatically well-formed sentences when they talk about minds and selves – they understand each other without too much difficulty, although they might occasionally contest the interpretation that another person gives of their mental state. Coulter argues that, from a Wittgensteinian perspective, the rules people *actually* and *pre-reflectively* use in referring to their minds and selves do not accord with the kind of entities that minds and selves are commonly construed to be. For instance, he says that the statement 'I think in my head' is grammatically incorrect in the sense that persons as thinkers think at home, on the street, in offices, etc. Coulter calls this a conceptual error because the rules people follow in talking about thinking should really be analysed as moves in a language game that consists of various publicly observable interpersonal acts (e.g., avowals, claims, etc.). In his view, selves cannot be talked into being because there is no *thing* to be talked into being. In other words, the reality of a sense-of-self is not the reality of a thing that could be observed in the way persons are observed.

Jonathan Potter and Derek Edwards counter Coulter's arguments by saying that they are only interested in how mental-state words are used, not in identifying proper and improper usage. However, this cannot be the full picture of their objectives because when they claim to be studying how mental-state words are used, they go beyond description and organise their observations systematically (Potter and

Edwards 2003: 173–4). They agree that people may talk *as if* their words are expressing inner thoughts and feelings and note that the use of a mental-state term is conceptually refutable. However, they are not prepared to engage with Coulter's arguments in the abstract. Therefore, they offer their own example of a 'real conversation' to illustrate their point of view. This was a clip from an interchange between a child-protection officer on a telephone helpline and a caller who reluctantly suspects that their partner may have acted abusively. The officer suggests that the caller's idea is in 'the very back of your *mind*' to which the caller half agrees. Potter and Edwards argue that it would not be useful to suggest that the officer really meant to say something that is best expressed in a language that does not presume the reality of a mind. But Coulter's point seems to be that there is an important difference between 'is' and 'as if' in reference to mental states. Talk about minds functions perfectly well but it is an 'as if' construction; it presupposes publicly warrantable acts which really 'are'. In any case, one can imagine other expressions the child-protection officer could have used which do not refer directly to a mind, e.g., 'You seem reluctant to believe that he might have done this', conjuring up the image of an actual confrontation and dialogue between the caller and her partner about events that may have actually happened.

The idea that self is an 'as if' reality is bound to meet with some resistance because, like the conjurer who explains how their trick is performed, the trick remains just as convincing the second time around (O'Connor and Hallam 2000). It is 'as if' only in contrast with a realm of things that we understand to exist in a concrete sense. Of course, philosophical arguments may not convince us that we can manage without illusions in a more literal world in which they do not exist. And this intuition is correct in the sense that 'as if' realities are real in another sense, just as the conjuror's trick really works (see Chapter 13). However, the everyday use of mental-state words cannot be made the final arbiter of reality if we have good theoretical and philosophical reasons for construing reality differently.

Self as narrative

Positioning theory could be accused of not paying sufficient attention to the fact that a person's life is necessarily structured in time, although the idea of second-order positioning and a reflexive self goes some way to meet this criticism. As noted above, when liable to being misconstrued, a person reflexively presents and defends their version of a 'true self', a notion that necessarily spans time and situation. This self might be the central character in a personal life-story with experiences and achievements that others might need to be reminded about. However, the idea of autobiography as second-order positioning differs from the theory that a person's life is structured moment by moment along narrative lines. The latter amounts to the view that life itself is temporally structured in a first-order sense.

A child at some stage in development must learn that its existence is temporally structured. The child has, however, always been surrounded by a universe structured by time. It is not as if the child at some point is, for the first time, living life as if there was a past and future, nor that it has never been involved in future plans made by others. It seems that a young child lives in the midst of actions that are temporally structured in a first-order sense as well as later on linking up events in a temporal sequence that can be verbalised. For example, children have to discover that death is the end of life and that they too will suffer the same fate. This realisation can be described as second-order, or retrospective, in the sense that it is a construction placed on experience up to that point. A second-order temporal perspective might extend over a very brief interval or might encompass a whole lifetime. For example, an elderly person might continue to muse over something that was said by a parent in early childhood.

Features of stories and a sense-of-self

A person's acts are usually linked to particular projects – as temporary as picking up a pen or as long-term as writing a book. It is therefore natural to understand persons as living out stories that structure a series of actions (O'Connor et al. 2005: 53–80). In order to have human interest, a narrative requires settings, characters and a storyline, with progressions, setbacks and a final denouement. Believable stories are ones that absorb our interest and transport us into the action. The claim made by narrative theorists is that our involvement in our own life can be viewed as dependent on precisely these self-same features.

A good story, then, stimulates the imagination. We are led into all kinds of possible scenarios through hints that take us beyond what is actually described into possible future happenings. We might identify with the projects of a protagonist, suspend disbelief if that is required, and find ourselves excited or deflated when our expectations are fulfilled or disconfirmed. Personal storytelling can be viewed similarly. For example, if we see a shadowy figure at night in a churchyard, this might arouse a number of imagined possibilities, from the vicar locking up to the wandering ghosts of our ancestors. Needless to say, the way we project these possibilities forward, and get absorbed in them, heavily determines our perception of reality at any given moment. The material for imagined possibilities has to come from somewhere. A person does not set out to make sense of the story of their life as if writing on a blank slate. To be born into a community and to share a language means that many of the tasks of ascribing meaning have already been accomplished for us. The categories for describing a life are there, ready for use, such as how others are to be regarded, how feelings are to be classified and what it is normal to want in the circumstances one finds oneself in. And imagination itself is also fed by the stories we have already heard and read.

Versions of the narrative self

The narrative metaphor can be understood to mean either that we act like a storyteller in relation to our self (the reflexive self) or that we live 'in time' and create stories as if we are the author of what is happening from moment to moment. In the latter case, narration is a covert or tacit metaphor, an organising principle for all of our experiences. On this view, temporal authoring is part of what it is to be human and underlies any reflexive storytelling that may later be superimposed on our lives. By contrast, in deliberate storytelling, a person attempts to narrate what they do as having a beginning, middle and end. Of course, as in a story, a character may be a passive victim of circumstances or fail to comprehend their own acts. A person may fail miserably in the process of constructing a coherent personal story but assuming that every act is structured by narrative, whatever a person does can be seen as an attempt to construct a plot.

The narrative concept is useful in both senses of living a life in time. The fact that a person is born into a certain way of life under unique circumstances is bound to constrain what narratives are produced and what it is possible to tell. However, the hypothesis that *all* of a person's experience is thematically organised along narrative lines seems improbable unless we assume that every form of temporal organisation follows a narrative structure. James Mancuso and Theodore Sarbin (1983) do seem to take this all-encompassing perspective when they conceive of a person both as an author (a first-order self) and as a narrative figure in a story (a second-order self). Presumably, the first-order self is usually singular whereas the second-order self can take multiple forms.

What role then does a principle of unruliness or chaos occupy? Mancuso and Sarbin cite Plato's allegorical character, the *epithumetikon,* as a source of unruly passions, suggesting that the naming of chaos as a character produces a script that a person can follow. They give the example of anger as one example of unruliness, and suggest that a display of anger can be viewed as enacting a role in a script in which the person as metaphoric storyteller has been 'overpowered, overwhelmed by the intrusion of passion' (Mancuso and Sarbin 1983: 252). Although we could interpret anger in this way, the idea that unruliness is scripted implies that a person as storyteller has to surrender control (as an ingenuous agent) to a force that is 'not-self'. However, it seems unlikely that all sources of unruliness take this scripted form.

Mancuso and Sarbin support their position by citing experimental evidence that subjects who view films of geometrical figures undergoing random movements tend to describe the movements as people engaged in human actions according to recognisable plot structures. This is indeed relevant evidence but snooker players do not typically endow snooker balls with a human personality. The expected temporal sequencing of events on a snooker table is a story of sorts but hardly one with a plot. Rather like snooker balls on a table, some people have abnormal experiences in which they say they are passively moved about by forces beyond their control. In so far as a person may learn how to predict the influence of these forces on them, the principles of their ordering could be said to structure experience, but it is stretching a metaphor to say that the forces necessarily have a narrative structure.

The question of the structure of action is unlikely ever to be resolved on an either/or basis, that is, as subject to forces beyond our ken or as narratively structured (wittingly or unwittingly). It is possible to interpret action as being structured in at least three different ways: by intrinsically unknowable mechanistic processes/events, by narratively structured forms of social life of which a person is unaware, and by deliberate attempts to shape a life in a desired direction (or by all three together). However, the question has sometimes been debated as an either/or issue. David Carr (1997: 7–25) discusses the problem in the context of historical theory and argues against those historians who believe that all historical reconstructions in narrative form are fictional because 'real life' doesn't have a beginning, middle and end. They seem to present the alternative to a narrative view as a series of meaningless events. Carr, himself, rejects a non-narrative conception of temporal structure while accepting that an author writing an autobiography might well produce an account that sounds like fiction to someone who has known the author well.

So, regardless of the fact that some historical accounts presented as truth are fictional, Carr still maintains that lives are narratively structured moment to moment. Carr follows the analysis of time provided by Edmund Husserl (1859–1938) who proposed that the experience involves the retention of the moments just past and the tacit anticipation (protention) of the future. Carr's point is that we cannot even experience the *present* moment 'except against the background of what it succeeds and what we anticipate will succeed it' (1997: 11–12). Although this point is well taken, we do not have to conclude from it that all temporal structure takes a narrative form unless we simply define Husserl's temporal structuring as a kind of narration.

Carr does not suggest that the means–end nature of human acts can *always* be mapped onto a story, or that the structure of action is tidy. In actual storytelling, the extraneous static is cut out, and the storyteller can be selective because, in a real sense, they know what the outcome will be. The author can conceal from the characters their ultimate fate. Carr points out that by contrast, in the midst of life, we are forced to take things as they come, like the author's characters, because we are denied the authoritative point of view of the storyteller. Carr does not imply that life is chaotic until it is transformed into a coherent story. In setting out on a project, we necessarily view life from the perspective of the project already having been completed. Along the way, there is constant revision and reassessment as we are forced to deal with accidental or chaotic circumstances.

In Carr's opinion, 'we are constantly striving, with more or less success, to occupy the storyteller's position with respect to our own lives' (1997: 16). For him, narrative is both a constitutive part of action and also constitutive of the reflexive self that a person takes to be the agent of their acts. Carr's position seems to leave open at least a possibility of a non-narrative structuring principle. For another narrative theorist, Alasdair MacIntyre (1981), human life is *only* intelligible as narrative and so it follows that a person's life is immanently structured as narrative.

According to MacIntyre, we are born into a 'tradition' in which we inherit certain identities, practices, purposes, virtues, etc., that are embedded in a hierarchy of narrative-like structures of meaning. He believes that all action is basically historical in character and that persons understand their own lives in terms of the narratives they live out (MacIntyre 1981: 197). He says that people project purposes concerning the right way to live and pursue them as a kind of quest.

MacIntyre distinguishes between the two concepts of identity that I outlined in earlier chapters. The first is strict or unitary identity, meaning that no matter how much a person changes from birth to death, they have to be regarded in their life quest as a unitary character. He says that a narrative history requires the concept of a person as a character

abstracted from a history. This character appears to be jointly constituted materially and conceptually. The second kind of identity is the
one we are at liberty to assume in ways that need not imply a unitary
person.

According to MacIntyre, the individual's task is to conceptualise their
'self' in the face of having to tie together a potentially fragmented set of
public and private roles, intended and unintended actions, completed
and uncompleted tasks, life as a child and as an adult, in other words,
a fractured set of possible narratives. One narrative may conflict with
another, and a person may be unaware of the narrative they are following. For MacIntyre, there is no such thing as 'behaviour' that does
not fall under the general description of narrative unless it is simply
unintelligible. Many retrospective accounts could be given, but there is
only one account, according to MacIntyre, that is closest to the truth
and renders a person's life truly intelligible. He also implies that a person can misread the narrative that is immanently structuring their life.
He stresses that the person as author is at best a co-author of their own
story, often entering a drama not of their own making.

MacIntyre's position appears to be overstated, for if we equate intelli-
gibility with narrative there is no other possible interpretation of human
life. In any case, there are events in human life that are not themselves
intelligible as a story, such as knee jerks or unexplained symptoms of a
medical disorder. They might be incorporated into a story, which is not
the same thing. The spontaneity of human dramas presumably has causal
origins (such as our biological constitution) that may have little to do with
our narrative history. If MacIntyre is essentially engaged in characterising
human sense-making, rather than explaining it, we are still left with the
problem of reconciling biological ordering principles with narrative.

The philosopher Paul Ricoeur (1991) also assumes that a person's
unitary character is constructed or entailed by the plot of the story that
a person tells. He puts less emphasis on narratives that a person lives
out without awareness. However, he sees literary narrative, like the narrative of real lives, as grounded in 'our unavoidable earthly condition'
(Ricoeur 1991: 78). Literary narrative is important as a source of self-
interpretation – as a kind of test bed of ideas – because 'the self does
not know itself immediately, but only indirectly, through the detour of
cultural signs of all sorts' (Ricoeur 1991: 80). He says that life and literature both testify to the meaningfulness (at least in our culture and
period) of the question 'Who am I?', for which any bare answer such as
a permanent material entity, or even a person known as X, would not be
sufficient. At the same time, there is not just one story that can be told
about self but a multiplicity of possible stories.

There is a lack of clarity in the narrative position concerning the way persons are related to selves. For example, what is the entity that generates self as a narrative? Self as narrative must depend on real persons because a story needs imaginary characters to act it out and these fictional actors are presumably based on actual actors. In this sense, the narrative metaphor sidesteps the question of the nature of selves by presupposing them. According to Dieter Teichert (2004 : 188), Ricoeur does not see it as a flaw 'that the identity of the person is constituted by a self-narrative and that the self-narrative is told/constituted by the person'. Presumably, this would be non-circular only if person and self were conceptualised differently.

Donald Polkinghorne's interpretation of the circular relationship between person and personal identity draws upon Ricoeur's concept of the hermeneutic circle (Polkinghorne 2004). A hermeneutic circle refers to the fact that in our dealings with the world (or a text), we project a meaning onto it in advance, perhaps without awareness, and then experience objects in a certain way. In the process of making sense of these experiences, we change the meanings we later project onto the world. In fact, we may deliberately experiment with what the world can tell us about this new meaning by seeking evidence to verify or contradict it. The progression in our understanding can be compared to a boot-strapping, circular process.

The hermeneutic circle is a partial answer to understanding the reciprocal relationship between person and self. For Ricoeur, there *is* human life outside language, but language helps to reveal to us what it is. The human imagination might produce wholly fictitious plots that cannot be sustained (or sustained only by going to great lengths) in actual experience. Ricoeur's analysis fits in with how many people experience their attempts at self-conceptualisation, a kind of fumbling in the dark that looks for validation in spontaneous feelings but also sees the need for reflection and reformulation. It is always unfinished business. A weakness of the hermeneutic approach is that it places so much weight on the powers of a person to articulate a unitary self-story, thereby underplaying the role of language, society and culture, emphasised so much by positioning theorists.

Cartesian influences on the narrativist position

One of the bequests in Descartes's legacy is the assumption that 'minds' are agents that perform 'mental acts'. In the cognitivist transformation of this terminology, 'cognitive systems' perform 'cognitive processes'. We can see a Cartesian influence at work in the ideas of

Dan McAdams (1996: 310) who takes from William James the concept of an 'I' that 'selfs' a personal identity. He quotes with approval Jane Loevinger's idea (Loevinger 1976) that the process of selfing begins with the establishment of an existential base – 'I exist', 'I am the source of my experience' – and then evolves over time toward more mature and complex modes of meaning-making that are characteristic of higher stages of 'I' development. As McAdams makes clear, he considers that infants and children are at a pre-narrative stage because their Me tellings do not require a consideration of life unity and purpose. This leaves unexplained the origins of the child's 'I' or any developmental account of the storytelling mode in infants (see Chapter 11).

McAdams treats the metaphor of person as author rather literally. The author seems to take full responsibility for creating a coherent and credible story with just the right amount of openness. From a constructionist standpoint, 'authorship' (i.e. taking responsibility and acting as an independent agent) is not something a child can acquire as an 'I' that kick-starts the whole process. I take the view that selfhood is acquired by being treated as a self by others. Moreover, although a person may contribute to authoring a life-story, the fact that a person is perceived as the same public person throughout life might be equally influential in producing a coherent and credible story by default. Rather than aiming to create a unity of meaning, a person's task could be construed as having to give a semblance of self-sameness for the benefit of others who demand it. We see this process at work in a person with brain damage who confabulates to cover up a memory loss. The biological reality is that death is the final denouement of anyone's story, but it hardly provides a neat ending to a unitary life narrative. Death may not be an element to include in a story but a fact of life that forces stories to be produced. This challenges persons to create a narrative setting in which death can be rejoiced, fought, welcomed, denied, laughed over, etc. Alternatively, it might be seen as a way station in a longer story.

Polkinghorne (2004: 29) states that narrative 'is the form of cognition that links one's life episodes into a whole and thereby gives one's identity a unity and self-sameness through time'. However, if meaning is assimilated as much as created, narrative is not simply the product of an individual person's cognitive processes. In fact, telling the story of one's whole life is something that one is almost never asked to do, except by narrative researchers, and, judging by some published transcripts of interviews, the telling is like extracting teeth. If we see narrative as a cognitive structure, we are likely to ignore the fact that it is co-produced and not just self-created. As well as directing a script, we are emplotted as a unitary person by the stage on which we are placed, the dramas that others have written and the typecasting produced by our inherited features, such as our biological sex, that may restrict the parts we can play.

Jerome Bruner's cognitivist interpretation of the narrative metaphor also obscures the relation between person and self. For instance, he describes self as 'both outer and inner, public and private, innate and acquired, the product of evolution and the offspring of narrative' (Bruner 1997: 159). On the one hand, self is said to be a 'preadapted processing system' that employs 'metacognitive skills', but, on the other, it is a narrative (a product of this system) that is imposed on a life, tying together the disparate strands over time. There seems to be two incompatible paradigms in this discussion: one that refers to human beings in a social context and another that treats people as self-contained minds.

The philosopher Daniel Dennett (2003: 245–55) has put forward the view that self is a fictional character at the centre of one's autobiography. At first sight, this seems to belong with the narrative position, but Dennett's main aim is to support a causal account of the person as a complex of 'brain plus body' mechanisms. The brain is where he thinks the real action is, and he compares the way in which we talk to ourselves with the way in which we interface with a computer, whose inner workings, like the brain, we do not need to know in order to operate it. All we need, metaphorically speaking, is an icon to be clicked, dragged and dropped. Consequently, he also describes self as 'the brain's user-illusion of itself' (Dennett 2003: 253). Dennett is therefore arguing that self is a fictional entity and the means by which a person interprets and controls their own activities.

Dennett acknowledges the source of these interpretations in human communication and interaction, but, at the same time, he seems to jettison these social origins when real persons act. The fictional nature of his concept of self has nothing to do with an imaginary character modelled on real life. Self is fictional because it does not truly represent how the brain's mechanisms *really* function. In his words, the person 'can control, to some degree, what goes on inside of the simplification barrier [i.e. computer interface], where the decision-making happens' (Dennett 2003: 253). It follows from this view of self that the brain-user's illusion of itself as a character in an autobiography is merely an accident of evolution – it could have turned out otherwise if a different sort of computer interface had evolved. One can therefore question whether this is really a narrative account of self at all.

Both MacIntyre and Ricoeur assume that persons really exist in storytelling mode, and so the narrative self does not just interface with the causes of action, it constitutes and coalesces with life as lived. However, Dennett is surely right to suppose that the causes of human behaviour shape action in ways other than providing a narrative structure. MacIntyre's top-down 'embedded meanings' approach is not consistent with much experimental evidence produced by psychology and neuroscience. But Dennett's description of self as a brain-user's illusion suggests that the person is a passive 'brain-user' who plays no role in seeking to explain and shape their own actions. Fictional or not, self as narrative is so intimately related to life as lived that we cannot simply regard it as fictional in Dennett's sense. A virtual self is not fictional if we regard it as a kind of shorthand way of making sense of something very complex. It does not lose all claim to be representing reality faithfully.

The positioned self and the narrative self

The positioning and narrative perspectives share much common ground. I have argued that, on the one hand, the narrative metaphor is too narrow to encompass all of the ways in which the lives of people are immanently structured. On the other hand, it rightly assigns to people a degree of autonomy in shaping their own life. To some extent, people negotiate their social positions while at the same time they are embedded in traditional social practices, grammatical constructions and mythic stories from which they cannot escape. Western selves tend to be constructed as authors of their own life stories, and it is difficult to see how human acts could lack storylike features altogether. The subject, verb, predicate structure of sentences already conjures up the image of a person doing something for some purpose.

Positioning theory does not directly theorise about natural causation, and it may regard itself as interpreting social life 'above' this level (see Chapter 13). Likewise, narrative theorists do not deal adequately with the non-narrative or non-discursive dimension of human life. It is only in the cognitivist versions of the narrative metaphor that natural causation is introduced. However, I have argued that these are mindist theories that obscure the relationship between person and self.

Part II

Person and self in science

One wou'd expect of these *Physiologists* and Searchers of *Modes* and *Substances,* that being so exalted in their Understandings, and inrich'd with Science above other Men, they shou'd be as much above 'em in their Passions and Sentiments. [...] But if their pretended Knowledge of the Machine of *this World,* and *of their own Frame,* is able to produce nothing beneficial either to the one or to the other, I know not to what purpose such a Philosophy can serve, except to shut the door against better Knowledge, and introduce Impertinence and Conceit with the best Countenance of Authority.

Anthony Ashley Cooper ([1713] 1981, Part [Soliloquy] III, Section I: 211–12).

There has been a long history of philosophical reflection on concepts of person, mind, soul and self, and in this chapter I try to show
how this legacy influences working assumptions in contemporary
science. Philosophers of science critically examine this legacy, but
many scientists do not venture deeply into the philosophical foundations of their theories. These foundations may now be taken as obvious truth when they were once put forward as an original response
to a meaningful question in a certain historical period. My aim is to
give an airing to some contemporary assumptions by examining their
sources.

I will focus mainly on the eighteenth century. This is an arbitrary
point of departure but it is a period in which philosophical arguments
about self began to assume their modern outline. Book titles such as
James Crabbe's *From Soul to Self* (1999) and Raymond Martin and
John Barresi's *Naturalization of the Soul: Self and Personal Identity in the
Eighteenth Century* (2000) point to a major transition from religious to
secular terms. The word 'soul' tended to drop out of use, except in
a religious context, to be replaced by 'self' and 'mind'. At the beginning of the century, matters that we now regard as psychological were
included in pneumatology – the study of spirits. By the end, this area
of study became the philosophy of mind. Psychology did not properly
emerge until the nineteenth century (Martin and Barresi 2000: 70).

In Part I, I distinguished between 'myself', used as a pronoun, and
my 'self' or 'the self' used as a noun. In the latter case, it may be seen
as something that belongs to us personally and towards which we hold
attitudes. Self has now become a theoretical construct, in which case
the noun names a process or principle of organisation. As far as I can
tell, there is nothing particularly novel in the seventeenth or eighteenth centuries in the grammar of reference to persons or speakers.
Self-referential attitudes, such as 'I am ashamed', do not seem to refer
to an inner self but to the attributes of the public person they are perceived to be. The key shift seems to be towards referring to self as an

entity distinct from the public person or personal attributes, perhaps replacing earlier 'inner' entities such as soul or spirit.

At least two historical trends may have contributed to this change of terminology. One was the growing belief that human beings could, by themselves, reason out the nature of things, including their own nature. The other was a materialist view of the nature of life that began to displace earlier religious conceptions. Many of the philosophers who were instrumental in contributing to these transforming trends combined a study of natural philosophy with a profound Christian faith, and they certainly did not propose to discard religion. Instead, they attempted to reconcile religion with materialism. The historical context for the discussion of mind and self was therefore far removed from the scientific context of today. And given real threats from established religion, what philosophers purported to be asserting at that time may well have been modified to conform to religious belief or at least to be less unacceptable to the Church.

The eighteenth century is close enough in time for us to feel that we know what the authors of this period actually meant by what they wrote. It is more difficult to get into the mindset of Aristotle's hierarchy of nutritive, sensitive and rational souls. While I intend to trace the origins of contemporary scientific conceptions of self, I do not assume that there can be a definitive history of 'the self'. Worldviews tend to come as a package, loosely parcelled up, so that untying one knot often causes the contents to spill out with unpredictable consequences. Continuity can be discerned in some of the main intellectual themes, such as the tension between naturalistic and religious accounts of human beings (including Christ's humanity), but the development of related concepts is not linear. A rather confusing mix of terms seems to have been endemic at all times. Self is one of a poorly distinguished family of concepts that include person, mind, the religious soul and consciousness. Bishop Berkeley (1685–1753), musing on the continuity and unity of the mind or self, wrote, 'This will, this Act is the Spirit, operative, Principle, Soul, etc.' (quoted in Martin and Barresi 2000: 67). The 'et cetera' seems to imply that all was up for grabs and nothing had been settled. This situation still remains, and there is often a sleight-of-hand substitution between person, mind, self and consciousness.

Classical precursors of self

Philosophical debates in the eighteenth century continued to express a number of interacting streams of thought in Classical philosophy and early Christianity. Human bodies had long been considered a part of material nature and, according to some philosophers, were composed of indivisible atoms. At the same time, people were thought to share in the nature of the divine, a realm of the immortal, perfect and eternal. But it was not until the seventeenth and eighteenth centuries that the materialism of the new scientific worldview began to seriously upset the Christian applecart. At the heart of the debate was matter – the stuff out of which the world seemed to be made. The idea that self was imaginary – a virtual reality – was vigorously debated at this time.

Martin and Barresi (2000; 2006) document a long trail of ideas going back to Ancient Greece, and I draw heavily on their writings in what follows. It was apparent from early times that the material body is subject to eventual decay and dissolution. But then the question arises: is the essence of a person – what animates them and gives them their moral worth – also a substance? As if recoiling from this possibility, the self (or rather the soul, spirit, etc.) was conceived as an *immaterial substance*. In common with most cultures, the Greeks were concerned with whether bodily death is the end of everything that concerns a human being. Plato (427–347 BC) formulated the idea that each of us has an immaterial and naturally indivisible soul that survives death.

Aristotle (384–322 BC), Plato's pupil, defined the human soul with greater subtlety; he saw it as an intrinsic power of the living body to act with reason and will (Bennett and Hacker 2003: 15–16). This power helps to define what a person is rather than being an entity within the person that exercises that power. As a power to exercise pure reason and gain knowledge of universal forms, it was impersonal. Personal identity was supplied by an animal soul that was not immortal. Aristotle's extant work did not become available until the twelfth century, and Plato's ideas were more influential on early Christianity. It was the idea of an immaterial soul reunited with the body after death that became the accepted doctrine of later Christian thought.

It may be comforting to think that part of us survives death as an immaterial, incorruptible and immortal substance. The Greeks were not alone in speculating about existence after death, but the post-death story varies a great deal. One thing that needs explaining is the connection between a soul that is immortal and the body it inhabits during a person's lifetime. The Ancient Egyptians took care to preserve the body for the afterlife (but discarded the brain) whereas Plato regarded the body as the prison of the soul. In Christianity, the soul's destination after death was a vital matter, and there was a concern that if humans did not care what happened to their soul, they would not be motivated to be good in this life. But if a person cares what happens, then presumably they will identify in some way with the manner of the soul's existence in the afterlife. Will it have a good or a bad time? Does it meet old friends? Can it remember its past life?

In the hands of Christian philosophers, such as Thomas Aquinas (1225–74), the soul after death existed at first by itself but then later on, at the general resurrection, it was reunited with its own body to make a complete person again. The general resurrection refers to the Christian doctrine that all humans who have died, whether elect or reprobate, will resume life with their old bodies in an immortal form to enjoy either endless happiness or a misery that is worse than death. This article of faith, if taken literally, produces its own conundrums. For instance, is the body reassembled from exactly the same particles of matter? Will it be the body at death or the body in its prime? If it is reassembled from new particles, will it have exactly the same characteristics as the person who died? If not, how might this affect decisions on the Day of Judgement when the person's lifetime acts are placed on the scales?

In retrospect, we can see that the metaphor of an immaterial substance to comprehend participation in the divine realm, and in human thought and reason, proved to be something of a curse. It generated endless debates about how a soul, which was both individual and universal, could be combined with what looked like a genuine substance (body) to form the whole person. The word 'soul' was also used to refer to aspects of humanity with which everyone was intimately acquainted and regarded as eminently real. As noted by Martin and Barresi (2006: 91) a common idea was that the essence of friendship was the development of a common mind, and that the basis for that was the love of Christ. They quote St Augustine, who, upon the death of a friend, remarked that it is 'well said that a friend is half of one's own soul' (2006: 91). Many meanings of the word 'soul' seemed to express human rather than religious sentiments.

The birth of self

René Descartes is the philosopher who is generally regarded as the seminal thinker who first presented mind and consciousness as objects for scientific study. According to Thomas Leahey (and sources he quotes), Descartes was a member of a group of reforming Catholics who were concerned about the tendency to assign sentient properties to animals, thereby removing the need for God in natural philosophy and threatening religious assumptions about the difference between the animal and human worlds (Leahey 2003: 43–5). Descartes made mind and body into two completely different kinds of substance, with the intention, it is supposed, of linking the religious soul to mind while preserving the freedom of scientists to develop purely mechanistic accounts of physical and bodily phenomena.

If we examine one of Descartes's final and complete statements of his philosophy of mind written in Latin (*Meditationes de prima philosophia,* 1641), we find that he dedicates the work to the Faculty of Theology at the Sorbonne in Paris and asks them to take it under their protection (Descartes 2005). He justifies the work as a means of persuading the faithless, by means of human reason, to believe in the existence of God and the immortality of the soul. Descartes is doubtful that without the Sorbonne's patronage his abstruse philosophical arguments 'will have much effect on the minds of men' (1901: Dedication, para. 6).

That Descartes's main interest lay in human nature rather than religion is suggested by the fact that he gives few arguments for the immortality of the soul, except to suggest that 'the destruction of the mind does not follow from the corruption of the body, and thus to afford to men the hope of a future life' (1901: Synopsis, para. 2). However, Descartes defines mind as an *unchanging and indivisible* thinking substance, and so it should follow that the contents of the mind (e.g., traces of good or bad acts) could, in principle, all be emptied out at death and the mind still remain immortal. His mind substance is hardly much of a guarantee for the immortality of the religious soul. Descartes uses the Latin word 'Animâ' only once, in the dedication to his Meditations, and in the French translation of 1647 the word 'l'âme' appears primarily in the dedication, preface and synopsis and only once in the Meditations. Thus, in the main body of his work, he uses words such as 'mens', 'animus', 'intellectus' and 'ratio', which are translated as 'esprit', 'entendement' or 'raison' in French, and in English by words such as 'mind', 'understanding' and 'reason'. The word 'soul' is used in the Second Meditation with reference to his *former* (everyday) conception of it and in the Sixth Meditation (para. 19) as an alternative to mind ('mind or soul').

These remarks are relevant because Descartes has been interpreted to be saying that self is consciousness or an observer of consciousness. In fact, he does not refer to an idea of self as an entity but simply uses the pronoun 'I'. He uses self-reflexive verbs such as 's'estime' to express esteeming oneself (Taylor 1989: 154) and he also defines self ('moi-même' as follows: 'there can be no doubt that my body, or rather my entire self (*ou plutôt moi-même tout entier*), in as far as I am composed of body and mind, may be variously affected, both beneficially and hurtfully, by surrounding bodies' (Descartes 2005: Meditation VI, para. 14).

In Christianity, a person's soul individuates the person, but the religious soul is hardly mentioned at all in the Meditations. Descartes's arguments are directed towards establishing the *kind* of thing he is, namely a substance that thinks, not that he is a particular mind or self. Mind is defined by the fact that it is indivisible, unlike matter. He says that although the mind thinks certain things, wills others and perceives others, the mind itself does not vary with these changes. He offers no grounds for individuating one mind from another (Martin and Barresi 2000: 129). This throws doubt on the assumption that his concept of mind is related to a concept of self because it does not account for the fact that each person's mind (though indivisible in itself) is divided from another person's mind. The cartoon picture it conjures up is of people surrounded by their own thought bubbles, but these bubbles are not given boundaries in Descartes's philosophy.

Descartes arrived at his conception of mind through his method of doubt, hoping to reach indubitable axioms from which further conclusions could be derived and tested. As is well known, he found that he could not doubt his own existence as a thinking thing, given that he interpreted doubting as itself a form of thinking. In the Synopsis, he states that his argument essentially shows that he is a something rather than a nothing. But this 'something', he implies, is his awareness of thinking a thought. When he compares his new conception with his former view, he considers that he used to think of himself as being stirred into action by his soul, which he imagined as 'something extremely rare and subtle, like wind, or flame, or ether, spread through my grosser parts' (Descartes 2005: Meditation II, para. 5). He argues that having discarded these ideas, he is still assured that he exists. Descartes's former interpretation of soul as a vaporous spirit reminds us again that the word 'soul' had several meanings which were only loosely connected with the Christian soul. For example, he refers to 'base and vulgar souls' (Taylor 1989: 153), but, in this expression, he seems to be using soul as a metonym for person, as we might use it in, say, 'ten souls lost at sea'.

According to Charles Taylor, Descartes's revolutionary move was to transfer the hegemony of reason as a certain vision of the (public) world to the hegemony of reason in the (private) world of the mind (1989: 147). What Descartes aimed for was a self-sufficient certainty of reasoning, even if secondarily, and by means of his own reasoning, he viewed God as the guarantor of the validity of his own beliefs. Reason is also employed in a new way to understand human beings. For instance, the senses are seen as providing ideas 'in the mind', as ideas that the mind can examine in a disengaged way (Taylor 1989: 162). Descartes allows himself to entertain the belief 'that body, figure, extension, motion, and place are merely fictions of my mind' (Descartes 2005: Second

Meditation, para. 2). He can also wonder, on the basis of his sensory experience, whether the hats and cloaks of human beings passing in the street below his window 'might cover artificial machines, whose motions might be determined by springs (Descartes 2005: Second Meditation, para. 13). The novel idea is that we can step back from direct perception of the world and study experience as 'sensations' with an intellectual part of the mind that is not itself an experienced phenomenon. In this last example, Descartes permits himself to compare humans with robots or animals; for him, animals were non-reflectively conscious and could act intelligently, but all this could be explained in entirely mechanical terms – they were essentially automata. Humans, by contrast, were not merely conscious but could reflect on their experience and think with reason about it. 'Animals do not see as we do when we are aware that we see, but only as we do when our mind is elsewhere' (Leahey 2003: 46).

Leahey (2003: 48–9) argues that by reasoning in this way, Descartes divides 'the self' from conscious experience, but it is not at all clear that Descartes does create a 'viewer, an inner self' as Leahey calls it, as a mental entity that observes experience. We can think of Descartes's combined mind and body as his 'unitary self' that can perceive, understand and judge at the same time.

However, it is certainly true that Descartes has been and is currently interpreted in the way Leahey depicts. As Leahey puts it, it is sometimes assumed that we see not an object but a projected representation of an object in a Cartesian mind-space and that a mental self is needed to view it. According to Leahey, mind, consciousness and self have all come to be regarded as objects (rather than personal powers) suitable for scientific study. And when the body is viewed as just another public object, as merely bits of colourless and odourless extended matter, the subjectivity and experiential richness of 'the mind' is emphasised. The biological organism is not, of course, this sort of lifeless material entity.

Matter and self

Over the course of the eighteenth century, the materialist view of the nature of life came to predominate. The soul itself passed away as the means by which persons and their mental powers were individuated. The words that substituted for soul still retained religious connotations. A self was something essential and unique to each person that could be moral or immoral. Selves could be good or bad as, indeed, they can be today. The belief in a permanent entity is nicely summed up by Thomas Reid (1710–96): 'My thoughts and actions, and feelings, change every moment – they have no continued, but a successive existence: but that self or I, to which they belong, is permanent, and has the same relation to all the succeeding thoughts, actions, and feelings, which I call mine' (quoted in Martin and Barresi 2000: 131).

The unique, unitary and immaterial soul had provided a convenient answer to many questions about identity and its post-death existence. It explained why it was reasonable to be rewarded or punished for deeds done. It also explained unique access to thoughts and feelings. Self has come to serve similar purposes.

Materialist philosophers were forced to rethink some basic issues about identity, and they focused their attention on the human body and especially the brain. Although society had already been described as a state of nature by Thomas Hobbes (1588–1679), it was the brain and body rather than a natural view of society that influenced their thinking. Persons and selves were not clearly distinguished; in fact, the terms were often used interchangeably. The materialists understood clearly that selves are not unique compositions of matter because, as a person grows old, matter is replaced. A self has to be a property that emerges out of matter: an arrangement or system of matter that stays the same or similar while individual components are replaced.

The problem now becomes this: what guarantees that these arrangements stay the same so that we can justifiably talk about the same person/self over time? John Locke's answer was that sameness of self depended on having a continuous memory (grounded in the material body and its previous actions) of one's past experiences.

Put differently, we are dealing with the same person when that person is conscious of having experienced or done what that person did at an earlier time. If a person has a memory of previous experiences – for instance, remembering on getting up in the morning what they did the day before – this implies that they have the same 'consciousness' (whatever that means) as the person who did it before. Locke's self was not just a passive recorder of experience; it was able to reflect on its thoughts and actions, suspending undesirable passions or habits, thereby allowing the will to execute reasonable and responsible acts. It could reflect on itself as the same being in different times and places and presumably, by so reflecting, could help to bring this unity and continuity about. The modernity of this idea is that the self is no longer a God-given soul, present from birth. It is cultivated and worked upon by the self, itself. The self is identified, more or less, with an area of conscious thought that is reasonable, reflective and moral.

Locke's notion of the person/self does not depend on the continuity of the material body in a concrete sense. Particles of matter can be replaced with new ones because what is important is their pattern and organisation not their individual identity. Locke distinguished between a man and a person. A man is the biological entity defined as a particular individual with the form and function of a human being. The person is a kind of legal entity, the human agent that is recognised by society as 'the same person', responsible in law for their actions and so forth. This makes persons into fictional or virtual properties of matter and allows for the possibility that the same biological man could deceptively (or by reason of mental disorder) act as two different persons.

Although Locke did not clearly distinguish them, person and self can be seen as the same entity viewed socially, from the outside, and self-consciously, from the inside. This is clearly implied by his hypothetical example of the prince and the cobbler (Siegel 2005: 100). The soul of a prince enters the body of a cobbler, while retaining consciousness of its previous life. In these circumstances, the prince would remain the same person but would be a different biological man. But he would only be a prince to himself; others would take him to be a cobbler, known both by his body and his previous personality. Locke has here set the stage for a great deal of later theorising about the way body, person and self are conceptually connected.

Locke was therefore quite prepared to view selves as discontinuous. He thought that in everyday use the word 'I' referred to the biological man and said that: 'if it be possible for the same Man to have distinct incommunicable consciousnesses at different times, it is past doubt the same Man would at different times make different Persons' (quoted in Martin and Barresi 2000: 28). Locke's thoughts on the subject are not at all far-fetched when we consider examples, produced from the nineteenth century onwards, of people with so-called multiple personalities. Apart from the prince and cobbler example, Locke elaborated on multiplicity with a number of other thought experiments of the kind beloved by recent philosophers of personal identity. His examples included the same body alternately shared, day and night, by a different person, and the same person (or consciousness) sharing two different bodies.

Locke's definition of self was soon criticised as circular on the grounds that if you know that your memory of a past self is a memory of you, you must already have a sense of yourself to know it. For example, I might have a vivid memory of an event that I had read about in a book. How do I know that this event is not something I have been involved in myself unless I am already able to distinguish certain memories as belonging to my own past and other memories as based on stories or hearing about other people's experiences? The adoption of any one of

Locke's criteria leads to paradox, but he does not manage to solve the problem of how Man, Person and Self should be taken together.

One of the paradoxes of the memory criterion led to a second objection voiced at the time. It was that two people might conceivably have exactly the same self (based on the same arrangements of matter) but this would make them the same person – which clearly they are not. They are two separate persons with the same self and so being a person must involve more than memory. As Samuel Clarke (1675–1729) in a famous debate with Anthony Collins (1676–1729) stated, 'you make individual Personality to be a mere external imaginary Denomination and nothing in reality' (quoted in Martin and Barresi 2000: 35).

A third objection was that if consciousness of self is constructed by memory, then personal identity over time may amount to no more than a series of consecutive fictions. There seems to be no guarantee that the person would continue to have numerically the same consciousness. And if that is the case, why should a person be concerned about what they had done in the past or plan prudently for their future selves? The memory theory seems to undermine our sense of responsibility for ourselves and weakens our accountability.

David Hume (1711–76) was even more radical in his approach to selves as illusions. The only reality for him was simple sensory experience he called 'impressions'. As far as he was concerned, the notion of material substance was equally illusory. He thought ideas of substance were merely verbal constructions of more basic experiences. Hume compared the mind to a theatre in which all we have are successive appearances and disappearances. Nevertheless, he did acknowledge that we believe in the illusion of the self as a persisting entity and also that we are concerned about it and in how others see us. He thought the illusion is based on our tendency to give an identity to impressions that resemble each other over time and also on a need to construct an explanation to tie the impressions together. For example, an identity is given to consciousness, even though this is a verbal abstraction based on a resemblance between all impressions as conscious experiences. Hume suggested other tendencies of the human mind that appear to contribute to seeing a 'bundle of impressions' as an entity. These included seeing a cause-and-effect relation between an entity and other impressions, by which he meant only that there was a predictable sequence of impressions. There is nothing *really* that connects objects together or selves together except our tendency to think they are connected! But Hume went beyond the idea that memory links up our idea of self by saying that we *discover* what our self/personal identity consists of by noting cause-and-effect relations between impressions (Martin and Barresi 2000: 89).

blic, we employ also when we deliberate in our own thoughts; and while we
ll eloquent those who are able to speak before a crowd, we regard as sage
ose who most skilfully debate their problems in their own minds (Nicocles,
ca. 88). (Nienkamp 2001: 18)

This conception of the relationship between language and thought
ts a different slant on the philosophical puzzles of self. The analogy
tween thought and conversation sidesteps many of the problems that
se from treating self as a substance – material or immaterial. In other
rds, we can treat talk about self simply as a 'form of talk' that has
 origins in actual conversations, without worrying too much about
 status as a thing. One problem with the metaphor of self as substance
:o find a plausible location for it. In fact, most non-philosophers are
bably not too exercised over the question of where thought resides.
t a brief examination of mental words quickly tells us that our meta-
ors for mind treat it as a container (e.g., 'I can't take it in', 'He's
ffed his head with facts').

It would be easy enough to discount the container metaphor as a con-
ient tool, but some philosophers and neuroscientists have taken it far
re literally. The mind for them really has become a place (Bennett
i Hacker 2003: 316–22). It is a place that contains mental entities
i mental processes, and, of course, the self. It lends credibility to the
blem of 'other minds' – how it is possible, if my mind is in my own
vate container, it can get to know what is in your private container.
The metaphor of a private conversation, in place of a mental con-
er, might not solve all our problems, but it transforms the kinds
juestion we ask. When we consider what function reference to self
ves in our beliefs and practices, it ceases to be such a slippery abstrac-
1. Moreover, there is no need to suppose a continuous history of an
ity (soul, mind, consciousness, etc.) that can be traced back across
 centuries as if there is some irreducible 'something' that acts as a
lge between all the peoples who have preceded us.
he reason that such a mammoth intellectual effort has been devoted
ebates about persons, souls and selves cannot be attributed solely to
scination with the niceties of philosophical analysis. These debates
iously mattered to people in conducting their lives. The religious,
ural and political contexts in which these debates were enmeshed
le them important. This is illustrated by the gradual withering away
he word 'soul', as noted above. It seems it no longer mattered as
:h to people to retain this concept (in non-religious contexts) or
/ found they could no longer ignore other ideas that mattered more.
ple began to refer to their self or their mind instead.

Hume's critics pointed out that he seemed to have
to be a rather disembodied, passive thing. We nor
self as having the power to make things happen. V
selves as agents and reward and punish them accordi
It seems necessary to put them into a real social con

A theory about the relationship between self and :
been proposed by Thomas Hobbes (1588–1679). H
of the natural state of human beings was one o
interest. According to him, it was self-interest, too,
the development of civil society. He thought life in
was so unpleasant, on account of violence, distrus
that humans contracted between themselves to obe
security and greater comfort. He imagined, therefc
in their natural, asocial state were capable of rationa
longer-term self-interest. Hobbes's vision was dev
de Mandeville (1670–1733), who produced an equ
humorous vision of how self-interest (and vice) cou
the public benefit. He did not think that civil societ
by a social contract, as in Hobbes, but by the mystif
self-interest. People do not compete, he thought,
sion. Instead, they engage in a hypocritical compet
virtue or become envious and avaricious, all of whi
economic wheels turning for everyone's ultimate t
1997). Mandeville's advanced ideas about the m
bodily needs behind acceptable social behaviour
social theories of self that were developed much lat

An alternative tradition for theorising

The thought of Plato and Aristotle was not the on
acy of Ancient Greece. The connection between tl
can be found in the ancient myths. The heroes of F
known for having conversed with the gods but the
aspects of themselves – their 'heart' and their 'spir
Nienkamp (2001: 10–12 and 141, Note 8), the Gre
Iliad can be translated either as 'to consider' or 'tc
gesting, it seems, that to consider something is to c
The idea of thought as internal dialogue was de
(436–338 BC) as follows:

With this faculty (logos) we both contend against othe
open to dispute and seek light for ourselves on thing
for the same arguments which we use in persuading o

Even though Locke clearly understood the virtual nature of the concept of person/self, his understanding of the role of natural causation was limited to biological Man, especially the human body and brain. Once we view social interaction naturalistically, the nature of the biological contribution to self has to be revised. If speakers, as natural organisms, play a necessary role in assigning the status of personhood and selfhood to members of their community, the biological view has to be extended to include the causal underpinnings of these personal interactions. A biological process is also needed to make the application of social criteria effective. So, although criteria for persons and selves are dependent on local norms (and to that extent constructed) there is a biological dimension to the conferral of identity, including the capacity to communicate and the biological efficacy of spoken words. The act of being confirmed as a person or self through social interaction is presumably not a one-off event but is continually re-enacted in an ongoing dialogical process.

Clearly, there must be a limit to the kind of persons or selves that others are willing to confirm. If a person exceeds them, they are likely to be committed to a psychiatric institution, and when there is a serious shortfall, personhood may be denied. The limits to personhood and selfhood, on a constructionist view, depend on the criteria that any community of persons is willing to apply. These criteria are likely to take into account our biological natures, its human frailty and the wish of most people to transcend the biological and social constraints placed upon them.

What kind of self is offered up to science on this constructionist view? Virtual selves are attributes of real people who have real histories and a real biological constitution, living in a real environment that limits their opportunities to express their potential. There are ample opportunities for the biological and social sciences to study processes that surround reference to self.

However, the answer to the question 'Who am I?', posed by a single individual, cannot be answered from the standpoint of naturalism. A person does not usually think that the answer to this question would be clarified by an appraisal of everything that has had a causal influence on them, together with an assessment of the likelihood that they will do X, Y or Z in future. A person's sense-of-self is generally constructed as a story that makes sense, leaving out shameful deeds and personal failures, embellishing the aspects that give a person a positive and credible identity and, quite possibly, retains not a few unrealistic dreams. The question concerns a person's *existence,* and access to an objective analysis of causal influences that have led to a person's current situation is unlikely to provide an answer to this kind of question. I am not suggesting that information derived from natural and social science is irrelevant to the existential question. A person might be ill informed about the causal influences on their current conception of self, and an expert might be in a better position to give a more accurate formulation, from an observer's perspective, of the events and processes that have produced it. And biological information pertaining to personal circumstances is obviously relevant in the case of disease and the possibility of a shortened life.

But, generally, the problem is more likely to be posed as, 'How do I go on from here?', that is, continue to be what I want to be or not to be what I don't want to be. I suggest that to answer these questions, a person needs a virtual self and a way of referring to it, to get them to first base. If, as I have repeatedly stressed, this virtual self is not an *entity* that is readily amenable to study within the framework of naturalism, the sort of problems that scientists are likely to inherit are ones of gross oversimplification. According to Martin and Barresi (2000: 1), the loss of the soul has left a yawning chasm, and, 'even those who accepted the new vision never came to terms with how they should feel about the self's possibly having only an imaginary or pragmatic status'. It is perhaps not surprising that scientists have resorted to fill the vacuum by searching for self in the brain – my topic for the next chapter.

9   Self in mind and brain

Given that 'the mind' is typically seen as a product of the brain, self has also become an important topic within neuroscience. It is, of course, vital to explore how brain activity relates to activities such as attention, perception and memory that are traditionally associated with *mental* processes. As parts of the biological organism, the brain and nervous system can be regarded as functioning in a similar way across all human beings, and there is an understandable tendency to assign to the brain the function of general coordination and control, a function that is similarly accorded to the notion of a self. I will argue that the equation between brain and mind has been made without sufficient regard for personal and supra-personal levels of explanation. Cultural variation in mind or self may be acknowledged, but the clear preference within neuroscience is to look for the sources of this variation in universal mechanisms of the brain.

As I made clear in Chapter 1, I am not setting out to preserve a certain level of phenomena (culture, norms, reasons, etc.) from the reach of natural explanation. My criticisms are directed at a tendency to confuse explanations at different levels or a failure to recognise that explanations are needed that interpenetrate different levels. As regards neuroscience, I attribute these failings mainly to the influence of Cartesian assumptions, and I will outline an alternative foundation that is heavily indebted to Wittgenstein. Few neuroscientists would deny that culture makes a major contribution to the development of a person's sense-of-self and concept of self. Nevertheless, mind and self are often reduced to mechanisms that are seen as innate or solely located in the individual's brain. One set of scientists believes that if we looked long and hard, we would discover the causes of all mental attributes in the structure and function of the brain. They assume that even if we are deeply influenced by culture, all causal influences can be understood as mediated by, or represented in, the brain and are therefore discoverable within it. Phenomena mediated by personal and supra-personal processes in my terms would be adequately captured as neural patterns or structures.

Philosophers and scientists influenced by Wittgenstein understand the relationship between mind and brain differently. For them, the 'mind' and 'mental states' are ways of referring to, and communicating about, personal powers, abilities and activities that are exercised in daily life. Reference to mind clearly serves pragmatic purposes, but the mind is regarded as a metaphorical entity. Of course, reference to mental activity has to be related, in a causal sense, to processes in the brain and to the behaviour of the person. However, in my view, mind and mental states are not the preserve of any one level of explanation. While the need for a brain is obvious, the *natural* significance of social practices and local norms means that mental phenomena must also be considered in their personal and supra-personal aspects.

The reduction of the mind to the brain simply seems to result in a loss of explanatory power. Any attempt to reduce 'mind' to universal brain processes would deprive it of its uniquely ordered historical nature. The pointlessness of reducing all levels of explanation to something more fundamental could also be applied to the brain – if brain-scanning techniques were developed to reveal a structure of subatomic particles, we might then lose sight of neurons, synapses, neural nets and other useful constructs.

The folk concept of mind and its relation to naturalism

Thinkers in the western tradition have played a very significant role in shaping how people generally conceive of 'the mind'. What I aim to explore in this chapter is how natural science has drawn upon the way ordinary people think about mind and self in an unreflective manner. Given that scientists study how ordinary people think, ordinary assumptions about mind and self are likely to find their way into science through the back door.

An extremely influential view is the idea that our common-sense understanding of the world can described as 'folk psychology' (Dennett 1991) and that the meaning of mental-state concepts is derived from an empirical 'folk psychological theory' that specifies how a set of mental concepts or propositions are functionally related (Stich and Nichols 2002). The underlying assumption here is that psychology can be an autonomous science. An individual knower is conceived as being motivated to understand the world, and the folk theory is a mental structure or system that intervenes between stimulus input to the individual's brain and their response output.

The fact that people do interpret each other's mental states with apparent ease has been understood in different ways by the natural scientists who follow this paradigm. One view is that folk psychology corresponds to the way everyone's brain is structured and, therefore, that it may represent an approximately true 'natural theory'. To think otherwise could potentially undermine the view that mind is innate and psychology is an autonomous science. Another view is that folk psychology cannot be relied upon to tell us much about the universal features of brains and mental processes. On the grounds that folk psychology could be regarded as just another theory, we might simply have got it wrong, just as ancient peoples got it wrong when they believed that human behaviour was influenced by an assembly of squabbling deities. On this view, scientists will one day get it right, and this new theory of mental attributes will win out over others and replace the prevailing folk psychology.

I will reject the idea that folk concepts of the mind comprise any kind of theory that is located in a person's brain. The belief that we need a theory to understand other people's minds is based on the idea that our world (including our knowledge of other people's minds) is represented inside a stand-alone mind/brain that processes input and produces an output. The neural and mental processes that are assumed to create an internal model or representation of the world then 'project it back', as if filling in a picture. One example of the belief that we create our world in this way is the idea that children, universally, have to learn a theory-of-mind. They are said to build up a picture of their own and other minds, by theorising on the basis of sensory input aided, according to some theorists, by an innate theory-of-mind module in the brain.

An alternative constructionist view, outlined in Chapter 11, is that children acquire their folk concepts largely by absorbing them in ready-made (cultural) forms and that they do not do so as independent information processors. The very idea of a mind could be regarded as a modern western concept. On these grounds, a constructionist might question the assumption that people everywhere (including our hominid ancestors) have held the belief that others have minds. And we know from anthropological studies of modern humans that common-sense understanding is highly variable. In some folk cosmologies, the cause of events is attributed to spiritual or communal forces rather than anything going on 'within the mind' of any given individual. Any explanation that puts forward the mind, and identifies it with the brain, could be confusing western assumptions with a universalisable theory.

As noted in the previous chapter, the writings of René Descartes have been a major source of scientific and folk beliefs about mind. His mind–body dualism has not gone away, and there remains a mountain of philosophical and scientific work that has been profoundly influenced by it. And, for the person in the street, the Cartesian view still sounds like common sense (we have all learned to be Cartesians). Authors influenced by Wittgenstein, such as Bennett and Hacker (2003), give the impression that it is an uphill task to introduce any opposing ideas, and their recent book quickly spawned rebuttals by Daniel Dennett and John Searle (Bennett et al. 2007). Dennett and Searle do not claim to be Cartesians but, upon examination (see below), their views are closely allied to the project of reducing psychological attributes to brain processes. In other words, having jettisoned Descartes's mind-substance, they still retain the *concept* of mind and put forward the brain as a stand-alone mechanism that is sufficient to account for human capacities.

Aside from disagreement over the philosophical foundations of neuroscience, there are other issues concerning the relative importance of universal and local (cultural) processes that are not directly related to founding assumptions. For example, authors may disagree over whether a cultural milieu should be considered as a *general* precondition for the development of a certain behaviour or whether the behaviour requires quite *specific* cultural inputs to emerge. For instance, with regard to self, does an infant develop normally just so long as it is raised in an adequately stimulating and nurturing environment or does it need specific inputs that allow it to symbolise self? Or, with regard to the acquisition of language, what is the relative weight to be given to the innate capacities of the brain and to exposure to speaking adults? Some skills, like learning to crawl and walk, seem to need minimal cultural input, but the same could hardly be said for many intellectual skills.

Similar issues arise with respect to human social evolution. What is the relative weight to be given to the biological evolution of new cognitive powers or to cultural practices that have perhaps contributed to the emergence of those powers? Primates reared by humans seem to gain enormously from their cultural enrichment. Some human-reared primates have learned to respond appropriately to spoken English, and they can communicate their wishes when taught to use signs. These are levels of communication that seem to go beyond the reach of their relatives reared in the wild. When primates have been trained to use arbitrary signs, they sometimes demonstrate very humanlike patterns of interaction with their human carers. If aspects of a human culture impinge in this way on primates, how much more must this have been the case in human social evolution?

Scientific consequences of adopting Cartesianism

The Cartesian influence on contemporary research has been described in a particularly illuminating way by Stuart Shanker (Savage-Rumbaugh et al. 1998). Although Savage-Rumbaugh, Shanker and Taylor write together, Shanker is the professional philosopher amongst them. He shows the connections with the neuroscience view that brain is identical to mind and the cognitive-science view that the mind is an organ of thought and voluntary conduct. Shanker notes that Descartes's thought arose in the context of an ancient doctrine that forms of life could be seen as progressing through different levels: inanimate, animate, human, spiritual and divine. Descartes's radical proposal was to draw a sharp distinction between mankind and the animals. According to him, both shared a machinelike body but only humans possessed a mind: the ability to reflect, to be self-conscious, to reason, to speak a language and to make conscious choices that direct the actions of the body.

Descartes assumed that 'states of mind' are private to the person experiencing them, implying that the minds of others can only be known second-hand, by making inferences from their behaviour. He acknowledged that some human responses are machinelike, as they are in animals, but he considered that voluntary acts are caused by the mind. He also argued that it is on the basis of a *similarity* between the acts caused by our own, known for certain, mental states (like wanting something or intending something) and the actions we perceive others performing, that we infer what mental state the other person must be in.

It follows from his philosophy that we cannot read the mental states of animals (they are mere machines). According to Shanker, Descartes reasoned on the basis that many of our own actions are automatic and habitual, that it was legitimate to infer that *all* of an animal's behaviour falls into the involuntary category. He considered that an animal's capacity to communicate is limited to natural expressions whereas human speech is something brought into play by communicating ideas and thoughts.

Descartes's thesis of discontinuity between animals and humans implied that any signs of animal intelligence 'would thus have to be explained away by showing either that the "animal" was a species of man or that the so-called "intelligent" behavior in question was really the result of instinct' (Savage-Rumbaugh et al. 1998: 80). As Shanker explains, philosophers and natural scientists have had two responses to Descartes's discontinuity thesis apart, that is, from accepting it. One response was to reassert the traditional view that humans are part of a divine order. Another was to go further down the mechanistic path and argue that humans, like animals, are also machines. Shanker also notes that acceptance of Descartes's thesis could be taken either in a weak or strong sense. In the weak sense, it could be claimed that we have no good evidence that animals have minds; in the strong sense, it could be interpreted to mean that animals cannot, by definition, have minds. Scientists who have followed the strong interpretation, and who have also considered that private mental states are not suitable to count as scientific data, have turned to observations of public events from which to derive a scientific theory of human psychology. Methodological behaviourists restricted themselves to observations of behaviour, and some neuroscientists focused only on brain tissue.

While many neuroscientists have treated the brain as a set of mechanisms, some cognitive scientists have, in parallel, treated the mind as a mental mechanism. They follow Descartes in assuming that the mind forms concepts that are derived from experience and that these concepts are linked to actions. Thus, in the case of voluntary acts, it is supposed that there is a mental state that initiates the act. Shanker argues that Descartes drew his conception of cognition from the model of science developed by Francis Bacon (1561–1626). It is assumed that the mind observes events and induces a concept from their pattern of occurrence. Accordingly, a person engages in a *mental act* of cognising, rather as a scientist does when forming a theory. The mental act is private, but the inductive process of making sense of reality can be studied objectively. Cognitive scientists have explored it experimentally by varying the conditions in which a task is performed. Shanker interprets this kind of experimental psychology as 'simply a more comprehensive and systematic version of what every human being does when she looks at reality' (Savage-Rumbaugh et al. 1998: 91) (according to Cartesian assumptions).

The cognitivist assumption that there is an entity called mind that can be explained mechanically also has implications for the way that the abilities of developing infants are understood. In effect, the infant changes from an animal reacting to events in an involuntary machine-like way to become a mini-adult with a mind. For Descartes, speech was the marker that indicated that there were thoughts (mental states) to be communicated and so 'the emergence of speech becomes the crucial indicator for whether, and if so when, the transition from reacting to acting has occurred' (Savage-Rumbaugh et al. 1998: 92). Speech was considered by Descartes to be the faculty that enabled a child to exercise voluntary control over its mind and therefore its actions. Ultimately though, Descartes's concept of mind drew upon the Christian notion of free will associated with the immaterial soul, and he retained this mental faculty as an essential source of volition.

Some cognitive scientists still hold to the Cartesian view that language represents mental states (thoughts, concepts, etc.), allowing them to be transferred from one mind to another when a person speaks. Shanker argues that there has been a concession towards allowing prelinguistic infants (and some animals) to have some basic 'first-order' mental states, but it is still maintained that to become a person in the full sense a child must develop a theory-of-mind based on an acquaintance with its own mental states. In other words, a child has to develop higher-order, meta-cognitive concepts inferred from observations of its own first-order mental states. It also has to learn what is meant by rational behaviour as defined by the community, inferring correctly which internal mental states are controlling another person's acts. A system of arbitrary signs (e.g., words in a language) is still needed to transmit these concepts to others.

According to the Cartesian model, to know the concept of, say, 'intention' is to be able to classify an experience (a mental state) as an example of intending something and also to be able to identify correctly when someone else's mental state is an intention to do something. It is assumed that another person's mental state can only be inferred once a child has developed its own theory-of-mind.

The concept of a mental state sounds like something that might correspond to a pattern of neural events, and, therefore, the Cartesian model holds out the prospect of finding the actual correlate of a mental state in the brain. If, instead, we adopt a constructionist view and reject the idea that a mental state is something that could exist apart from a person acting in a certain way (e.g., adopting practices in which the use of a mental-state term is embedded), then the idea that brain events simply mirror mental states or, from a scientific perspective are sufficient causes of mental states, is mistaken.

Shanker himself draws upon Wittgenstein's notion of a language game to describe what it is for a person to possess a certain concept. Possessing that concept and using it in a grammatically correct way would differ for different societies of speakers. For instance, in child-development research, it may be necessary to appeal to social criteria to decide when a child is 'pretending' and when it is 'lying'. Is a child who is claiming to be ill in order to avoid going to school pretending or lying? According to Shanker, it is not the facts of the matter that decide the criteria for applying psychological terms – the facts lying buried in mental representations and cognitive processes – but it is the social criteria for the possession of a concept that decide whether someone possesses it. In addition to the process of learning how to be a person with a mind, a child has to acquire the reflexive ability to talk appropriately about its own mental concepts. In western culture, this may entail talking in a Cartesian manner. However, this ability need not be thought of, in Cartesian terms, as an innate, meta-linguistic, cognitive capacity but as another example of talking in certain ways, for certain purposes, in social contexts that happen to call for it. Given that this is a local, historical conception, no universal theory (in psychology or sociology) can completely account for it.

Mental terms and social acts

Wittgenstein's understanding of meaning as use carries the implication that it is persons who act and create meaning, not brains or minds. Max Bennett and Peter Hacker (2003) argue that neuroscientists commonly ascribe to the brain what can only rightfully be ascribed to persons. If we assume that an ordinary language term is only used meaningfully when its use conforms to social criteria for its correct application, Bennett and Hacker argue that it simply makes no sense to say that *brains* believe, know, assume, intend, infer, categorise, decide, initiate, symbolise, etc., etc. They regard this as a failure to speak meaningfully, save for when scientists use these terms metaphorically or metonymically (Bennett and Hacker 2003: 72). Scientists may argue that they are only using their terms in a technical sense and following an accepted scientific practice of using convenient analogies. In fact though, as Bennett and Hacker show, in many cases this is not what they actually do. The terms are used illegitimately in their customary senses. For instance, it might be assumed that the activity that shows up in a brain scan when a person is thinking is evidence of the *brain* thinking. All that can rightfully be claimed is that the scan indicates the neural correlates of a *person* thinking.

Before considering objections that have been made to Bennett and Hacker's arguments, I will enlarge on the assumption that everything an organism needs to know for successful adaptation is located inside their brain or mind. The assumption rests heavily on the concept of representation. The essential idea is that humans are not automatically linked to the events that they perceive around them. In its simplest and unobjectionable application, the term 'representation' refers to the way physical events at the sensory organs are transformed into a new (neural) code. A more sophisticated meaning is that behaviour is *mediated* by representations (or models) of external events that are 'decoupled' from any simple reflex mechanism. A representation is decoupled in the same way that a map represents the terrain it describes, allowing a person to plan a route rather than follow their nose or the sun. The same representation could guide a range of different responses, just as different routes could be taken based on information contained in a map.

The concept of representation has been used to explain how a person learns to speak and act in ways that are appropriate in their culture. For instance, the potential to be a self could be described as the internalisation of cultural imperatives stored in the form of representational knowledge. But *in* what is this representation of self stored? Conceiving of the container as 'the mind' makes knowledge into a personal possession, on the assumption that it is persons who possess minds. One can see how people might naturally infer that their thoughts and feelings are contained 'in their mind', and if mind is equated with brain, their capacity to act in a culturally appropriate manner might also be understood as knowledge stored as neural patterns.

Bennett and Hacker (2003: 159) criticise this representational view of knowledge. They point out that *storage* is a metaphor, maintaining that remembering a fact or an experience, or knowing how to do something, are powers or capacities demonstrated in behaviour. They note the ancient ancestry of the storage metaphor. It is found in Plato as an impression on a tablet of wax, and the metaphor has been used in various forms ever since. One popular current idea is that knowledge is stored in the brain as an encoded description representing what is remembered, e.g., a complex pattern of synaptic connections. Recollecting then becomes the recreation of the original pattern of neural activity, a concept that Bennett and Hacker (2003: 163) set out to criticise.

They have several objections to this notion. First, they say that retention is confused with storage. Although storage may sometimes imply retention, retention does not imply storage. If we think of memory as a power that a person demonstrates as an ability, it is not an ability that is stored but only the causally necessary neural structures for the possession of that ability. Moreover, they argue that even if the structure of the storage mechanism bore some resemblance to a picture or written record, it would not be available to the person needing to use it because persons do not look into their own brain or read 'neuralese'. Even if this were possible, a person would have to *remember* how to read it or recognise it. For example, the storage of information about people as photos in an album does not guarantee that one will remember what names to attach to the faces. Similarly, mental representations 'in the brain' cannot guarantee that their possessor remembers what they represent. And

in some cases, such as the retention of an ability to draw logical inferences, it is quite unclear what it is that is being represented and stored.

These arguments can be extended to remembering who one is; enacting a self is not a matter of reactivating neural events that represent my
knowledge of who I am, such as a self-schema. The attraction of the
storage metaphor rests on a process of reading off information from
something that has been encrypted in neural processes. As already
noted, many instances of memory do not entail recreating an original
experience or act, nor is the ability to make use of information necessarily the recreation of past events. This must be true when envisaging
the future. Enacting a self does not seem to be a matter of activating
self-knowledge and trading information with other people.

An alternative dialogical interpretation of this process would depend,
rather, on a view of the person as engaging in complementary acts; a
person's brain is only enabled (as a self) by events occurring outside it,
the most general of which would be fellow human beings who recognise
that person as a person. On this view, self is co-constructed in a coordinated sequence of events. Moreover, the social practices in which self
is implicated depend on shared knowledge in an objective, public form
(a shared language, the written word, codified procedures, etc.) that are
co-opted rather than internalised in mind or brain. In this light, mind
is a participatory activity rather than a model, theory or representation
that mirrors either my 'mind' or the 'mind' of another.

Objections to Bennett and Hacker's arguments

The response to Bennett and Hacker's book published in 2003 provoked the American Philosophical Association to organise a meeting in
2005 at which Dennett and Searle replied to criticisms levelled against
them (Bennett et al. 2007).

Dennett's riposte first of all agrees that any talk couched in terms
of what *persons* do should not be transferred to a *sub-personal* level of
explanation. He is equally concerned about 'Cartesian leftovers' in
neuroscience. This still leaves us, as Dennett says, with the problem
of relating the personal to the sub-personal level of explanation. By
sub-personal, he means how neurons actually behave together or how
scientists interpret this behaviour in terms of processes, mechanisms
and modules. But Dennett is still willing to put his money on a form of
cognitive neuroscience that treats the sub-personal as if it were a set of
intentional systems which do things 'strikingly like' deciding, believing, guessing, etc. He believes it is justified to stretch ordinary usage
to cover the sub-personal on the grounds that adopting this method

has led to scientific discoveries. By taking the intentional stance, we are able to get 'whole wonderful persons out of brute mechanical parts' (Bennett et al. 2007: 89).

The upshot of this position is that Dennett has backed a methodology that still assumes, in Cartesian fashion, that there is merit in conceiving of the mind as a mechanism composed of parts mediated by the brain. As a methodology that may happen to pay off, there can be no objection in principle to the attempt to explain the personal as if it could be reduced to the level of sub-personal mechanisms. Bennett and Hacker are not offering a better scientific methodology, and if we remained at the personal level of explanation, wholly guided by ordinary grammatical usage, we could give up on any attempt to understand human beings in the language of science. However, the point Bennett and Hacker seem to be making is that some of the concepts used by neuroscientists do not cash out, and could not be cashed out, at the level of explanation for which they were intended. I give some examples below to illustrate this point.

John Searle counters the Wittgensteinian argument that there have to be public behavioural criteria for ascribing mental states to human beings by saying that a person still has private mental experiences, like pain, as well as using public criteria for ascribing pain to oneself or another. Moreover, he says that the argument says nothing about *where* pains are located. He maintains that 'pain is a real event in the real world, so it must have a location in real space-time' (Bennett et al. 2007: 118). He is unambiguous about the location – it is in the brain. In the case of a pain in a phantom limb, the pain is said to be located in a body-image constructed by the brain. Similarly, with regard to thought, he says that through neuro-imaging techniques, we can say, 'exactly where in my brain the thoughts occur' (Bennett et al. 2007: 109). He acknowledges that it would be odd to think of the decisions that a person makes as a rational agent as being located in the brain, especially for a decision like purchasing a property. However, Searle says that neuroscientists can ignore this because a person can be regarded as an embodied brain, and decision-making is a psychological process that occurs in the brain. Searle defines self as a purely formal postulation: 'a kind of principle of organization of the brain and its experiences' (Bennett et al. 2007: 121). Searle is here reflecting the assumption that psychology can be an autonomous science.

Bennett and Hacker regard Searle's views as a materialist version of Cartesianism (Bennett et al. 2007: 159). They argue that the brain is not an organ of consciousness. The fact that neural events in the brain may be causally necessary for a person to report being consciously aware is not the same as saying that the brain is conscious. The location of a thought, if we ordinarily think about this at all, is where the person is, not somewhere in the frontal lobes (Bennett et al. 2007: 142). Moreover, a thought is not a locatable thing in the sense of an entity *within* the person. It is not this kind of event. The location of phantom pains is where they are felt to be located, not in the brain, even if the location of the pain is illusory. The cause of a pain in an unamputated limb might be located in the foot, but Bennett and Hacker argue that ordinary grammatical usage does not permit us to say that the pain is located in the boot in which the foot is placed. Pains are real, but they do not behave like physical objects that can be located in space and time.

They also object to Searle's definition of a human being as an embodied brain (Bennett et al. 2007: 159). Abbreviating their detailed arguments, they say that 'I' (if I *have* a body) cannot at the same time be *in* my brain. Nor am I my brain together with my body. This is simply my body. Although 'I' am a body, this is insufficient to define a human being as a person. For this status, we need to endow the body with capacities such as intellect and will. Bennett and Hacker do not go on to explain how the status of person is acquired because this is not their purpose. They are content to state that a normal human being can be described as an agent that acts according to reason, has desires, intentions, etc., and acts in accordance with social norms (Bennett and Hacker 2003: 365). While this is an accepted definition of personhood, it does not take us very far in reconciling personhood with naturalism. In fact, Hacker (2001) does not see any room for this ambition at all. Bennett and Hacker's aim is to proscribe nonsensical natural science rather than offer a theory of their own.

Monism and reference to 'the mind'

Most scientists of human behaviour would probably say that they aim to explain rather than explain away the fact that we refer to our desires, our intentions and our rich experiences. Human experience is not equivalent to, or identical with, the processes and mechanisms put forward to account for them. At the same time, nearly all scientists are monists who assume that there is a single and unified natural reality. For many of the objects we perceive (e.g., tables), it makes sense to account for them in terms of known physical principles. If minds or selves could be treated as objects like tables, a search for their natural substrate in the brain might make sense. If, on the other hand, mind or self are constructs, and therefore ways of talking about the world that serve practical purposes, I believe that any attempt to account for them scientifically would have to consider the sub-personal brain along with personal and supra-personal natural processes.

The idea of self in the brain is the dominant view. A recent article entitled 'In Search of the Self' reported the results of scanning the brain by the method of positron emission tomography while participants judged lists of personality traits (Craik et al. 1999). Some of the traits were personally relevant to the participants, and others were not; of some interest, the former, in contrast to the latter, were correlated with activation of the right frontal lobes. But perhaps more interesting is the title of the article. Are the authors intending us to think that the self is in the brain or are they just trying to catch our attention? To be generous, we might assume that this 'self in the brain' is a convenient conceptual hook, not to be taken too literally. Theoretical constructs can be useful for prediction, even if they do not refer to real existents. Thomas Leahey takes this position when he writes: 'Therefore, a respectable scientific psychology might be constructed on the notion of mind whether or not "mind" or minds exist, as long as it is capable of adequately dealing with human behavior' (2003: 73, Note 18). The criteria for respectable science that Leahey cites are grounded in judgements of adequacy and capability. As I hope to show in the next section, it would be hard to claim that these criteria have been satisfied in some current examples of neuroscience theorising about mind and self.

In his consideration of mind as an object for science, Leahey (2003) considers various possibilities for explaining how folk concepts arise. It might be supposed, as noted above, that people develop a folk theory and that 'the mind' awaited discovery just as atomic particles awaited discovery. On these grounds, a good folk theory would mirror natural processes. A second stance is that folk concepts of mind are human artefacts – conceptual tools with practical applications. Leahey says that this stance shades into the third, which is mind as a social construction. On this third view, according to Leahey, mind could be a 'profound illusion' (2003: 36), unlike the interpretation of mind as an artefact tied to real human interactions. However, it is not clear how illusions could be unrelated to human practices. Leahey cites Greek gods as examples of profound illusions, but these gods were surely human artefacts and also tied to social practices.

Leahey (2003: 54) draws further on the concept of an illusion when he makes a distinction between types of materialism. He defines materialism as the belief that the only substance that exists is matter. First, he says there are those materialists who want to eliminate mind in scientific explanation, viewing it as an illusion (eliminativists) and, second, those who grant mental states and processes some reality and therefore think they are worthy of a genuine scientific explanation (reductionists). Leahey regards constructionism as a version of eliminativism (2003: 55). As argued in Chapter 1, I do not hold to an eliminativist version of constructionism, and mental states and processes could be considered 'real' under a different description. Moreover, if organised matter has emergent properties, it may be possible to develop a non-reductionist unified science that is compatible with constructionism (see Chapter 13). In that chapter I also attempt to deal with the tricky distinction between virtual reality, illusions, and fictions (see also Held 2002).

If self is a virtual reality, it may be necessary to eliminate it for *certain kinds* of scientific analysis. This is not because self is an incorrect theory or misrepresentation of reality (like the concept of phlogiston) but because it represents reality in ways that serve a variety of purposes at the same time. In other words, the practice of referring to self is simply too complex a natural phenomenon to reduce to any one level of explanation. It would simply be poor science to look for 'self' in the brain. The self could be justifiably eliminated as a scientific object not because it is illusory but because, as the fabled Irishman is supposed to have said, 'If you want to get to Cork, I wouldn't start from here.' The whole field of study may need to be reconceptualised before it becomes amenable to scientific investigation.

I suggested in Chapter 1 that an interpretive analysis of concepts of mind and self might be the most useful (and only feasible) approach to take in certain circumstances. To adopt methods of interpretation need not imply that other approaches to investigating and explaining self are illegitimate. Just as an anthropologist might recontextualise witchcraft, a constructionist could do the same for mind or self. The aim in this kind of analysis is not to eliminate or replace a concept like self or to deny that people are being truthful when they say they are bewitched. One aim would be to bring to people's attention how reference to mind and self (like witchcraft) is related to the three levels of explanation I have described.

Mind, self and brain: A critique of neuroscience theorising

One of the striking features of much of the neuroscience literature is the assumption that it is blindingly obvious that mind equates to brain. Of course, when scientists refer to mind/brain identity, they do not mean by it what we normally mean by identity (Velmans 2000). No one 'in their right mind' answers the question 'Who are you?' with the answer 'The activity of my neurons.' I can be a person or self without knowing anything about my brain, and so, if I am neuronal activity, this is not a relationship of logical identity.

The case for a degree of correspondence between brain events and a person's reference to mental attributes is incontrovertible but we need only infer from this that the brain plays a necessary part in any causal explanation. There is simply no reason to make the assumption that the workings of the brain are sufficient to explain everything we need to know about minds or selves if the brain is only one element in a larger natural system. Brains are not stand-alone devices that exist outside a social matrix of events. Yet some neuroscientists really do seem to take seriously the possibility that everything a person needs to be a self could be supplied to a brain that exists in a vat of nutrients (Ramachandran 2006).

I have decided to critique several neuroscience theories in order to illustrate the general points I have made so far. I have singled out theorists whose views have been influential. They are more accurately described as examples of *cognitive* neuroscience.

Nicholas Humphrey

In essence, Humphrey believes that self is part of the mind and mind is identical with brain. He compares self to an 'inner eye' looking into and reporting back on what is in the mind (Humphrey 1993). The analogies he employs to understand mind are drawn from the information-processing computer. According to this popular analogy, the brain is compared to a computer's hardware and the mind to its software. New software can be installed (for instance, by learning a new habit), and this software is inscribed in the brain's neurons, just as computer software has a physical basis in hardware. The organisation of the whole hardware/software complex becomes the basis for mind. Humphrey's view is that at the highest level of organisation there is a master program that gives orders to lower-order programs that carry out their duties in a more automatic fashion. In short, the complex operates rather like a civil service in relaying commands up and down a hierarchy of executives and minor officials. A person's self is said to be in some way connected with the operation of the master program.

More recently, Humphrey (2002: 9) has modified this view and described the development in infancy of a unified self that 'moulds the whole system into one'. He believes that a baby does not at first have experiences that are perceived as their own. Unification is the result of 'the power inherent in all his sub-selves for, literally, their own *self-organisation*' (Humphrey 2002: 13). They unify under the influence of a unitary life project that is 'self-made'. However, bearing in mind the existence of multiple personality, he accepts that for some babies this 'solution to the problem of selfhood' is not always attainable (2002: 46).

Humphrey's views amount to a radical reduction of mind and self to the brain. For Humphrey, as an identity theorist, any mental state has a corresponding brain state (or set of such states) so that, at some stage in the future, we will find a way to translate mental descriptions into brain descriptions, and vice versa. But this view is inconsistent. If selfhood is a 'problem' for the organism, how do we understand this problem as belonging to the brain as a bodily organ? The problem seems to belong to a person. He sees multiple personality is a *way of coping* with childhood trauma (2002: 46) and so the self-organisation that produces unitary selfhood cannot simply be a brain process.

Humphrey refers to the master program as Head of Mind, which he characterises as an inner figurehead that 'represents the person to himself and to the world' (Humphrey 1993: 30). The language of self, the 'I' statements that connect a person to the real world are demoted to the level of a self-confirming 'language apparatus' that is controlled by input from various subsystems of the hardware/software complex. In other words, language is just one more module that exists within a flow diagram of the mind.

As Humphrey acknowledges, people often feel like different selves, implying that there could be different Heads of Mind. He proposes that the solution to the puzzle of multiple personality is that a brain is not originally endowed with a single Head of Mind but slowly gets acquainted with various possibilities of selfhood until one of them, by majority verdict, gets elected to be the 'real me'. In the brains of people with multiple personalities, he suggests that the various candidates in the election are so evenly balanced that they take it in turns to be Head of Mind (or less politely oust each other out of position).

In this hypothesis, the whole person is smuggled in surreptitiously. If a person represents themself by a Head of Mind, in what sense is the Head the Head? Moreover, the 'I' in I statements properly refers to the speaker as a whole person. How can 'I' be a sub-module of the self as Head of Mind? To propose that brains hold elections for a Head of Mind has all the hallmarks of ad-hoc theorising to make good a gap in mind/brain identity theory.

Bernard Baars

Coming from a slightly different direction, Bernard Baars has argued for 'a cortical self system' (1997: 144). Baars makes out a convincing case that attending consciously to events has a special role to play in the control of animal and human behaviour. According to him, self is not like Humphrey's 'inner eye', an observer of our conscious states. Baars equates self with a set of mechanical entities of a cognitive or neural kind, such as pattern recognisers. This cortical self system produces consciousness, and, following identity theory, Baars assumes that to be conscious simply implies that it is 'I' that has access to conscious experience. If this were true, there would be no need to postulate further observers of mental states or brain states, but nor would it be necessary to postulate the existence of persons, which is a less acceptable conclusion.

The assumption of a self that has access to its own mental states raises the question of a difference between conscious and self-conscious experience. Humans can identify their own point of view and compare it with another's point of view, and this capacity seems to go beyond the mere fact of being conscious. Baars could be interpreted as saying that there is an entity, an 'I', that has access to conscious experience, or that persons (and perhaps many animals) *are* simply creatures that are normally conscious of events around them. A constructionist might agree that humans, like animals, are conscious of events, feelings, etc. At this pre-reflective level, there is presumably no need for an additional 'I' that has access to these experiences. But if Baars wishes to establish 'I' as an entity, it would have to be, for a constructionist, a product of reflection, i.e. a person conceiving of themselves as an entity like a self. The speaker imagines a fictional mental entity when, using the personal pronoun, they make a claim to be conscious of something. If a *person* does this, it is not clear how that function could be reduced to a sub-personal mechanism.

In whatever way self-consciousness is understood in theoretical terms, it is clearly a complex biological and social phenomenon that includes anomalous experiences of a sense-of-self. Baars accepts this and notes the existence of fugue states, depersonalisation, multiple selves and other strange syndromes that reveal how complex the phenomenon of self-awareness really is. Baars' explanation for these anomalies is that they are associated with disruption to a largely unconscious, stable framework of taken-for-granted expectations, intentions or assumptions, which he calls 'deep context'.

Baars' suggestion of a deep context does not sound at all like a neural process. It is difficult to see how assumptions about the world could be translated into cognitive or brain mechanisms. These seem to be properties of persons in a social context. 'Deep context' therefore sidesteps the important issues. The chapter of his book in which self is discussed is entitled 'The Director', but this way of conceiving self would only make sense if cognitive mechanisms could write their own scripts. A person level of description seems to be needed for this activity.

Jeffrey Cooney and Michael Gazzaniga

Not all neuroscientists propose a central executive that controls the action. An alternative position is that the outputs of various modular structures interact in a central 'neural workspace', eventuating in a kind of integrated and composite control by a set of relatively independent neural structures. Cooney and Gazzaniga (2003) argue for this position on the grounds that it helps us (as theorists) to interpret the effects of localised neural damage to specific modules, such as the one for face recognition. In addition, they suggest that an 'interpretative module' located in the left hemisphere of the brain is involved in helping us (as ordinary persons) to make sense of the integration of modular activity and to mediate conscious perceptual experiences that result from damage. For example, in left visual hemineglect, a patient fails to perceive the left side of the visual field, and, according to these authors, the cortical damage may also cause the patient to neglect any memories of how this left field used to function. Looking around, a scene appears normal, and rotating the head simply brings objects into view. In the absence of a discrepancy between present input and past memory, no problem is detected. There is no higher-order executive to check the adequacy of the interpretation.

In some rare cases of neglect, the denial of a problem seems quite bizarre, for example, when the whole left side of the body is paralysed. When asked to explain why they are unable to perform a task requiring two hands, a person with paralysis might simply claim, 'I did not want to do it.' Cooney and Gazzaniga (2003: 164) note that the capacity of these apparently deluded persons 'to create a subjectively rational story out of seemingly incoherent information is startling', and they draw the conclusion that an interpretative process must have an overwhelming influence in shaping our own 'normal' experience of the world.

This conclusion cannot be disputed; there must be numerous occasions on which a person's perception seemed self-evident but could have benefited from doubt and further questioning. However, to regard interpretation as merely the function of a part of the brain leaves out the role of persons as disputants in social contexts. Neural tissue cannot decide what is rational or what information is incoherent, but it may cause behaviour that is judged to be so by independent criteria. These are judgements that people make about interpretable situations using their whole brain, however deficient its abilities. The interpretation

'I didn't want to do it' makes some sense in a human social situation. Conceivably, even these delusions are not immune to argument. The general point is that neither a central executive nor modular interaction is sufficient on its own to explain the control of behaviour.

Antonio Damasio

Damasio, a neurologist, has put forward another highly developed conception of self as a neural and mental phenomenon. He draws upon a body of literature on learning, memory and consciousness, as well as clinical syndromes associated with damage to the human brain. His views are especially interesting because he excludes language from his account of self (but brings it in to explain personhood).

Damasio (2000) tackles head-on the material basis of self yet understands self to mean a conscious feeling, or a feeling of knowing, that is purely private. He builds up an account of the evolution of consciousness, a process that eventually led to a level of complexity that distinguishes human from non-human primates. Essentially, Damasio defines self as the 'feeling of what happens'. He deliberately chooses the term 'sense of self' to underline the fact that self is a form of knowledge based on a feeling and not on a conceptual distinction. His theory treats knowledge as neural patterns or mental representations.

Damasio does not suggest that animals function at one level and humans another. Humans function at complex and simpler levels simultaneously, depending on the task and the degree to which any particular habit is exercised automatically. At the simplest level, he regards learning as taking place by means of unconscious processes, a kind of learning that is concretely adapted to the specific setting in which it is needed. Many, perhaps most, animal species are said to function in this way. At this level, an animal has no sense of itself learning, and its behaviour is controlled by its biological needs and the situations it encounters. Damasio calls it the proto-self.

This kind of learning was said to have been given a major boost in evolution with the arrival of 'core consciousness', a kind of second-order knowledge in which an animal is able to represent itself to itself when interacting with the environment. Damasio assumes that this development allowed animals to be more flexible when adapting to a new situation. In first-order knowledge, the animal simply learns which habits work best in particular contexts, selecting from a limited range the one that is most likely to succeed. With second-order knowledge, an animal is said to represent itself when interacting with objects, and Damasio assumes that it is these representations that control behaviour, rather than the object the animal confronts. The animal reviews the possibilities prior to acting, selecting some habits and inhibiting others, releasing it from the influence of whatever external stimuli happen to be present at the time.

Damasio believes that core consciousness corresponds to the activity of second-order representations. He sees it as consciousness of the here and now, based on a feeling of knowing, in which the sense-of-self is a biological given. Damasio describes it as a wordless feeling of the relationship between an organism and the object it is in the act of knowing at the time. He assumes that it grows out of the bodily sense an animal must possess if it is to select from a range of potential bodily movements, such as planning a route when jumping from tree to tree. A response of this kind requires an implicit body/other distinction, entailed in a range of anticipated movements. How far core consciousness extends down the evolutionary scale is not known, but, according to Damasio, an organism that possesses it knows that it is itself that knows. He considers that core consciousness *is* simply a feature of all second-order representations and is identical with an as-yet-unidentified brain process.

One criticism that can be levelled at the concept of core consciousness is to question whether it is meaningful to say that an animal knows that it knows something. Human beings are capable of intuiting the difference between knowing something and knowing that one knows, but is an animal equipped to make this distinction? Damasio claims that core consciousness is private and personal, but this idea is difficult to accept when the feeling occurs in an instant of time and cannot be linked consciously to anything that comes before or afterwards. He says that 'a sense of self informs mind non-verbally of the existence of the organism in which mind is unfolding' (Damasio 2000: 89). But is this saying anything more than an animal is aware that its body is attuned to the world and that it has a sense of its own ability to manipulate the world it inhabits? Any talk of 'minds' or 'awareness of its own existence' seems redundant.

As humans, we often carry out quite sophisticated acts that must require second-order representations but without focal awareness of what we are doing. Damasio may assume that these acts have become automated and that a feeling of knowing only arises when an act is initiated or interrupted. So, for instance, when a person suddenly feels that they are about to fall over, their awareness of what is happening might enable them to select corrective movements in addition to any reflex adjustments. But on the assumption that people anticipate situations and select finely tuned responses without awareness, the operation of a second-order process cannot be a sufficient explanation of core consciousness.

The idea of core consciousness carries with it the Cartesian assumption that there is an observer that continually perceives its own state, as if the perception is a reflection in a mirror. How otherwise could it be personal and private? But if this accompanies all states of consciousness, it is a trivial sense of privacy. As Damasio emphasises, an animal must represent its body in space and time, implying a self/non-self distinction. This could be experienced in a pre-reflective way as a feeling, as Damasio suggests. A question that needs addressing is whether lower mammals, primates and humans differ in the way this body/world discrimination is made. I assume that a human is conscious of itself as an object in the world in the way that a lower mammal is not.

For higher primates at least, there is evidence that they react as if possessing some knowledge of another animal's field of view (see Chapter 12). This might indicate an incipient understanding of a personal realm as opposed to a public realm of experience. It is possible that an animal is intimately acquainted with its feelings, but this does not imply that it knows that it knows in the sense of symbolically representing itself in awareness. At best, there is a tacit corporeal sense.

Damasio goes on to argue that humans possess 'extended consciousness', a state of the brain in which a temporal dimension has been added to core consciousness. For all humans with intact brains, consciousness is normally extended and so it is difficult to describe what unextended (core) consciousness might be like for a human being. Damasio calls the extended, temporal consciousness possessed by humans 'the autobiographical self'. The latter is said to arise with the reactivation and 'display' in consciousness of selected sets of memories. The metaphors he employs are those of theatres, panoramas and landscapes. He assumes that pulses of core consciousness extend into sets of pulses that may represent events over minutes, hours or years. Damasio asserts that autobiographical selves do not require language, yet he wants the concept to include agency and ownership. He states that an autobiographical self consists of a repository of memories for fundamental data that define personal and social identity (Damasio 2000: 223).

These proposals are fundamentally at odds with a constructionist position. Bennett and Hacker's critique of memory as storage applies to Damasio's concept of autobiographical memory. The idea that a person's sense of being a self with a history is equivalent to the reactivation of past experiences sounds distinctly peculiar when his analogy conjures up a comparison with the structure of personal profiles held in government databases. We normally think of our identity as lived, not as known by reading off information from a file. Damasio admits that the autobiographical self needs to have its memories organised and presented in a temporal framework, but he doesn't show how this is achieved. Selves are future-directed, and Damasio conceives of the future as 'memories of the future'. An imagined future certainly has to be based on past experience, but it cannot consist simply of the reactivation of a memory. The sense of being a self existing through time requires a temporal framework for memory. The need for a marker of time is vividly illustrated by the intrusive memories of people who have been traumatised. They sometimes relive a memory of a past trauma but do so as if it were a present experience. These reactivated memories are regarded as pathological because they are not placed within that person's usual framework for time, even though they are experienced as presently occurring. The reactivation of a memory does not, in itself, constitute a sense of time.

When Damasio tackles the concept of personal identity, he finds it difficult to relate to neuroscience. He thinks it is almost astonishing that we have only one identity, and he is forced to revert to everyday language to make sense of it. An example of this is 'the idea each of us constructs of oneself' (Damasio 2000: 224). Damasio says that our idea of self is based on autobiographical memories, but who is it (presumably not a memory) that is doing the constructing? If self is a feeling, a biological given of core consciousness, how does it do anything as sophisticated as construct an idea of itself?

The conceptual problem is compounded in the case of persons who have multiple personalities. Like Humphrey, Damasio follows Dennett in proposing that the mind prepares multiple drafts of its life script but is pushed biologically and by the need for survival into one draft. Possessing only one self has 'advantages to the healthy mind' (Damasio 2000: 354). The unhealthy mind of the person with multiple personalities has managed to create more than one control site: 'the switch from one master control to another enables the identity/personality switch to occur' (Damasio 2000: 355, Note 14). According to Damasio, each separate autobiographical self uses the same core consciousness, but how does this core self know which self it is? Who presses the switch?

Chris Frith

Frith's views are interesting because he speculates about each person having a stand-alone brain and how separate persons interact to produce culture. He attempts to build a social world from a solipsistic Cartesian world. He posits a mental world and a physical world (essentially the world as it is described by physicists); our brain is part of the physical world, and it produces for us a mental fantasy or illusion that coincides with physical reality (Frith 2007: 111–38). Brains have no direct connection with physical reality so they have to build up models on the basis of 'crude and ambiguous cues from the outside world' (Frith 2007: 132). The model predicts what something is or how it will behave, based on the brain's innate 'prejudices' or on the most probable hypothesis generated by a pre-existing (acquired) model. Models are fine tuned by the success of their predictions, in other words, whether they lead to consequences that are valued or avoid consequences that are not valued. The only causal reality is the physical and so minds, selves and our conscious perceptions are all, in some sense, illusions that are more or less functionally adaptive. Frith claims not to be a dualist (2007: 184), and he is not especially interested in explaining consciousness. He is a materialist, and so the mental world is presumably identical with a yet-to-be identified brain process. Accordingly, he states that he, as author of his book, is an 'I' that is an illusion that has been created by his brain (Frith 2007: 185).

There is clearly scientific merit in the idea that a brain builds a model of the world that is external to the brain. Frith demonstrates its explanatory value through many fascinating experiments. He also casts light on the causal origins of a sense of an action as 'mine' or 'intended' rather than passively caused. However, there is something odd about his claim that when he refers to himself, Chris Frith, and uses the words 'I' and 'his', he does so by virtue of illusions created by his brain. On the contrary, we feel that Chris Frith is actually a real person in the physical world. He is real by contrast with his fictional protagonist, a professor of English, who disapproves of his neuroscience reductionism. Everything in the mental world cannot be illusory because we would then lose sight of important ontological distinctions. If the mental world is created from models that the brain builds up, many of the assumptions that Frith makes could also be illusory. For example, the idea that more than one mind exists could be illusory; the distinction between 'in my mind' and 'in your mind' might not make any sense in the physical world, since we cannot point to any physical boundaries to which the boundaries of minds correspond. As his experiments show, the boundary between mine and not-mine could be constructed, but Frith assumes that each mind/brain is separate.

Frith would probably say that some 'illusions' correspond to the material world and others don't. The inference that each person has a mind is consistent with sensory feedback. However, if brains are sub-units in a larger physical reality, we have no firm grounds for believing that brains, as stand-alone entities, are entirely responsible for creating the models that yield the mental world we share. He bolsters his own argument by describing sensory input as crude and ambiguous, seeming to imply that the stand-alone brain has to do all the hard work. In fact, sensory input already has a latent order, especially when structured by language.

Frith grants that perception of causality depends on point of view (2007: 187). Thus, willed action is always constrained by the physical and social context, and these aspects of the situation could be focused upon as causes. An experimenter instructs a participant to 'freely' lift their finger when they feel like it, but, as Frith points out, the experimenter would be upset if a participant never lifted their finger at all. He concludes that concepts such as 'will' arise from interactions with other people. He says that: 'One important result of our experience of being free agents is that we recognize that other people are free agents just like us' (Frith 2007: 191). An implication of his phrasing seems to be that our brain creates a model that supplies us with an illusory experience of freedom from which we infer that others have similar experiences of freedom. As he puts it: 'This final illusion created by our brain – that we are detached from the social world and are free agents – enables us to create together a society and a culture that is so much more than any individual' (Frith 2007: 193). Just as Frith fails to follow Wittgenstein (2007: 150), at this point I fail to follow Frith. If our separation from the social world is an illusion, why attribute this illusion to a creation of our individual brains?

Constructionism and a natural science of society

There remains the problem of reconciling a socially constructed self with naturalism. This is a problem that faces evolutionary biologists and archaeologists when they try to account for transitions in social organisation between primate, hominid and human societies. There is general agreement that the account has to explain functional relationships between organisms, their brains and their environment, including artefacts in the environment fashioned by the organism.

Despite this broad conception of a functional system, it is the brain that has received overwhelming attention, presumably on the basis that self is something mental and mind is thought to equal brain. Like Frith, the anthropologist Dan Sperber (1996) assumes mind/brain identity. As he says: 'Our individual brains are each inhabited by a large number of ideas that determine our behaviour' (Sperber 1996: 1). Sperber's conception of mutual understanding, like Descartes's, is the successful transfer of mental ideas. The metaphors he uses are 'contagion', 'invasion' and 'epidemiology'. Sperber advances his views with the intention of locating anthropology in the natural sciences. Although he does not want to reduce all cultural phenomena to facts about brains or minds, he does seem to accept mind/brain identity without question: 'the material basis of psychological processes is obvious enough' (Sperber 1996: 14). He points out that the material bases of cultural processes are more mysterious and notes that anthropological accounts are wonderfully free of ontological commitments. Sperber's aim is to find an ontological anchor in mental representations that exist, according to him, in people's minds and brains.

How does culture fit into a framework of mind/brain identity and mental representations? One of Sperber's illustrations can be used to state the problem concretely. He argues that when a man and a woman marry, the only thing that can be stated for sure is that some mental representations 'are being circulated' (Sperber 1996: 23). However, it is not clear why people as functioning human organisms are not assigned equal causal significance. Representations like marriage presuppose the existence of embodied persons who understand what it is to enter a legal commitment. The same argument could be applied to primate colonies that are described as possessing a culture (e.g., a type of tool-use not directly mediated by their genes). The role of one primate imitating another has to be proposed as a potential explanation for this phenomenon. A primate may have to represent tool-use in its brain but this is only half the causal picture.

Sperber grants that representations in minds depend on functional relationships between 'brains, organisms and environment' (1996: 26) and so it is not clear why brains should be sufficient to explain culture. In developing his position, he assigns a regulatory role to representations themselves. As he puts it, 'some of the representations involved may play a regulatory role by representing how some other representations are to be distributed' (Sperber 1996: 29). Institutional phenomena can now be placed at the top of a causal hierarchy, with human mental representations as simply more complex than animal representations. One form of complexity is the fact that they may represent the causes of human behaviour as being located in entities/forces that are not the 'real' material cause, which, according to Sperber, are representations in the brain. Sperber could be interpreted as saying that the members of a culture believe that the institution of marriage involves, for instance, a union between ancestral spirits, yielding representations as to how marriage should be regulated. Presumably, in Sperber's view, the members of the society would be wrongly attributing the cause of their behaviour to immaterial spirits when the real cause was a brain event.

From a constructionist standpoint, to represent something is not simply a brain process and so what is happening when people 'misrepresent' is a question that is much more difficult to answer. They are representing what happens in their culture but not, of course, as natural scientists. If we extend the search for natural causes from brains to the environment, including its cultural artefacts, the people may be accurately representing what they have played a part in creating.

From a standpoint of naturalism, the conceptual boundaries of a persons-in-society functional system could be placed at different locations for different theoretical purposes. In contemporary society, the biological person is treated as a functional unit by the health services, and this is for good practical reasons even though a person's health is known to be a function of environmental factors as well. However, a group of persons could also be viewed as functioning as a unit when they share a system of symbols and normatively regulated practices (or indeed when they simply exchange diseases). If common-sense ideas are socially constructed, minds and selves do not have a concrete spatial location, and so we should not worry about locating them solely in heads. One possible reason for the excessive focus on heads is that, traditionally, philosophers have considered the problem of knowledge from the point of view of a relationship between a knower and the known, i.e. between subjects and objects, a person and their world, etc. A knower in this relationship is identified with a person or part of a person, usually their brain.

Philosophers such as Ruth Millikan (2004), who have considered the acquisition of human knowledge from an evolutionary standpoint, conceive of the knower as a single organism. Millikan distinguishes between 'inner' representations that serve the function of tracking 'real' natural properties of the environment and representations that are equivocal, redundant or empty. Millikan must be right that animals that track the former are in a better position to adapt successfully than those that produce empty representations. Millikan does not think there is anything wrong with 'defective' mental representations, but she clearly wants to ring-fence representations that, for the animal or human, render it better adapted to the environment.

Millikan defines mental terms as empty if they don't enable a person to reidentify what is referentially the same thing as the same again. It might be thought that things like ancestral spirits would fail on this criterion. However, if people act according to conventions that allow for consistent reference to the existence of spirits, they can be reidentified. The spirits may not represent contingencies in the physical environment but they do track social contingencies, and, on my interpretation, the latter are also contingencies between natural events. If one person responds to another, contingent on their norm-following behaviour, there exists a natural (physical) correlate of this contingency.

On another interpretation of Millikan's argument, she is saying that spirits would be defective as representations if they were represented, not as the product of social conventions but as having immaterial causes. For instance, we know that a 'centimetre' only exists by virtue of an agreed convention. We do not assume that a centimetre is a natural entity but accept it as a useful social fiction that can be reliably reidentified. But many of the first attempts at science were probably based on shared beliefs that were *not* understood to be merely social conventions. Defective representations may have enabled imperfect prediction of real-world events (including social behaviour) and therefore may have offered biological and evolutionary advantages. To regard representations of immaterial entities as empty or defective is to privilege one kind of explanation of reality based on recent scientific theory.

Sperber's representations that 'misrepresent' are analogous to Millikan's defective representations. It seems inevitable that any natural-science account of human behaviour is led into a position of pointing out a discrepancy between a person's understanding of how they their 'mind' functions and how a scientist understands it. A constructionist account of a person's reference to self is in the same position. Most people do not think of their self as a virtual reality. But this particular folk representation is not 'mistaken' if a plausible account can be given of the social processes that lead to its origins and maintenance, and self bears a meaningful relationship to life as lived. If we give up the idea of mind or self as an imperfect attempt at scientific theorising, the question of its correspondence to natural reality falls away.

Rather than conceiving of representations as 'inside' a person, they could be viewed systemically and functionally in a wider social system (see Chapter 13). Accordingly, a person's 'self' need not be thought of as existing either 'in' the person's brain/mind or 'in' the world. It could be viewed as being continually recreated and redefined as a virtual entity in a system of socially interacting persons. The position I have just sketched out implies that mind and self are not purely personal possessions. Some philosophers have recently grappled with this notion under the general heading of the 'extended-mind hypothesis', to which I now turn.

The extended-mind hypothesis

One means of grasping this hypothesis is to think of its opposite, an unextended mind. Presumably, this would have to consist of a flux of mental states, in essence, a stream of consciousness. Mindists generally assume that a person intuits or deduces that other people have minds as well. Nevertheless, this knowledge would also have to be a mental state, and a conscious state of an unextended mind would reveal all there is to know about it by introspection. If it wanted to know whether it believed something or felt something, the mind would simply consult its own mental state. Evidence for beliefs might be sought from relevant information, but this would be fed into the mind as further states of conscious awareness and perhaps subjected to a process of reasoning.

If we now consider how an unextended mind might be explained as a natural process, then the mind/brain identity hypothesis proposes that any mental state is identical with or caused by events in the brain. So, for instance, a mental experience of a tree would be constructed by the brain from a model that what is being perceived is indeed a tree. The mind is therefore extended to include unconscious neural and cognitive processes, all of which would exist in the brain. Of course, some mental states are judged to be perceptions of public events, and other mental states are understood to be events private to the mind. Nevertheless, the assumption could be made that the experience of something as public or private could also be explained in terms of neural correlates of these perceptions. According to the mind/brain identity hypothesis, we do not have to consider events outside the head as direct causes of mental states. The unextended mind, on this view, begins to sound like a solipsistic universe although it could be supplemented by assuming that there are non-neural events that act as remote (indirect) causes of mental events. In other words, it would not have to be denied that physical trees actually existed.

There are various ways of extending this rather odd conception of mind outside the head. For instance, it is generally accepted that most mental states are causally determined, at least in part, by the environment at the time. So one means of extending the mind would be to say that a mental state of, say, a 'tree' is partly determined by the presence of an actual tree. Moreover, this removes the need to say that a tree is mentally represented *as* a tree in order to be perceived as such. All that is required is for an organism to track features of the environment and to retain a sufficient neural trace for the feature to be recognised as the right kind of feature when next encountered. Events in the environment may be assumed to be sufficient to prompt this recognition in the same way that, say, a painting of Picasso is recognised as one of his, without being able to represent the entire corpus of his work or even give any account of the features that lead one to judge it as Picasso's.

Going a bit further, it might be claimed that one couldn't even know about trees at all unless there was some state of affairs (natural and social) external to the person that determined what it was to have a mental state of a tree. Presumably, an actual tree can only prompt recognition of a tree if it reliably conveys information that it is a tree of the kind perceived. Animals that live in trees presumably acquire reliable knowledge about trees, enabling them to alight on branches or swing from one branch to the other. Similarly, humans undoubtedly acquire reliable knowledge about the environment without knowing how they do so. That is, they need have no corresponding conscious mental state that informs them of this knowledge. Humans may, without having to justify it, truthfully believe that something is the case without introspecting about the rational basis of their belief. In other words, we do not have to suppose that a mental state of the unextended mind, or internal reasoning, is the only means by which a person arrives at true belief.

So, just as actual physical trees may reliably lead to perceptions of trees, it could be argued that social and normative regularities of the environment make a necessary causal contribution to the ascription of mental states even if we are not aware of these causes *as* mental states. Consequently, we are led to question the meaning of mind as something a person possesses ('in their head') and also the equation between mind and brain. We can also reconsider how nature and culture can be combined in a causal explanation. How, for instance, do cultural artefacts like language and tools, existing outside the head, relate to a person's mental attributes, like believing something or thinking something?

This is the kind of problem considered by Andy Clark and David Chalmers (1998), two proponents of the extended-mind hypothesis. Without going into the details of their philosophical reasoning, their main arguments are revealed in a discussion of an illustrative example – a somewhat forgetful man who relies on information he has written down in a notebook to help him successfully reach a destination. This illustrates the idea that an artefact in the world is a part of thinking when it 'functions as a process, which, were it to go on in the head, we would have no hesitation in accepting as part of the cognitive process' (Clark 2008). In other words, the idea that thinking goes on in minds in heads is an overly restrictive interpretation of what thinking is. Things external to the head are part of the cognitive process and so we should consider the mind to be extended. Clark and Chalmers do not include *any* cultural artefacts in the cognitive process but only ones, like personal notebooks, that are reliably available, trustworthy and easily accessible.

The extended-mind hypothesis does not imply that 'the mind' (whatever that is) now has a new spatial boundary, as Coulter and Sharrock (2007: 214) seem to assume in their criticism of the idea. Rather, it is to suppose that what goes on in brains or heads is insufficient to account for cognitive activities, a position with which they must be sympathetic.

In the illustration just provided, a person who has a better memory than this forgetful man (a memory supposedly located 'in their head') might simply rely on what they know to be the case, without resorting to memory aids. Clark and Chalmers do not seem to be claiming that a physical artefact *is* a mental state but only that the physical artefact could be an essential physical cause or correlate of a mental state in the same way that the brain presumably plays a necessary (though not sufficient) causal role in all mental states. They acknowledge that the occurrence of any conscious mental state might still depend on events in the brain.

The extended-mind hypothesis is credible from a constructionist standpoint with the proviso that mental states are redefined as ways in which persons express themselves through language and in relation to social practices. In fact, the extended-mind hypothesis is understated when considered in a broad evolutionary perspective. Kim Sterelny (2004) points out the many ways that animals and humans create an environment in which they are better adapted to survive by manipulating it to ease burdens on memory. For example, 'In songs, stories and rhyme, the organisation of the information enables some elements to prime others' (Sterelny 2004: 243). Sterelny refers to portable epistemic tools as 'decoupled representations'. Nonetheless, he argues that external cognitive tools are in the public domain and therefore not 'literally parts of the minds of the agents that regularly use them' (Sterelny 2004: 250). This might be a sound objection to the extended-mind hypothesis if one could actually define the mind literally. With Sterelny's argument, we are back with the unextended mind and its mental states, with each organism carrying its mind around in its head.

Many scientists have assumed that it *is* possible to create a unified science of mind confining itself to inner (neural and mental) goings-on in brains. Clark (2008) counters this argument by refusing to limit the explanation of mind (and intelligent behaviour) to any one causal paradigm, such as biological processes in our brains. His preferred scenario is an extended functional system in which what is out there in the world can guide and control our reasoning and our disposition to believe that something is the case. This does not imply that he believes that a notebook (or presumably language) *on its own* constitutes a functioning cognitive system.

One objection to the extended-mind hypothesis is that the biological brain has the final say and controls and chooses actions in a way that anything external cannot. Clark counters this by questioning the assumption that the 'inner' is unified. He asks which part of the brain has the final say or whether neural sub-systems ever have a say. Clark believes that to view the agent as some distinct inner locus of final choice and control is deeply mistaken. This is 'to shrink the mind and self beyond recognition' (Clark 2008). The source of the self cannot be found, he says, in mental states that happen to be controlling action at some particular point in time.

The extended-mind hypothesis conjures up a functional system of 'information flow' without a clear-cut boundary around mind. Clark (2008) concedes that it is not easy to achieve a consensus amongst philosophers and scientists about the distribution of minds and mentality in nature and cultural artefacts. Clark does not want to ditch the concept of the mental altogether, suggesting that 'there will be a science that needs to cover a wide variety of mechanistic bases, reaching out to biological brains, and to the wider social and technological milieus that (I claim) participate in thought and reason' (Clark 2008).

Clark's arguments do seem to imply an agent that is presumably a unique biological organism or person. His emphasis on trustworthy information (internal or external) that guides reasoning and behaviour implies that the information is trusted by an organism and used for some purpose or other. Any functional account of human behaviour seems bound to acknowledge the organism as a functional sub-system. It is hard to conceive of the evolution of the human brain without supposing (1) that the brain is a discrete organ with its own internal systemic principles of organisation, and (2) that whole organisms, as unique entities, rely on external sensory information with the consequence that some of them with advantageous characteristics survive to reproduce more successfully. However, at some point in our evolution, it seems likely that ancestral humans identified each other as individuals belonging to social categories. Social categorisation might have been associated with new conceptions of agency that referred to non-individual powers (the divine, the spiritual, the mental, etc.). This would have had the effect of extending the causal influence of the environment beyond the 'niche creation' typical of most animals (see Chapter 12).

The extended-mind hypothesis could be interpreted as extending the cognitivist assumption that the mind is a self-sufficient system of formal properties and functional relationships. On this conception, cognitive science does not attempt to account for the *semantic* features of mind (e.g., the content of beliefs), a task that would have to be assigned to additional historical analysis. If the extended-mind hypothesis is cognitive in this sense, cognitive assumptions simply have to be broadened out to include functional relationships in the environment. Would this conception of the extended mind be vulnerable to the criticisms that Wittgenstein directed at the possibility of an autonomous science of psychology?

In Wittgenstein's footsteps, Meredith Williams (1985) has trenchantly criticised the cognitivist view, and, by extension, we might conclude that her criticisms apply also to the extended mind. In essence, she argues that semantic mental content can only be individuated in a social process. A mind, as a set of modular closed systems, could only be understood as operating in a predictable fashion on predetermined types of sensory input. Williams argues that this does not accurately describe mind, which is, instead, heterogeneous. She concludes that a cognitive conception of a unified and autonomous science of psychology is untenable, thereby undermining any claim it might have to be an independent *component* in a monistic scientific account of reality.

In my view, Wittgenstein did point to a universal mechanism of sorts, that is, the manner in which psychological properties are acquired, even if he left it up to ideographic analysis to elucidate what any local folk psychology might amount to. In line with this perspective, I will take it that the extended-mind hypothesis expands our conception of what we need to include in a unified science of human beings but does not remove the need for a situated, historical analysis of any particular psychology.

Having made a case for discarding (1) the Cartesian notion of a mind composed of states and (2) the assumption that states of mind can be explained as brain states, I will go on to consider the implications of this position for scientific conceptions of human agency, for the development of a 'self' in childhood and for accounts that have been given of the way apes evolved into humans.

10   Self, person as agent and natural causation

A person's agency – that is, their power to act with deliberation according to the demands of a situation – is difficult to reconcile with naturalism. One contentious issue is how we can be both naturally determined and morally responsible. I will deal with the subject of agency very broadly and try to put the question of causality in a philosophical and historical context. Personists assign the power of agency to the person. This leaves them with the task of explaining how persons can be causes and how the agency of persons differs from the agency of animals. Sub-personal theories have to show how an 'executive mechanism' in the mind or brain can account for the sense people have of being aware of their reasons for acting and their belief that it is *they* who are in control. Supra-personal accounts of agency face similar problems in so far as they dissolve distinctions between events caused by persons acting intentionally and natural processes taking place between persons. And when agency is explained as the product of social practices and social structures, the sense of a person having any autonomous control seems to disappear.

Some psychologists, such as Jack Martin and Jeff Sugarman (2003), take a middle position between biological and cultural determinism. They adopt a systems view (see Chapter 13) in which levels of reality are nested. Martin and Sugarman nest psychology within society and culture, and they conceive of agency as an emergent psychological property that can independently feed back on society. This view would be compatible with naturalism if a mechanism of emergence for agency could be found. A concept of emergence seems to be needed to avoid reducing agency to sub-personal mechanisms. I assume (see Chapter 11) that infants, even if innately predisposed to become agents, acquire agency in the full sense when parents and carers treat them as agents. A child cannot acquire agency by exercising *personal* capacities that it does not yet possess. Consequently, I will maintain that agency is a property that emerges out of interactions between persons, and it is the latter who also transmit its historical character.

191

As already noted, sociologists are confronted with the problem of reconciling the relative autonomy of individual and social processes and their interaction. In an extensive review, Mustafa Emirbayer and Ann Mische (1998) detail sociological opinion. They believe that a 'radical reconceptualisation' of agency is needed and base their own analysis on a set of descriptive dimensions. While insisting that agency, as we now conceive it, is a product of history, they also seem to be proposing agency as a universal process (or dimension?) that takes variable historical forms. They conceive of the 'transpersonal context' as a constraining factor and situate the origin of agency in 'self-dynamics' (1998: 974). If they are correct, agency needs to be conceptualised jointly at suprapersonal, personal and sub-personal levels. However, Emirbayer and Mische do not show how agency is related to personhood (except for certain historical associations) and do not attempt to deal with subpersonal (biological) mechanisms.

I do not intend to be drawn into philosophical debates about free will versus determinism. I will simply take it that human agency is compatible with naturalism and discuss some of the problems encountered when working out the implications of this position. Although belief in a God-given free will has declined, most people still maintain that they can freely tailor-make their life according to personally chosen designs. This is one of the foundation stones of the autocentric perspective, and autonomy is essential to the western concept of self. As Charles Taylor sees it, we cannot escape making sense of our lives in terms of a framework of beliefs and values that, in some sense, we have personally chosen. In orienting ourselves to a concept of 'the good', he thinks that we see our life in story form. Taylor states that this is 'an inescapable structural requirement of human agency' (1989: 52). The alternative for him would be an amoral existence in which people choose only on the basis of natural likes and dislikes, desires and aversions. He presents the alternatives as a cultural/moral order versus a natural order that reduces people to the level of animals. My aim is to muddy this distinction rather than take up one of his options.

Westerners tend to feel most fulfilled as a self when they exercise their power to act. Determined, decisive and 'in charge of themself', are all positive attributes unless they spill over into obstinacy. The question 'Who are you?' is often answered by a list of things a person has done or intends to do. Our institutions are built around the assumption that people consider their options, make choices as rational agents and act on them. It is generally expected that the choices people make will accord with prevailing notions of what it is sensible for people to do. Anomalous or eccentric choices may be tolerated, but we still expect to be able to trace their links to an understandable rationale. If we cannot, we may simply regard the person as mad.

I think it is also generally accepted that the capacity to choose rationally and morally is rather fragile. In the first place, we are constantly reminded that some of our behaviour, like eye blinks and swallowing reflexes, does not distinguish us from animals. And human desire, like a desire for affection, while less obviously reflexive, is often compared to a biological force and experienced as beyond personal control. In the second place, it is recognised that rational acts, and even moral sensitivities, can develop into rigid habits or compulsions. They lose the quality of being freely chosen. While freedom and choice are often flagged up as uniquely human, we do not see as much need to explain these phenomena naturalistically as we do when a person's acts cease to be rational or sensible. However, there seem to be no good grounds for producing a different kind of explanation for how a sense of freedom can be fostered and how it can be lost. The only clear-cut exceptions would be cases of organic disorder or addiction to chemical substances. In any event, the traditional framing of the issue as a battle between animal passions and human reason seems to be inadequate.

The expectation that people will act reasonably on the basis of their beliefs and desires belongs to explanation at the personal level. But in order to enact a reasoned choice, sub-personal mechanisms are needed to explain how the body functions to sustain the chosen activity. Sub-personal mechanisms are also typically invoked, correctly or not, to explain dysfunctions and compulsive habits. The supra-personal level of explanation is more rarely introduced to explain human agency although Daniel Dennett appears to do so in his book *Freedom Evolves* (2003). Wolfgang Prinz (2006) and Guy Claxton (2005) take a similar view, but all three authors seem to be wedded to the primacy of sub-personal mechanisms that, in my view, undermine their own thesis (see below). Before proceeding to discuss natural theories of agency, I will give a brief historical survey of how agency became a philosophical and scientific issue. Human volition and reason were formerly understood within a theocentric perspective on the world. They were not personal attributes by virtue of the fact that people were persons; they were granted to people on the grounds that they participated in a divinely constructed universe. Seen in this way, it would have made little sense to explain them personally or sub-personally.

Historical development of the ideas of reason and will

In the opinion of Hannah Arendt (1906–75), the concept of volition did not arise until well into the post-classical era:

[T]he idea of freedom changed from being a word indicating a political status – that of a free citizen and not a slave – and a physical fact – that of a healthy man whose body was not paralysed but able to obey his mind – into a word indicating an inner disposition by virtue of which a man could feel free when he was actually a slave or unable to move his limbs. (Arendt 1978: 30)

Arendt links volition to a new conception of time and a new conception of the agent. Her thesis is that the concept of time in Ancient Greece was cyclical, and, as with night and day, birth and death, all was repeated in an endless cycle without beginning or end. In this folk cosmology, the idea that people shape their future is likely to be greatly diminished. Arendt (1978: 15) points out that Aristotle conceived of human affairs as accidental or contingent rather than essential and necessary. So, even when mankind produced something original, Aristotle considered the new creation to have pre-existed as a 'potentiality' before being actualised by human hands. These beliefs clearly undermine the idea that humans have a role in choosing their own future. This does not mean that the Ancient Greeks failed to recognise that they could exercise a preference, or did not distinguish voluntary from involuntary acts. However, these were underdeveloped notions from a modern standpoint. Arendt believes that it was Aristotle's concept of *proairesis* (in Latin *liberum arbitrium*) that opened the way to free will. Proairesis was a faculty of choice that Aristotle developed to solve the problem of how a person arbitrates between reason and desire, *both* of which for him were unmediated and compelling. This 'opens up a first, small restricted space of the human mind, which without it was delivered to two opposed compelling forces' (Arendt 1978: 62).

Arendt notes that Christianity introduced a rectilinear concept of time. The world had a beginning, and singular, non-repeatable events, such as Christ's death and resurrection, influenced the future. Eventually, a calendar was developed with Christ's birth set at time zero. According to Christian belief, everything that happens is under God's oversight, and people would have been naturally reluctant to assume that their actions had much significance in the larger picture. However, as Christianity developed, it promised an individual resurrection. Whereas for the Greeks what mattered was the eternity of heroic values and the civic state, in Christianity the possibility of eternal life for the individual person was now raised. To earn this, the individual had to commit to doing good and being good in this life. The future then really became an issue for the individual person.

In Arendt's interpretation, Saint Paul was instrumental in stressing a person's mental disposition towards obeying divine law. In face of the impossibility of obeying law at all times ('evil dwells within'), it was not enough just to obey law but to voluntarily submit to obedience – to say, in effect, that whatever I feel compelled to do, or have done, I can still *will* to be obedient or disobedient. This was thought to be necessary in order to be forgiven through God's mercy. The philosophy of volition was developed by Saint Augustine (354–430) who also stressed that freedom of the will was an inner power of affirmation or negation, rather than an ability to put an act into effect. The importance of a disposition to act is implied by present-day concepts of being a person of goodwill or ill-will. Similar considerations were evident in Stoic philosophy. People could be educated to determine what attitude they would take to reality, or to their own distress, regardless of what was actually happening to them. For Christians and Stoics, self-monitoring and self-control were encouraged for religious and ethical reasons, or simply to achieve a calm and tranquil life.

The Christian way of construing agency, perhaps like any construction, has some paradoxical implications. In Christian doctrine it is God who invests humans with the faculty of free will – the freedom, in other words, to choose between good and bad acts. This causes theological problems in so far as God is thought to be all-knowing and would presumably design human affairs to preclude evil. Why then should he have ordained evil if he wanted humans to choose good? Some evils, like earthquakes, appear to have nothing to do with human intentions, and so they have been designated Acts of God to absolve humans from possible involvement in causing them. However, this has not stopped human beings reading divine reason into natural disasters, for example, as a collective punishment for wrongdoing. Some Christian sects have escaped the heavy consequences of free will by assuming that they are members of an elect group, chosen by God, who will go to Heaven regardless of the evil they perpetrate in this life. It seems that however the human capacity for choice is conceptualised, it is likely to lead to paradox and special pleading.

It is of interest, as well, to trace back the modern concept of reason to its origins in a theocentric world. According to Taylor (1989: 115–26), Plato was influential in shaping the much later western view of mind as an *inner* location and in the possession of a person. Plato thought that people should aspire to perceive the world rationally, as it really is, an ordered world of eternal Truth and Goodness. To place oneself in harmony with this external reality, it was necessary for people to employ their reason to exert mastery over their capricious and insatiable desires. Taylor argues that Plato's view, 'because it privileges a condition of self-collected awareness and designates this as the state of maximum unity with oneself, requires some conception of the mind as a unitary space' (1989: 119). As Taylor points out, we often talk about being swept away (by passion, excitement, etc.) from this special location. A plurality of loci for thought and feeling becomes a kind of error or moral lapse.

Taylor makes clear that Plato's vision of truth, morality and order belongs to the cosmos. Thus, in developing their wisdom and their harmony with the cosmos, people had to aim to be connected in the right way with something external. But they do not start off in an 'inner place'; Taylor believes that the process of internalising the mind arose out of later developments in the early modern period that placed the powers of reason within the person. In the interim period, the move to a concept of an internal location was aided by Stoic philosophers of the classical period who viewed reason in a more practical way: as a means to correct false opinions about the nature of the Good. A decisive transition was St Augustine's integration of Greek thought with Christian theology.

As Taylor sees it, St Augustine projected a vision of the eternal, the good and the true onto the Christian God; experience of God's presence inspired love for him. In the Christian worldview, Plato's concept of an immortal and immaterial soul has been individualised as a personal soul that is promised an afterlife in Heaven if certain conditions are met (baptism, faith in God, confession of sins, etc.). It was by the grace of God that a person was endowed with a soul, and along with it came the soul's power of reason. Reason was seen by St Augustine as an inner light that was implanted by God as a potential to judge rightly. Augustine believed that it was necessary to be self-reflective to find God. Reason 'illuminates that space where I am present to myself' (Taylor 1989: 131). God was the source of the light because God was the fundamental ordering principle within the soul. God's light was a kind of inner eye, and, therefore, a person found God, or 'saw the light', through self-reflection in an act of knowing. This truth was not seen as a personal attribute because it was God who animated the soul. Augustine taught that it was necessary to turn inward and reflect on the truths that God had implanted. Reflection was necessary because truth may be distorted by false images. However, Augustine believed that when the truth was witnessed, it would automatically inspire a love for God.

The transformation of reason into a personal attribute took place in succeeding centuries as natural philosophy transformed the image of the world as God-given to a Nature subject to its own laws. It was possible to know these laws by the application of 'ordinary powers' of human reasoning. Reason became an instrumental power to exert control over nature, including the passions of 'human nature'. The soul was naturalised as a self-sufficient attribute of the person, and reason was exercised in an inner space, the so-called mind. In order to follow this story to the present, we need to consider how volition became a faculty of mind and how it entered into theories in the human sciences. I will also consider how it came to be criticised by personists such as Gilbert Ryle. Before doing so, I will outline some common presuppositions about agency as expressed in ordinary discourse.

Agency in everyday discourse

I think it would be hard to maintain that people have any clear idea about how they acquire a sense of personal agency or why it is that they sometimes lose it. In the human sciences too, there is no agreed theoretical explanation for the loss of a person's power of agency when they act 'compulsively' or 'irrationally'. People may express strong opinions about what acts are within a person's capacity to control (for which they are likely to be held accountable), but people make a variety of causal attributions about behaviour like drinking heavily, being a poor parent, gambling or driving dangerously. Of course, certain criteria for being normally competent are laid down in law but these, in turn, depend on judgements that are rather difficult to make, like being in possession of one's reason and knowing what one is doing.

There is a strong and a weak sense of talking about one's actions as controlled by oneself. In the weak sense, people recognise their actions as their own whether or not they intended to produce them. For instance, a person might refer to an unauthored act as follows: 'I didn't mean to say it, it just came out.' It is their own act but not one they intended to produce. Unauthored actions can vary from harmless sneezes through to overwhelming compulsions that are disowned and unwanted. In the strong sense of agency, an act is deliberately chosen. However, even chosen acts seem to vary in the extent to which a person endorses them as their own. People sometimes say that they assent to their compulsive habits rather than succumb to them.

The strong sense of agency seems to be closely related to a person's idea of their ideal self. A person acts so as to constitute and strengthen that 'self' and may realise that certain acts have weakened it. The western ideal of an autonomous person is usually understood to mean someone who shapes their actions to conform to the kind of self they would like to express. However, people are sometimes rather circumspect when claiming authorship for expressions of a desired self. For instance, a person might be remarkably competent at doing something but still say: 'It's a gift – I don't know how I do it.' Or a person assigns authorship by default: 'I suppose I must have done it.' People may fail to act in the strong sense of agency when they expect it of themselves or others expect it of them. Under these circumstances, people might discount authorship, perhaps claiming that their action was caused by a disorder or an inherited defect for which they were not responsible. Alternatively, a person might believe that their deficiencies really do define their self: 'I am useless, inept, and it's my fault.'

On all of the aforementioned grounds, it becomes difficult to draw a sharp boundary between acts that are willed or intended and those that are not. Causal attributions are often negotiated or made retrospectively. We cannot simply rely on the fact that a person 'felt' that their act was intended. It is common to question people by saying: 'Yes, but did you really *mean* to do it, say it, etc.' Bertram Malle (2006: 209) argues that we have to demonstrate folk concepts empirically, by systematic description and analysis. However, he later draws an unproblematic distinction between those acts that are attributed to the agent's reasons (intentional acts) and those behaviours (unintentional) that have mechanical causes or do not involve awareness or choice (2006: 217). Although people do classify in this way, the distinction seems too neatly drawn. People do believe that they direct their own lives, but there is still plenty of room for direction by God or by external or alien forces. Belief in the magic arts has not disappeared. Some personal powers are described as being of a mixed intended/unintended kind. The poet might think that they are the instrument of a muse but still set to work to polish up the words that first came by inspiration. It is too easy to conceptualise western notions of agency narrowly, leaving out concepts of self-understanding that include being possessed, chaotic, divided, compelled and so forth.

Even more suspect is the idea that intention can be detected as a mental state. Malle (2006: 219) says that there is no evidence that 'will' is actually a folk concept, but he does believe that there is a folk concept of intentional agency (i.e. acts done on purpose) that includes an awareness of fulfilling the intention. Granted that this is so, it is not quite the same as claiming that people are aware of 'mental states' such as *experiencing* a desire for something, a reason to want it and a belief that it can be achieved. However, in his critique of some natural-science experiments on human agency, Malle does think it justifiable to speak of mental experiences and how long they last. For instance, he distinguishes between the time it takes to experience a 'desire to act' from the time it takes 'to act consciously' on that desire. But unless we can really measure these episodes of mental activity, they are merely speculative. Nevertheless, Malle is surely right to deny that the experience of intending an action is an illusion or that conscious thought has no role to play in causing actions (2006: 222).

The usual starting point for an investigation in natural science is a fairly well defined and empirically observable phenomenon, but these requirements are hardly met in studies of human agency. Given the powerful influence of mindism and a long history of western thought about free will and a mental faculty of volition, the search for 'executive mechanisms' could be interpreted as simply a continuation of that philosophical and religious tradition. Without these historical antecedents, it seems unlikely that scientists would have searched for the neural correlates of an act of decision. It might be preferable to set causal questions about agency into the broader context of animal behaviour and to attempt to explain differences between animals and humans with respect to the initiation and maintenance of action. For example, what are the causal antecedents that distinguish between a primate deciding to request a banana from a machine by pressing an icon (see Chapter 12) and a person deciding to buy a banana in a shop?

An examination of neural activity in primate and human brains may not get us very far in answering this question. A more obvious difference concerns the variety of conditions that influence behaviour in humans, such as the cost of bananas, whether they are grown by a multinational or by local small producers, the nutritional value of bananas, and so on. The neural mechanisms relating to the control of behaviour are certainly of interest in both primates and humans, but searching for the distinctive properties of human agency at this level may not be very fruitful.

Viewed historically, the chief interest in human agency has revolved around what makes humans unique in the animal world. These concerns can be traced back, as we have seen, to Plato, Augustine and others. Modern philosophers, such as Harry Frankfurt (1988) have continued to pursue these ancient questions and have analysed criteria for referring to an act as freely chosen. Frankfurt can be interpreted as developing Augustine's line of reasoning that free will is connected with an attitude towards one's choices. He makes the point that we wouldn't want to say that a person exercised freedom of choice when they merely acted on their desires, any more than we would want to say that an animal 'freely' fulfilled a desire. He reserves the concept of freely choosing to what he defines as second-order wants. The want is second-order because it consists of wanting to want something and knowing that this want could be expressed in future action. The primate who presses the icon for a banana just happens to want it. It is not, it seems, expressing an attitude to this want in future. Unlike the primate, the human is sensitive to a much wider range of conditions (temporal and spatial) in which the want is expressed or suppressed.

Frankfurt views the capacity for second-order wants as essential to our idea of being a person. He would argue that young children, responding to their impulse of the moment, do not yet possess this capacity. Freedom of choice is being in a position to compare and evaluate our choices and to translate first-order wants into actions (i.e. literally being free to do as one pleases). A person who 'does not know what they want' would be deprived of freedom of choice on this criterion, and also their personhood, because they could not translate first-order wants into action.

Frankfurt's concept of 'wanting to want' may be essential to personhood and morality, but, according to Taylor (1977), it doesn't give enough significance to the 'strong evaluations' that he considers to be so important in personal identity, such as the moral virtues, family honour, etc. After all, criminals also want to want things. I will not pursue this line of thought, which would take me off the main topic, and so I will turn now to the influence of mindism on philosophical and naturalistic accounts of agency.

Mindist accounts of agency

Contemporary concepts of person, mind, volition and reason are very closely interconnected. The inclination of scientists has been to take mind as a given and to seek sub-personal explanations for volition. Philosophical conceptions of personhood also exert a strong influence on an understanding of volition. Descartes had equated the person with a thinker and denied reason to animals. The reasons for intended acts came to be seen as originating in the minds of persons. In John Locke's philosophy, the identity and continuity of a person were made to depend on the contents of the mind, as if those mental contents were mental states that could subsist independently of the person who experienced them. Voluntary action was the power to form 'preferences of the mind' and 'to do or forbear any particular action' in light of them

(Locke 1959: 113). The Lockean model of personal identity has been developed by philosophers such as Darek Parfit (1984) and Michael Bratman (2007).

A mindist assumes that the mind is a part of the person that possesses the power to select and execute acts. On this view, a person's actual act is preceded by a mental act that the mind performs rather than the person. For instance, I may be pretty sure I can decide to get up in the morning or stay in bed and that this decision depends on a mental act of choosing.

William James discusses this very situation in a passage from his book, *The Principles of Psychology* (1890). He imagined getting out of bed in an unheated room on a frosty morning, wondering whether he would ever muster the resolve to get up rather than lie there cosily under the blankets. He put the capacity to act down to a kind of momentary and fortunate amnesia for warmth and cold and the capture of his consciousness by the clear idea of what he had to do that day, untrammelled by competing contradictory and paralysing suggestions. James describes well what 'passes through the mind', and we should, like him, reject the idea that mental activity is unconnected with action. But James does not actually describe a mental act consisting of a decision to get up. His general point seems to be that vividly recalled ideas or memory images simply cause a person to act. This is to suppose that 'mental events' act as causes in a stand-alone fashion.

The weakness of James's argument is shown by the ease with which counterexamples can be produced. There are, for example, unfortunate individuals who endlessly juggle their thoughts, and these thoughts do not issue in a positive act. Or, if the individual does act, they reverse their previous decision by 'changing their mind' and doing the opposite thing. It seems that the only way we can judge whether someone acts decisively on the basis of their reasons for acting is by noting what they actually do, regardless of the thoughts they entertain. Entertaining thoughts may play a causal role, but it is not an adequate explanation for choice.

In James's scenario, whatever passes through the mind, a person must at some point jump out of bed. An employer would not be content to hear about mental struggles and good intentions – an employer wants to see that person sitting physically at a desk. The employee might come to the conclusion that they are conscientious and only rarely laze in bed, but it is only in retrospect that this can be known for certain. This is not to deny the existence of good intentions to go to work on time. But in the wider social context, what probably gets a person out of bed is the mortgage that must be paid, what others would think if that person were to stay in bed, the tediousness of lying endlessly in bed, and so forth. These distal causes, even if mentally represented, are not simply mental causes of an act of getting up. They are real events that are likely to befall a person. They may be supplemented by actual proximal causes such as opening bank statements in bed or having the bedclothes removed. These distal and proximal events are directed towards a person, and they have real consequences. From a natural-science standpoint, it is more reasonable to suppose that these are amongst the major causes of a person getting up rather than the thoughts through which the reasons for getting up are mentally represented.

The existence of mental acts of volition is one of the chief targets for attack in Gilbert Ryle's well-known book, *The Concept of Mind* (1949: 62–82). Ryle does not deny that we deliberate, choose and act in the light of reasons. Ryle is concerned to show that voluntary and involuntary acts are routinely distinguished on the basis of what can be publicly observed, for instance, actual behaviour, the situation, the kind of act and what we know about the agent's competence to do something. Ryle says that we do not need to refer to the occurrence of any episode in a person's stream of consciousness, such as a 'volition', a mental event that precedes a choice. He maintains that this concept is a myth, largely on the basis that no one ever describes their conduct in this idiom. Doing something deliberately can be adequately described, he says, in action terms such as paying heed, not relaxing one's efforts and resisting temptations to abandon a task. He argues that, in any case, we can only infer the existence of volition in another person from their observed acts, that is, after the fact. We recognise intended acts when we see them, but we don't see volitions. Volition may be a useful abstraction to cover intended acts, but, for Ryle, to speak of *a* volition as a mental act would be to commit a category mistake. Volition is a person's disposition to behave in a certain way, not a mental event.

Ryle argues that we are more likely to pay attention to involuntary acts, or acts of omission, than to willed acts. This is the case when a person fails to act within their competence and is therefore potentially culpable. For example, we do not take note of the freely chosen acts of mothers who love their babies, but we are concerned with a failure to show motherly love when we expect it and see no obstacle to its demonstration. The belief that an act is freely chosen has been defined as a belief that a person could have acted otherwise, but, for many routine or conventional actions this belief is purely theoretical – it is never tested out. In a different world in which devotion to babies was seen as a weakness, mothers might be classified as suffering from a compulsion to love their babies.

I will follow Ryle in claiming that the classification of a type of action as intended can be taken to mean that it is the kind of act that people are generally expected to be capable of intending. Although we may have this expectation, a person might fall short and be shown to be incapable of 'acting freely'. Ryle's emphasis on public criteria for classifying acts as voluntary and involuntary shifts the burden of explanation onto the social processes that lead to voluntary behaviour and the way in which such action is construed. A period of acculturation is needed before a child can be said to produce voluntary acts. We may routinely treat young infants as if they were persons, but we do not expect them to have all the volitional powers of an adult.

Although Ryle tells us where to look for public evidence of volition, he does not thereby furnish us with an explanation as to why some individuals possess a behavioural disposition to pay heed, put in effort, etc., and others do not. He gives no empirical theory of volition. This leaves it open to the mindist to accuse Ryle of behavioural reductionism and to argue that internal (sub-personal) organismic events are still needed to provide a causal explanation of the disposition (Sprague 1999: 114–15). Sprague counters this objection by denying that a person's acts can be detached from the actor as if there are human acts in the abstract for which separate causes must be produced. Sprague admits that a person learns how to act in a certain way by attending to the practices and procedures for doing so. However, at the level of description appropriate for acts, it is logical to ascribe them to the person.

Voluntary acts could be said to be voluntary because the individual and others perceive them in this manner. They are not acts that can be divorced from personal evaluation. However, we need not conclude from this that voluntary and involuntary actions cannot be distinguished in terms of mechanisms at the personal and sub-personal level. And it is obvious that a person has to rely on all sorts of mechanisms of perception and motor control in order to exercise their agency. On this view, the personal level of explanation does not preclude the sub-personal but is not reducible to it.

The causal factors I cited in the decision to get out of bed in the morning might be seen as ruling out any role for a person *forming an intention* to act. An intention doesn't seem to be needed if a person is just responding to the longer-term consequences of either getting up or not getting up. On this view, by getting up reliably, a person simply recognises retrospectively that getting up is part of their repertoire of voluntary acts. And if a person persists in saying that they *really tried* to get up, and fails to do so, the belief is formed, all round, that the person is incapable of acting freely in this regard. However, in reasonably familiar circumstances, people do manage to predict reliably what they are capable of doing when they try to do it and are able to state the circumstances in which their volitional powers are exercised. The causal efficacy of an intention to act could be attributed to the past consequences of an act while at the same time a person quite reasonably claims to be acting on the basis of desires and beliefs. There is no need to suppose that the process is a series of mental events that are the sufficient causes for the intended act.

Johannes Roessler (2003: 386) points out that there is also a sense in which a person can have a purely practical grasp of what they are capable of accomplishing without having any first-person thoughts about it, e.g., they can treat an object as 'within reach' without thinking that it is within *their* reach. He suggests that infants' grasp of the causal significance of their own actions may be practical in this sense. Later, an infant becomes *reflectively* aware of intending to perform certain acts.

Roessler rejects the idea that when a person is reflectively aware of intending, they are, first, introspectively aware of the intention and then, second, perceive that the intention has been translated into the act. This way of conceiving of intending suggests a third-person spectator attitude with respect to oneself. Roessler argues instead for 'direct self-awareness'. In his example of driving a car and intending to take the next left turn, there is no further decision to act on the perceived information when the junction appears – the driver simply expects to see when to turn (Roessler 2003: 392). On this account, personal and sub-personal explanations are combined. But as Roessler states: 'it is rational to form an intention only if you think you will (or at least may) be able to execute it' (2003: 393). Presumably, a belief of this kind depends on a retrospective analysis of previous acts, which, in some cases, is a non-reflective registration of perceptual feedback and, in other cases, a deliberate review of the evidence. There is a sequential blending of personal and sub-personal events rather than a strict division between 'willed acts' and 'automatic responses'. Roessler (2003: 394) also points out that being irritated with oneself on perceiving the consequences of certain automatically controlled responses (e.g., driving into the left-hand turn too fast) demonstrates a personal-level evaluation that continually monitors the sub-personally mediated response.

What turns this evaluation of perceptual feedback into a person-level act is the introduction of inferences that relate to wider self-referential beliefs. For instance, a person might reflect that they have no wish to be killed when cornering. But to be in possession of a sense of voluntary control over one's safety is to know (i.e. directly from previous experiences of driving) that cornering at a slower speed will render one safe. However, the person-level inference seems to require an explanation that differs from an *automatic* sub-personal mechanism that provides perceptual feedback of the consequences of cornering at different speeds.

The 'mental acts' approach to understanding volition still has its exponents. According to Myles Brand (1984), the traditional notion of free will is a free, uncaused mental act, a volition, causing us to do A rather than B. One reason why Brand takes this notion seriously is that he sees problems in viewing the embodied person as the human agent. His objection is that it is unclear what an agent is. If it is a substance, he asks how a substance can cause human acts since substances and acts belong to different logical categories. But this line of thinking continues the dualist assumption that a person is a mind plus a body, and so, if mental acts are denied, only the material body remains as a cause. Abandoning dualism, we can say that persons simply are agents who happen to express their acts through their body. In the respect of being active organisms, we resemble the higher primates and other animals. We may not wish to assign self-conscious choice to primates, but we simply accept that being active in different ways is part of their nature, as it is ours.

Richard Williams (1992) also presents us with a stark choice between a causal realm of things and a human realm of discourse that is concerned with morality and being true to oneself. In order to illustrate his argument, he says that an act of charity would lose its meaning if it were to be analysed as the necessary effect of some necessary set of causes. Part of the meaning of an act of charity is that it doesn't *need* to happen – charity cannot be *compelled*. However, this argument assumes that a natural scientist has to reduce moral compulsion to the manner in which one billiard ball compels another to move in a particular direction. But in complex and dynamic living systems, there is no reason to assume that an act is determined in the manner of a billiard ball. If Williams objects to naturalism *in principle,* then there is, of course, no possible response. Williams believes that if an action is naturally caused, 'it is worthy of neither blame nor praise' (1992: 758). However, it is just not clear why any natural scientist should give up praising and blaming actions on the grounds that they hold to the position of naturalism.

A different strand of mindist thinking derives from John Locke's views on personal identity. It leads to the conclusion that agency is a sub-personal mental faculty or brain mechanism. Derek Parfit's views have been particularly influential (Parfit 1984). He has developed the arguments of empiricist philosophers and linked them more closely with the brain. He accepts the Lockean view that a person is defined by psychological continuities in mental contents (including memory) but goes on to claim that these continuities are not fixed, although they must overlap sufficiently from one life stage to the next. This largely depends, he says, on having enough of the same brain to maintain this continuity and a body in which the brain can function. In other words, he assumes that a brain in a body is a sufficient cause of psychological continuity. Included within Parfit's continuities are intentions to act that get translated into future acts. In other words, psychological continuity depends on agency, which for Parfit is a function of a brain.

In one of his many thought experiments, Parfit entertains the possibility of a person's brain being divided into two halves and transplanted into two separate bodies. If there was sufficient psychological continuity, so he maintains, it would be legitimate to argue that one person had become two – numerically different but qualitatively the same persons. Parfit's work is a conceptual analysis of the criteria we apply when granting personhood, but he also makes sweeping assumptions about the role of the brain. Apart from some incidental remarks, he leaves out any mention of the role of other people and of society in making a necessary natural causal contribution to personhood and agency. His stand-alone brain/mind is no less hypothetical than his idea of being tele-transported to Mars (the basis of another of his thought experiments). As Sprague (1999) remarks, Parfit is claiming that experiences and brains can be impersonal – they do not have to belong to any particular person. This is a very strange notion, and, in my view, a continuing sense of person/self must include particular other persons.

For instance, Parfit would agree that in the case of the divided brain, a person would not continue to exist as two identical selves because their new environments would be different. He would presumably have to say that any new social environment would do just as well as any other as a home for each person because, for him, *particular* other people are not necessary for the maintenance of personhood. In order to go along with Parfit, we would have to assume that the new social environments provided sufficient psychological continuity to be able to refer to the same person. But if in a new environment no one is willing to confirm a person's beliefs (e.g., they are treated as completely deluded), can personal continuity be maintained? The brain and its former intentions would be of little help in these circumstances. In Parfit's terms, are the psychological characteristics sufficiently continuous? The answer is surely no. The agency that guarantees continuity is not just a sub-personal mechanism.

Michael Bratman, a philosopher of agency, also refers explicitly to a Lockean conception of the person. He wants to develop a theory of agency that is 'fully embedded in an event causal order' (Bratman 2007: 22). In line with Frankfurt's views, he presents the problem as getting from the lower-order desires to the higher-order attitudes of persons who endorse or reject those desires. This seems to require an agent who 'must be seen as a separate element in the metaphysics of agency' (Bratman 2007: 24). Bratman believes that positing an independent agent is incompatible with embedding agency in a causal order. He avoids this conclusion by giving 'plans and policies' a basic explanatory role in a theory of human action. In other words, Bratman seems to make the move of attributing agency to sub-personal cognitive mechanisms. Thus, in place of a person who monitors their motivations and plans, he substitutes 'relevant states and attitudes that play appropriate roles in the agent's psychology' (Bratman 2007: 31). Bratman expands this position when he says: 'This makes it natural to suppose that for her to endorse a desire is, roughly, for that desire to be endorsed by attitudes whose role it is to support the temporal organization of her agency by way of constituting and supporting Lockean ties characteristic of her temporal persistence' (2007: 31).

To claim that a person's 'attitudes' endorse an intention is really just a cognitivist translation of the idea that a person's 'will' endorses an intention. It reduces the personal level of explanation to the sub-personal. In order to preserve Bratman's preference for a natural causal interpretation of agency, it would be necessary, in my view, to turn to a supra-personal level of explanation (see below).

Mindist accounts of agency in psychology and neuroscience

I think it is fair to say that many psychologists do not see any theoretical difficulty in assigning agency to persons. Todd Little and colleagues review three psychological approaches to agency and argue that individuals are inherently active and self-regulating (Little et al. 2002: 390). While there is little to disagree with in this statement, their view that 'an individual's actions result from selective choices that emanate primarily from the self' (Little et al. 2002: 390) begs a number of questions. For instance, in 'self-determination theory', actions that are classified as intrinsically motivated 'are done of the self, by the self, and for the self' (Little et al. 2002: 392). In their integration of the three approaches, the authors reduce agency to a cluster of dispositions and biological needs. In this kind of theorising, proposals for universal processes seem to be so deeply intertwined with western cultural assumptions that it becomes impossible to disentangle them.

Some cognitive scientists and neuroscientists have sought to explain human agency in terms of brain events and the circumstances that instigate them. They claim to have discovered the *real* causes of voluntary acts, thereby showing that the experience of willing is an *illusion*. Daniel Wegner has expressed this idea in his book *The Illusion of Conscious Will* (2002). Timothy Bayne (2006) offers a detailed philosophical critique of what Wegner might mean by an illusion of will. First, Bayne says we might wrongly believe that the experience of consciously willing an action *causes* the action. Bayne argues that people do not normally believe this anyway. Second, Wegner could be interpreted as arguing that we have no direct evidence that the experience of willing something causes any act. But Bayne responds that we have many experiences in which there is no *direct* evidence of a causal relationship, although we might still assume, on other grounds, that, for example, light waves striking the eye cause us to see. A third possible interpretation of will as an illusion is that our experience of doing something may be illusory in the sense that it can be proved, in carefully designed experiments, that what we *thought* we were doing was actually performed by someone or something else. Bayne points out that just because examples of an illusory sense of authoring an action can be found, we cannot conclude that *all* of our experiences of being the author of an action are illusory.

Nevertheless, we are left with examples of acts that a person *believes* to have been intended but which, in reality, appear to have been caused by mechanisms of which the agent was entirely unaware. This encourages researchers to suppose that it just *seems* as though we are a self that has the power of agency. Although I have argued that self is virtual, this does not mean that real persons do not possess agentive powers. It is just that self, amongst other entities and forces, is one way people comprehend those powers. Wegner is committed to the idea that authoring an action has complex natural causes and so it is not unreasonable to suppose that authored and unauthored acts have different causal antecedents. Bayne suggests that people need not be committed to any particular kind of account of their power of agency or even what kind of 'causal thing' they are when they cause things to happen (2006: 180). He says it is quite unclear what causal mechanisms actually differentiate authored from unauthored actions. If a causal difference exists, there is likely to be something of a causal nature 'really' going on when a person thinks that a (virtual) self intends and executes an act.

There is other research showing that the reasons people give for, say, choosing something, are often spurious because it can be proved that

other factors have causally influenced their choice without their awareness. One aim of this research is to discredit the mindist assumption
that human acts are preceded by momentary mental states that track
an intention and account for the act. They try to show, instead, that
the act has causal antecedents of which a person may be unaware. For
instance, it can be shown that the reasons a person gives for having
selected one item amongst a group of items are spurious. It can be
demonstrated that the choice is actually related to variations in the
conditions of choosing (e.g., physical arrangements) that predict quite
well what the choice will be (Nisbett and Wilson 1977). The results
of this kind of study are incompatible with a simple mindist assumption that our expressed intentions cause us to act or that our reasons
for acting are necessarily related to the causes of our acts. However, if
there are no sound theoretical reasons for giving credence to the mindist position, the findings of the studies, although certainly interesting,
assume less significance.

However, it would be to fall into a dualist trap to substitute the proximal natural events or conditions (in the brain or the immediate environment) that predict an act's occurrence for the 'real' cause of the act.
A predictive relationship between events leaves wide open the causal
mechanisms that may be needed to explain it. At the very least, distal
as well as proximal events are likely to be implicated. It is most unlikely
that we can simply ignore people's stated reasons and intentions as not
contributing to any causal explanation. People's stated reasons and
intentions have a long causal history that is likely to be relevant to what
they do.

Granted that people do explain their acts with reference to their
reasons and intentions, the question arises as to whether the causally
relevant influences that people identify should demonstrate any logical
connection to other kinds of causal explanation produced by, say, social
or biological theorists. Theories of natural causation do of course influence reasoning. For instance, if I express an intention to lose weight,
it would be inconsistent of me not to exercise and to eat fatty foods. It
is to be expected that people form their intentions on the basis of their
knowledge of natural causation. However, there is no reason, as Malle
(2004: 220) points out, why there should not be natural causes that are
unrelated to the content of intentions, especially when people could not
be expected to have any knowledge of them. Malle says that a person
can make meaningful choices without needing to know, or wanting to
know, the causal history of their choices.

However, if the criteria for describing an act as intended are publicly
shared, the criteria are likely to be connected with widely understood

natural constraints on human behaviour. In a game of tennis, I might claim to have originated a brilliant shot, and my opponent might claim it was a fluke. To prove that I was really trying, I could attempt to justify my return shot as a finely honed skill by showing that I was naturally capable of repeating it. Public criteria for an intentional attribution often entail knowledge of natural causation and also concrete evidence, that has to be applied correctly in the circumstances. The fact that the reasons for intended acts may be based on false causal reasoning does not make them any less intended.

Some scientists have denied a causal role for intention on the grounds that a better causal explanation can be found in brain mechanisms. Experimental evidence has been produced to suggest that our self-reported intentions to act do not correspond in the required way with recordings of brain activity (see Malle 2004: 207–31). The findings have been taken to prove that people report their intentions *too late* to account for the initiation of their stated actions. In one of these studies (Libet 2000), the participants had their brain electrical patterns measured at the same time as they flexed their wrist at roughly self-chosen times. The participants noted when they initially became aware of wanting to flex their wrist and read off the timing of these moments from a rotating clock display. The main finding was that there were characteristic brain changes *before* the participants ever even noticed becoming aware of wanting to flex their wrist (the difference in timing was very small of course).

The rationale of these studies rests on an assumption that an intention to act is a mental event with a direct correlate in the brain. However, if we consider behaviour interpersonally and acknowledge a wide array of natural causes of human acts, there is no need to suppose that the momentary neural events that are precisely correlated with any particular act are 'its cause'. This would potentially contract the scope of any causal theory to an infinitely brief period of time. And if, instead of a 'mental cause', it is supposed that neurons 'make our decisions' for us, it is hard to interpret what this means. It may make sense to say that neural control mechanisms operate automatically (on our behalf) in the case of, say, a change in pupil size with changes in light intensity. But only persons make decisions in a literal sense. Neurons do not act on the outside world: their relationship to the world outside the brain is mediated by impulses in afferent and efferent nerves. These, in turn, are related to the resources of the body that a person has to employ in stating intentions and acting on them. And if the classification of an act as intended is mediated by the evaluations of other persons, intended acts only make sense in a supra-personal social world.

Supra-personal accounts of agency

In my view, the supra-personal level is implicated in agency if intended acts are, in part, an effect of the natural causal effect of one human being on another acting as whole organisms. This level is relevant to the evolutionary origins of personhood. In his book *Freedom Evolves*, Dennett (2003) provides an explanation of this kind. The general thrust of the argument is that ancestral humans who believed in free will would have had survival advantages – or at least this belief would have conferred advantages if shared by members of a social group who were genetically related. It certainly makes sense to hold a version of a belief in free will. As Dennett says, if we were all fatalists, believing that whatever we decided to do was determined by a roulette wheel spun by God, our inclination to praise or blame, or to attempt anything new, would diminish to vanishing point.

Dennett also argues that acts we understand to be freely willed can be explained as naturally caused. One step in the evolution of free will might have been an awareness of the possibility of cultivating freedom rather than letting it happen 'naturally' through child-rearing and social intercourse. Educational practices refine choice by controlling natural inclinations and fostering behaviour that is only weakly related to bio-logical impulses. Dennett's ideas, as best I understand them, imply that believing we are free to make certain choices and acting so as to enforce this freedom by praising good choices and punishing bad ones (which in my view would be a supra-personal process), makes us free or per-mits us to be free in the desired ways.

To express this somewhat differently, a shared belief that people are capable of acting in accordance with norms for acting in one way or another influences behaviour between persons in such a way that the belief is self-fulfilling. The assumption we usually make is that most people, most of the time, will act as they are expected to act when we assume that they will. People approve of acts that conform to expect-ations of reasonableness and disapprove of 'unreasonable' acts. From the standpoint of naturalism, it could be assumed that the effects of social evaluation keep the required acts in place. It is a commonplace that sanctions may have to be adjusted to encourage 'reasonableness'.

This hypothesis is compatible with the idea that concepts of human freedom and choice are constructed and also with Sartre's suggestion of a virtual self as a false representation in which the distinction between 'the willed and the undergone' is a form of self-deception (Sartre 1992: 101). However, it is a moot point whether a person's belief in a power of agency, even if constructed, is a self-deceptive one. A person is being authentic in adopting it, and the power is not illusory if a person, conceiving of themselves as a moral agent, responds to what is happening from this perspective. If we were to consider agency as an illusion, we would probably have to abandon a person discourse altogether.

And if a belief in free will is regarded as a false causal attribution in relation to a scientific account of agency, there are very few folk beliefs at all that could survive this test. This is not to say that theocentric, autocentric and ecocentric worldviews are without implications for practices that sustain agency.

If I understand him correctly, Dennett seems to be claiming that a belief in free will is a political ideology. Clearly, freedom of choice has a much wider connotation than the power to choose to get up in the morning. We project possible futures and therefore view ourselves as future agents. A person's agency is closely connected to the construction of time and a self that continues to exist. The self as a theme is constructed out of past acts and possible future acts. A personist would claim that it is persons who construct a self of this nature. To be consistent, Dennett ought to explain the temporal self as a supra-personal phenomenon. However, Dennett is not consistent, and, when he discusses a self in time, he reverts back to a sub-personal explanation. This is revealed in his discussion of absent-mindedness.

Absent-mindedness is a phenomenon in which one finds oneself doing something but not remembering why one is doing it. It represents a breakdown in the temporal construction of self. Dennett discusses its implications for his conception of an agent that chooses. Dennett says that there is a 'larger me that does the policy-making' (2003: 252) that temporally loses track of the context of an earlier thought, which remains conscious but is no longer meaningful. He suggests that there is a part of me that 'is unable to gain access to another part of me that is the author of this thought' (2003: 252–3). Linking the two acts is the same embodied person who, Dennett says, creates 'the brain's user-illusion of itself' (2003: 253). This illusion (i.e. Dennett's concept of an agentive self) provides a person with a means of interfacing with actions performed at other times. Dennett's scenario suggests that agents are persons who may utilise illusory crutches in order to make sense of their own actions, and this gives them a sense of coherence. At each point in time, it is the same embodied person who acts, but the person's acts are linked by an illusory self that exists in a temporal framework in which a person's acts are placed (and in absent-mindedness this goes slightly awry).

On one interpretation of Dennett's views, it is the person who acts and shares a belief in a socially constructed self with agency. It is not something in a person's brain or mind such as a faculty for practical reasoning that invents the self. However, Dennett backslides from this position when he later refers to the cause of actions as taking place in a 'central-processor' in the brain (2003: 254). We are, he says, brain-and-body activity, but, on this assumption, it is not clear how all the social and political factors he gives so much weight to actually become internalised in the brain. It does not seem to be theoretically desirable or necessary to introduce the idea of a central processor at all. This conception simply substitutes brain events for mental events (volitions).

Wolfgang Prinz also reverts to sub-personal causes of agency while at the same time maintaining that 'free will is a product of collective endeavour' (2006: 259). He views the constructed sense-of-self and agency as acquired cognitive representations which in turn represent sub-personal processes (that 'really cause' behaviour) (Prinz 2006: 270). Prinz believes that the social process breaks down the 'solipsistic closure' of this system, but it is not clear how he deals with this problem naturalistically. Guy Claxton (2005: 341) also speculates about human agency from a position in which 'no intention is ever hatched in consciousness'. An intention is just a premonition about what may be about to occur. He defines self as an 'agglomeration of both conscious and unconscious ingredients' (2005: 348), and he asks whether a ghost in the machine is really needed to read the conscious signals, a doer behind the deed. He opts for Dennett's solution that we treat people 'as if' they were morally responsible and then the brain takes this into account in making its computations. Morality becomes a form of cognitive bias. A weakness in this argument is that the person as a whole organism sneaks back into the reasoning. Who makes cultural agreements? Or what is it that categorises another organism's acts as moral or immoral? To suppose that the brain makes decisions of this nature is to commit the mereological fallacy (Bennett and Hacker 2003: 68).

When it comes to matters of legal responsibility, it is clear that it is the person and not an illusory self (and certainly not a brain) that takes central stage. People are usually prosecuted for their public acts, or planned acts, not for their cognitive processes. They are occasionally punished for the kinds of thoughts they harbour but usually on the presumption that certain thoughts are closely associated with acts (e.g., acts of terrorism or paedophilia). The evidence considered in court is, nonetheless, of a public nature – possession of material indicating incitement to violence or evidence of computer access that implies an illicit interest.

Of course, not all forms of moral accounting are so severe; the *kind of self* one expresses might also be subjected to approval or disapproval.

I might be accused of being a lazy so-and-so for not getting up in the morning, but I can defend myself by referring to what I actually did as a person. Many acts of approval or disapproval have neither legal standing nor a strong moral message. However, they are still addressed to persons not selves, i.e. it is you, the person, who is a lazy self. These public construals may be internalised and become the kind of person one thinks one is. If a person dislikes the self they believe they have become, it is the person as agent who sets about changing this state of affairs. A person eats less, has a nose operation, seeks a therapist and so forth.

The supra-personal level of explanation comes into play when models of personhood and selfhood receive general endorsement. What a person actually does to alter their view of their self will no doubt depend on what powers of agency, what scope for change and what future purposes are valued and held up as typical for the kind of person they are in their particular cultural and historical setting. Constructions of selfhood are therefore powerful influences on a person's agentive powers and choices.

However, explicit models of person and self may not be the most powerful influences. People may acquire a sense of themselves as agents without conceiving of 'the self' at all. We frequently act without a clear idea that we intended to do something as an expression of our 'self'. As mentioned in Chapter 2, the Baining people of Papua New Guinea seem to show little interest in anyone's motives or in historical events that might explain their current behaviour (Fajans 1985). Persons are expected to behave in certain ways, and they describe themselves and others as 'shameful' when they break the rules. There is no reason to deny that Baining people make choices and have a sense-of-self but not, it seems, to express their 'self' or to plan a personal life project.

I have come to some tentative conclusions in this tour of human agency. I think it is evident that religion and philosophy have shaped the way that agency has been conceived as a problem amenable to investigation as a natural process. Mindist assumptions continue to have a profound influence on natural enquiry, whether in philosophy or science. In the final chapter, I will return to the related topic of reasons and causes and also consider dynamic systems models that tend to erase the distinction between human agency and other kinds of causation. A different avenue into a science of agency lies within the field of animal behaviour. Here, the focus is placed on differences between primates and humans as agents (see Chapter 12).

11   Self in child development

A study of the developing child promises to hold the key to what it might mean to acquire a sense-of-self and knowledge of self. At some point, the child must realise that its own perspective on the world differs from that of others. Putting this differently, we could say that the child becomes reflectively aware of itself as a unique individual with a unique perspective. The evidence from developmental research indicates that this is a long drawn-out process not a magical transformation. Moreover, there does not seem to be a fixed progression of stages, with each one replacing the last. And it is likely that modes of awareness, from simple to complex, coexist throughout life. As we all know, adults can be childlike at any age.

It is certainly difficult to project oneself into the mind of an infant. As adults, we are aware of existing in time, and the absence of a sense of temporal continuity is barely conceivable. Nonetheless, the evidence points to early infancy as being a time lived unreflectively in the present moment. This conclusion does not sit easily with the Cartesian assumption that consciousness is inherently self-reflective – that humans know that they know when they are conscious – whereas animals just 'know' and may indeed lack consciousness, responding like automata. Since the time of Descartes, research on animals, especially the primates, has led us to revise our assessment of their intellectual powers and capacity for conscious awareness. Just as we might question the presence of reflective awareness in early development, we might question its absence in primates.

It is reasonable to assume that close observation of the developing child would throw some light on this problem. We cannot consider the origins of reflective awareness too narrowly because the first signs that the child is expressing a unique point of view is preceded by several years of general intellectual development. The infant can be interpreted as expressing desires and beliefs – what we commonly understand as signs of having a mind – long before it may know it 'has a mind'. Observations of infants and young children are not, unfortunately, easy to interpret. Research is influenced by different philosophical assumptions leading to divergent interpretations of the same observation. The philosophical problem of the existence of other minds is expressed in the form of questions concerning the criteria for a child possessing or having acquired a 'mind'. A related issue is whether awareness can be differentiated into levels of increasing reflexivity.

What does a child have to learn?

The world of infancy brings us face to face with fundamental philosophical questions and empirical uncertainties. How does the child become aware of its own thoughts, desires and feelings and a sense of time? Infants become increasingly sophisticated in their verbal reporting of experience, eventually referring to past events and anticipating future events. The child also becomes aware of itself as a being with a continuing identity. This kind of reflective awareness is not needed, at least in animals, to adapt successfully to the environment. Pre-reflective animals can learn, and implement what they have learnt, without needing to 'know' that they have experienced something. The animal does not have to be aware that it is engaged in a temporal process or reflect on the fact that it is learning. The human newborn is probably in a similar mode of awareness, which may persist for many months or even years. An explicit sense of time seems to develop between the ages of three and five.

Research on memory has a direct bearing on the distinction between awareness in general and awareness of self. Apart from retaining a *tacit* memory of how situations have been successfully handled in the past, there seem to be two main kinds of long-term memory – semantic (or declarative) and episodic. The first kind operates when we are asked, say, to give the name of the capital of Brazil. Success in producing the answer does not depend on remembering how, when or where the correct response was learnt. The essential requirement is to retain the memory and remain sensitive to the appropriate cues for calling it up. It need not make reference to self (as it clearly would not in animals). By contrast, remembering, in the sense of a person recalling a particular sequence of events from an episode in their past life, has been called episodic memory.

Endel Tulving has defined and investigated these two kinds of memory. He believes that episodic memory is present in many highly evolved species, and this presumably implies that they can engage in a kind of simulated replaying of earlier events without necessarily acting on them. In humans (and perhaps only humans), Tulving has proposed that episodic memory is accompanied by 'mental time travel' (2005: 14). The person who remembers is said to be able to travel back in their mind to an earlier occasion and mentally relive it. Possible future scenarios can also be entertained and experienced in the present.

As Tulving remarks, time travel needs a traveller, and he assigns this role to self. If this self is not there at birth, it must at some point appear in the child's life. But what is it that makes its appearance? Experimental psychologists are unhappy with poorly defined concepts, and Tulving thinks that 'self may turn out like phlogiston or aether – a convenient temporary prop' although he does not want to 'exorcise' it yet (2005: 15).

Tulving is clearly expressing some embarrassment in plucking a concept 'out of the aether' and implanting it into a model of the human mind. An alternative way of looking at this supposed dilemma is simply to declare that self is a social and linguistic phenomenon. We do not have to think of the child acquiring an entity that *does* anything like travel through time. 'Going back' in one's mind or 'projecting oneself forwards into the future' are ways of talking or thinking, not ways of travelling. Travel is an apt metaphor for time, but it needs only a speaker, not a traveller. We can think of this self as an analogical person who does the travelling.

Most specialists in child development assume that neonates live initially in a permanent present and then acquire the ability to develop into a being that 'knows' that it lives in time. A human baby has to learn to distinguish self and world and learn the extent of its power to manipulate what happens. As is true of any animal, human infants have to be self-referentially aware in so far as they sense the world from the unique spatio-temporal location of their body. Infants are born equipped to respond to the human face and human gestures but there is a long period of physical dependence in which it must learn to acquire a wide range of competencies. I am going to assume (and this is hardly controversial) that the child comes to know its powers tacitly before being able to refer to them explicitly, that is, before it reflects on self as an *object* of awareness. I will focus on a child's capacity to take a perspective on its experience *as* a self, acknowledging that this is grounded in a tacit bodily awareness and behavioural competencies.

Philosophies of mind have been influential in research on child development, and, to simplify matters, I will group the latter into internalist and externalist schools (see Carpendale and Lewis 2004 and Sodian 2006). I will describe each one before offering a critique.

Internalist approaches to development of self

One form of internalism is based on the assumption that a child knows itself 'from within', which follows from conceiving of the mind as given to each and every human being as a private and individual faculty. In the mental simulation version of internalism, the child develops an understanding of what other people are thinking and feeling by analogy with an introspective analysis of its own 'mental states'. Thus, on the grounds that others are human like them, it is reasoned that what is going on in other people's minds bears a strong similarity to what is going on in the child's mind. Mental states, such as beliefs and desires, are understood to be evident to oneself but only indirectly observable in others. This means that an inference is needed to understand another person's state of mind. Simulation internalists assume that the infant's development is somehow lopsided. It has to work out that others have minds on the basis of its own resources, that is, by means of experiences that the brain furnishes for it. A different internalist position emphasises the child's general cognitive abilities and processes that allow it to develop a 'theory-of-mind' (see below).

Differences between internalists have been described as strong and weak versions of the general position (Gergely 2004). Expressed strongly, even very young infants know innately their own mental states and can simulate, on the basis of their own experience, what others are experiencing. An intermediate position is that infants only gradually acquire a sophisticated conceptual understanding of their own mental states but still attribute them to others on the basis of their own introspection. In the weakest form, the child uses its intellectual powers to develop a grasp of its own and other minds – a kind of a scientific theory consisting of conceptual propositions and representations that enable a child to predict and explain another person's behaviour on the basis of their inferred mental state (e.g., 'Why has Mum turned off the TV? Because *she wants* me to go to bed'). In other words, the child is thought to behave rather like a scientist, gathering evidence about other's mental states, forming hypotheses and abandoning them when the evidence doesn't fit. This theory-of-mind is said to continue to mature and incorporate others' beliefs about its own mental states (e.g., 'I believe that Mum *believes* that *I don't want* to go to bed'). At some point, usually between the ages of three and four, the child is said to acquire a truly representational theory of how someone else's mind is thinking.

Externalist approaches to development of self

Externalists stress the importance of social learning and cultural influences on the transmission of mind while not denying that innate biological factors are necessary for development. Most externalists abandon the Cartesian tradition and take their lead from Wittgenstein.

They deny that a child learns to recognise its own 'mental states' through introspection or by means of an innate theory. Philosophers influenced by Wittgenstein simply dismiss that idea as misconceived (Bennett and Hacker 2003: 348). Wittgenstein did not deny that one could experience sensations privately or that one could introspect. His arguments were concerned with the manner in which a child learns to refer to private experiences, i.e. by participating in a shared language and seeing how words are used in an everyday context. Accordingly, it is assumed that minds, and the very notion of a mind, are constituted by ways of talking about experience within a public context. Whatever is *felt* privately or interpersonally, *knowing* a mental state means recognising the *public* signs (situations and overt acts) that are, by convention, referred to as expressions of that state. Therefore, the meaning of someone else's mental state is not *inferred* from their behaviour, as if we have to decode what is 'in their mind'; how others express themselves publicly is simply a *part* of the meaning of the state. The child has to learn the criteria that apply to the local vocabulary of mind and refer to their own and others' mental states correctly. This does not reduce mental states to linguistic conventions because reciprocal emotional bonds inevitably contribute to the public behaviour so labelled. The externalist accepts that humans share a common biological potential for sensory, intellectual and emotional responses and that these form the public and private basis for social learning. Consequently, there is no reason to assume that the vocabulary of mind in different cultures will be totally different.

The externalist position in developmental research draws heavily on the writings of the Russian psychologist Lev Vygotsky (1896–1934) (see Vygotsky 1962). The general thrust of the socio-linguistic position is the idea that we have to move from the external to the internal, from human acts to mental life, and not the other way round. It assumes that the origins of a child's mental concepts are social. The focus is on explaining what we commonly understand to be 'our mental activity'. Parents lead the way in prompting this learning, gearing their assistance to the child's level of understanding. In so doing, parents naturally pass on their own understanding of mind. The child is drawn into activities that it will only come to understand fully later on. Learning is assumed to take place when parent and child jointly engage in practices such as pointing things out, describing objects and doing things with them. The parent's linguistic commentary is interpreted theoretically as a prop to the child's thinking about a task rather than an exercise in providing names for concepts or an exchange of information (Carpendale and Lewis 2004).

Psychologists influenced by Vygotsky stress that children imitate adult conversation, in effect, giving themselves instructions to complete tasks by talking to themselves as proxy adults. At a later stage, this self-talk becomes inner speech or what we normally understand as thinking things through in one's head. A key point about the internalisation of dialogue is that it can bring to bear the perspectives of *different* people for solving the task in hand (Fernyough 2004).

One implication of the externalist's focus on the social origins of mental concepts is the need to take account of a culture's history of accumulated reflections on the nature of their reality. Compared to evolving humans, modern infants have the great advantage of being surrounded by linguistically sophisticated adults, with access to the written word and other forms of human knowledge objectified in visual media, sound recordings, the architectural landscape and so forth. In a sense, the child is force-fed millennia of cultural achievements, packed into just a few years. For this reason, the process of developing into a modern infant cannot be compared directly with the evolutionary development of the human species. At best, the former might give us a few clues about the hurdles that evolving humans had to jump.

A critical appraisal of internalism and externalism

Theorists of all persuasions assume that the infant develops on the basis of its experience, and so differences of interpretation derive from the way experience is utilised. The key stage in development for the internalist is the child's ability to represent mind as a model of reality, implying that the child is aware that others may hold a different model of the same reality. Internalists who believe that children develop this model by means of sub-personal neural mechanisms run into the objection that the personal level (i.e. the concept 'person') is essential to the acquisition of any mental concepts worthy of being included in a theory of mind. If personhood is assigned by others, a stand-alone brain is not sufficient. For the externalist, the pre-verbal infant has to be treated 'as if' it was a person by adults who already possess the concept. All of this must be facilitated by innate mechanisms of mutual affective responsiveness of the kind also found in primates. However, 'mind', in so far as it entails propositions about being a person, cannot be explained purely sub-personally.

The simulation version of internalism also runs into the problem of ascribing powers to infants that they are unlikely to possess, such as drawing analogies and making inferences. Moreover, the ability to introspect does not develop until the ages of six to eight, and even children of five do not have a clear idea of what it means to be conscious or unconscious (Flavell et al. 1999). Furthermore, if a child understands another by simulating their experiences on the basis of its own, this must create a barrier to understanding any mental state it has not already experienced itself. On the externalist view, a child is taught how to differentiate mental states (its own and others), and a shared language allows it to comprehend mental states it has not yet experienced. This is typically how adults extend their understanding of other people's experience – through poetry, literature, etc.

Internalists defend their position by supposing that the brain has unconscious mechanisms to simulate mental states without need of introspection (Sodian 2006: 121). There is also evidence that there are specialised neurons in the brain (mirror neurons) that fire off either when certain primates (and humans) engage in a movement (like grabbing) or when they watch another animal carry out the same movement (Rizzolatti et al. 1996). This process suggests that, at some level, human beings intuitively understand what another is doing. However, a correspondence between neuronal activity in two brains belonging to two interacting organisms may only tell us something about a very direct form of social influence, unmediated by perceptions of self and other as whole organisms. The neurons are presumably indifferent as to *who* is exercising the movement that is mirrored (see Gallagher 2005: 220–3, for an extended discussion).

The philosopher Peter Carruthers (2004: Section 2.5) has analysed the problem of children's minds, starting from the Cartesian premise that there is a logical problem in explaining how a child or an adult understands another person's mind. He argues that a belief in the existence of one's own mind does not justify (given that it is a sample of only one) the belief that other people are similarly endowed with a mind. This, for him, is too great a logical leap. Instead, he suggests that there is a much stronger case for arguing that a belief that other people have minds is based on a child developing a theory-of-mind.

Carruthers objects to simulation theory on the grounds that the bare recognition of a 'mental state' is too meagre a basis to ground a rich understanding of 'the mind'. He points out that an infant might be able to simulate what another is thinking in a particular situation but only by imagining itself in the same circumstances. But this process of imagining seems to be informed by a conceptual understanding of what causes experience, not simply the simulation of an experience. He therefore favours the view that a child has to develop a theory of the structure and functioning of a mind, including concepts that allow it to recognise a mental state as a certain kind of mental state. He concedes that infants are not mini-scientists, and so he is left with the position that children are either *taught* theory-of-mind or that it is the product of an innate cognitive module in the brain that operates largely unconsciously.

He regards the first option as a complete non-starter, stating (rather puzzlingly) that there is not a shred of evidence that children are instructed in the way mental-state concepts function (Carruthers 2004: Section 3.2). He prefers the second option because it accounts for why our understanding of mind feels like a given. However, it is not clear why this option should be any less of a non-starter. As noted above, an innate mechanism would consist of general postulates and algorithms, and, before they could be applied, the child would have to identify itself and others as particular entities to whom the theory was applicable. Moreover, the hypothesis of an innate capacity would lead to the prediction that anyone's mind, anywhere, could be understood fairly easily on an innate basis, and this is transparently not the case. This is not to deny the importance of innate mechanisms that may contribute to the mediation of bonding or antagonism between members of the same species.

Common to all schools is the assumption that an understanding of the development of psychological states has to be sought in the mutual responsiveness of a child and its carers. In the next section, I attempt to balance internalist and externalist insights into the development of self-awareness.

An outline of the development of a personal perspective

The following outline is based on the work of several developmental psychologists but principally Katherine Nelson (2001; 2005). Nelson believes that the infant, in its earliest stages of development, is an experiencing 'I' that lives only in the present. She maintains that this form of awareness initially provides the basis for learning elementary conceptual distinctions such as differentiating body-self from the world and grasping that carers (and other less significant objects) are permanent entities. Towards the end of the first year there are signs that the infant is learning to share its understanding of the world with its carers (see also Carpendale and Lewis 2004). It may look to see how a carer is reacting to a situation, follow the carer's gaze and begin to point to objects. Infants appear to direct the adult's attention, either to make requests or point out something of interest. It is assumed that this capacity for joint attention is essential for subsequent learning.

Nelson argues that the infant in its first year is principally getting to know the routines that underlie the regularities of its daily existence, such as feeding and bathing. It learns what follows what and also learns its own role in an activity as a whole, for instance, learning to hold a cup to its lips. The next stage in acquiring knowledge is imitating the acts of others, such as throwing a ball or singing a song. By the end of the first year, the infant can imitate an action some time after first observing it. Actions can now be practised on their own. Imitation (mimesis) emerges at the same time as the child's first words, and it is presumed to play a large part in learning to talk. The significance of mimesis, unlike learning routines, is that the child learns the role of others as well. Thus, in symbolic play, the child may enact the role of another, for instance, playing at food preparation and feeding with a doll. In doing so, the infant is learning a differentiated view of self as like others (doing the same things) but different from others (doing the same things but at a different time and under its own control).

Amongst the child's first words are nouns that refer to persons (e.g., the child's own name and 'Mama') and pronouns that indicate the speaker and their personal perspective. The child may first refer to itself by name (e.g., 'Judy wants ...') before using 'I' correctly. Personal pronouns mark the beginning of a symbolic understanding of self, but the earliest verbal expressions of 'mine' are centred, as one might expect, on objects – searching for, grabbing and claiming an object, very often when the object is *not* the child's (Hobson 2000). This employment of 'mine' is not evidence that an infant knows it is 'a self'. In order to refine its symbolic understanding, the child has to move from a situated, concrete understanding to an abstract or decontextualised use of symbols. 'I', 'me' and 'mine' are first observed in concrete interpersonal contexts, but the use of pronouns later broadens out to signify the acts and attitudes of the speaker who is being referred to.

Expressed differently, there has to be a shift at a conceptual/symbolic level in addition to simply learning how to use pronouns to signify particular persons. This was demonstrated in a study of families who all used sign language to communicate on account of their deafness (Petitto 1987). In American Sign Language (ASL), personal pronouns are formed by pointing directly at the addressee rather than by using arbitrary symbols. One might think that pointing to indicate the person referred to was simpler than having to learn 'I' (or 'Me') and 'You'. The verbal symbols 'I' and 'You' have to be reversed in order to signify correctly. In other words, the child is addressed as 'You' but must learn to use 'I' to refer to itself (Oshima-Takane 1999). By contrast, pointing is just pointing. Hearing children, when learning to speak, often make errors that involve a failure to reverse 'I' and 'You'. Surprisingly, children using ASL who, like hearing children, acquired pointing at around nine months of age, later avoided pointing and seemed to make the same kind of reversal errors once the pointing gesture became an abstract symbol and part of a linguistic system. There seems to be an important difference between pointing out a person or speaker and representing that person's point of view.

Towards the end of the second year, the child has knowledge of an adult's intended goal for an activity, as shown by its anticipation of the adult's reaction when the goal is frustrated by failure to achieve it. It begins to represent another's intentions independently of what the other is actually doing. This achievement coincides with the child's ability to recognise itself in a mirror. A test for recognition is performed surreptitiously by placing a mark on the child's forehead while they are otherwise engaged and then allowing the child to view itself in a mirror. The critical test is whether the mark is ignored or the image is simply viewed as another child or whether there is evidence that it recognises itself (e.g., by pointing to the mark in the mirror, touching its own forehead or trying to rub off the mark). Mirror recognition is assumed to signify an understanding of self as seen by others, that is, as an object of another's attention.

Nelson does not draw the inference that a two-year-old, even one that recognises itself in a mirror, has advanced beyond an experiencing I. She says that for the young child, 'I am who I am right now.' The child lives in the midst of its own actions and interactions, following rules and predicting an orderly sequence of activities but is not yet able to survey these activities in a reflexive manner. It generalises from its experience and uses this knowledge for prediction, but Nelson assumes that there is no personal memory of an episode of activity. Children at three, when asked to say what happened at dinner the previous evening, tend to report what *usually* happens at dinner. They may use the objective 'You' rather than 'I' as in, 'You eat and then you go to bed', suggesting that their knowledge is neither personal nor temporal. It is a shared memory, neither mine nor yours.

Nelson argues that the learning that makes it possible for the child to reflect on past experience is constructed through a dialogue with the child that places events in a temporal framework. This is 'episodic memory' referred to earlier. The transition to a continuing sense-of-self is believed to take place between the ages of two and five.

A personal and temporal perspective is developed when adults and siblings engage in dialogues that refer to past events and upcoming activities, reinstating through language past selves and projected futures. Different persons, each with their own continuing identities, form a part of these scenarios. The use of names and pronouns in a narrative context emphasises both time and different experiential perspectives.

The talk is usually organised as a story in which the adult refers to goals and evaluations, sometimes highlighting the child's perspective (e.g., 'That was fun wasn't it?'). The narrative also introduces mental state terms such as thoughts, feelings, hopes, efforts and disappointments. These are terms that the child can begin to apply to itself, producing an incipient understanding of its own mind. Unlike the child's grasp of daily routines, the narration of episodic memories emphasises specific events and unexpected outcomes. A framework for a continuing sense of identity only emerges when the child constructs a narrative of its own experiences. A child's commentary on itself, spoken out loud at first, will naturally include evaluations of goodness and badness from which later attitudes to self may be derived.

Nelson steers a middle course between internalism and externalism. Researchers of an internalist persuasion, such as Michael Tomasello and colleagues (2005), believe that it is the infant who must work out what others are doing and why they are doing it. They assume that the child's ability to read others' intentions is largely innate, requiring no specific cultural input. Their view is that 'infants begin to understand particular kinds of intentional and mental states in others only after they have experienced them first in their own activity and then used their own experience to simulate that of others' (Tomasello et al. 2005: 688). Having mastered this, it is supposed that the child can begin to have intentions about the other's intentions. They see this ability as being crucially dependent on a close relationship with a caregiver but, oddly enough, don't view this input as making a *specific* contribution (Tomasello et al. 2005: 689). Tomasello's interpretation is an individualistic one, highly dependent on the infant's innate potential. From an externalist perspective, the idea that the child acquires a mentalistic understanding of a carer's intentions on the basis of its own experience is to put the cart before the horse.

At the opposite end of the spectrum is the position put forward by Kenneth Kaye (1982). He argues that in order to understand intentions, an infant must be treated as intentional in the sense that an adult interprets its actions in adultlike terms. The child, day by day, receives acknowledgement for its fledgling, but growing, grasp of the mind. The child has to learn to distinguish its own intentions from the intentions of others – it does not know them 'from within'. It has to learn to differentiate what is 'in its own mind' and what is 'in the mind of another', and the outcome of this process will depend on the parent's style of childrearing. The differentiation of self from other will be poor in a child that is not treated as an independent entity but rather as an extension of its carer's own needs.

As can be seen, there is a striking difference between an internalist and externalist conceptualisation of the way a child develops a personal perspective (see Costall and Leudar 2004). For the internalist, a child has to learn to represent another's mental state, enabling it to understand that another's perception of reality differs from its own. This is a process of inferring from another's observable behaviour to their unobservable, private mental state. By contrast, the externalist does not consider that mental-state concepts are *in* minds at all, implying that one person has to infer what is in the privacy of another person's mind. As Wittgenstein argued, the criteria for correctly ascribing mental-state concepts are assumed to be public (i.e. in behaviour and situations) rather than private. Consequently, a grasp of mental concepts is demonstrated in interpersonal behaviour and, in fact, is constituted in joint action.

The debate between internalists and externalists has crystallised around interpretation of a test that has come to be known as the 'false-belief task' (see Reddy and Morris 2004). Children at some stage in their development comprehend that different persons may hold different beliefs about the nature of a state of affairs. This enables them to influence another person's beliefs by manipulating the information the other is exposed to. The false-belief task tests whether a child has insight into whether another child acts on the basis of a mistaken view (false belief) about the world. In one of these tasks, an experimenter enacts a story and then questions the child to determine what it believes to be the case. An example of such a story is as follows: a doll protagonist (let's call him Joe) puts an object (e.g., a toy) in one container, and then Joe 'doesn't see it' being moved by the experimenter into a second container. A child who observes all this and registers the new location is then asked by the experimenter where Joe will now look for the object when he returns. Most three-year-olds do not realise that Joe has a false belief and wrongly claim that Joe will look for the object in the second (new) location where the observing child knows it to be. By contrast, most four-year-olds grasp the idea of false belief and point out the original container.

The introduction of a concept of belief into the interpretation of this task is not without its problems, especially when experimenters have sought to investigate the beliefs and mental states of primates, and have devised an equivalent false-belief task for them (see Chapter 12). Beliefs have to be inferred in animals because they cannot state them in a language shared with humans. However, perhaps infants younger than three, like primates, can make use of experience in order to act in ways that can be interpreted as holding a belief, even though they cannot verbalise it. On a cognitive interpretation of a child's mastery of the false-belief task, it is inferred that by the beginning of the fourth year, a child entertains a belief that others can hold a model or representation of reality that differs from its own. This accomplishment is understood as a new ability to disengage from the immediacy of what is experienced and to suspend judgement on its truth and reality. Prior to this time, the child is assumed to comprehend the world in the way it literally appears or is said to appear if pretended. Happenings can be recounted, but there are no 'inaccurate' renderings of events.

In a cognitive perspective, the child's belief about the other is inter- preted as being able to read or predict their 'mental state', where mental state means something private and unobservable inside them. However, in terms of success in the false-belief task, it means answering a ques- tion (or pointing) correctly or acting in accordance with a prediction that the other will behave in a certain way. It is certainly true that a child younger than three behaves in a way that is strikingly different to an older child. It may think that others' knowledge cannot deviate from its own, or, when a true state of affairs is revealed, it may deny holding an earlier false belief (Kuhn 2000: 305).

However, an externalist could offer an explanation of these develop- ments without resorting to a concept of mind or mental state. Reference to the mind could be interpreted as evidence of the child having learned to talk in a certain way about experience by adopting the concepts of rationality supplied by its local language. And a concept of the other, and how the other behaves, could be seen as an expression of skills that lie on a continuum with primate behaviour. Young infants (pre- sumably like any animal) operate from a default position that there is no perspective other than their own. Consequently, anything that they may happen to learn about the world as an inductive generalisation from their own unique experience is not automatically generalised to particular others. Any such transposition seems to presuppose mastery of personal pronouns and appropriate reversal of 'I' and 'You' as a con- ceptual/symbolic shift. A child can then generalise what she or he has learned to do to what another (or a doll) can do. This is unlikely to be a watershed acquisition of a theory-of-mind but a gradual refinement of skills.

Psychologists influenced by Vygotsky have pointed to the close asso- ciation between mastery of 'theory-of-mind' and the development of language. Janet Astington (1996) points out that an understanding of mental concepts seems to be grounded in shared activities with older children or adults. For instance, children younger than four under- stand the idea of playing a trick on another person and that it is possible

to do this by inducing a false belief. Astington suggests that 'participating in pretend situations, where representations are socially shared,
helps children understand situations where representations are not only
different from reality, but are not shared in a social pretend domain'
(1996: 193).

Mastery of the idea that others may hold different beliefs about the same
reality does, of course, have major implications; the child can deny what it
is feeling or tell lies and imagine others doing this as well (Marková 1987).
This does not mean that the child can yet conceive of being unaware of
its feelings. In other words, the child does not actively self-deceive but just
realises it has been wrong or that its feelings have changed.

From around seven years of age, the child begins to see itself as others
see it, for example, as putting on a façade to hide inner feelings, thereby
recognising a difference between inner feeling and outward expression.
The child is sufficiently detached from its own perspective to persuade
itself to believe what does not appear to be the case – that there may be
a different truth about its behaviour or feelings – and to achieve this,
it doesn't have to change its own opinion. The child learns to take the
position of another person so that it is able to see how others are trying
to influence it from their perspective.

From around ten years of age, a third-person viewpoint develops.
The child is able to view itself (I) interacting with another (You) from
the position of a third party (Him, Her, Them). An example might be
to imagine what a team is thinking about the interactions of the members of the team. The third-person view can step outside what I want
or what I think You want and see what is, say, good or bad for the team
as a whole. Ultimately, the child (by now a young adult) can see itself
in an abstract way, for example, as a legal entity or the subject of a psychological theory.

The intellectual flavour of these developments suggests that internalists have a point in stressing the growth of the child's reasoning abilities. For instance, Philip Zelazo and Jessica Sommerville (2001) argue
that self-reflection is as much a sign of the power of reasoning as it is
a social and linguistic process. They agree with Nelson that the child
does not think of itself as existing in time until the age of three to four
years. However, they propose that the way in which time is expressed
symbolically (e.g., now, yesterday, tomorrow) is an intellectually complex frame of reference because the child has to understand eventually that 'now' will become yesterday and tomorrow 'now'. Moreover,
it has to learn concurrently that there is a separate stable framework in
which events are ordered along a continuum of fixed reference points
(e.g., their date of birth or a particular Christmas in a certain year).

Zelazo and Sommerville's model of self-reflective consciousness is based on a set of increasingly complex stages or levels. The lowest level is simply substituting a symbol for the thing symbolised such as the word 'Dad' for seeing Dad. Another example at this level would be pointing to a thing as a way of indicating it. A symbol can be stored in long-term memory and, when recalled, can itself become an object of consciousness and a potentially enduring memory trace. For instance, the child becomes capable of imitating an action some time after first observing it. They argue that the importance of symbols lies in the fact that they can be decoupled from the thing symbolised. As stored symbols, they become available to stand in for direct experience and can be related to other symbols. In their view, self-reflection is a recursive process in which a symbol mediates a conscious experience that, in turn, may become an element in additional degrees of recursion. The higher levels include action-oriented rules that can be applied to the symbolic description of events. Each higher level entails greater breadth or abstraction than the previous one, and the level of embedding signifies, in their words, 'psychological distancing' (Zelazo and Sommerville 2001: 230).

These authors have studied children's mastery of rules and conclude that by two and a half to three years, a child can sort pictures according to a simple rule, like putting different colours in different places (analogous to a rule relating now, yesterday and tomorrow). Later on, the child can consider two rules in relation to the same events but has difficulty alternating rules and cannot represent the two rules contrastively. The latter ability would be required to contrast the history of the world as an objective series (e.g., events in their family history) to the history of self as a subjective series (e.g., a memory sequence of what has happened to them). Seeing the *relationship* between these perspectives entails an even higher degree of psychological distancing. Not until the age of four or five does a child know when it is appropriate to reference an event according to its own history or to world history. At an earlier age, a child may remember what they did but not understand the temporal-causal connection between past and present experience.

The concept of levels of consciousness and embedded rules reminds us of the fact that, in western culture, self is constructed in the image of logical operations and the ideals of abstract thinking. Saying that someone thinks like a child is often a form of condemnation. However, it would be overstretching a point to say that reflection on self necessarily requires embeddedness in higher levels of abstraction. Presumably, self-reflection could circulate recursively at a single level of abstraction, simply offering up different points of view on the same theme.

An implication that can be drawn from studies of reasoning is that conceptualisation of self continues throughout development and cannot easily be separated off from reasoning about reality in general. Self-reflection is perhaps best thought of as a lifelong process without obvious endpoint. As a recursive process, thinking could get stuck in a cul-de-sac or diversify into forms that have happy or unhappy endings.

Nelson's interpretation of knowledge of self as a narrative is consistent with how most western adults think of themselves – as having followed a unique trajectory of experiences over their lifetime. Autobiographical memory does not get established until four or even five years of age (Nelson 2004). This may explain why the early years are usually a blank, except perhaps, for a few vivid visual images. Events have not yet been placed in a story. Adults introduce the child to the concept of being a person who has a past and can expect good or bad things to happen in the future. This narrative construction of self should be distinguished from simply referring to oneself as a speaker, which is acquired much earlier and need not be reflective.

Nelson does not think that the construction of narrative is an innate characteristic. In western culture it is important to construct a self-story, but we need not assume that this has always been so – or at least not to the same degree in childhood or in the history of our culture. Nelson argues that in pre-modern societies, narratives were largely communal, with little need for individuals to construct a story for their own lives (2003).

In contemporary society, individual life stories may find their source in myth, literature, heroes or celebrities. Shared myths are often about the life of a single individual, and they embody the values and beliefs of society. In the early years, children model themselves on their parents in their imaginative play, but later on peers and cultural sources become increasingly important. The construction of an autobiography demands a protagonist – 'a self' – that undergoes the trials of life and comes out of it heroically or tragically. I suggest that self is an analogical entity that emerges around the age of four when language skills have advanced sufficiently to engrave it in memories that can be recalled at will. Narrative creates self as an entity to reflect upon but it is the biological individual, as speaker, who is needed as the narrator. In other words, the self we *imagine* to be our central core is not the self that reflects. There need be no single scriptwriter but a multiplicity of voices conversing 'in our head'. If we internalise other's responses to us, the story of our self is more like an improvised play than a single narrative.

12   Self in human evolution

The constructionist perspective has been a fairly small voice in the recent explosion of interest in human social evolution. The scope of this interest has been broad, covering transitions from our primate ancestors to hominids, and on to modern *Homo sapiens*. It has included cultural change as well as the evolution of biological traits. The hard sciences of genetics, evolutionary biology, palaeontology, neuroscience and primate psychology have linked forces with anthropology, archaeology and philosophy. The consensus view is *co-evolution*, a synergistic interaction between biology and culture. If culture were to be ignored and mental life viewed simply as the product of innate neural mechanisms, we would have to look no further than the evolution of the brain and processes of Darwinian natural selection. However, most specialists believe that cultural innovations, passed on from one generation to another, conferred biological advantages on human groups and thereby influenced survival. It is possible that different biological capacities evolved concurrently, and this may have created an opportunity for the relatively sudden appearance of behaviour that could be culturally transmitted.

It is neither possible nor necessary for me to summarise what is known about human social evolution but I can at least attempt to place ideas about person and self in an evolutionary context. I will begin by charting a few of the key landmarks in the development of the human species and then restrict my focus to person and self. The topic has been particularly divisive because it concerns speculation about the relationship between self, language and culture. Some of the questions being addressed are: When did language evolve and in what form? How did this achievement relate to prior cognitive abilities and to consciousness? How did early humans understand each other as separate beings with psychological attributes? At what point can we say that this understanding was articulated by means of symbols? How much does an awareness of self depend on mastery of a language, structured by grammar?

The familiar Cartesian assumption that humans have innate access to a first-person perspective once more comes to the fore. My emphasis on participation in a world of shared symbols that relate to persons and personal perspective does not imply that primates are unable to read the behaviour of other animals or that they lack culture altogether. It may be legitimate to refer to primates as understanding the perspective or intentions of other animals, or even 'reading their mind', if we are clear what we mean by mind. The constructionist case can only be strengthened by showing continuity with the abilities of primates.

Another area of debate is how early humans developed a sense-of-self as existing continuously through time. We take it for granted that we can review our memories over a span of years and also project our existence into the future. This ability is underwritten by concepts of personal identity and personal history. In this respect, we apparently differ vastly from the cleverest apes. Is this ability innate or does it depend on learning a narrative identity and the stories a culture tells about itself?

A brief synopsis of human social evolution

Although the consensus is a synergistic interaction between biology and culture, opinions differ on the weight to be given to innate capacities and the need for a cultural milieu in which human capacities were first acquired and expressed.

Taking a broad perspective, 5 million years is 'a higher estimate for our last shared ancestor with the chimpanzee' whereas 30 million years separate us from monkeys (Byrne 1999). Very early on, our ancestors developed a bipedal gait. An upright posture might have increased the salience of full eye contact and perhaps gave greater scope for the emergence of hand gestures and the flexible use of tools and weapons. There was a tripling of brain size around 3 million years ago, and this was accompanied by adaptations in female anatomy. The narrow hips associated with an upright posture were not compatible with delivering large-skulled babies; the hips broadened, and babies were born at an earlier stage of maturation when their skulls were smaller and their bones more flexible. They were also quite helpless to look after themselves for many months, if not years, and so childrearing became excessively prolonged in comparison with other primates.

With regard to culture, the overall picture is that for long periods of evolution there were spiralling advances that resulted from a process of natural selection occurring in synergy with cultural change. Our own species, *Homo sapiens sapiens,* first appeared around 200,000 years ago (MacWhinney 2004: 397). The archaeological record shows that the development of a larger and more complex brain did not lead quickly to new cultural achievements – the time lag seems to have been in the order of tens or hundreds of thousands of years later. And for about half the time our own species has lived on the planet its mode of living was virtually indistinguishable from that of *Homo neandertha-lensis,* now extinct. The first stone tools date back 2.4 million years (Holden 2004), but evidence of major cultural change, such as bone, antler and ivory technologies, did not occur until the Later Stone Age (Palaeolithic period) around 400,000 years ago in Europe. Cultural revolutions seem to have happened too quickly to be explained primarily as the outcome of evolved bodily changes (Johnson 2005: 506). Steven Mithen (2000) believes that it was not until between 60,000 and 30,000 years ago that the archaeological record 'is transformed in a sufficiently dramatic fashion to indicate a distinctively modern type of behavior and mind'. Mithen notes that *Homo sapiens* had already been around for at least 70,000 years and that evidence for modern culture was not associated with any change in brain size.

A variety of selective pressures have been put forward to account for the evolution of intellectual abilities, complex social relationships and cultural innovation. The widespread use of stone tools probably meant that there were advantages to be had from the ability to imitate others and see things from their perspective. Hominids presumably developed the skill of recalling a series of motor actions aimed towards a desired endpoint, like fashioning a tool. Brian MacWhinney (2004) points out that hominids who could imitate well would probably have been more successful as toolmakers, and, as infants, they would have bonded better in the early risky phase of development. Moreover, the ability to communicate would have become more significant as groups of hominids used signs to establish social ranks, to distribute food and to compete over access to mates.

As soon as our human ancestors began to initiate *planned* excursions into the environment, they would have required some kind of representation of themselves in relation to the space and distances around them. It is thought that by linking systems of spatial navigation with a growing ability to imitate the actions of others, hominids were increasingly able to predict their position over longer periods of time. Robin Dunbar (2000) emphasises a different influence in social evolution – the need to increase the size of the group as a defence against predation. He argues that, in primates as a whole, there was a selection pressure for increased brain size in order to mediate the social interactions of a larger group.

Hominids presumably built on the extensive social repertoire of the primates. Richard Byrne (1999: 74–5) describes modern primates as showing the following social behaviours: formation of alliances in the competition for resources, cooperation in the acquisition of rank, investment in social grooming as a way of building up 'friendships', selective reconciliations after conflict, knowledge of personal characteristics and affiliations and techniques of social manipulation such as deception. The skills listed presuppose an ability to discriminate other members of the group as individuals and as kin, a memory for ranks and past affiliations and, in some cases, a memory for personal histories of help given and received.

Communication

There are a number of competing views on the factors that led to the evolution of language and communication. Bo Gräslund (2005: 115–17) emphasises bipedalism and its consequences for the position of the throat and windpipe that made it possible to produce more finely articulated sounds. He dates the beginning of this development to at least 4 million years ago. Others propose that the important anatomical changes began around 300,000 years ago and continued to perhaps 50,000 years ago. In addition to changes to the vocal tract and reshaping of the larynx (Lieberman 1994), there was an increase in the neural control of the muscles of the chest so that breathing could be modulated for phonation (MacWhinney 2004: 384).

An upright posture may have increased the salience of face-to-face communication. It is supposed that facial expressions and gestures became increasingly differentiated and under voluntary control. Hand gestures, facial expressions, clicks or lip smacks that do not involve the larynx may all have played a part in hominid communication (Pennisi 2004). But in hominids we are still likely to be dealing with a system of iconic signs, used in concrete situations. Iconic signs such as hand-waving (and rude gestures!) have by no means lost their significance for us today.

Merlin Donald (1991) stresses an early mimetic system of communication. This system uses icons such as stylised gestures to represent actions or objects. They would be employed to give information and to support plans or group activities. The individual who attempts to provide information to an audience through mime has to re-enact a scenario and imagine how it would be perceived as a series of events by the audience for whom it is intended. This implies a need to understand an analogical relationship between the performance and the scene it represents – a mapping of actions onto performance (Donald 2001: 269). According to Donald, mimesis would have been central to chant, song, ritual and warfare.

Donald believes that a reflexive awareness of self has its roots in the cognitive capacity to control mime, requiring as it does the integration of different sensory modalities in a virtual mind-space and the ability to voluntarily express or inhibit complex muscle movements. Donald believes that the significant break with our primate past came when hominids redirected attention away from the external world and onto their own actions (2001: 270).

From proto-language to a language with grammar

Opinion is especially divided over the evolution of language. Some experts think that genetic changes, associated with a 'language module' in the brain, were crucial, the most recent occurring perhaps only around 40,000 years ago. Others see language as a gradual cultural/historical development once the brain became biologically ready for language use around 200,000 years ago (Arbib 2005). Gräslund (2005: 114) puts this readiness much earlier at 500,000 years ago.

In any event, it would appear that over several million years, our ancestors communicated by means of signs that lacked any grammatical structure. The development of language may have depended on a number of co-evolving bodily adaptations and cognitive abilities. One of these has been described as the ability to recognise that others have intentions to achieve a common goal. It must have been necessary for hominids to share plans for hunting, migrating and for an endless number of other activities. All of this is facilitated in a modern language by the use of grammatical conventions to indicate who is doing what, where and when. It is at this point that psychological concepts creep into the discussion, as early humans begin to refer to each other's actions and make plans together.

According to Donald (2001: 75), conscious awareness preceded language; it evolved as an essential element in the construction of meaning in general and allowed hominids to think over intermediate periods of time, introducing deliberation over action. He believes that language evolved later as a capacity subservient to wider symbolic purposes (Donald 2001: 119). In other words, hominids would at first have communicated by using icons that did not amount to a system of symbols with a syntactic structure. Donald's views do not imply that communication involved hominids introspecting on their own 'mental states' and inferring like-mindedness in others. This is the way some theorists influenced by theory-of-mind have regarded the matter. For instance, MacWhinney (2004: 395) talks of mental models of the self's activities that 'could then be projected onto the other'.

Daniel Hutto (2008: 227) speculates that attempts to communicate through mime would have led to a standardisation of forms of expression, prompted by evident failures to communicate on certain occasions. He believes that this 'would have been a crucial step on the road from contextual, indicational communications to true predicative symbolic use'.

Clearly, there are limits on mimetic representation as an efficient system of communication. Each separate meaning or intention would need its own icon, each of which would have to be learned and stored in the brain as a holistic and independent sign. It seems likely that there was evolutionary pressure to develop a more efficient brain with greater storage capacity. It was our own species that apparently carried this development forward.

A problem for theorists of the evolution of language is to understand how a system of iconic signs (e.g., vocalisations) became divorced from their fixed meanings, to produce, in effect, two separate systems, a vocalisation system and a meaning system. To explain further: modern humans are capable of two separate abilities, one of which is talking gibberish (producing arbitrary combinations of sound) and a second is having a meaningful thought that is difficult to put into words. With separate systems available to us, even slight variations in sound can have a different significance (Knight 2000: 99–119). To put this more technically, our ancestors evolved a code, based on a finite set of meaningless units of sound, and acquired the ability to rearrange them into clusters (words) which in turn could be rearranged, according to rules, into sentences. So, from simple beginnings, a complex hierarchy of communicative tools was constructed (Studdert-Kennedy 2000). This transition was most likely built on prior abilities to understand symbols, but it was perhaps the remapping of these symbolic capacities onto words, and sequences of words, that led to the rapid development of culture.

Cartesian thinking is evident in this area, as in others. Ray Jackendoff (2002) refers repeatedly to speakers and hearers, but his overall stance is to purge linguistic theory of intentional terms such as 'symbol'. For him, communication between humans is about the cognitive capacities of individual humans and the 'state-space' of their brains (Jackendoff 2002: 34–5). As he says, 'issues of social identity' are 'relative remote from my concerns' (Jackendoff 2002: 37). This follows from his position that 'language is instantiated in the minds and therefore the brains of language users' (Jackendoff 2002: xiv). Consequently, the role of speakers and hearers in the evolution of the linguistic expression of personal perspective gets neglected.

The vocalisations of most animals are concerned with weighty matters – their survival and basic needs. It is therefore important to understand how, in human evolution, vocalisation became more playful. Of course, animals are no strangers to play. They may signal to other animals that what is to follow is going to be play: 'these bites are not real bites'. But human communication developed into a system that is far more creative, reflexive and devious than anything seen in the higher primates. For example, in modern infants, speech is incorporated into pretend play and supports the imagination. It has been assumed that language evolved to expedite rather concrete and pragmatic everyday activities but at some point in our history, symbols must have acquired a non-literal (metaphoric) significance. Indeed, Giambattista Vico (1668–1744) suggested that metaphor is the normal way of experiencing 'facts' and that a distinction 'between the literal and metaphorical is only available in societies which have acquired the capacity for abstract thought' (Hawkes 1972: 39; Vico 2000). It is possible that language has always been a creative tool, enabling our ancestors to compare situations that are only remotely similar in physical terms.

With a means of producing a set of phonetic contrasts, and a set of conventions for grouping them into words that signified things of importance, modern *Homo sapiens* had a virtually limitless system for learning, storing and retrieving information. MacWhinney (2004: 398) argues that the new lexical power was linked to the older mimetic system of a string of represented actions, and he suggests that the syntax and grammar of sentences emerged from the online tracking of the flow of perspective in action sequences. Whereas this ability had formerly been achieved mainly by a visual display of simulated actions, it was now transferred to speech. It became possible to explain verbally where to find things, how to do things and when to do things.

Reading purpose into primate, hominid and human behaviour

Some of the most complex and intriguing questions in human social evolution revolve around a theoretical understanding of purpose in animal and human behaviour. Purpose is related to the philosophical concept of intentionality, understood to be a property or power of 'mind' (Jacob 2003). Animal behaviour is clearly purposeful but whether that is evidence for 'mind' is a separate question. Intentionality is a power to represent, or have something stand for things, properties or states of affairs. In contrast, 'an intention' has been thought of as a specific state of mind that plays a role in carrying out an action. The nature–culture debate finds expression in this area of philosophy in the form of questions about the existence of intentional mental states and whether they can be reduced to natural states of an organism. My aim in this section is to draw inferences from the empirical evidence and to relate them to the philosophical assumptions of researchers.

Put concretely, how does one animal or human know what another is about to do? Does it know that the other individual knows that it knows its intentions? Is a human in a better position to read what a fellow human is up to than one of our close primate relatives in a comparable situation? Speculation about evolutionary transitions is hampered by lack of agreement when these issues are discussed with respect to modern humans. Once more, the main battle lines are drawn up between internalists and externalists, and the prime cause of the tussle is a dispute over the meaning of mind and mental state. Internalists assume that reading someone's mind is about knowing what mental state they are in. They assume that private access to our own mental states or an innately grounded theory allows humans to understand what others know, believe, intend, desire, etc.

Drawing on Wittgenstein, externalists assume that the meaning of mental-state concepts is learned in a public context and that, therefore, a mental state is not in some private place, the mind, but is, in important respects, publicly observable. To be in a certain frame of mind is to stand in the right (normative) relationship to agreed criteria for making the ascription to that frame of mind. Bennett and Hacker (2003: 97–107) point out that many of the terms in our psychological vocabulary, such as 'belief' or 'intention', are not the names for a private experience. They suggest that these terms express, in a certain linguistic idiom, human attributes that could be described differently, without significant loss of meaning. When philosophers and scientists do not agree about the meaning of mind in modern humans, it is no surprise to find a lack of consensus in discussions of the transitions in mentality between primates, hominids and humans.

'Personal' perspectives in primates

The field of study that is interested in the way primates share perspective is known as 'shared intentionality'. For humans, purpose may be inferred when behaviour indicates a strategic and flexible pattern of acts dedicated towards the achievement of some particular end. Dennett, in his book *The Intentional Stance* (1987: 246) describes different orders of intentionality, the lowest, zero order, being a mere tropism, which he describes as an absence of intentionality, or any mentality. A dog barking for the sake of barking might be an example. A dog, 'believing' that it is about to be attacked, and barking to ward off another dog, could be interpreted as exhibiting *first-order* intentionality. It is first order because it appears to be directed towards a desired end. To express *second-order* intentionality it would have to be assumed that the dog is also attempting to influence the other dog's 'intentions' (which we may assume it does not have the capacity or desire to know). The main aim of Dennett's reasoning is to dissolve the barrier between human, animal and machine, and he advocates the use of intentional language when we do not possess detailed knowledge of how a complex system actually works in terms of natural processes.

In other words, Dennett advocates interpreting the behaviour of both animate and inanimate systems in intentional terms *as if* they were expressing beliefs and desires. This recommendation still leaves us with the problem of explaining the difference between zero-order and first-order intentionality in the case of animate creatures. The dog's purpose in barking to ward off another dog could be explained either in terms of automatic brain mechanisms (a complicated tropism) or as the expression of a first-order intention. If the latter, is the dog in a particular mental state and does it 'know' what mental state it is in? Knowing in this sense seems to presuppose a capacity to symbolise. However, some theorists do not think that an intention has to be represented by a conventional symbol, and they apply the term 'mental representation' to purely mechanistic processes built into the brain. The capacity to use public symbols moves us into new territory because it potentially allows an animal to indicate its own purposes to itself. Although it is difficult to imagine a dog mastering the latter feat, some higher primates have been taught to use symbols in order to communicate with their trainers (see below). With this kind of evidence, we have more justification for theorising about an animal engaging in foresight or symbolising the purposes of other animals.

It is widely recognised that some animal behaviour that appears highly intelligent can be explained by showing that it is the outcome of systematic training; the animal is responding to subtle cues and merely obtaining a reward in a rather convoluted, instrumental manner tied to a particular context. Perhaps much of our own intelligent behaviour could be explained instrumentally without our awareness of how an end is being achieved and without symbolisation of the activity. We do of course share the simpler learning mechanisms of animals. I will take a symbol to mean a perceptible object that has a conventional and abstract significance; it has a multipurpose use in so far as it can be adapted to provide a mediating role in many different chains of complex behaviour sequences.

What may cause us to doubt that we humans respond to others by inferring or predicting their mental states is the ease with which we give a plausible explanation for almost anything we (or they) do. We may begin to wonder whether conscious deliberation or particular mental states are needed for purposive activity at all. The almost seamless communication that can take place between a dog owner and their pet suggests that the projection of conscious intentions may have little to do with the actual mechanisms underlying shared human activity. If that is so, the argument could run, primates may act in a purposeful and humanlike manner without any of the reflective 'self-awareness' involving the mental states (beliefs and desires, etc.) that seem to accompany human acts. And we humans may be capable of communicating in a human way without having to label our 'mental states' as beliefs or desires, or reflect on them as such.

If there were agreement about the explanation of human behaviour, it would be easier to decide whether apes are like humans or whether humans are more like apes. The difficulty is compounded by the tendency of theorists to borrow the language of human minds to describe 'mental' mechanisms in animals. Theoretical terminology becomes ambiguous in the sense that it does not easily allow us to distinguish between acts that are guided by thought (i.e. states of which the organism is aware and may, in fact, symbolise) and acts that are controlled by automatic brain mechanisms without an organism's awareness. There is no reason to put an embargo on theorists to prevent them conceiving of unconscious brain mechanisms that involve inferences, theory building or even desires and beliefs, but unless this technical employment of everyday concepts is clearly marked, it can be highly confusing.

The differences between primate and human behaviour can be explored by considering the collaborative hunting activities of chimpanzees (Boesch 2005). These animals adopt distinct roles (driver, blocker, ambusher) and may shift roles during a given hunt, presumably because they 'share' a common goal and 'know' how it can be achieved. Meat is distributed to the contributors after the hunt, not being reserved by the animal that captures the prey. It is tempting to assign mind-reading to the chimpanzees, but is this actually necessary and what would it mean anyway? In one sense the animals are reading the purposes of their fellow hunters because they are collaborating to achieve a common goal. But dogs, too, can read the 'intentions' of their owners. It is far from clear that the communication of the chimpanzees can be called a sharing of perspectives in the sense that one chimpanzee is able to represent to itself what it is doing or to perceive its own behaviour from the perspective of another.

According to Daniel Povinelli and Jochen Barth (2005), chimpanzees use cues from each other's behaviour to act in a purposeful and collaborative manner but they do not represent each other's 'mental states'. This does not imply that they act robotically with no awareness of what they are doing. The suggestion is that chimpanzees in the hunt do not have a means of labelling their own experiences as being of a particular kind although they do recognise other chimpanzees as individuals, interpret their behaviour and facilitate their role in the hunt. Without responding to visible cues indicating purposive acts, they would not be able to cooperate. Povinelli and Barth argue that the categorisation of experience requires a symbolic system.

Primate researchers who have been strongly influenced by experiments on theory-of-mind in children (see Chapter 11) hold a different point of view. They are led to think that a primate understands that it has its own perspective on a situation (perhaps accompanied by a distinctive experience) and that another animal has a different perspective. Celia Heyes (1998) discusses evidence that non-human primates conceive of mental states like 'believe' or 'know' and use them to predict and explain the behaviour of others. Heyes is highly sceptical, but even the premises of the research that she reviews can be questioned. We cannot be sure that even *humans* know that they believe something by recognising a 'mental state' or adopt a theoretical attitude in order to predict the mental state of another human.

We could assume instead that purpose in animals and humans is expressed and therefore read from observable behaviour, regardless of whether or not it is accompanied by 'mental states', whatever they are. If by mental state is meant sensory or affective experience associated with behaviour, we could interpret this feedback theoretically as having a similar function to the self-produced muscle sensations that play a role in controlling motor acts. Although it is natural to infer that a primate expresses a state like 'fear', we may only be justified in categorising this experience as a 'mental state' because we possess, as humans, a symbolic means for doing so. A primate may well experience pain, hunger, sexual desire, etc., and observe corresponding signs in other animals. But it seems improbable that a primate could learn to distinguish different kinds of bodily feedback and associate them with a concept of itself as a unique organism ('its own mind') and transpose them into 'the mind' of another animal that it also recognises as a unique individual.

An externalist rejects the notion that humans *infer* a mental state of fear in another human by using observable cues to *predict* an unobservable mental state of fear. A certain pattern of behaviour *means* fear, not that a terrified look or running away *implies* fear. If observable cues are part of the meaning of a mental state, humans may simply take it for granted that others have corresponding and similar feelings in the public situations in which the state is observed. They do not *predict* another's mental state and do not need to *know* it when the other produces all the appropriate and relevant observable cues. Similarly, in primates, the emotional bond between mother and infant or the 'anger' of competing dominant animals could be interpreted as revealing a reciprocity of acts and a correspondence of feeling, not mind-reading. A primate might adopt a strategy to achieve mating but it is not obvious that it needs to predict what its potential partner might be feeling; it only needs to interpret public cues in terms of the next step in the strategy.

Many forms of human social behaviour don't seem to require a form of mind-reading that is mediated symbolically. Robert Gordon (1998) mentions a number of responses that seem to be cued by external situations in an automatic way. These include responding emotionally to vocal and facial expressions, turning one's eyes to triangulate with another's gaze and alternating one's glances between the other's eyes and the surrounding scene to confirm convergence on the same target. He notes that we may share these behaviours with non-human primates and in neither case do we have to suppose the discernment of mental states or the employment of a theory of mind.

On grounds of parsimony, it seems preferable to follow Povinelli and Barth and assume that primates and humans can only be said to communicate *about* mental states when they possess a means of symbolising them through conventional gestures or signs. The crucial difference would be between a natural sign (e.g., signalling a food source or presence of a predator) and a gesture indicating, for instance, 'I'm hungry, let's stop to eat'. The interpretation of primate behaviour in this regard is by no means clear-cut because some higher primates reared in a human environment have been taught to use signs (see below). They can indicate what they want to happen in certain situations or indicate some of their own states, such as hunger. Some primates socialised in this way are closely bonded with their carers and so it is interesting to speculate whether their considerable abilities enable them to refer to the purposes of other animals or persons. Being in possession of signs for different individuals, can they refer to a particular individual when that third party is not physically present?

The evolution of human mentality

One of the first questions to consider is whether hominids, when they began to symbolise the purposive behaviour of other individuals, did so in ways similar to our own. In other words, did they represent intention as individual beliefs and desires? A cursory examination of anthropological studies of pre-literate people shows that the anthropologist and indigenous informant can often agree about what events have taken place, but the reasons they give for their occurrence may not correspond at all. On these grounds, we should not privilege the beliefs and desires of modern individuals as explanations of human behaviour. It would be unsafe to assume that our mental-state concepts are universal or timeless.

We are on safer ground in assuming that ancestral humans inherited the cognitive abilities of the higher primates to read or predict the behaviour of other members of their social group. If we assume that this can be done 'naturalistically', that is, without the benefit of conventional, multipurpose symbols, we need to ask what difference the availability of a symbolic system might have made to the process of reading intentions. In other words, what kind of relationship might have existed between natural signs for predicting what another hominid is doing and the first cultural symbols used to categorise human behaviour and interpret its cause?

One possibility is that ancestral humans observed regularities in the behaviour of others and acquired a 'natural theory', much as they would have done for any animal in their environment. The arrival of linguistic symbols might have facilitated this learning by codifying natural categories, permitting predictions and inferences of a more precise kind in a wider range of situations. For instance, perhaps individuals could now more easily communicate their intention to seek a food source in a new location. Terrence Deacon (1997) seems to argue along the lines of symbols producing greater efficiency of communication, even though he believes that the advent of a language structured by grammar amounted to a radical change of cognitive strategy. Although this generated novel types of communication, he nevertheless argues that the strategy evolved out of, and was grounded in, the ability to learn natural contingencies between events (in his terms, 'indexical learning'). According to Deacon, there is a hierarchical relationship between symbolic and indexical reference, which suggests that its purpose is the same – to communicate about 'physical referents'. Words are said to form a higher-order system of relationships that are *about* indexical relationships. As Deacon puts it: 'indexical power is distributed, so to speak, in the relationships between words' (1997: 83).

Deacon is a cognitive neuroscientist and so he is presumably theorising about a sub-personal mechanism. Words that are dissociated from
fixed referents are understood to form a system of combinatorial possibilities upon which to base a more efficient mnemonic strategy. A problem with this hypothesis is that it does not provide an account of how
words evolved in relation to communicating hominids. Furthermore,
once human groups came under the influence of symbolically mediated
norms, the concept of a 'natural contingency' takes on an indefinite
meaning. Rule-governed social practices would have created a new set
of natural and social contingencies in a complex dynamic system. It is
unclear how the hierarchical relationship between levels that Deacon
proposes could be sustained. Unless it is simply assumed that 'mind' is
a natural phenomenon, that gives rise to certain kinds of natural contingency, there is no reason to assume that a more efficient symbolic
cognitive strategy was the means by which humans discovered a more
accurate 'theory-of-mind'.

Furthermore, Deacon grants that symbols may refer to non-physical
entities, such as angels, and that new logical groupings may be discovered amongst relationships between words. He imagines the symbolic capacity to be a new level of self-determination, liable to virulent
compulsions. At the same time, he wants to ground it in a real, physical world that includes other persons, because symbols are shared. He
regards self as a virtual reality that belongs to a cultural tradition, a self
that is 'on loan' and may migrate to other persons. This view is essentially mindist, and Deacon does not really show how his virtual self is,
as he says, 'grounded in a personal subjective experience' or, for that
matter, related to other attributes of persons, like agency.

A different line of thinking is based on the supposition that a sign with
a fixed meaning could acquire new symbolic power if it came to be used
figuratively to draw attention to abstract similarities between quite dissimilar situations (Foster 1994). For example, a stick could be compared
with a finger, or vice versa. A stick and a finger might have analogous
uses such as getting something out of a crack. A less concrete example
might be a hunter's mimicry of animal behaviour to represent figuratively an activity in a completely different situation. Foster assumes a
gradualist approach in the evolution of an ability to make use of analogy,
in which 'the body' was the original icon. In the finger–stick analogy,
the symbol is not physically arbitrary because both share the property
of tools. Mary Foster (1994) makes the sweeping claim that analogy
is the foundation of culture, a claim that is closely related to the views
of cultural anthropologists such as Claude Lévi-Strauss (1963), who
suggests that analogy organises systems of thought on many cultural

levels. For instance, homologies have been inferred between elements in myth, the naming of clans, the spatial arrangement of human habitation and the structural relationship between architectural features within dwellings.

For any animal whose behaviour is not innately triggered by fixed signs, there is a need to generalise what has been learned in one situation and apply it in another, similar, situation. For most animals, this generalisation is achieved by producing similar responses to physically similar situations. An animal behaves as if one nut can be cracked open in the same way as the last similar nut. In addition to stimulus generalisation, animals such as primates can extend their repertoire of behaviour by imitation and emulation. An animal can imitate when it reproduces a sequence of responses that it has just observed in another animal. Emulation refers to an ability to grasp the end-point of an activity that has just been modelled, and to vary somewhat the means of achieving it, rather than imitate all of the details previously observed. Chimpanzees can both imitate and emulate (Horner and Whiten 2005). Whether and in what way these processes might entail an ability to draw on analogy is unclear. Perhaps language is not needed for the latter ability. For instance, pointing to a body part such as the mouth to indicate a feature of an unrelated situation (e.g., a cave) could be interpreted as a communication that does not require a contrastive set of linguistic symbols. As noted earlier, the use of mime for communication might have led to a standardisation of gestures, thus promoting the development of decontextualised, general-purpose symbols.

Although it is possible that communication by mime or analogy might have enhanced the learning (and transmission) of natural contingencies, its significant consequence may have been a more creative understanding of personal perspectives. We need not assume that analogical thinking corresponded to, or refined, pre-existing knowledge. On the contrary, its application to the comprehension of the natural and social world could have had unpredictable and idiosyncratic consequences. Given that a symbol has a conventional (arbitrary) meaning, and a similarity can be perceived between quite dissimilar natural events, efficiency of learning may not have been its main advantage.

Events understood in symbolic terms could have had a justifying or persuasive function. Moreover, as social life became more complex, the demand for technical terms that facilitated communication in local, idiosyncratic situations could have led to the evolution of group differences in 'mental states' themselves. Although the oldest categories of human thought may have corresponded to perceptions of entities in the natural environment (air, fire, water, etc.), it is quite clear that these categories have since been exploited for their figurative potential.

One possible implication of the above is that the idea of a 'human mind' cannot be taken for granted as an obvious next step in an evolutionary sequence that begins with a primate understanding of mentality. Ancestral humans might have attributed the cause of an individual's acts to impersonal or unseen forces or made interpretations on the basis of group membership. If so, it would follow that theories that concern the learning of mental-state ascriptions in modern infants may have relatively little to tell us about the transition from hominid to human mentalities.

A constructionist perspective on evolutionary development does not take anything away from the significance of primate studies of mind-reading. It just means that hominid and early human symbolisation of the causes of behaviour may have been far more exotic than the literal thinking of earlier higher primates. As far as we know, chimpanzees are rather concrete thinkers who are not in the habit of creating effigies of superchimps. Authors who espouse theory-of-mind tend to assume that reading the intentions of humans can be interpreted as a natural activity because the capacity for theory-of-mind is seen as universal rather than culturally specific. There are certainly examples of primate behaviour that support the assumption that they can use data (natural observations) to make predictions. For instance, a primate may exploit regularities in nature to manipulate another animal. It has been observed that a male Vervet monkey deterred a rival male from joining his group by giving a leopard alarm call whenever the rival crossed some open ground that lay between them (Cheney and Seyfarth 1990). This suggests that natural contingencies between events can be exploited to predict how another animal will behave, but it is rather doubtful that the monkey is making predictions on the basis of another animal's state of mind. Ancestral humans were presumably similarly endowed to manipulate their social environment. However, normatively controlled behaviour, mediated by symbolic or analogical reasoning, might have produced a situation in which it cannot be assumed that mind-reading was based on an instrumental mastery of how humans 'naturally' behave. Human attributes may not have mirrored 'nature' in this sense.

In order to bridge the gap between primates and our more recent ancestors, adherents of a predominantly cognitive approach to social evolution have speculated about intermediate stages in a theory-of-mind. Thomas Suddendorf and Andrew Whiten (2003) argue that even if primates don't possess a theory-of-mind, the great apes (and also human infants at an early stage) might have an 'intermediate theory of mind' (2003: 181). They cite evidence produced by Michael Tomasello and his colleagues (see Tomasello et al. 2005) that chimpanzees can understand the nature of goal-directed action. For instance, Tomasello argues that chimpanzees can tell the difference between being refused something and someone *trying* to give them something and clumsily failing. They are also said to know whether or not another chimpanzee can see something that is hidden from view. When describing the behaviour of apes (in carefully controlled experimental situations), Tomasello and colleagues use terms that we would normally reserve for modern humans, such as apes making inferences: 'the subordinates knew what this meant for the dominant's goal-directed action: if the dominant could see the food or had seen it just before, subordinates could infer that she would go for it (whereas they would not make this inference if what she saw was instead a rock)' (Tomasello et al. 2005: 684).

Tomasello grants that there is no evidence that apes can generate action plans based on a rational assessment of reality, an ability that he regards as a 'more mental dimension' (Tomasello et al. 2005: 685) of intentionality. He therefore draws the implication, like Suddendorf and Whiten, that mentality is on a continuous dimension rather than being stepped. He states that one feature lacking in apes is the motivation and skill to share their mental states with others. He assumes that chimpanzees in a collaborative hunt have intentions to reach goals, which they somehow recognise as a mental state, but are not able to share a joint commitment to reach a goal.

Suddendorf and Whiten (2003) argue that the great apes are capable of going beyond instrumental knowledge and can entertain what could be or might be the case. In support, they cite evidence that apes will search for an object that has been invisibly displaced; that human-reared apes treat dolls and toys as if they were animate characters; that they enjoy watching television and interpret photographs appropriately. They also have a limited ability to engage in do-as-I-do imitation games. The great apes can use different tools for different tasks and modify a tool for the task in hand. A high proportion of chimpanzees, gorillas and orang-utans are said to pass the classical mirror recognition test (see Chapter 11).

Suddendorf and Whiten are undecided on the best account to give of the evolution of, in their words, theory-of-mind. As the authors say when discussing the role of language: 'How would one agree on a symbolic system to exchange ideas about minds, if no one believes the other has a mind?' (2003: 189). But if mind is culturally constructed, it is not true that there is an entity, mind, waiting to be symbolised. To speak of an 'intermediate theory-of-mind' is to assume what needs to be demonstrated – that ancestral humans needed some kind of theory-based method for understanding each other in terms of mental states.

Of course, for a concept of mind to develop, it must be assumed that there is a capacity for symbolic communication and a social life sufficiently complex to require articulation. The evolutionary process could be compared with the way persons engaged in specialised tasks develop technical terms that only they fully understand on the basis of close familiarity and daily practice. The externalist argument is that mind does not lie waiting to be symbolised but that increasingly complex social practices give rise to the conditions in which mind is symbolised for pragmatic purposes. If there is an intermediate stage here, it lies in the development of symbols and a proto-language.

Symbol-using primates

We may be able to learn something about human social evolution from studies of primates who have been taught some of the elements of human culture. We should at least be able to estimate the potential for intellectual development and speculate about intermediate stages of mentality. Early attempts to teach chimpanzees to communicate with spoken words led to failure, perhaps because these primates lack the ability to articulate human phonemes (Terrace 2005). Since chimpanzees are able to discriminate sounds in the range of frequencies employed in human speech, sensory discrimination should not be a limiting factor. Beginning in the 1960s, gestures (ASL) and an artificial visual language consisting of plastic chips began to be used in training. Later still, computers were used to display 'lexigrams' and to record responses. A lexigram is a combination of a particular geometric configuration and a particular coloured background. Portable devices are now available, displaying up to several hundred signs.

Typically, chimpanzees require hundreds of trials of training and intermittent rewards (food, etc.) to learn to make a range of requests by pressing a particular lexigram sign. Having done so, they have been able to combine two or three signs when interacting with their trainers and with their dispensing machines, e.g., 'Please machine give X'. Herbert Terrace has critically reviewed the evidence of over thirty years' research and has concluded that the signs uttered by an ape are merely imitative of the trainer's signs and that their sole function is to obtain rewards (2005: 88). In effect, he says, they are complex discriminations, and he denies that there is any evidence that apes in these studies share knowledge for its own sake, e.g., pointing out, as a child does, that there is something interesting to look at 'over there'. He argues that apes do not use signs referentially, by which he means presumably that the sign does not stand in for the object symbolised, independently of a context in which it is instrumental in obtaining a reward.

Terrace's rather uncompromising position leaves him with little alternative but to suppose that some ancestral group of humans acquired the capacity (in some unspecified way) to use an utterance 'to influence another individual's *mental state,* rather than behavior' (2005: 102). Once they had they evolved this remarkable ability, they were able 'to share their thoughts, perceptions and desires and to comment about events and individuals of mutual interest' (Terrace 2005: 102). Terrace grants that primates who have been socialised in a human environment occasionally point to an object when they are not actually interested in gaining possession of it. He also acknowledges Tomasello's conclusion (see above) that a subordinate chimpanzee 'knows' (without training) when a dominant animal can see a hidden food and only goes for it when the dominant's line of vision is obstructed. Terrace is therefore also committed to the idea of an intermediate theory-of-mind.

Some of the strongest evidence for ascribing minds to apes comes from a study of Kanzi, a Bonobo chimpanzee reared by a foster mother who was, at the time, being trained in the use of lexigram symbols by Sue Savage-Rumbaugh (Savage-Rumbaugh et al. 1998). Kanzi's mother learned relatively little after hundreds of trials, at which time baby Kanzi had been present as an observer. Following a separation from his mother, Kanzi rapidly acquired the meaning of the lexigrams, without formal training, although he was intermittently rewarded with human attention, sweets and prizes. He has readily added new lexigrams to his vocabulary. He also comprehends the meaning of several hundred words of spoken English and understands the meaning of many nouns, verbs and noun–verb combinations. In a test for the comprehension of 660 different sentences presented by the experimenter from behind a one-way screen, he carried out 72 per cent of the requests correctly, e.g., 'Pour the coke in the lemonade.' (The experimenter in the room with Kanzi was unable to hear the request.) A two-and-a-half-year-old child responded correctly to 66 per cent of the same sentences.

Some of Kanzi's errors could be interpreted as unconventional but meaningful responses, as mishearings, or as a confusion between homonyms, e.g., can (able) and can (trash can). Both Kanzi and the child understood the difference between sentences of the form: 'Go to location X and get object Y' and 'Take object X to location Y.' Kanzi also understood embedded phrases of the form 'Get the X that's in Y.' However, unlike the child, he had particular difficulty understanding 'Give (or show) someone X and Y.' He did not remember both items and normally gave only one (correct) item. Savage-Rumbaugh notes that the grammatical structure of a sentence like 'Feed the doggie some milk' actually seemed to facilitate his understanding of the sentence, while a sentence with a simpler grammatical structure, like 'Show me the doggie and the milk' was more difficult for him.

Savage-Rumbaugh points out that Kanzi's ability to *communicate* meaning, in contrast with his ability to *comprehend* English sentences, may be underestimated because he can only do so by pointing to symbols on the lexigram board. This is intrinsically cumbersome, and searching through the symbols takes considerable time.

Reactions to the claims that are made of Kanzi's abilities range from Terrace's dismissal that they are just conditioned discriminations to the wonder of some visiting academics who, after becoming personally acquainted with Kanzi, came away with the distinct impression that Kanzi was reading their mind and reading the intentions of other animals. For instance, Stanley Greenspan and Stuart Shanker (2006: 152) state that: 'Kanzi had been glancing at me surreptitiously all morning. By choosing me to be the chasee, Kanzi was actually testing me out to see how I would respond. He was also drawing me into the group, both physically and psychologically.' This kind of projection seems to be as wide of the mark as Terrace's dismissal.

Terrace (2005: 99) predicts that a withdrawal of rewards would lead to a collapse of Kanzi's skills whereas it would not do so in the case of a child. However, the role of motivation can be separated from the question whether a lexigram is being used as a symbol. The communicative responses of a child would also likely collapse if all attention were to be withdrawn. Terrace cites B. F. Skinner's view (1957) that verbal requests (*mands*) are produced in any situation and are maintained by a primary reinforcer (e.g., food, comfort, a smile). He compares an ape's use of a lexigram with a mand. By contrast, Skinner's concept of a *tact* requires the listener's attention and is only produced in a specific context. He says that a tact is maintained by a secondary reinforcer, such as verbal acknowledgement. Terrace argues that tacts are not followed by primary reinforcement and their sole function is to share knowledge, e.g., in his example, a child says 'blue jay' and points to it, and the listener acknowledges the identification of the bird. In Terrace's view, apes never learn to tact.

The contrast between a mand and a tact, as it applies to non-human primates, seems overdrawn. Savage-Rumbaugh's observations of Kanzi suggest to her that he requests actions in which he is neither the agent nor recipient, such as requesting merely that he observe that A chase B. He is also said to be curious to see what happens when roles are reversed in games such as chase. He will also note relationships between symbols, photographs and objects. For example, if Kanzi is playing with a ball, he may touch the ball lexigram or point to a photograph of a ball if any are around (Savage-Rumbaugh et al. 1998: 50). Also, when in pain, he is said to point to the location that hurts and show it to his trainer. If Kanzi's behaviour is sufficiently humanlike to dupe visiting professors of psychology, we might be inclined to conclude either that all human behaviour follows simple operant principles or that Kanzi shares at least some of the human capacity to use symbols.

It is of more interest to ask what Kanzi is unable to comprehend. If he is curious about role-reversal in a game of chase, can he take a perspective on what he observes and reflect on the intentions of the participants? Although this seems likely to be beyond him, he does possess lexigrams for 'being good' and 'being bad' and applies them to his own behaviour. According to Savage-Rumbaugh, he sometimes evaluates his own actions before he does them, and he is also said to appreciate when others are in pain by acting in an appropriately caring manner, attending to their injury. However, it does not follow that Kanzi evaluates another's performance and compares it with his own. And, in apparently empathising with human pain, he may simply be imitating human social acts. Neither of these behaviours need be interpreted as an ability to *represent* the perspective of another. Nevertheless, it would appear that Kanzi's abilities, and those of other trained Bonobo chimpanzees, far exceed an instrumental response to cues that are subtly picked up from their trainers.

Savage-Rumbaugh points out that Kanzi, unlike other primate subjects in language experiments, was exposed to human speech and lexical training from an early age. His achievements might suggest that there is a sensitive early period for language learning, as seems to be the case for humans. Moreover, like human infants before they learn to speak, he was exposed to the spoken word on a daily basis for an extended period of time. The linguistic achievements of a human child are rapid and dramatic between the age of eighteen months and four years, but the production of words is preceded by a lengthy earlier period in which it learns to comprehend the significance of what is said.

It is by no means clear that Kanzi is capable of second-order intentionality – in other words, shaping a message to another individual under the control of a symbolic representation of its likely reception by the other. If he could do this, it would imply Kanzi's ability to see things in advance from the other's point of view and to tailor the message depending on how he wanted the other to receive it. This kind of abstract symbolisation of persons and their intentions seems to be limited to humans. Primates are clearly capable of pointing to themselves (or a lexigram) as a sign of their wishes, but they do not seem to be capable of pointing to indicate the wishes of another animal. Kanzi has been observed 'trying to help out his wild-reared friends when they have difficulty understanding what their human caretakers might be asking' (Donald 2001: 130), but this is not strong evidence of second-order intentionality.

Higher primates in the wild can, of course, size up a situation as it unfolds, enabling them to get their needs met. They have to remember their previous encounters with other members of their social group so that they do not, for instance, 'upset the boss'. Some animals in the wild may practise little deceptions to achieve personal goals, such as acting friendly and then thrashing a rival when it comes close (Donald 2001: 130, quoting the work of Richard Byrne and Andrew Whiten 1988). Given that our ancestry lies in the ape line, it is not surprising to find evidence of continuity with the advanced mental capacities that we like to think of as being exclusively human. Although there must have been intermediate stages in the ability to read the intentions of others and to symbolise human acts, we need not conceptualise these stages as progressions towards a theory of something (a mind) that was waiting to be discovered. I will now criticise some further proposals that have taken this cognitivist approach to social evolution.

Theory-of-mind in human evolution

The view taken by many evolutionary psychologists is that the mind is the activity of the brain, and organisms have innate access to some of their own mental states. Evolutionary psychologists have quite reasonably argued that the brain is not just a general, all-purpose processor of information and point out that different cognitive 'modules' have evolved under various circumscribed environmental pressures (Gander 2003). This has resulted in specialised brain structures for tasks such as spatial orientation. A module is conceptualised along the lines of an unconscious mechanism that receives input on which it performs operations according to rules (algorithms). The product is some kind of representation of the input or an instruction to produce a behavioural response.

If modules are impersonal, modularity does not get us much further forward in thinking about persons and selves. Some psychologists make the assumption that there is a module for theory-of-mind, but there remains the problem of moving from a module to the individual who possesses it. Even if the module enabled recognition of mental states and contained an inbuilt inference rule allowing it to infer that other individuals were similarly endowed with a mind, the organism still has to symbolise *itself* and *others* as whole, unique organisms to whom a mental state belongs.

It is essential that primates and humans perceive each other as whole individuals because they interact socially (or compete) in such a way as to imply unique identifications. They harbour intentions towards each other as individuals. Innatist theories simply presuppose reference to whole individuals as well as mental states. For instance, Pascal Boyer assumes that 'person' is an element in an 'intuitive ontology'. He defines the latter as 'a set of categories and inference-mechanisms that describe the broad categories of objects to be found in the world' (Boyer 2000: 100). Humans can, of course, learn to discriminate categories of objects, but Boyer seems to want to regard persons, like plants, as an intuitive category. In my view, to regard a human as having a mind is intimately linked with categorising them, symbolically, as a person. Although ancestral humans (like primates) must have identified unique individuals in their social group, this is not the same as saying that they categorised them as persons.

The existence of symbolic categories presupposes a group of interacting individuals who adhere to norms and rules of communication. However, theorists who speculate about the evolution of person/self are inclined to look for mechanisms within the individual organism that predate the emergence of symbols. For instance, Natalie Sebanz (2007) wonders about the evolution of a 'mental self', meaning an awareness of our own mental states. She distinguishes a mental self from simpler forms of self-awareness or 'basic sense of self'. Her aim is to explain the evolution of self on the foundations of individual cognitive mechanisms of an intuitive (non-symbolic) kind. Sebanz suggests that one of these mechanisms is a sense of agency in joint actions, such as discovering the difference between acting alone and acting with others. However, this would appear to take us no further forward in evolution than chimpanzees who collaborate when hunting. Sebanz goes on to argue that, by some incremental means, a stable sense of being an acting entity emerges, together with an awareness of the accomplishments of other unique individuals, their biographies, their preferences and all without a symbolic language. The underlying assumption is that 'mental states' became more complex, diverse and temporal before humans attribute them to a 'mental self' belonging to a person as their source and owner. Quite apart from doubts about the meaningfulness of intuitively sensed complex mental states, it is their attribution to persons that we need to explain.

254 Person and self in science

Once symbolic categories had evolved, an understanding of the physical world in these terms may have coexisted in parallel with, and sometimes in conflict with, intuitive (non-symbolic) concepts. For example, symbolic representations of physical principles may not have captured the essence of what was known tacitly about the physical world and could have been entirely misleading. A fellow human might have been perceived naturally as a human (*qua* species of animal) and at the same time be represented symbolically as an animal of a different species. It seems essential to keep natural concepts and symbolic categories theoretically distinct, although in practice they are jointly expressed.

Constantine Sedikides and John Skowronski (2003) adhere to the innatist path in evolution and claim that the 'symbolic self' is the result of a fortunate accident – either a mutation or favourable mating – producing hominid individuals with the capacity for a symbolic self. In a similar style of reasoning, Mark Leary (2007: 21) imagines a 'cultural big bang' produced by an evolutionary change in the brain and believes that in a transition period 'some people had a self and other people didn't.' Leary equates the self with the ability to self-reflect.

Sedikides and Skowronski define self as a reflexive entity with a 'sense-of-self' and charge it with representing a person's attributes, future goals, beliefs about how others might perceive them and, in sum, initiating, mediating or moderating thoughts, feelings and behaviour. Their argument virtually pre-empts the need for any further thought on the subject. They propose that 'the private self emerged first and the public self component was superimposed on this private self by means of processes such as reflected appraisal' (Sedikides and Skowronski 2003: 602). Reflected appraisal is defined as an individual's ability to assimilate the perceptions of others into the self. We can only make sense of this ability if self arises in some miraculous way without origins in social communication. In effect, they assume an innate theory-of-mind in which the mind of others is understood by analogy with one's own mind.

A speculative constructionist approach to the evolution of 'mind'

The essence of the position I will put forward now is that our early ancestors acquired explicit forms of self-reference on the back of their ability to relate to each other as public speakers (or communicators) and not by virtue of an innate ability to read their own minds. Julian Jaynes presented a version of this thesis in a ground-breaking book *The Origin of Consciousness in the Breakdown of the Bicameral Mind* (1976). He maintained that self-consciousness developed out of a virtual relationship with speaking statues, and in the spirit of this conjecture but not the substance, I will throw in my hand with the idea that the invention of selves (and gods) was a by-product of a public language.

This reverses the intellectualist or cognitivist view that ideas about mind were grounded in consciousness of self and its mental states. One early example is the theory of animism made popular by the nineteenth-century anthropologist E. B. Tylor (1832–1917). He assumed that early humans were like us and formed their beliefs on a rational basis, asking themselves questions like 'What is the difference between life and death?' and 'What is it that appears to us in dreams?' In the view of animism, our early ancestors had a personal psychology that they projected onto nature, infusing it with spiritual beings that exercised their will over human affairs.

A constructionist alternative is that an inner life of self-reflection is a late development in cultural terms, built in part upon the invention of ever-more-complex imaginary entities and ways of referring to them through language. In other words, we need not assume that there is a primal experience *by* self *of* self. Although experiential knowledge of the body, and also concepts of the objects we experience, cannot be reduced to language alone, I will assume that the contemporary concept of self presupposes millennia of accumulated cultural achievements. This position is not at variance with the view that language, although recent in evolutionary terms, required several million years of communication and proto-language in order to develop (MacWhinney 2004).

As Donald expresses it (2001: 150–1), 'our dependency on culture is very deep and extends to the very existence of certain kinds of symbolic representation.' He assumes that cognitive activity is shared between many brains and that our symbolic resources are distributed in all kinds of external storage devices. Donald argues that human society behaves like a distributed symbolic system whose properties cannot be predicted from what individual brains can do in isolation. What this thesis implies is that contemporary self-reference can be compared with the mastery of a set of conceptual tools, tools that depend on external support. A similar statement could be made about the accomplishments of contemporary physicists. However brilliant the physicist, they have to work with a prevailing set of theories and the tools for taking them forward. Referring to self is not, of course, an advancing science, and I make no claim for the superiority of modern selves over earlier selves. The similarity between self-reference and physics lies in the fact that both depend on earlier cultural achievements and a methodology that is shared with others.

In its widest connotation, a concept of self includes any means by which the individual organism acts on the basis that it is a unique object amongst other spatially distributed objects. At a more sophisticated level, it identifies its own perspective and contrasts it to the perspective of other organisms. Many self-referential abilities only manifest themselves in behavioural discriminations. The attainment of what might be called self-awareness rests on an ability to signal a personal perspective by means of substantive markers such as gesture or language. Given all the various meanings of self-reference, we cannot discuss its evolution as if it were a unitary trait. As we have seen, Donald assumes that the development of language was superimposed on an earlier phase of mime and gesture and served to clarify and sharpen up the meaning conveyed in a sequence of re-enacted movements. Mimesis is inherently self-referential if an individual is conveying something they have done or witnessed. Personal perspective can be reinforced by pointing to self or particular others. But pointing to third parties or things is more ambiguous, especially if the requirement is to indicate particular individuals in the past or future. Pointing is oriented to the present, and it is only by analogy that it could be used to indicate what *has* happened or *will* happen. The arrival of spoken names and a language with tenses to indicate past and future would have greatly extended the possibilities for precise communication about particular actions and particular individuals.

Donald does not deny a role to conscious experience – he affirms it – but we do not have to assume that experience automatically discloses concepts of either privacy or self. Animals can function perfectly well with a tacit knowledge of themselves as objects in space without needing to *conceptualise* their experience as 'theirs' as opposed to belonging to another animal or person. The externalist attempts to show how early humans conceptualised self as a personal entity by first learning about themselves as public (primarily social) objects. By contrast, many writers who adopt an internalist position do not discern a problem in explaining the evolution of self-conceptualisation. For example, Gräslund (2005: 126–7) baldly states that even the great apes 'clearly possess an inner consciousness', 'have a grasp of their own personality's relationship to the world around them' and possess 'a basic notion of self-identity'. He says 'It is also clear that all the great apes perfectly understand the meaning of a proper noun, and that they can cope with personal pronouns such as I, my, and you' (2005: 126–7). He claims that, by contrast, monkeys are hardly aware of their own awareness and lack the ability to place themselves in another individual's position. As we have already seen, these claims for the great apes are not justified by the evidence. Before I develop an externalist view, I will examine ways in which social theorists have conceptualised the relationship between persons and the social groups they compose.

Personal perspective in the context of the reproduction of the group

The question of the origins of the category of the individual, subject or self is obviously a fundamental one in human social evolution. It is taken for granted in philosophy and social theory that subjects can be distinguished from objects and that a boundary can be drawn between subjects and the natural and social world in which they exist. It has been assumed that a subject encounters the world as a knower, acts on the world and thereby derives knowledge about it. This knowledge enables the knower to operate successfully within the world and to categorise and label its objects. Expressed in the most abstract terms, we have to assume that there are reciprocal relationships between subject, object and world. For the natural scientist, the subject is simply an individual organism observed from a third-person perspective. For most animal species, the reciprocal relationships between subject, object and world can be specified without the additional complication of the subject's ability to symbolise its relationship to objects and world. By contrast, the human subject can symbolise itself as both a subject and an object and think in a variety of ways about subjectivity and objectivity.

This does not mean that animals lack the ability to perceive themselves as an object and navigate the world as an object. However, there is a strong presumption that this ability is tacit, dependent on innate mechanisms that continue to mature after birth, becoming ever more finely developed through trial-and-error experience with the world. Research suggests that an awareness of being a body in space becomes more sophisticated as the evolutionary scale is ascended (Parker et al. 2006). Some primates appear to recognise that a mirror image represents their own body, implying that the animal perceives its body *as* an object. This ability goes beyond the obvious capacity to *use* the body to explore the world. However, the ability of humans to conceptualise themselves as objects interacting with other objects, or sharing properties with the world, adds a completely new level of complexity to the way reciprocity needs to be explained theoretically.

The ability to symbolise self and world has important implications for cultural and biological reproduction. However, the distinction between biology and culture is to some extent artificial. As Tim Ingold (1994: 9) puts it, 'For human history is but the continuation of the evolutionary process by another name.' Many organisms can construct their environment to some degree, and culture is not restricted to humans because primates can learn about features of their environment and model the use of tools, passing on skills to succeeding generations (Fragaszy and Perry 2003).

Despite the difficulty of drawing a line, I will assume that the ability of humans to perceive other humans in terms of their local symbolic significance, that is, in arbitrary and conventional ways, does mark an important boundary in social evolution. Obviously enough, an animal might learn about the significance of natural signs, but the meaning of an arbitrary sign for humans is negotiated and fixed by the group. For instance, the sun might be viewed as a life-giving force by one social group and as a devouring monster by another. The point at which human beings are assigned to arbitrary categories is the point at which they cease to be merely other natural organisms to, say, bond with or attack.

I am concerned here with how categories pertaining to the world, and to the humans within it, can be placed in an evolutionary sequence. Tylor's conjecture that the earliest beliefs in spiritual entities were the projection of a personal psychology is one such speculative sequence. It seems likely that some ways of objectifying the world are more basic, primitive or intuitive than others. Humans and animals share the capacity to discriminate what is useful to them in the environment and may, in effect, 'objectify' the environment perceptually. For instance, gatherers of food in the wild would have learned to 'see' food sources, and this knowledge could have been transmitted as part of a local culture. Other features of the environment may have stood out as objects on the basis of responses under genetic control. For instance, humans and chimpanzees have an innate tendency to fear snakes (Mineka and Cook 1988). One implication of these remarks is that the cultural reproduction of knowledge is dependent on both social learning and genetic influences, the balance varying with different kinds of behaviour.

Social theorists have employed a variety of concepts to describe cultural reproduction, a popular one being 'objectification' and 'incorporation'. The general idea is that humans gain knowledge of the world as if it is composed of 'objects' (e.g., material artefacts or symbols such as words and images). Human subjects are conceptualised as being born into a cultural world composed of objects and 'incorporating' these objects as knowledge. The significance of incorporation is that subjects are enabled to reproduce objects for the next generation. The

activities of cultural transmission presumably range from tacit and natural ones to explicit and educational ones. Subjects are not completely
constrained by the knowledge they incorporate (they may produce new
cultural objects), and objects are not completely constrained by the
subjects who reproduce them (for instance, natural events, such as a
depletion of resources, will constrain this process). Consequently, cultural reproduction is never simply a process of replication.

How might we understand the origins of concepts of person and self
in this process of cultural reproduction? Social theorists have regarded
these concepts as being of paramount importance, especially in modern and post-modern societies, where they are understood to play a
large part in reproducing relationships of power and social control
(Giddens 1991; Rose 1998). For the moment, I am concerned with
pre-history.

With respect to *categories of thought* about subject and object, there
are two principal ways of understanding their origin: anthropomorphism and physiomorphism. An anthropomorphic concept of the world
(and its objects) means that the world is classified in terms of human
characteristics. A physiomorphic concept of human characteristics
(of the subject) means that they are classified in terms of features of
the world. Interest in ways of thinking in pre-literate societies was
brought to a head by the philosopher and sociologist Lucien Lévy-Bruhl
(1857–1939) who drew upon numerous anthropological studies to show
that human characteristics were often ascribed to the world and vice
versa (Cazeneuve 1972). He cited many examples of peoples who identified themselves with objects in the world, especially with animals,
in fact often claiming that they *were* a certain kind of animal. Lévy-
Bruhl described these observations as 'mystical participation', meaning that humans were demonstrating a kinship with all things animate
and inanimate. In mystical participation, the spiritual and the material
are not distinguished (in the way we are accustomed to do), and both
humans and the world are assumed to be controlled by the same invisible forces. Lévy-Bruhl did not believe that categories of thought were
the projection of an individual mind upon the world because he saw
them as collective (social) representations. He therefore left open their
anthropomorphic or physiomorphic basis.

Nevertheless, it has been customary to interpret the population of the
natural world with invisible forces, gods and humanlike wills as being
the result of the projection of a human psychology. Graham Richards
(1989: 6) points out that one problem with simple anthropomorphism
as an explanation for the origins of categories of thought is that it presupposes that humans were able to identify these forces in themselves

to begin with. This is not easy to comprehend if, like Richards, we follow Wittgenstein's argument against the possibility of a private language. Anything purely internal, private or invisible could not have provided the primary basis for a set of linguistic terms describing human attributes. Richards argues that humans first learned signs for communication by sharing ways to denote *public* objects, suggesting a physiomorphic origin even for attributes of the subject. In other words, shared meanings for features of the public world, such as animals, fire and water, were incorporated as signs for human characteristics.

In fact, as Richards points out, the argument cannot be that simple because humans possess innate propensities to act towards the world, and this can be interpreted as a kind of projection of human attributes. As noted above, humans have a genetic predisposition to fear certain objects and situations (and unfamiliar places in general), and so it is not too surprising to find a universal tendency within people around the world to be subject to attacks of intense fear when they move away from the safety of their domestic habitation, especially at night. This tendency could be interpreted as an example of projection, although people themselves often attribute the experience to external invisible forces. The derivations of the modern words 'panic' and 'phobia' are from the Greek gods Pan and Phobos who provoked these responses, presumably by invisible means (Marks 1987). The word 'fear' derives more prosaically from Old English 'faer' that referred to actual sudden calamities or dangers. The existence of innate human predispositions, like fear of unfamiliar places, is undeniable, but we need not explain the perception of 'external forces' as a projection of private psychological feelings. This presupposes that these feelings have already been identified as private entities. The identification of fear could be explained physiomorphically as introjection in the form of names for public happenings – either gods with human-like features or actual physical attacks or calamities.

Richards argues that physiomorphism is not an intrinsically linguistic process (1989: 32) although a fully fledged language must have enormously facilitated the transfer of meaning from events in the public domain to attributes of the human subject. But physiomorphism can also be enacted by, say, imitating an animal's behaviour, wearing its skins or a body part (e.g., a bear claw) or by eating and drinking natural products or intoxicants. Richards' general argument is that comprehension is sought either by *being* like something in the public domain or *identifying or comparing oneself* to it. Richards is not claiming that early humans did not experience hunger, fear, lust, etc., but that communicating about them entailed their mapping onto a public phenomenon.

The private experience is not so much created as objectified. However, by so doing, the experience becomes something that can be reflexively evaluated as an 'object'. In other words, the mode of referring to things in the world (as objects) is reflexively borrowed to talk about private experiences as objects. It can be argued that the same reasoning applies to entities like a mind or self. Language facilitates the move to 'I am X' (metaphor) or 'I feel like X' (analogy) where X is a public phenomenon and where the transfer of meaning may be experienced as something like Lévy-Bruhl's mystical participation.

Richards believes that the transfer of meaning is also facilitated by the unique status of the human body as both the subject and object of consciousness. For instance, the hardness and softness of things in the world is also experienced as hardness and softness of the body. These qualities can be experienced both objectively and subjectively. The meanings encoded by language do not, therefore, intrinsically refer to either public *or* private phenomena. Moreover, words for body parts (head, mouth, etc.) can be transferred to the natural environment. And with regard to animal behaviour, there are clearly many commonalities between humans and animals and so the same terms can apply to each. Identification with categories for animals is not necessarily anthropomorphic except when meaning is transferred back from the human to the animal world, projecting onto it attributes which, from a modern scientifically informed outlook, it seems most unlikely to possess.

Physiomorphic origins of signs for personal perspective

Richards believes that syntactic and lexical language created new opportunities for the identification of personal perspectives. Prior to an advanced language, individuals presumably gestured and spoke in a proto-language that enabled forms of personal identification. Humans were recognised as individuals, and it is easy to imagine a sign developing for 'No, that's mine.' However, as well as standing in for other objects (persons, etc.), signs for the communication of public identity and personal perspective have a double existence as objects that are themselves in the public world. Linguistic signs were public phenomena, just like the things that signs referred to in the world. This meant, according to Richards, that language itself was available for physiomorphic assimilation. In the same way that 'fear' was labelled and spoken about as the presence of a god, a person could reflexively identify themselves as the particular speaker who was publicly identified and referred to as that speaker. Thus, instead of 'I am identical to X (a type of animal, etc.)', identity is established by: 'I am identical to a speaker (of a particular type, etc.)'. Others would be identified through their role as speakers.

The internalist might view these conceptual manoeuvres as unnecessary, but the externalist is seeking an explanation for a human ability to take the position of another that does not rest on a simple interpretation of projection. It certainly seems to be the case that great apes can make requests to indicate their own needs, but it is not clear that they can reflexively use signs to convey meanings about their own identity and wishes as a particular animal. In other words, making one's needs known and getting them fulfilled is not the same as knowing oneself as a particular individual with needs. Moreover, apes reared in a human environment do not seem to exchange messages about the wants of different animals (or their human carers). The externalist argument is that once ancestral humans identified a personal perspective with an individual as a named public speaker, further human attributes could be referred to as 'my', 'your' or 'their' attributes. The subject becomes an object, and other speakers, as objects, may be perceived as sharing similar attributes with oneself. The proposal is that 'personal' attributes are first objectified by means of a shared language, meaning they are not 'private experiences' projected on to the world. Consequently, they need not be viewed as attributes (like mental states) that others *must* share on the basis of an inference that others are human beings like oneself and therefore have similar private feelings.

Richards makes it clear that when a human's way of being is represented by (or identified with) a property of the world, such as an animal, the source of that way of being is ascribed to the animal. As noted earlier, public speech is a world property, but, at a pre-linguistic stage of evolution, a variety of physiomorphic identifications may have existed. Humans shared ways of being with animals and so the *form* of a human being would not necessarily have provided the primary basis for physiomorphic assimilation. Consequently, the argument that humans just knew their own mental states and attributed them to other humans by drawing an analogy between self and other on grounds of physical similarity is not convincing. An analogy could have been drawn between self and animals – even though one might not have understood their 'language' very well.

What language provides, according to Richards, is three possible roles: speaker/listener (subject), things referred to (objects) and utterances (signs requiring interpretation as subject, object or further signs). He notes that these roles are extremely flexible in normal conversation. For instance, speakers can become objects, as can their psychological attributes. The 'passions' are viewed, in part, as objects that move the subject who is 'passive'. Public objects may be interpreted as utterances (e.g., physical omens), and utterances might themselves be perceived as speakers (e.g., the words of a god). Some phenomena, such as dreams, have an ambiguous status that could be assigned to subject, object or sign. Is a dream oneself on a journey, a message uttered by another being or just the sign of a bad digestion?

Consequently, utterances do not have fixed meanings: their mode of referral may have to be negotiated (Richards 1989: 33–42). For example, the utterance 'It is cold in here' could be taken to be referring to an objective state of the world (temperature), to an attribute of speakers/listeners (an emotional atmosphere) or interpreted as a sign ('You haven't fixed the heating yet'). This approach to the negotiation of meaning complements the open-ended, dialogical conception of self described in Chapter 2. Richards argues that he is not dividing phenomena into three types. He says there are only phenomena that can be interpreted in three ways, implying, for instance, that attributes of speakers could be assigned to animals and gods.

Richards speculates that in the course of human evolution diverse physiomorphic identifications finally narrowed to language-mediated categories, such as types of speaker. 'Identification of self as speaker can finally triumph over all other identifications as the core of selfhood' (Richards 1989: 114). This identification may have facilitated the emergence of culture because shared language categories ensure a transcendent group identity. Language confers the evolutionary advantage of binding the group together because it is external and collective and firmly embeds the individual within the group.

A speculative illustration of Richards' ideas

The following imaginary scenario attempts to illustrate Richards' thesis more concretely. We can assume that in order for a group of humans to refer to each other's actions and place them in a temporal framework several interdependent elements are needed. The first element is some kind of gesture or vocalisation (an utterance) that by convention has a common meaning for other humans by virtue of referring to a public entity (the second element) such as deer in the next valley. The third element is the identification of the source of an utterance, the speaker, as a public individual with whom the meaning of the utterance is shared. It is also necessary to assume the existence of some means of indicating whether the deer have been seen (past) or are likely to be found (future).

From these beginnings we can begin to speculate further. If Jack from the Upper Cave is recognised as a named individual, he can recognise himself as a unique speaker with an identity. His sense of being Jack is talked into existence by being called Jack by other members of the group. Self-reference becomes possible in the sense of being a body with a certain voice, physical appearance and a name. 'Jack found the deer, and I am Jack.' 'I' refers here to the speaker, and the context of speaking removes any ambiguity as to whom 'I' refers to: it is the person speaking referring to themselves as a speaker or actor. Other personal pronouns (or grammatical or gestural devices serving the same purpose) presumably evolved to refer to other identified speakers: 'you' to whom I am talking, singular or plural; 'we' as more than one person speaking with a common voice; and 'she/he' or 'they', a person or persons talking among themselves or who collectively form a group of potential speakers or actors.

We are probably safe in assuming that Jack could 'decide' to speak or withhold speech if it was not his turn, but it is not at all obvious that Jack would need to reflect that, apart from being a person, he was also a self that decides to speak. It must have occurred to him that when he stubbed his toe that the pain belonged to him and not to the others who sympathised or laughed. But it seems unlikely that Jack reflected on the nature of self-reference apart from identifying his acts, feelings and utterances with his public person. In other words, Jack lacked the modern sense of having a 'self' within his person that decides, feels, thinks, etc.

In fact, it cannot be assumed that utterances were always seen to belong to particular persons as such – which they clearly do not in the case of chants or epic poems. Charlene from the Lower Cave would have recognised the quality of Jack's voice, but the meaning of an utterance is communally negotiated and so Jack's voice partakes both of Jack as an individual and of the community to which he belongs. Utterances have an ambiguous status in the sense that they do not seem to belong unquestionably to speakers or to the world. A voice can take possession of a speaker's body, and this is sometimes fostered in a trance state when it might be spoken publicly in a different voice. It is still quite common for certain people to hear voices as if coming from gods, devils and ancestors.

It is likely that Jack became known by other characteristics as well. A phrase like 'one of Jack's deer' implies that Jack has acquired personal characteristics and not just a personal identity. And by reflexively applying these social evaluations to themselves, a public speaker may acquire the capacity to reflect on their personal attributes. Jack perceives himself with the tools employed to refer to people talking. 'I am Jack talking' begins to create a distance between just talking (which may be performed without self-reflection) and perceiving oneself as a talker. 'I, Jack, have just said that.' The notion of being distanced from one's own experience is presumably an extremely important one in the evolution of the capacity to think about self and also to disengage from that thinking when it becomes an encumbrance. In Jack's case, he has acquired the ability to take the role of another speaker and to look at himself through the eyes of another ('So, I'm a speaker like them and can describe myself in the way they would describe me').

We may speculate that the 'I' that indicates the speaker may then become an analogical 'I'. Rather than the person simply talking, with 'I' indexing the identity of the speaker, 'I' can become an analogical person or self behind the speaker. This is a natural jump to make if speech can be prepared in advance of speaking and withheld until 'I' want to say it. There is, of course, no actual speaker behind the speaker. Utterances can refer to states of affairs that are not actually present, for example, to entities like gods that are modelled on publicly available experiences. And, as we have noted, this second analogical speaker may have a completely different public identity – an ancestor, for example. When the distinction begins to be drawn between Jack in the here and now and Jack's ancestors, such talking in tongues may have been encouraged. Ceremonies may have developed to promote this communion, the quality of the voice changing as contact is made with the author of the voice.

Figurative extensions of the literal use of language may have played a large part in the way that Jack's other characteristics were referred to. Jack may have proposed a hunt for deer. If Jack was known to be an unreliable companion in the hunt, he might have been compared to other features of an unsuccessful hunt. To slip and fall at the crucial moment of throwing a spear would have been a publicly available experience that readily identified a person like Jack. He became known as Slippery Jack. This process is not an idiosyncratic transfer of meaning because it is based on a common experience. Everyone knew what it was like to slip on a wet rock. In some ways, aspects of this experience captured one's interactions with Jack. You never really knew where you were with him; you might, metaphorically, slip at any moment.

The further possibility that an utterance itself becomes a sign of another state of affairs (rather than a subject or object) can be illustrated as follows. Jack's utterance that there are deer in the next valley, if repeatedly proved false, might have been referred to as just one of old Jack's mutterings. The utterance 'One of Jack's deer' could then come to refer to the absence of a sought-after quarry. This way of talking is of a more abstract nature than simply taking Jack's utterance to be factually false because it no longer refers to Jack as a concrete individual. The utterance itself is treated as something to be interpreted, regardless of who says it or why. Utterances become messages – in the same way as the message spelled out by a ouija board has to be interpreted by the circle of people who lend their fingers to the glass.

All such proposals about the origins of person reference are inevitably speculative, and some readers might regard them as purely fanciful. However, Richards' framework of persons, objects and signals provides a way into a rich interpretation of references to personal perspective in a range of contemporary and historical circumstances. The inherent flexibility of modes of referring can clearly make it difficult to distinguish between literal and figurative uses of words. We are accustomed to using metaphors such as 'My heart bleeds for you' knowing that blood will not gush forth, but alien linguistic references do not always provide the same opportunity to disambiguate literal and figurative uses. Richards' thesis has the advantage that it accommodates so many of the features of a virtual self.

13   Loose ends and split hairs

I will now return to some of the theoretical issues I raised in Chapter 1 and review them in the light of arguments presented in the intervening chapters. The issues are complex and unresolved. This chapter is a set of 'loose ends' rather than a list of tidy conclusions. I will focus on what I consider to be the leading issues. The first of these is the problem of locating persons and selves within levels and types of explanation. The second is to consider whether a dynamic-systems perspective and the concept of emergence offer a solution to this problem. I will then go on to discuss some of the finer points of using words such as 'fiction', 'illusion' and 'virtual' in relation to self. Finally, I comment on the way authors have historicised the self and worried about its future.

Explaining persons within levels

It is difficult to produce a view of persons that integrates all three levels of explanation that I have identified: the sub-personal, the personal and the supra-personal. My aim was to bring them together in a common framework for the natural and social sciences. It is at the personal level that explanations are most familiar. Personists refer to personal attributes such as holding beliefs, acting on desires and making rational plans for the future, but there is a problem in relating this kind of discourse to causal theories. The personist stance is potentially undermined by higher and lower levels of explanation; if social determinism is adopted, the person becomes an identikit social product; if personal powers are reduced to sub-personal mechanisms, persons are dehumanised. As I pointed out in Chapter 1, personists do not buy into the idea of 'the mind' as a meaningful way of putting a boundary around personal attributes, but they share certain concerns and difficulties with mindists. In what follows, I will focus on how personists have attempted to preserve the autonomy of the personal level and go on to discuss this issue in relation to the distinction between reasons and causes.

267

Many of the terms in which people justify their acts or describe their sense-of-self fall into the category of reasons. Reasons, in turn, may refer to mental attributes such as desires and beliefs although they typically incorporate occasional reference to natural influences such as 'a low blood sugar level'. The distinction between explanations in terms of reasons and natural causes has a long ancestry, receiving an early expression in the hands of Wilhelm Windelband (1848–1915), a philosopher of history. He distinguished *Naturwissenschaften* (natural sciences), which are concerned with a search for universal laws of nature, and *Geisteswissenschaften* (human sciences), concerned with understanding things in relation to a specific (socio-historical) context. My review of the literature in previous chapters illustrates the difficulty of bridging the gap between these orientations. In some cases, theorists do not identify the distinction when it may be necessary to do so, or they may not perceive a need to bridge it anyway.

Interpretation builds on everyday practices of understanding people in terms of their unique reasons for acting, and I argued that, for certain purposes, it is the most sensible method to adopt. The method has been viewed as a literary rather than a scientific enterprise (Geertz 1983). Interpretive analysis can be performed well or badly; it can be refined by attention to detail; and it is likely to be improved by a theorist's intimate acquaintance with the people or culture under study. Interpretation is needed when the focus is on the fine detail of personal and social phenomena. It is suited to the open, indeterminate and creative quality of social interactions. It is usually employed when we know independently (and perhaps because we have been similarly acculturated) the kind of rules that persons of a certain type in certain circumstances are likely to follow. It is for these sorts of reason that we might choose a motor mechanic familiar with the idiosyncrasies of French engineering to repair a French car. If the mechanic has had to *learn* to be a member of that culture to do the job well, it would hardly be a surprise to find that another mechanic, armed only with the principles underlying the design of the internal combustion engine, would not get very far with the repair. They would be attempting to negotiate the alien culture of French methods of motor manufacture.

I have assumed that interpretive methods yield results that are compatible with the operation of natural causation. I do not mean to imply that it is therefore justifiable to ignore the fact that a person's acts are finely tuned cultural performances and go on to treat them as mere 'responses' from which general laws and mechanisms can be inferred. I only claim that an explanation in terms of natural mechanisms is possible in principle. The same might go for explaining an event such as an unexpected collapse of a house. We would normally assume that it had a natural cause even though we could not determine what it was.

This is the kind of argument employed by the philosopher Donald Davidson when he asserts that reasons are causes (2001). He is not claiming that beliefs and desires are 'events' that could be entered as terms in a natural theory (Davidson 1994: 287). He acknowledges that reasons have a justifying character that is absent in natural causal explanation but he does not think that the concept of cause is thereby ruled out as illegitimate. Reasons could justify *and* be causes, even though a causal sequence of events is simply assumed, as in the case of the collapsed house. Davidson also points out that polarising reasons and causes produces a major difficulty (2001: 19). If it is argued that a natural causal explanation reduces a person to the status of helpless victim (the passive effect of a prior cause), the riposte can always be given that the alternative leads to an infinite regress of reasons or other mental states. The alternative would be an agent who did it for some reason, but then the cause of that agent doing it would have to be explained by events that are permanently insulated from a level of natural causation. Davidson supposes that free and intentional actions could be explained by agent-less causes that are *both* reasons and causes.

Philosophers influenced by Wittgenstein, such as Rom Harré, have viewed the matter differently. One of the aims of linguistic philosophy is to dissolve hitherto intractable metaphysical questions by appealing to the rules of the grammar in which an argument is couched and examining how the terms are ordinarily used to make sense in a non-philosophical context. It may then be possible to account for a conceptual difficulty as a misuse of language. Thus, in the case of whether a reason could be considered a cause, it should be possible to appeal to the way people use words and then see if the problem revolves on the use of language. However, although a linguistic analysis may warn against nonsense, it presumably cannot rule out the possibility that people speak about reasons and causes in contradictory ways. In other words, people may combine the different grammars of reason and cause but be quite unaware (or unconcerned) about the metaphysical implications of doing so. For example, it has been assumed that God both created the world (presumably a feat of natural causation) and had a 'reason' for doing so. Reasons and causes are quite happily combined in this instance.

Harré (2005) is concerned primarily with the problem of relating the terms of discourse in one discipline, such as biology, with those of another, such as psychology. He recognises the desire to develop a common discourse – a unified and coherent system of concepts – of which a reconciliation of reasons with natural causes might be one example. Harré's arguments are mainly directed against reductionism in which there is an attempt to replace a concept like 'thinking' with a concept like 'brain process'. In reductionism, the new conceptual system essentially eliminates the old by replacing it with a set of concepts at a lower level. Throughout this book, I have also resisted the reduction of the personal to the sub-personal. At the same time, I have argued that natural mechanisms need not be considered as always operating at a level *lower* than the personal, and the merits of reduction can be considered on a case-by-case basis. The behaviour of complex systems has become a science in its own right, and it would be inappropriate to reduce, say, a natural description of the ecology of a pond to a description of the physiology of individual organisms within it. In the sciences, mixed levels are the norm, and the sort of problems that arise concern the way explanations interrelate. I conclude that it is not necessary to insist that a discourse of reasons be *replaced* by a discourse of causes, although the aim would be to find a way of relating them that was not reductive.

Harré's discussion of the problem (2005) seems to have the aim of preserving the autonomy of reasons over causes. He says that the rules of grammar underlying some discourses are relatively permeable to the rules of the grammar of other discourses, whereas some boundaries are impermeable. He argues that certain propositions within a discourse set up 'presuppositions', or 'ground rules', for what can be stated within it. For example, to talk about human beings presupposes life. He draws upon and elaborates Wittgenstein's distinction between 'hinges' and 'frames' (Wittgenstein 1953). A 'hinge proposition' (e.g., the existence of life), once it is taken up in a discourse, is not subject to empirical test. A 'frame proposition' is defined as that which fixes the grammatical rules for the use of words, that is, how the concepts are internally related in a system. Harré notes that a hinge proposition for biological discourse is the concept of a bounded and self-sustaining individual organism. He points out that biological discourse does not typically incorporate hinge propositions relating to morality.

Harré argues that there are three hinge-specific grammars in discourse about human life: a molecular, an organismic and a person grammar. His aim is to relate these discourses without adopting the concept pair 'reduction/emergence'. If I understand him correctly, Harré argues that a common set of concepts cannot be found, each level of explanation possessing its own set; the direction of his argument appears to be that the three discourses are incommensurate or impermeable to each other. Nevertheless, Harré asserts that we can talk about persons in terms of different discourses if we make clear the conditions that allow the relevant properties to be displayed. He compares the situation to the one faced by physicists when it was discovered that the precise location and momentum of a subatomic particle could not be determined in the same experimental set-up. In another illustration from physics, Harré notes: 'A cloud chamber reveals particle-like phenomena, whereas a diffraction grating reveals wave-like phenomena. No apparatus can be built that would reveal both at once' (2005: 9). A common discourse is only possible for, say, particles and waves, if the *conditions* that allow for the display of the properties concerned are included in the discourse; there is no *third* conceptual system to give a common account of the properties.

Extending this general argument to animals and humans, Harré adopts the concept of affordance from the psychologist, James Gibson (1904–79). An affordance is that which allows a disposition to be displayed, as in the example of 'a hand affording grasping'. Harré goes on to argue that different set-ups might yield incompatible affordances in the sense that properties are revealed that are jointly *possible* but cannot be actualised simultaneously, as in the illustrations from physics. In other words, Harré argues that it is possible to say that thoughts are psychological attributes under one description and brain processes under another. These would not be self-contradictory predicates because each is just a *possible* description of persons.

Harré's conclusion appears to be that hinge propositions of organism talk and person talk cannot be adopted in the same discourse. 'Organismic' affordances are not realisable under the same procedures as 'moral' affordances. To accept this conclusion appears to rule out the possibility of developing a third discourse, differing from both, that affords reference to moral acts and organismic behaviour within the same frame. Harré's move to preserve the autonomy of moral discourse is not entirely convincing when actual examples of human behaviour are examined in detail (see below). In the examples from physics, there is a hinge proposition that it is *matter* that is being conceptualised, and this is presumably the metaphysical assumption that links waves and particles. It could be argued that it is a concept of *causation* that links reasons and natural-science explanations. And again, with respect to human organisms and persons, I assume that both are manifestations of life. Indeed, I have followed Harré in assuming that persons are *jointly* constituted at biological and social levels. The latter are not simply *possible* alternative discourses for theory-building. It is true that we are yet to discover how the biological and personal levels could be integrated in a discourse that affords both. So far, I have simply rejected some possibilities, like a discourse that takes seriously the notion of the thoughts of a brain in a vat of nutrients (e.g., Ramachandran 2006). However, it seems to me possible to regard moral and natural descriptions as complementary predicates of human life, without thereby reducing moral values to a description of sub-personal events.

Harré (1998) reserves a special place for the socio-cultural level of explanation by deploying his task/tool metaphor. He suggests that cultures afford *tasks* whereas brains afford *processes* or *skills*. The brain and body are, metaphorically speaking, tools utilised in the pursuance of culturally determined tasks, including moral projects. I will now consider this proposal in some detail.

Harré's task/tool metaphor

The alleged value of this metaphor rests upon the distinctive grammars of task and tool and what this implies for the problem of integrating different levels of explanation (1998: 44). Tasks are performed by *persons* in accordance with conventional reasons, purposes and rules; tools are employed as the *means* for completing tasks. One implication of the metaphor is that a grammar of personally intended acts stands in a hierarchical relationship to a grammar of natural causes. Accordingly, Harré argues that psychological phenomena are *enabled* by natural conditions of the body, brain and environment of those engaged in an activity. In his example of a game of tennis, the game is controlled by rules but enabled by physical objects (racquets and balls, etc.). He construes the brain and body of the tennis player as amongst the tools employed in playing (Harré 1998: 44). So, just as the hand enables (affords) tool use, so the brain can be addressed as a tool to produce answers to tasks like remembering someone's name. In principle, the brain is seen as equivalent to an address book that could have been consulted in the same circumstances.

Several criticisms of this metaphor immediately suggest themselves. First, the task/tool metaphor would have us suppose that the body is a multipurpose tool under a person's command. This is to stretch the meaning of tool to include non-intended functions that accomplish tasks for which a person is clearly not held accountable, such as digestion. I might *try* to remember something but I cannot consult my brain. Its operations are as mysterious as digestion. A neuroscience account of how a brain functions to enable memory is simply not part of an account of everyday remembering and so a brain is not a tool.

Second, grammatical rules are embedded in 'forms of life' that are largely inscrutable with respect to how the rules are produced. In other words, it is not obvious that different grammars imply anything about underlying causal mechanism at a different level of explanation. It seems rather likely to me that brains are causally implicated in constituting tasks as well as the tools to achieve them. The fact that we don't refer to our brains when making up the rules of a game like tennis does not imply that the brain is not causally implicated in making up the rules. As Feest (2003) argues, we could explain human activity as a functional system and claim autonomy for this level of explanation, while not ignoring the need to identify the physical, causal processes that realise the variables specified within the system.

Third, it is not obvious that the grammars of tasks and tools are clearly separable. A tool is used by an agent for a purpose, that is, a person adopts a tool for a task. It becomes a tool as part of the intentional description of the task being performed. A piece of rock could become a tool (e.g., a hammer) but it ceases to be a tool when the task has been completed. Similarly, hands only become tools when they are functional. Frozen fingers cease to be useful tools if they lose their sensitivity. And if a brain is only metaphorically a tool, we do not have any solid grounds for placing it in a hierarchy in which it is the task that has the 'upper' hand. Harré states that: 'the rules of tennis are not some conjunction of the laws of physics and neurology' (1998: 44). It is certainly the case that a rule is not a factual statement or an attempt to explain underlying mechanisms in terms of natural processes. However, it is not clear how this difference translates into a hierarchical relationship between levels of explanation, especially if rules and laws are alternative possible accounts in the manner of wave theory and particle theory in physics.

The task/tool metaphor is also contradicted by the way we routinely mix the grammars of natural causation and personal intention in ordinary talk. Harré points out that when we switch grammars in human affairs, there is often a ritual to go with it. For a surgeon, the person is first prepared as a body on a table, and everyone understands the necessity for this. However, it is far from clear that persons undergo any ritualistic switching when they move between referring to themselves as objects subject to universal natural processes and persons subject to moral obligations. It is quite typical to say, 'I feel awful – it must be a virus.' Feeling awful is an avowal that is validated by social criteria. Having a virus is an assertion that is validated by laboratory tests. A blended reason/cause discourse is simply endemic. People mix their metaphors, and they do not seem to be necessarily aware of this or mark it out linguistically.

The choice of an appropriate grammar becomes acute when the objects of the discourse are anomalous experiences of self, as found in some so-called 'mental disorders'. We are not sure which grammar to apply. For instance, on what grounds do we say that a person who claims that their thoughts are controlled by aliens from outer space is following our own grammar, expressing a new and interesting grammar of their own or not following any consistent rules at all? Perhaps, in the last case, they are simply expressing a disorder of their brain, in which case neurological processes might provide the best account of what is happening. We have to be careful not to prejudge anything that sounds 'odd' as a new grammar, and a pathological one at that. A person might be stretching a familiar rule or misapplying it in the wrong context. Or a person might not have grasped a rule or might have combined rules to produce gobbledegook. To this extent, they are not expressing a disorder or a new grammar but have simply not yet mastered the rules.

It is widely accepted that psychotic experience can be interpreted in a variety of ways: as a brain disorder, as a meaningful response to earlier trauma or, perhaps, as a routine expression of practices, such as witchcraft, that may have been learned elsewhere. A person controlled by aliens believes that they are the passive recipient of the thoughts of others. On one hand, this could be seen simply as a variant of familiar forms of passive influence such as being overtaken by a strong emotion or 'hypnotised' by a charismatic personality. On the other hand, there might be no discernible rule in the psychotic person's discourse, and we might infer that there *is* none.

A key issue seems to be whether a reliable means can be found for distinguishing the class of actions that are instances of following a rule from the class of actions that are assumed to be caused 'naturally' (see Chapter 1). A detached observer could do this, presumably, by noting reference to local reasons or rules and confirming that an appropriate following of the rule was approved or enforced and that mistakes were corrected. There seems no reason to suppose that this process falls outside natural description or explanation even if the rule itself is contextual and justified by the people concerned through reference to other reasons. A reason that conforms to following a rule can be described as a certain type of behaviour whether or not the observer considers it rational or not to follow the rule (Calvert-Minor 2008: 6). What makes it descriptively a reason is the fact that it is caused and maintained by social consensus. This renders the reason open to natural causal explanation.

In contrast, Peter Hacker (2001) assumes that any contextually bound or historical custom is resistant to explanation by universal scientific laws. But this is probably also true of local and contextual *natural* events whose origins are multiply or historically determined. Complexity of determination, even taking account of a string of rules or provisos, is not a knock-down argument against natural causation; it just points to the difficulty of the enterprise. The description of a general class of events with a purely local meaning (e.g., 'thumbs up') would be of little value as a term in a natural explanation, but this class of event could be grouped with others (or redescribed) in order to subsume it within a natural theory of general applicability. The two types of explanation (local versus general significance) would of course have different functions.

Hacker grants that there are different types of explanation of human behaviour and that Wittgenstein did not examine how they are related. Hacker does not deny nomological laws to historians, but he says they are not like scientific laws or explanatory in the same way. His concept of a natural law is 'blind movements of matter in space' (Hacker 2001: 73). However, this is an oversimplified view of nature. He considers that psychological generalisations are only *constraints* on what a person can think or do but a psychologist would probably be only too happy to be able to specify all the constraints on a person's behaviour in a given situation. Hacker implies that a great novelist would be in a better position to explain behaviour, but, of course, this is likely to be true only in the cultural context with which the novelist (and their readers) is familiar. Moreover, there is no reason to attribute the novelist's supposedly superior ability to an explicit knowledge of the rules that are followed locally. They might have learned to read behaviour by means of the same universal learning processes that permit a primate to predict the behaviour of other animals in the social group to which it belongs.

Harré emphasises that grammars are prescriptive and that this is not true of natural causal explanation. However, it is not always possible to say what is prescribed merely on the basis of what is said. For example, he claims that it makes no sense to say 'I know I am the same person I was yesterday' because our normal framework presupposes the continuity of personal singularity. If we begin to doubt our self-identity, Harré argues, then we enter 'a new pattern of language games and the grammar of the old no longer guides us. By the same token, the fact that there are possibilities of pathologies of self does not cast into doubt the framework with which we ordinarily live our lives' (1998: 84).

However, it has made sense to a number of philosophers, as well as to apparently psychotic individuals, to ask questions about how they know that their identity is continuous. An appeal to grammar can certainly put an end to unnecessary questions that both rest on and subvert the way language is normally used but it cannot be meaningless to reflect critically on the grammar of normal usage. Harré quotes with approval Terry Warner's paper on 'Anger and Similar Delusions' (Warner 1986) that makes *explicit* certain rights, duties and assumptions that seem to be *implicit* when persons express anger. Warner's conclusions are counter-intuitive in relation to our normal understanding of anger, which we usually construe as a state in which we are 'passively' taken under its sway. In other words, we often say that we are 'overcome' by anger when, on examination, a display of this emotion seems to be far from reflexive. Warner's arguments amount to a claim that we are 'normatively' deluded into thinking we are passive. This is an example of the strategic employment of a grammar of natural causation to conceal a grammar that is intentional and rule-governed.

One implication we can draw from Warner's work is that following a rule does not mean that we are always aware of doing so. Consequently, we cannot easily distinguish between habits that develop from trial-and-error learning (as in many animals) and the habitual following of rules that are tacit but nevertheless exquisitely sensitive to social norms. It is indeed one of the aims of psychological therapy to disambiguate behaviour that is caused 'naturally' (e.g., dizziness resulting from vertigo) and behaviour that may seem uncontrollable but is in fact amenable to self-reflection and potential voluntary control (e.g., dizziness that is a feigned illness – swooning – and a means of managing a difficult situation).

Not only are apparently involuntary habits potentially rule-governed, but, furthermore, the most deliberate and rational following of rules can, for some people, become habitual and compulsive. The person who compulsively checks five times (or in multiples of five) that their front door is locked is following a rational and normal convention the first time they check but subsequently cannot be described (nor do they describe themselves) as following a rule but obeying one. Whether we describe this behaviour as part of a person discourse or a discourse of natural causation is a moot point. Some people with obsessions are described as delusional because they insist that their perfectly reasoned thinking is a valid description of reality.

There is a real difficulty, then, in describing human 'passivity' in relation to some acts that are examples of the tacit following of rules and some acts, like habits, that have only the outward appearance of following a rule. In both cases, people position themselves as passive. There is little doubt that a grammar of moral discourse differs from a grammar that pertains to natural causation but whether our choice in using one or the other says anything much about the way human behaviour is actually caused is a different matter. Acts that are *actually* under normative control may be very similar to acts that are reflexive. The problem arises for psychologists who study eye blinks: some appear to be reflexive, others intended, and others are presumably blended. Reflexive and normatively controlled acts need not be constructed as either/or in a hierarchical relationship but as either or both in a parallel relationship.

It is true that only persons are held responsible for their acts, that is, only persons are considered suitable subjects for normative control. If this is what defines the personal level, it is a process that could be studied naturalistically even if this process does not make reference to the moral criteria that govern it. And if the further claim is made that people autonomously choose their moral criteria when passing moral judgements on themselves or on others, this makes the source of morality utterly mysterious. In fact, the claim seems inconsistent with the many natural causal explanations put forward to account for *immoral* or *compulsive* acts.

When normative control fails, as in the example of a person with an obsession described above, Harré resorts to the idea of a defective tool (1997b). But a person might construe an action as governed by a rule when other evidence can be produced to show that it is not – or perhaps the converse might apply. For instance, a person might believe that their unassertive behaviour is due to a brain defect – say, a deficit in certain neurotransmitters. After training, and having learned how to act assertively, the person can tell a voluntary story about their acts of self-assertion, a story that is likely to be validated by others. Attributing unassertiveness to the possession of a defective tool would be to draw unnecessarily on a sub-personal explanation when the unassertiveness in question could be interpreted as a poor voluntary (personal) strategy for achieving desired effects. This is not to suggest that only one kind of account is 'correct'. The brains of unassertive people may well differ from the brains of assertive people, and their 'deficit' may be a contributory cause of their behaviour. But assuming that training people in acts of assertion is generally effective, it would seem that treating them as persons who are responsible for their acts would be a better way of construing and remedying their problem. The question is not so much which grammar is appropriate but which strategy is causally effective. It is quite conceivable that there are biological differences between persons that would make the training more or less effective. Alternative accounts can be placed in a parallel or complementary relationship rather than a hierarchical one.

Systems, emergent properties and levels of explanation

I will now explore the idea that levels of explanation can be related to what has been called 'a dynamic systems perspective' on the human sciences (Sawyer 2003a). My objective is therefore to examine the possibility of situating persons and selves within functional systems that can accommodate both biological and social concepts. This is such a complex issue that I can only touch on some of the main considerations. The broader context for this discussion is the problem of social causation. The position taken by methodological individualists is that all social phenomena are caused by the actions of individuals in response to the situations they encounter. They resist the idea that social processes have some kind of independent causal efficacy in the form, say, of a 'group mind'. For instance, does an organisation as a unitary entity cause effects or are the actions of an organisation entirely reducible to the individual acts of its members (Tollefsen 2002)?

The position I have so far taken is that interactions between persons – the supra-personal level – should be considered as generating phenomena that cannot be explained as (or reduced to) the properties of persons taken singly or in aggregate. Deborah Tollefsen's interpretation of social causation is to consider a group like an organisation as having rational intentions that may, in fact, depart from the preferred reasons for acting of the individuals who make up the group. Tollefsen's basis for interpreting a group's intentions is drawn, by analogy, from a person-level understanding of a person's reasons for acting. In other words, the group 'has its reasons'. Agreeing (or disagreeing) on an interpretation rests on the existence of social norms that, in my view, are already supra-personal phenomena and therefore something that already needs to be explained from a naturalistic perspective. Consequently, I will simply regard the natural effects of one individual on another as a form of natural causation and assume that these interactions have emergent systemic properties. On these grounds, chimpanzees that engage in collaborative hunting activities (see Chapter 12) are exhibiting a 'supra-personal' process because their social behaviour cannot be reduced (on one interpretation at least) to an aggregate of individual-level responses.

For many sociologists, social mechanisms have their own reality and causal efficacy. They are considered to be emergent properties of interacting persons. It is assumed that social structures as well as individuals exert agency, although these two forms of agency are conceptualised as being in a reciprocal relationship. Dave Elder-Vass (2007) has set out some of the key terms in this sociological perspective. The 'total system' in a dynamic systems view includes events and processes at all levels, some of which, like human beings, can be considered as sub-systems because they have at least some self-organising properties. A conceptual distinction can be made between those factors that generate and structure a system into its characteristic form and those factors that elaborate or change it. Change in a social system therefore depends on the co-determination of antecedent structures and what it is the partici-pating agents do to act upon it. Structures like organisations are said to be emergent properties of the interactions between individuals and are not simply reducible to the conjoint acts of individuals. Elder-Vass (2007: 27) notes that similar arguments could be applied to the living human body as an emergent property of its individual biological parts. A person-level of explanation can be considered distinct from the sub-personal because the *parts* of a person's body do not possess the causal power of a person. It is only through the interaction of biological parts (in conjunction, as I will argue, with supra-personal influences) that the person exists.

A natural living entity such as a human being can be said to exist as a unique biological system when it maintains a boundary between itself and its medium or environment. The environment may also be a biological system when the system is itself a sub-system in a larger whole. Obviously, the boundary generated by a system is permeable to exchanges of various sorts with its environment, and the bound-ary is lost when these terminate (e.g., when an organism is starved of oxygen or food, or when internal organisation breaks down). A self-organising living system has been defined as 'autopoietic' if it continually regenerates its components and their processes of inter-action, the whole being considered as a unity on this basis (Maturana and Varela 1980). According to Keith Sawyer (2003a), social sys-tems differ from natural systems in the sense that (1) they are not physically locatable (i.e. they have no obvious visible boundaries); (2) communications between the components are not physically observable and describable; and (3) individual members of the system can represent characteristics of the whole, subjectively 'understand' it and hold intentions towards it.

As I have already attempted to show in this book, acknowledging these differences does not necessarily make social systems immune to naturalism. For instance, the description of a system in terms of func-tions, or the intentions of its members, does not imply that a function or an intention is not realisable as a natural process; personal interactions are accompanied by biological processes whether or not we are in a position to describe them. With regard to the third difference, I will suggest that intentions are not properties of individuals per se. They can be regarded as properties of the social system as well.

The argument I have been putting forward is that the person is not an autonomous system because personhood is a function of a larger social system whose boundaries are set by interactions within a group of human beings. In other words, a person is not like a cell in a tissue culture in a Petri dish, maintaining itself by exchanging inputs and outputs with its environment. A person is more like a semi-independent cell (sub-system) in a social organism that partly controls its inputs and outputs. This organic metaphor for society is by no means new but it can be newly interpreted. A major problem is that of discovering where the boundaries of a system lie or where to place them if approaching the problem on an a-priori basis. Another is to determine whether systems are hierarchically embedded or emerge from a set of parallel sub-systems in a common environment. For instance, as I have frequently asked, what is the boundary of the *mind?*

One solution has been offered by Niklas Luhmann who applies the concept of autopoietic systems to biological, psychic and social levels of explanation (see Moeller 2006). Luhmann treats communication, mind (consciousness) and life (body/brain) as autonomous, operationally closed systems in the sense that they are not related in a hierarchy. Instead, they provide an environment for each other, 'irritate' each other and are structurally coupled without having any direct relationships. This leaves the concept of an environment in a fuzzy state, especially as Luhmann regards language as a medium for both consciousness and communication (Moeller 2006: 19). Although Moeller (2006: 10) argues that this systems theory supersedes mind–body dualism, it is hard to imagine a conception more Cartesian.

Another solution views systems as embedded and relies on the concept of emergent properties to account for the higher-level system. This solution would still allow independent, semi-autonomous entities to exist within a common medium provided by either a lower- or higher-level system. Emergence therefore holds out the possibility of integrating biological and social sciences while at the same time retaining their relative autonomy. As I suggested above, the fact that a discourse of reason is impermeable to a discourse of cause need not imply incompatibility at the level of physical instantiation.

As systems themselves interact, a number of systemic levels could emerge and produce novel properties. The assumption can be made that the interaction of entities at the higher level cannot be predicted in advance on the basis of properties of lower-level entities (see Benton and Craib 2001: 119). For instance, we could suppose that a social process like language emerges as a consequence of interacting organisms that, individually, do not (and could not) express it. This sounds like a more promising basis for a unified system than reductionism, which asserts that all properties at a higher level can be fully explained by more basic laws at a lower level.

However, until it can be shown how emergent mechanisms actually arise, the concept of emergence remains as a speculative and promissory suggestion. For instance, a reductionist could still argue that language is an organismic potential fully explicable in terms of an innate brain structure, which, in turn, is explained by neuronal systems, physiological processes, biochemical reactions and so on down to the molecular level.

Attempts to integrate levels of explanation within a systems perspective have been met by attitudes that vary between vigorous opposition to a form of acceptance that trivialises the issues. Hostility may be related to the fact that humans are, in some measure, self-defining animals. For instance, Keith Webb (1995: 10) states: 'What is incomprehensible is that biological approaches still have sufficient credence to warrant serious discussion in contemporary social science.' Webb's speciality is conflict resolution and so his concern about biological reductionism is understandable if, as he surmises, this view encourages the belief that aggression and violence are inevitable in human affairs. However, it is also incomprehensible that biology should be ignored. Webb considers its influence to be so slight as to be negligible (1995: 18). He does concede that personal biochemical imbalances might cause aggression but Webb regards these instances as accidental occurrences, unrelated to a general inherent tendency to display aggression. He states that: 'Conflict is not inherent in human nature but rather in the condition of man' (1995: 12). This begs rather a lot of questions about how to define the human condition.

At the trivialising end, Ronald Mallon and Stephen Stich (2000) think that social constructionist and evolutionary psychology are, at least as far as emotions are concerned, quite compatible. They say that any disagreement could be regarded as a semantic issue. This would be true if, as they argue, social constructionists are just concerned with the unique local circumstances that trigger emotions and shape their expression, while evolutionary biologists have the serious task of discovering universal mechanisms in the brain that underlie the core of any emotion. I do not question their assumption that there are innate neural predispositions to express an emotion such as fear. But it is far too easy to equate the brain with a natural universal component and local modes of expression with the cultural component. Giving them a spatial location, inside and outside the brain, contributes nothing to understanding the relationship between culture in its natural aspect and nature in its cultural aspect. The view I have taken is that persons are jointly constituted as biological and cultural creatures. Likewise, all cultural artefacts are simultaneously material and semiotic.

It would be neat if the different sciences could be differentiated on the basis of emergent levels of explanation for each one. However, in a system with emergent properties, it can be postulated that there is 'upward' and 'downward' causation between levels. For instance, if language is an emergent property of interacting individuals, it exerts downward causation on the properties of individuals (e.g., on their cognitive strategies for solving problems). There is also upward causation; this can be illustrated by the example of a community of non-hearing individuals that learns to communicate by signing rather than by spoken words. These interpenetrating causal influences can be allowed without abandoning the idea that systems retain functional integrity.

The systemic level I have called supra-personal would possess functional integrity to the extent that relationships between persons were reliably maintained (as a stable pattern that reproduces itself) by reciprocating events that could be described conjointly at a personal and biological level. This view entails the assumption that the expression of socially significant responses, gestures, words, etc., in systematic association with social and environmental contexts, could be considered from complementary perspectives as semiotic and biological processes. A supra-personal system therefore refers to 'behaviour of persons in context'. The processes/mechanisms that maintain it as a stable pattern cannot be observed (they have to be inferred from observed relationships) but they are clearly tied to empirical referents, such as features of persons and their practices in relevant contexts. Given that a total system of the kind just described is made up of semi-autonomous sub-systems (e.g., persons) interacting in an unpredictable and changing environment, the system remains an 'open' one (Benton and Craib 2001: 129). However, while a system may be open from the perspective of its sub-systems (e.g., persons and institutions), it could perhaps be considered closed depending on the timescale and the medium in which it is understood to operate. The relative stability of the supra-personal system could be attributed, in part, to the sedimented nature of historical mediating factors such as a society's language and institutions. Put differently, the system retains its past states in the face of new inputs (what is technically referred to as a hysteresis effect).

Persons as natural causes in a systems perspective

I have assumed that persons have natural causal effects on each other and that their interactions are mediated by language and other social practices. Supra-personal processes, in turn, react back on the person and contribute to the constitution of personal attributes. This conception is clearly incompatible with methodological individualism. The latter approach explains a person's acts in terms of the beliefs, motives and intentions of the individual actor. Peter Manicas, a philosopher of social science, states that 'the primary causal agents in history are persons' (2006: 115). He believes that 'social structure' exists only virtually because it enables and constrains, but does not cause, action. Later on, he refers to constraints and enabling conditions as social mechanisms (2006: 124), in which case it seems that their influence *could* be regarded as causal.

There should be no objection to treating a social constraint, like a threat, as one of the causes of behaviour in context. It is only on autocentric assumptions that the buck stops with a person making a decision, that is, that causation is given a primary locus in the person. However, once it is assumed that there is downward causation from an emergent supra-personal level on many personal attributes, including intentionality, the social cannot be built up only from the personal. The 'invisibility' of supra-personal influences, like a threat that has not yet been exercised, may explain why they have sometimes been disregarded and methodological individualism has remained popular. Of course, the invisibility of a social process does not undermine its efficacy in shaping social practices.

Some attributes of the person-level system must be intrinsic to that level; at a minimum, an embodied person has self-organising systemic characteristics as a material body. In constructivist (rather than constructionist) theories, there is a tendency to regard the brain as an autonomous system whose relationship with the environment, though permeable, is always indirect, that is, mediated by 'models' of the environment; I rejected this conception in Chapter 9.

I will now examine and criticise several attempts to conceptualise persons within a functional framework that demonstrates emergent properties. Keith Sawyer (2003a; 2004) is an emergentist who considers that the properties that emerge at a social level are real mechanisms that participate in causal relations. In other words, a social phenomenon like 'social class' is not just an abstract aggregation of occupational titles but could be viewed, potentially, as a social mechanism. Sawyer defines a mechanism as 'a detailed description of the system's components and their interactions' (2004: 261). Sawyer therefore also rejects methodological individualism. If there are emergent social mechanisms, there are some social phenomena that cannot be reduced to, or do not comprise, interactions amongst persons considered as self-sufficient individuals. Sawyer argues that what is needed is some means of distinguishing those emergent properties that are reducible from others that are not.

He calls his own position non-reductive individualism, thereby acknowledging that socially emergent properties are embedded in individual interactions but insisting at the same time that the properties have autonomous causal power. He assumes that an emergent property could be realised by different social mechanisms that are not similar in a descriptive sociological sense. For instance, ways of 'being a church' could be realised in different manifestations but still share a common emergent property. Nor need they be similar, according to Sawyer, at the level of the social mechanism that glues together each church. The separate examples of any emergent property could be 'wildly disjunctive', implying that a social property like 'being a church' could be theorised about at a higher level of explanation without reducing it to the social interactions that go into any exemplar of the property. This higher-level property could have an autonomous downward causal effect at a lower level, implying also, it seems, that it could be realised in as-yet-unidentified forms. Sawyer (2003a: 220) notes that 'social-level causal explanations may be possible even when individual-level causal explanations for the same events are not possible.' It also follows that a property of a social group need not necessarily be observed in its component individuals.

Is the concept of emergence useful in thinking about person and self? In the way I have presented matters, individual persons and selves are concrete expressions of processes that can be theorised about generically. I have also assumed that many personal attributes are the consequence of emergent supra-personal mechanisms. Put differently, there are universal processes that will generate new specific forms of person and self. Social theorists who build their models on the properties of persons as we currently conceive of them would likely pick out properties like a person's intentions. An example might be a person's intention to consume a product on the grounds of their knowledge of its existence and its cost relative to similar products. However, if we take emergent properties seriously, we cannot say that a person's intention is a property of the human organism per se. It could just as well be an individual (personal) expression of the downward causation of an emergent social mechanism. The whole concept of a 'human nature' comes into question. If emergentism is accepted, we cannot easily determine (at least at present) what properties are intrinsically personal and what are not.

Viewing a person's intentions in this way flies in the face of autocentric assumptions. The preponderant view is that intentions belong to the mind, and the mind, if it is an emergent property at all, emerges only from the brain. Neuroscience emergentists place the human mind and consciousness at the pinnacle of a hierarchy of each person's brain system. Todd Feinberg (2002: 125) points out that this was the concept put forward by C. Lloyd Morgan (1852–1936) and also by Roger Sperry (1913–94), whose view was a version of Cartesian dualism. Feinberg (2002: 127) rejects dualism and the idea that there is some place in the brain where all the brain's activity comes together, as if at a pinnacle. He substitutes the idea of a nested hierarchy of sub-systems in which there is no 'top command' and the controls or constraints are distributed around the sub-systems working interdependently. Yet Feinberg returns to his Cartesian bunker when he asks 'What is the "inner I" that pulls together the mind and controls our actions' and 'What keeps the millions of neurons in our brains from all going off in their own directions?' (2002: 131).

His answer takes the form of non-neurological concepts, such as meaning, conscious purpose, self and will. He defines 'the' self as a property that emerges from 'a nested hierarchy of meaning and purpose' that is created, he says, by the brain but is not reducible to the brain (2002: 131). Unlike the brain that is grasped by an outside, objective perspective, the self is said to be the inside, subjective perspective. Feinberg says that feelings like pain do exist but only for the subject who experiences them. In other words, one's own material brain produces one's mind, 'but for the observer that mind does not materially exist' (2002: 148). Feinberg admits that 'There is a certain loneliness to all this', especially as anyone's inner self is no more than an illusion to someone else, but he comforts himself with the idea (unexplained) that 'we partially merge with another person's mind' (2002: 152). At the same time, he denies that this has anything to do with material, physical transfers between persons. In Feinberg's hands, emergentism at the sub-personal and personal level is transformed into an incoherent form of Cartesianism. I have argued that a version of emergentism that might go some way to rescuing this self in a bubble would have everything to do with material, physical transfers between persons.

If this version of neuroscience emergentism is unsatisfactory, can the same be said of behavioural and psychological versions?

With an integrative perspective in mind, Michael Mascolo and Kurt Fischer (1998: 332) set out to construct self within a dynamic systems model of 'weakly connected control systems'. In the way that I have done, they differentiate the agentive organism or person from self-awareness or self-representation (i.e. a person's representation of their own powers and attributes). Persons, as self-organising systems, are said to co-act with other persons, meaning that persons and selves are simultaneously individual and social. The total system is conceived as a hierarchy of levels with the genome at its base and the cultural-linguistic level at the apex. Levels operate according to their own principles, but they are only partially independent because they mutually regulate each other, vertically and horizontally. Mascolo and Fischer propose four levels of the organism-environment system: the bio-genetic, the organismic-agentive, the social-dyadic and the cultural-linguistic. Systems are assumed to be controlled by hierarchically embedded feedback loops.

Mascolo and Fischer decompose human behaviour into sets of skills, understood as properties of 'persons-in-context' (1998: 339). They refer to 'the mind' as being inherently fractionated into separate control systems, and, although it is not clear what they mean by mind, they do conceive of it as extending 'beyond the skin' (Mascolo and Fischer 1998: 375). Persons are said to mutually regulate each other during communication, and this implies, presumably, that minds are simultaneously individual and social. The environmental context includes the influence of shared goals and meanings that participate 'virtually from the beginning of development' (Mascolo and Fischer 1998: 348).

Mascolo and Fischer refer to a construct of self in several ways. First, the person functions as a distinct and integral system, and, second, self refers to the agentive system's capacity to become aware of its own processes, products and identities (i.e. a person has a sense-of-self and can reflect on their own constitution). This latter self is jointly constructed between persons. A shared representation such as a standard for civilised behaviour can then come to serve as a reference value in a feedback loop for the person as a semi-independent system. Activity and self-representation are conceived as emergent products of the co-action of all levels of the total system. However, the individual as a semi-independent system contributes to its own development and self-representation. As they phrase it, 'Such a self is neither an autonomous center of control nor a decentralized product of social forces' (Mascolo and Fischer 1998: 377).

This dynamic-systems model is in broad accord with the way I have conceived constructionism in relation to naturalism. However, in terms of figuring out functional relationships between the biological and social elements, the devil presumably lies in the detail of interpenetrating causal influences, both vertical and horizontal. For instance, there is a risk of individualising social (dialogical) processes when 'social values' are transformed into reference standards for the person-level sub-system. A person may act on the basis of reference values retained from previous interactions but the values are maintained dialogically. And how exactly does the agent's capacity to reflect on aspects of its own existence feed in to the functioning of the system as a whole? It is also difficult to grasp the implications of separating the cultural-linguistic level from the social-dyadic level. If cultural and linguistic influences exert their effect through dialogical interactions between persons, the two levels are not systemically autonomous. Mascolo and Fischer exploit the model primarily in its application to child development, on which I will not elaborate here.

The radical behaviourism of Burrhus F. Skinner (1904–90) can also be regarded as a viable functional model of the relationship between personal and supra-personal levels. Although radical behaviourism is often derided as a simplistic reduction of human behaviour to stimuli and responses, rewards and punishments, this is a misrepresentation of Skinner's views (Blackman 1991). Skinner studied behaviour as a naturally occurring biological phenomenon, and his concept of operant behaviour, selected by its environmental consequences, was intended as a direct parallel to Darwinian natural selection over an evolution-ary time span. He then generalised principles inferred from patterns of behaviour in contrived environmental contexts to far more complex human activities such as self-control and verbal reference to reasons and private events. Skinner denied the possibility of reducing dynamic patterns of behaviour in an environmental context to sub-personal mechanisms, and so he remained opposed to a cognitive science allied to brain science.

Skinner's functional analysis of behaviour is essentially as a dynamic system. At a social level, it is the reciprocal interactions between people-in-context that comprise the system. The system has emer-gent properties even though some of its explanatory principles, such as reinforcement, were originally inferred from the behaviour of animals in isolated laboratory conditions. It would be a mistake to conclude from this that the social level is reducible to the administration of 'rewards and punishment'. Reinforcement is inferred from the effects of sets of complex behaviour-in-context contingencies, distributed spatially and temporally. As an inference from observations, forms of reinforcement are equivalent to the invisible structuring principles or mechanisms that have been proposed by some social scientists. 'Reinforcement' is not visible in the way that a concrete reward, like a food pellet, is visible.

It can be compared to the relational mechanism that has been proposed by Elder-Vass to explain the emergent properties of a group of individuals who all hold, and uphold, the same normative belief. The relations that make the individual belief causally effective are the commitments of members to endorse it by advocating it, praising it or criticising those who fail to enact it, etc. (Elder-Vass 2006).

Derek Blackman (1991) argues that there are strong parallels between the ideas of Skinner and G. H. Mead. Both were centrally concerned with self. For instance, Skinner speculates about the genesis of self-directed speech and the conditions under which persons could exercise control over their own behaviour. He attempts to explain the transition from external control to self-control in a biological framework, without resorting to sub-personal mechanisms. As we have seen (Chapter 7), Mead's objectives were similar. For both thinkers, meaning and consciousness are constituted within social interaction – meaning is not a process of transmitting ideas from one conscious mind to another.

In 'About Behaviorism', Skinner (1976: 119) gives a speculative account of the genesis of reasons from causes. He suggests that language enabled people to describe the effects of external contingencies on their own behaviour. He believes that the first verbal practices involved giving commands, advice and warnings. A command informs another person what to do, usually with an understanding of the consequences of not doing it; advice and warnings prescribe behaviour to be executed if certain consequences are to be obtained or avoided. Commands and advice, if heeded, lead to external consequences that then serve to control and maintain it 'naturally'. Commands to a motorist like 'Stop at the junction', which may be naturally reinforced by a reduced probability of having an accident, might need to be supplemented by contrived social contingencies, such as the imposition of a fine for disregarding it. Generally useful advice may get to be enshrined in folklore. This amounts to instructions for following a rule that not only speeds up the acquisition of new behaviour but also attunes a person to the environmental contingencies that typically control it. With regard to rules or laws, these may either specify contingencies that exist in the social environment (by design) or to contingencies that exist in the natural world (as discovered by experiment or trial and error). According to Skinner (1976: 129), the causal efficacy of a reason for a person lies in the *actual* consequences that adopting the reason (advice, warning, etc.) has had in the past.

In the same book, Skinner is less convincing in his account of persons and selves. In fact he just substitutes 'person' for human organism. Persons and selves are simply various behavioural repertoires of the organism elicited under various circumstances. He denies that a person is an originating agent (1976: 168) but in so far as a person is an integral organism, this statement ignores self-organising principles in the person as a sub-system. However, he rightly stresses, in my view, that self-descriptive behaviour had to await the evolution of a verbal community. A person gets to know themself through first knowing others. Self-descriptive behaviour, in which the person reacts to themself as an object, allows for different repertoires of behaviour to interact and compete with different strengths, according to the environmental context and its historical association with each repertoire. Skinner's approach has, of course, been developed by other authors (e.g., Hayes et al. 2001).

Is a virtual self a fiction or an illusion?

I have maintained that self is virtual and a person (as embodied) is real. This distinction is implied in the contrast between 'my self' and 'myself' and also in the suggestion that self is an analogical person. I will now say more about a virtual self, bearing in mind John Austin's caution that any assertion that 'X is real' is not worth stating unless we can point to a contrasting sense in which X might not be real (Austin 1964: 77). For instance, he says that the meaning of a 'decoy duck' depends on a contrast with a real duck. But in another context, a decoy duck might be considered real in contrast with, say, an image of a decoy duck in a person's mind. The contrast between real and virtual I have made in this book arises out of adopting Harré's proposal that persons are doubly constituted. On the one hand, a person is a biological organism. They are a real example of living matter, neither a collection of inert matter nor a contrived mechanical object like a robot. A person is also *really* a person by virtue of the fact that other people regard her or him as fulfilling the social criteria for personhood. Here the contrast is between real persons and humans who fall short of the criteria (e.g., newborn babies) or 'simulated persons' who deceive us into believing (sometimes with our acquiescence) that the criteria have been satisfied.

The distinction between human beings and robots concerns living matter, whereas the contrast between persons and non-persons does not depend crucially on life. A non-person like a zombie is represented 'as if' living. The virtual/real distinction, as far as it applies to self/ person, could be made as follows. A virtual self is an 'as if' or analogical person that lacks certain features of real persons such as embodiment. I have assumed that this way of talking enables real persons to represent a great deal of what they do in a symbolic manner by referring to the activity of a virtual entity (and sometimes a force). When self is compared metaphorically to an analogue person, virtual selves behave in much the same way as real people in the world. For instance, a person might 'sow the seeds of an idea' or 'weave a plan for the future', but it is a metaphorical entity inside them that sows and weaves. In Chapter 3, I expanded my definition of the generic Self to include all of the possible ways in which persons comprehend their relationship with others and with the world. The characterisation of a virtual self that I have just given may be peculiar to western culture. In other words, it is possible that the familiar autocentric western self as a kind of analogue person is a historically contingent manifestation of selfhood.

Some manifestations of an 'as if' person, like a stage actor playing a role, are perhaps best described as virtual persons (or personages) rather than virtual selves, but these are simply terminological refinements. The reality of the actor as a unique human being is not essential to the performance because we might be quite content with an understudy. The reality of the actor might reassert itself if the actor forgets their lines or steps out of character for whatever reason. Besides playing a certain character, an actor can take on additional optional personas – ploys, masks, deceptions, ironic characterisations – in effect, 'playing' them within the play. I have made a similar argument about people: that they are jointly constituted biologically and socially and possess the option to present themselves as various 'as if' persons or 'selves'. A properly constituted person has a unique body and a credible history. As described in Chapter 4, some biological individuals constitute themselves as more than one credible individual on account of bodily dysfunction, psychological trauma or plain deception. They may be regarded as pathological or criminal, and we may be at a loss to know how to relate to them.

The stage analogy is, of course, an old one, but people may not feel the least like players as I have portrayed them. Their analogical self feels quite real. A distinction that is commonly made at a phenomenal (sense-of-self) level is between an authentic, familiar or true self in contrast with an anomalous, false or unwanted self. When I claim that a virtual self is based on an analogy, this implies nothing about its felt reality. A virtual self is neither a mere theoretical conception nor a literary flourish; in other words, it 'really' does constitute an unquestioned sense of the self's reality despite its metaphorical origins. And once a figurative connection has been made between unrelated semantic domains, such as the world and a stage, new metaphors tend to spring from it. A person 'in the spotlight' stands in the same relation to the world as the player does to the stage. At times, we seem to be in the thrall of figurative language; at other times, we employ it deliberately.

The idea that ancestral humans experienced the world through metaphor (that is, had not yet distinguished the literal from the metaphorical) was proposed early on by Vico (2000). We can understand this process as a fundamental cognitive operation because, for Vico, to imagine is immediately to believe (Haskell 1993: 27). Vico also thought that metaphors sometimes become fossilised in speech despite having once been the live embodiment of perceptions whose existence we are now unaware. Sarbin (1968) provides an example of this process when he carries out an etymological analysis of the word 'anxiety' which supposedly refers to a literal mental state. He traces it back to Middle English and Old French words for a choking sensation. He suggests that people who were suffering spiritually reported that they were 'as if' choking physically. Later on, anguish (anguisse) became a 'real' property of the mind. In a similar way, we can say that self has become a part of the mental furniture. Self is not *fictional* if by fiction we mean something invented arbitrarily – metaphor does communicate something that is 'really' sensed or intuited. A metaphor can be dead and still refer to something that has a basis in reality, as in the case of anxiety. However, its reality may not be that of a literal 'thing' or 'entity', like 'the cap' of a bottle. To suppose that a metaphor does refer in this way is to reify it. Choking does enable us to refer to real circumstances – 'I (really) felt choked!' – but a person does not necessarily literally choke.

Why should people resort to metaphor to understand their experiences? I assume that for linguistically competent humans, some aspects of reality are easier to grasp conceptually than others. Derek Melser (2004: 166) argues that the specific usefulness of metaphor is to refer to features of things that would be difficult or impossible to refer to otherwise. Abbreviating Melser's discussion considerably, he explains the process of metaphor as follows: there is a general referent, the topic under discussion, and a specific referent that is a feature of that topic that is rather difficult to pin down. However, this feature is captured by a metaphorical word or phrase in which the feature is more obviously present. It is understood from the context of communication that the metaphor is not to be taken literally. The listener grasps that a feature of the metaphor is applicable to the topic under discussion. In Melser's illustration, the metaphor is the Taj Mahal and it is used to describe a hat that someone is trying on in a shop.

Applying this general approach to self as a metaphor, there must be an aspect of human affairs that asks to be comprehended, to which an idea of self (as a proxy person) might provide a convenient answer.

The state of affairs that is conceptualised metaphorically is surely not just mundane activity but rather subtle interactions between persons or between a person and their environment. In Chapter 2, I argued that it is difficult to define self in any literal sense and eventually I arrived at a dialogical conception. Speaking persons are of course usually presented to us concretely, and the ordinary features of conversation lend themselves as metaphors to capture more nebulous features of persons and their relationships. The following illustration should suffice.

In a real activity like 'man smashes bone with stone', the parsing of a sentence into subject, object and verb obscures the total and interactive quality of the experience. When we examine what persons do, it is not as if they are literally separated, as subject, from the world as object (Merleau-Ponty 1966). Our perceptions and doings are always the product of an interaction. For example, we might agree that a road is twisting and its being twisted is a public property, but it is not one that could easily be defined in physical terms. The road is twisting because we have to adapt our movements towards it: twisting roads, twisty pieces of wood and, of course, twisting ourselves around reliably generate a bodily sense of twistedness. Twistedness is neither purely in the world nor purely in us. It is a common experience elicited by situations with certain physical properties that become salient in relation to the design of our own bodies. Labelling this experience as 'twisting' makes it available as a potential metaphor for talking about less obviously locatable experiences – some people are simply 'twisted' or make us feel that we have to adapt ourselves to them by 'twisting' our normal reactions.

Lakoff and Johnson (1980: 192), in their well-known book *Metaphors We Live By,* carve out a similar path between objectivism and subjectivism when they adopt an 'experientialist account of understanding'. As I have just portrayed it, they assert that a human being's experience of reality is a product of their interaction with the natural and social environment, constrained by the properties that human beings naturally possess. As they put it: 'there are many things we understand directly from our direct physical environment' (1980: 176). These understandings may form the basis of any conceptual system we devise, whose truth is tested against further experience. They take these foundational assumptions for granted and assume that we have real experiences of a real world. However, according to Lakoff and Johnson, metaphor is employed to conceptualise that reality because we do not understand it directly in its totality. We develop an 'indirect' understanding when we employ one kind of thing to understand a completely different kind of thing. One implication of this process is that metaphor may hide reality as well as 'revealing' it, and so in order to bring out the fullness of reality, we may need to employ several complementary metaphors or even ones that are frankly inconsistent. For instance, these authors point out that an argument can be compared to a journey (it sets out, progresses, comes to an end, etc.) or it can be compared to a container (it is empty, has holes in it, won't hold water, etc.).

Lakoff and Johnson (1980) do not get down to specifics with regard to the categories of person and self. What, for instance, are our direct and indirect understandings in this domain? A person can be understood as a 'participant' in an experiential gestalt (1980: 176) but Lakoff and Johnson say that much of the time the experiential background is never noticed because it is simply presupposed. We have to turn to a metaphor like 'the mind is a container' to see how we *indirectly* understand a process like memory. As noted above, their idea is that metaphor both reveals reality and constructs new realities. But it seems to me that Lakoff and Johnson do not supply us with a way of knowing whether the categories of person and self reveal reality directly or whether they have been constructed to reveal reality indirectly. Given that customary usage may reify metaphors, we have little to go on in deciding the issue. In fact, Lakoff and Johnson go as far as to say that metaphors 'have little to do with objective reality, if there is such a thing' (1980: 184). They consider that all truth is relative to a conceptual system, but, if this is the case, their other notions are incoherent.

Lakoff and Johnson (1980: 180–2) grant that their experientialist theory of truth has elements in common with a correspondence theory and with classical realism. This must be so if they are right in assuming that we have direct knowledge of the world and the world has a feedback, corrective function. Their concept of realism also extends reality from the physical world to the cultural world. But if the cultural world is, in part, an expression of a conceptual scheme framed by unacknowledged metaphorical presuppositions, it becomes impossible to disentangle direct and indirect experience. We are left uncertain whether metaphors of person and self are creative constructs or could, in principle, be shown to fail the test of 'reality'. For instance, what might the metaphor of 'mind as a container' conceal or reveal about reality?

More recently, Lakoff (1997) has explored the metaphors that, he believes, structure our experience of self, gleaning them from a spectrum of expressions that include such exotic examples as 'If I was you, I'd hate me.' Lakoff wonders whether 'these metaphors are tapping into some sort of real human experience' (1997: 110) reflecting, it seems, the intuition that human beings have a sense-of-self as experienced and also try to structure that experience with whatever linguistic tools are available. However, his formulation of the matter begs the question whether a metaphor constitutes the experience in an unquestioned form or simply helps to convey it. It seems impossible to separate out 'real' from 'conceptual' bits of our experience unless we possess an independent basis for drawing this contrast. It is not clear which scheme Lakoff is using to distinguish ordinary experience from 'real' experience.

Lakoff analyses the metaphors we use for person and self and concludes that we adopt a 'divided person metaphor'. He says we think of a person as being an ensemble of (1) one Person; (2) the Subject (a locus of consciousness and rationality); and (3) at least one other entity, a Self that 'includes at the very least our bodies, our emotions, and the part of us that acts in the world' (1997: 94). He then goes on to say that the Subject is normally thought to be contained in the Self and also to be in possession of, or above, the Self. He asserts that expressions such as 'Step outside yourself' and 'Take a good look at yourself' suggest that Self is conceived as a container for the Subject and that being Subjective is staying inside the Self. The container metaphor indicates that one cannot see the outside of the container, although Lakoff believes that, with effort, one can think outside it.

It is not immediately apparent that this is an accurate representation of western metaphors of person and self. The metaphor of division does not indicate what a self is – surely it is not just a *part* of a person. His emphasis on *one* person and *a* self suggests that the first refers to a singular body whereas there may be more than one self, although Lakoff portrays a self as an acting body. Moreover, when we express emotions (part of Lakoff's self), we are surely also a locus for the consciousness and rationality that fall under his description of the subject. If there are inconsistent metaphors at work here, what are they? We do use metaphor in many of the ways that Lakoff describes, and the expressions he considers that invite people to see themselves as others see them certainly employ metaphors of looking and space. This metaphor implies containers, or boundaries to be crossed, but it doesn't suggest as much difficulty in getting outside the boundary as Lakoff imagines. We can see 'eye to eye', 'be like-minded' or 'be at one' with another person just as easily as we can see things differently.

My suggestion that self is an analogue person is broadly in line with the theory put forward by Julian Jaynes (1976) in his book *The Origin of Consciousness in the Breakdown of the Bicameral Mind*. Although Jaynes' psycho-archaeology of consciousness has received most attention, he preceded it with a general theory of self. In fact, to speak of the creation of consciousness or things 'happening' in consciousness could be seen as a diversion from his central argument. Jaynes himself points out that a metaphor for consciousness does not make sense because there is nothing that 'consciousness' (i.e. a quality shared by all immediate experience) is like. And to speak of consciousness *doing* anything is already metaphorical because (and I agree) in the human realm it is only real human beings who *do* anything (1976: 54). His proposal is that the concept of self evolved as an analogue person: 'Mental acts are analogs of bodily acts' (1976: 66). The theory has a strong behavioural flavour to it, reminiscent of Vygotsky's concept of internalisation in child development (see Chapter 11). He describes an analogue as a special kind of model in which there is a point-to-point correspondence, as in a map, between the features and the terrain it charts. Perhaps a good illustration would be a child doing an arithmetical sum by imagining counting its fingers instead of actually counting them. The external world is the source of the analogue in the mental world, including, of course, an analogue 'I' moving about in the world. Once the analogue has been created, it can, like a map, be used to imagine 'as if' journeys or 'as if' decisions at various choice-points. Consequently, some so-called 'mental entities' may be viewed as agents, just like real persons, and many 'mental states' can be regarded as intentional because acts in the real world normally progress to the attainment of some end.

Jaynes argues that the analogue 'I' inhabits the 'mind', which is conceived as a metaphorical space in which the 'happenings' are abbreviated excerpts of what happens in the real world. The analogical 'I' may 'see' an analogue 'Me' acting in the world although perhaps only in the barest of shadowy details. In this mind-space, excerpts may get 'conciliated', in Jaynes' terms, and perhaps put into a story. How things get conciliated (i.e. accommodated, narrated, integrated, etc.) reflects structures in the real world. Jaynes senses that there is a profound problem in conceiving of an analogue 'I' seeing an analogue 'Me', although he leaves this problem to one side. In my opinion, if we think of the mental world as an analogue of the real world, there is no problem of an 'I' perceiving a 'me'. In the real world, 'I' is a grammatical device for indexing the speaker (see Chapters 2 and 3). It is, after all, as a person that 'I' create my mental world but I do not catch myself doing it. In my metaphorical doings, I imagine an objectified me.

The analogue 'I' in Jaynes' theory does not necessarily have to employ abstract categories like 'twistedness' as part of its analogical doings. The child that imagines counting its fingers can use its own behaviour in a concrete situation as a model not itself as a speaker with other social characteristics. However, Jaynes does equate the evolution of consciousness with the invention of an analogue world in which language is essential. Jaynes does not believe that language is sufficient by itself for conscious awareness because he does not think that the characters of pre-history, such as the figures in Homer's *Iliad,* had a conscious mind as we do, did not introspect, and 'did not have any ego whatever' (1976: 73). Instead, they listened to and obeyed the hallucinated voices of gods. Jaynes denies that humans projected their own psychological nature onto the world – rather, they learned to become self-directing (like gods) by modelling themselves on events that they understood to be caused by forces external to them. I presented an argument of a similar kind in Chapter 12 although I see no reason to deny a conscious sense-of-self to Homer's characters, however much it may have differed from our own.

Like the 'mind', self is a remarkably robust reification. Mark Leary (2007: 13) believes it to be a recent evolutionary adaptation with a neurological basis. Leary reverses Jaynes' reasoning when he argues that having a self allows people to create an analogue-I (2007: 5), whereas Jaynes claims the opposite: an analogue-I allows us to have a self.

Disbelief that self is virtual

What do we say to the person who complains, 'Of course, I have a self, and know damn well I *am* a self.' As stated above, there is no reason to deny the felt reality of virtual selves. The complainant might still bridle at the theoretical implication that selves are historically contingent. We get a sense of this resistance when the tables were turned on an anthropologist, Dorothy Holland, when she was asked by one of her Korean colleagues, 'What does it feel like not to have a soul?' (Holland 1997). Perhaps this question stems from the idea that without a (real) soul a person would be a zombie. It is simply very difficult to imagine a different sense-of-self. However, with or without a soul, the western self seems to be a rich enough concept to satisfy most people that it is real.

The significance of pointing out that self is virtual is to prompt people to consider the role of reification in their taken-for-granted sense of reality. It is not to suggest that any experience grasped figuratively is illusory or fictional. The woman's hat that looks like the Taj Mahal really is a monstrosity. When using metaphor, we are attempting to pin down a real quality in our experience. Even the events occurring in a metaphorical mind-space are based on the activities of real persons. When we do mental arithmetic or say that someone has a twisted mind, we are really doing something.

To give a more abstract example, when a person uses an expression like 'It felt like I was an intruder', we assume that reference is being made to an actual situation in which another person was, say, being asked about their salary or marital situation. The metaphor of an intruder identifies a feature of the situation that was really present (some unease or embarrassment) that was difficult to describe. Unlike the intruder, a person is real. If this was not so, the metaphor of interiority/exteriority (e.g., seeing things *as if* in someone else's shoes) would not make much sense. In other words, I can readily put my self (but not my person) in someone else's shoes. It would be literally possible for me to step into your shoes, but this is very unlikely to help me to see things from your perspective. In other words, we can step inside someone's conceptual world but not inside their body, for obvious literal reasons.

Derek Melser (2004) is a personist who does not think that any kind of location (like self or mind) is needed as a place in which thinking, feeling, believing, etc., occurs. He takes the view, similar to that of Jaynes, that thinking is a form of covert action, an internalisation of interpersonal acts. Thinking is a 'token activity', but he still understands it as an action. Melser describes mental states as entities constructed by converting verbs into nouns. He believes that it is a widely held but mistaken assumption, that 'mind is the name of something abstract, which we are initially acquainted with, and form a concept of, without the metaphors' (2004: 179). While fully endorsing this position, I disagree with Melser's assumption that 'thinking is an action and not a natural process' (2004: 13). He adheres to the personist credo that thinking is the act of a person that can only be understood in terms of empathy and interpretation. If I understand him correctly, he does not regard thinking as natural because we have to learn how to do it. However, all kinds of natural capacities must be needed to learn cultural practices. We may not have much of a clue how overt acts become covert acts, but I assume that it can be explained, at least in principle, by natural processes.

Melser argues that 'the layperson's notion of mind does not amount to a concept or theory' (2004: 187). It is 'a whole lot of *as-ifs* and *so-to-speaks*' (Melser 2004: 187). He describes mind as a 'raggle-taggle' collection of incompatible metaphors that include agent, place, repository, mechanism and instrument. As he rightly points out, even though there is no coherent lay theory of mind, it is generally assumed, without justification, to be a *location* for all of the covert activity that goes on. Melser notes that it is extraordinarily difficult to get across the idea that the 'mind' might not exist. After all, what are cognitive scientists studying?! But as noted earlier, a metaphorical understanding of experience need not be seen as an attempt to point to a 'thing' with a location. It can be directed at aspects of reality that are difficult to grasp in any other way. It seems to me that a personist need not deny the reality of natural mechanisms causing experience. The mind and the self are folk constructs, but it is not as if they bear no relationship to the way people function as biological organisms. In an earlier period of our history, a spiritual soul was thought to animate and control the body and was also thought to be the seat of intellect, imagination, feeling and will (Macdonald 2003: 245). Some writers in the fourteenth and fifteenth centuries came up with an alternative proposal that the brain was the internal site of the power of cognition (Macdonald 2003: 258). Although we may have forgotten that 'mind' does not literally exist, there is clearly an area of human affairs that really does call for an explanation.

Virtual selves in virtual worlds

A fascinating property of human thinking is its recursive nature. Having created virtual selves in a real world, it becomes possible to think of virtual 'virtual selves' in an imagined world. For instance, in the board game Monopoly, I might point to a top hat and say, 'This is me.' It stands in for the moves I might make in the game. Imaginary worlds are not limited to forms of play but may also be generated in a private world that is not shared with others. When adults do this for too much of the time, they are often said to have lost contact with reality.

The technical capacity to create imaginary worlds has been greatly enhanced by animated simulations of virtual locations on the World Wide Web. Participation is not, however, a purely solitary activity because imaginary worlds, like games, have agreed rules. In a virtual-reality world, it is my avatar that represents my involvement in that world. 'My avatar' is equated with 'my self' but '*my involvement in the game*' is something I have to do as a person, 'myself'. So what I am doing is not unreal (I am certainly sitting at a computer screen), it is just that I am not 'really' purchasing a chain of hotels. Money may exchange hands in virtual worlds, and the telephone or cable company has to be paid for connection to the Internet. In this sense, involvement in a virtual world does not differ, in principle, from other kinds of game-playing.

However, just as people who fantasise too much may be viewed as having forfeited a credible public identity, fears have been expressed that involvement in computer-mediated virtual worlds puts people at risk of psychological maladjustment. It seems undeniable that easy access to the Internet has created new opportunities for addiction to, amongst other things, gambling and pornography. However, I will restrict the present discussion to an effect on concepts of identity and a sense-of-self.

John Bargh and Katelyn McKenna (2004: 575) point out that each new technological advance in communication was met with concerns that it would weaken community ties. They cite evidence that this was in fact true in the case of television, but internet use seems to be associated with the formation and maintenance of close relationships. People may spend a considerable amount of time on the Internet, but this is at the expense of watching television or reading newspapers, not socialising (2004: 581). The relative anonymity of the Internet can also have the advantage of making talking with strangers easier although it also carries the risk of exploitation.

The more relevant issue in the present context is whether the creation of a new 'as if' self, such as an avatar, begins to compete in a negative way with self as presented in other work, home or social contexts. It is quite normal (e.g., when acting) for a person to 'put on a self' to create an illusion for others. If I was one of a pair of identical twins, I could play the part of my twin without believing I was the twin. This enactment becomes delusional if I really believe I am the twin, a real person. Putting on an 'as if' self to create an illusion of being my twin is quite a different matter. An illusion is something that is really perceived by others, and it is contrasted with the perception of an object in a set of conditions taken to be the 'standard' way of perceiving it (Austin 1964: 62–77). I might be perceived as my twin but there would be 'standard conditions' in which my real identity could be known.

The boundary between creating an illusion for my own or other's pleasure, and my 'real life', has the potential to break down during participation in a virtual world. Richard MacKinnon questions whether involvement in virtual communities is just 'role-playing' and asks 'How much of one's day does someone have to spend playing a game before it is fair to call it a "life"?' (1997: 232). This question applies to many aspects of life apart from cyberculture. We are not infrequently reminded: 'Don't take it too seriously – it's just a game.' MacKinnon discusses some actual examples of the crossover between real persons and their personas in virtual communities. The University of Michigan expelled one student for committing a virtual rape when a member of the cyber community concerned (not the 'victim') made a complaint. Police also arrested him for making threats to injure another person, although the charge was eventually dropped. This is certainly a striking example of the potential consequences of taking 'a game' seriously but it is perhaps not different in kind from over-involvement in a game such as Monopoly or poker. If involvement in a virtual community reaches the point of a loss of contact with a quotidian reality, then presumably the same sort of criteria would apply to these cases as in similar forms of behaviour classified as deviant by psychiatrists.

Self: Diagnoses and prognoses

My analysis of concepts of person and self has assumed that we can think of person/self both generically (or universally) and specifically (or historically). Adopting this standpoint, I will now consider the many attempts to produce a history of self. It is the biological constitution of human beings, including their nature as social beings, that forces us to recognise some universal, generic or essential features of persons and selves. At the same time, I have argued that people can only be fully understood in culturally relative and historical terms. Ian Fraser (following Ruth Abbey 2000) endorses this two-dimensional approach to self (Fraser 2007). There is both an *ontological* dimension (biology, the role of language, dialogical relations, etc.) and a *historical* dimension that charts world historical stages, cultural histories and unique biographies.

It is presumably the human capacity to reflect that allows us to think historically at all. When the object of reflection is our 'self', I have followed Mead, Ryle, Sartre and others in arguing that the act of reflecting is unknowable, implying that we only catch ourselves as objectified reflections that are already retrospective. An opposing view that I have consistently criticised is that we can really introspect on what is happening right now at this instant. In the Cartesian tradition, self is transparent to itself: it is assumed that we simply know what 'mental state' we are in, including an awareness of self. The closely related notion of a minimally aware self or 'core consciousness' (see Gallagher 2000) has no extension in time and for this reason is not relevant to the present discussion.

There is another sense in which self has been understood as immediately knowable. It has been argued that a person is not mistaken about who is the subject of experience when they have learned to use the first-person pronoun correctly. A person who makes appropriate use of the grammatical 'I' seemingly cannot be mistaken about who is speaking or reporting an experience. The person or speaker knows that they are a subject of experience in this sense. However, I do not see that this is knowledge of a *self*, an entity within the person, that is the subject of experience. It is just myself not my self that perceives or acts. Self, in my view, is always *spoken of*. So, while it is likely to be universally true that in any language there are means of indexing speakers, there is likely to be considerable variation in ways of characterising the speaker as a reflexive object through different modes of address. Moreover, children have to learn how to use personal pronouns, and the process can go awry in childhood and adulthood. Some adults use personal pronouns in anomalous ways, and the question of *who* is the owner of, say, a thought that is perceived as having been 'inserted' into a person's mind is not easy to answer (Gallagher 2000). In effect, a person is saying 'I am having a thought' but 'I am not thinking it.' 'I' may index the speaker and little else.

The indexical 'I' therefore leaves considerable scope for historical variation. The person as speaker acknowledges that they are the locus of awareness of a thought, but this is an attribution that, in principle, could be extended to everything, including external voices. An attribution concerning the internal or external source of an experience seems to be based on an inference rather than direct knowledge because we know that in some cases people may be convinced that their inserted thoughts have an external source but then later go on to believe and feel that they are self-produced.

The example of inserted thought illustrates two aspects of self-reflection. The first is motivated by an ontological question such as, 'What are the origins of my experiences?' or 'What makes it possible for me to reflect at all?' The second aspect concerns the *content* of experience, e.g., 'What does this thought mean?' It is possible to describe thoughts and also to construct them, without necessarily reflecting on who or what originates them. Traditionally, the source of experience has been located externally within the framework of theistic worldviews. More recently, the answer has been given in terms of a natural constitution or the social relations in which a person is nurtured.

Attempts to define self as the content of experience or, as David Hume sceptically concluded, 'a bundle of impressions', have been criticised as unsatisfactory because it puts the person in far too passive a role in relation to their experience. People have powers to *construct* their future acts and therefore to determine, in part, their future experiences. I therefore propose that human reflexivity is a historical constant, whether or not this power is self-reflectively conceptualised. In other words, people are always self-shaping to some degree, whether they know it or not.

As noted above, ancient views of the ontology of person/self are usually theocentric. The idea that people are autonomous, reflexive, self-shaping creatures did not really surface in the common language until the seventeenth century. I have called this the autocentric perspective. Alfred Tauber (2005) states that the word 'reflexivity' was coined in this period as a new term for introspection and self-awareness. He also points out that an obscure English minister, Henry Jeanes (1611–62), appreciated the fact that a self that knows itself carries the problematic implication of an infinite regress of selves, thereby flagging up a puzzling ontological question at this early date. A major break with the autocentric perspective came with Georg Hegel (1770–1831) who thought that self-consciousness was an empty idea 'if considered apart from intersubjectivity or outside its historical community' (Tauber 2005: 53). According to Fraser (2007), Karl Marx (1818–83) also criticised the prevailing notion that the essence of human nature was to be found in each individual, and he emphasised historical influences in the form of the social relations in which people lived (Fraser 2007: 14–18). These new ontological conceptions effectively decentred the self from its locus solely within persons. I have called this new western perspective 'ecocentric'. This does not mean that persons are now more aware of their *location within* an ecology; rather, this is a theoretical awareness that self is a *function of* an ecology.

One of the histories that can be told about self is a history of the development of conceptions of reflexivity. Another is a history of the *content* of reflection – the way people understand the world and represent their own attributes. The content of these reflections is usually allied to conceptions of the sources of morality and to models of ideal personhood and so the history of ontology and content are not easily separated. Beliefs about the source of self and its powers are closely related to models of what it is possible and desirable to construct as a person's aims.

The conceptual tension that has generated topics for the present book has its origins in the idea of a universal human nature conflicting with (or difficult to integrate with) an understanding of people as autonomously producing their unique historical circumstances. As Fraser (2007: 16) puts it, 'we need to understand the self dialectically as a general and determinate abstraction'. For a theorist such as Foucault, the conflict between a conception of humankind (universal) and person (historical) reflects a stage in western thought. In *The Order of Things*, he states, 'man is only a recent invention, a figure not yet two centuries old, a new wrinkle in our knowledge, and that he will disappear again as soon as that knowledge has discovered a new form' (Foucault 2004: xxv).

If this observation were to be accepted at face value, it would reduce the theoretical issues I have discussed in this book to a clash of conflicting discourses. However, without dismissing Foucault's point that 'man' is a discursive invention, I will continue to maintain that the intellectual project of naturalism is unlikely to disappear even if the concept 'man' disappears out of naturalistic discourse. For instance, there are attempts to speculate about the natural origins of discourse itself.

Like Foucault, the philosopher Charles Taylor, whose influential history of self I have frequently quoted, refuses to engage with naturalism while having a great deal to say about people's response to 'Nature' as a source of moral inspiration. His view is that concepts of person and agency have to be interpreted within a largely philosophically defined moral framework. He rejects the idea that this kind of framework could be reduced to a language of natural causation (Taylor 1989: 19). According to him, there are moral goods or standards that command our respect regardless of any ordinary reasoning about one thing being more desirable than another (or, presumably, having a greater 'natural' affinity to people's biological predispositions). Taylor's history of the western self is an interwoven tapestry of many strands of ideas in religion, philosophy, literature and the arts; he sees these ideas as coexisting, conflicting, diverging, coalescing, etc., in different ways in different historical periods. Taylor does not attempt to relate them to social mechanisms or technological change. However, he attributes many of the dilemmas of modernity to scientific and technical forms of instrumental reasoning that he calls 'disengaged reason', by which he means processes of thought or a cannon of trustworthy principles. Taylor emphasises the rhetorical power of scientific reasoning in shaping modern selves but he declines to employ it himself as a way of theorising about a generic Self.

There are few theorists who dispense altogether with a concept of a universal human nature – a set of biological predispositions that must find expression in some form. Universalist assumptions are not always stated explicitly of course. For instance, an idea of what is 'naturally' satisfying is implicit in Marx's concept of alienation. This sets out some generally desirable conditions of human existence (see Fraser 2007: 24). These are (1) a direct and controlling relation between a person's work and what they produce; (2) a need for a personal creative input into work; (3) a cooperative rather than a competitive relationship with others; and (4) an opportunity to express a personal capacity for self-determination.

I mention alienation to show how 'human nature' inserts itself in most historical perspectives on social change. The reflexivity of human beings is a rather subtle example of a power that can be theorised about as a universal human potential. For instance, it could be argued that people who do not appear to be alienated from a form of life that is 'naturally satisfying' to them (however alienation is defined) do not necessarily reflect on their role in producing these circumstances. They may certainly register joy, pain or suffering, but, in so far as these states are represented as objective conditions of life (e.g., reflecting the state of their relationship to social or supernatural influences), they are not elements of a reflexive representation of self. Steven Lukes (1985: 300) argues that once the historical transition was made to a self-reflective individual (i.e. a sovereign chooser of actions) from an individual whose identity was ordained by an inherited history, we were irrevocably transformed and cannot now reverse time and return to our former state. I will now discuss some histories of self that view self-reflection as a historical development.

Histories of self-reflection

Considered in its dual aspects, an *awareness* of human reflexivity is a cultural expression of an inherent power and not simply a cultural invention. In other words, an awareness of the power of self-reflection can be viewed as an unveiling or realisation of powers. On these grounds, it could be argued that *self-conscious* attempts to produce social change are a recent phenomenon. I assume that people have always referred to some of their inherent powers, but this does not mean that they have always planned their acts in reflexive projects. This kind of joint universalist/relativist approach is adopted by Don LePan in his book *The Cognitive Revolution in Western Culture* (1989), an analysis of changes in modes of thought from the Anglo-Saxon period through to the seventeenth century. He is primarily interested in concepts common to most speakers of the language, but he admits that a tiny elite of educated individuals might have been familiar with more sophisticated ways of reasoning that had their origins in Ancient Greece and Rome. This is consistent with his emphasis on cognition as a set of intellectual tools that are developed through exposure to relevant cultural input.

Self-reflection seems to require a form of intellectual detachment from immediate involvement in experience. Although LePan does not deal with this topic directly, he discusses a related development in the appreciation of time. Based on an analysis of literary texts, he documents a transition from a pre-modern concept of *expectancy* to a modern concept of *expectation*. The latter concept entails a prediction about what is likely to happen in given circumstances: 'it requires the ability to combine various and often disparate pieces of information, which may have been received at several different times and places, in a particular way; to draw inferences from these data; and to project these inferences into the hypothetical realm of the future' (1989: 75).

Expectation implies an understanding of the means by which ends are achieved whereas expectancy (or prophecy) just refers to end results.

LePan points out that the Latin verb *exspectare*, meaning 'to look out' or 'to wait for', was retained in the Latin used throughout the Middle Ages to refer to waiting for the resurrection of the dead and the life of the age to come. Expect, in this sense, is an expectancy and not an expectation (1989: 79). According to LePan, literary evidence of the use of the verb 'expect' in the sense of 'to look forward mentally' does not exist before 1578. There are many examples in the literature of words with a related meaning but these are interpreted by LePan as forms of expectancy ('expectant', 1393; 'hopeful', 1393; 'anticipacioun', 1450; 'look for', 1513). LePan claims that there were abundant linguistic resources to express purpose, desire or fear but none to express disinterested expectation. The latter would appear to be at least one component of a modern reflection on self.

LePan is making the counter-intuitive claim that most people who spoke Old or Middle English merely hoped for things to happen but verbalised no specific probabilistic expectations, or rational calculations, for future events. An important aspect of forming an expectation would be to have, or to weigh up, human intentions in such a way as to predict how the future might unravel itself. In effect, he is saying that there were no Sherlock Holmeses or Agatha Christies in this period.

Expectation is oriented to the future and so conceptions of time are intrinsic to its meaning. On the one hand, patterns of human behaviour are inevitably sequential, and those habitual patterns that have certain purposes (the rituals of social greeting, farming practices, tool-making, etc.) follow a predictable sequence although this may, at times, be contradicted by experience. Repeatable patterns can be described as generating expectations in a rather mechanical way that applies as much to animal as to human behaviour. On the other hand, planned behaviour usually entails a non-repeatable sequence of acts, or several interlocking sequences, individually or jointly performed. In so far as group coordination is required, a temporal framework is needed to cue each action. These cues may consist of natural sequential events (e.g., the movement of the sun or the full moon) or conventional signs (e.g., a calendar or beacon), none of which supply the precision of modern forms of timekeeping. According to LePan, without precise temporal markers, simultaneity is difficult to comprehend, and plans are complicated to devise. He provides illustrations of these difficulties from medieval texts.

Although in Latin the future tense is indicated by the inflection of a verb, Old English (c. 450 to c. 1150) did not have a separate future tense as such, and, where the future was intended, the present tense was used. The verbs 'wille' and 'sceal' meant 'to wish to do' and 'to have to do' respectively. They became verb auxiliaries to indicate the future in Middle English (c. 1150 to c. 1500) and Modern English ('will' and 'shall'). It is clear that 'wille' and 'sceal' suggest the experience of being involved in the fairly immediate future (wanting something, promising or being obligated). Shall is still used to denote force in Modern English ('You *shall* obey me'). It could be inferred that the language of Old English was not developed to deal with detached reflection on future matters.

An absence in the early medieval period of future-oriented words that concern calculated planning could perhaps be explained by a limited scope for choice beyond the immediate exigencies, poor inferential reasoning or the lack of a concept of probability. LePan focuses mainly on the unavailability of a reliable chronology and, more fundamentally, on the absence of a concept of objective time. He suggests that the implicit point of reference for time was the Divine Order which was literally 'out of time', while time existed only in this world (1989: 84). The passage of time was linked to experience of the physical world, whereas in eternal life, time came to a stop. LePan argues it was not until the sixteenth and seventeenth centuries that the idea of time as an infinitely flowing 'objective quantity' was widely assumed (1989: 86). For illiterate peasants who had limited access to temporal markers and little ability to record events, there must have been a diminished sense of history or their own history. Activities like building a simple house could be conducted by exercising traditional skills developed through trial and error without rational calculation. This statement is consistent with evidence of excellent memory for sequential events as recounted in stories, poems or the Bible. These recitations do not presuppose an accurate chronology or the abstraction of themes that are related through inference. An implication we may draw from LePan's analysis is that thinking of self in the way we are now wont to do presupposes that our cognitive powers have been shaped by many centuries of literacy, education and scientific reasoning.

Richard Logan (1987) offers another history of 'the self' that focuses directly on reflexive self-representation. Logan bases it on the I-Me distinction of G. H. Mead, which he interprets as a distinction between 'I' that can behold the world and 'Me', a self that is an object of reflection. I think this is a misrepresentation of Mead's theory (see Chapter 8) in that I understand Mead to mean that 'I' can only catch itself in a reflected Me. However, we may take it that Logan means that 'I' in early post-classical western history was simply a conception of the acting person beholding the world rather than a self beholding the world. So, according to Logan, people recounted their own history in a non-self-conscious manner in terms of deeds done framed within an externally provided model of the virtues. A person's public self was reflected in the images and judgements of others. In a later period, Logan suggests that more emphasis was placed on an individual perspective in the sense of making known where the subject stood as an autonomous, perceiving and reasoning being confronting the world. The individual marked out their viewpoint as distinct from that of the group. He believes that despite Renaissance individuals becoming increasingly assertive, they were still 'non-reflective and un-self-conscious' (Logan 1987: 17) by today's standards. 'Self-awareness appears to have been most saliently a matter of beholding one's *actions* and *effects* on the world and beholding other's *re*-actions to same' (Logan 1987: 17–18).

Of course, a non-self-conscious mode of awareness is still alive and well in contemporary society. There is nothing especially odd about a community of persons without selves. One example is the community of car drivers. This community follows rules more or less courteously, exchanges signals that have a shared significance, and there is a tacit hierarchy of mutual fear organised principally around size of vehicle. Only rarely do drivers lose control in fits of shouting or rage, and, even then, we may not need to speculate about their inner selves. Car drivers face situations that must have been commonplace since prehistoric times: for instance, when the way gets narrow, a human being has to face the question, 'Should I go first or let the other one through?' We are largely interested in car drivers as individuals following a public code, not as selves. They do not need selves to control their cars or to relate to each other in a civil manner. If we take Logan's argument seriously, what appears to have been lacking in the early modern period was a person acting on behalf of an inner self. 'Self-willed' dates back to Old English when it meant following one's own desire or being obstinate. I assume it acquired new significance when employed in connection with the self described by John Locke several hundred years later. Locke's person possesses a self that directs its own will on the basis of its own understanding.

Logan, in common with many other authors, argues that over the course of the seventeenth and eighteenth centuries, people came to identify their own mind as the source of powers to reason, choose and 'construct' the world. In Logan's words, the individual does not just behold the world but now observes it as a detached 'I'. 'I' is conceptualised primarily as a mind (a competent reasoner) that is beginning to be understood as something like a personal, inner object. He cites

Kant (in the eighteenth century) as the first philosopher 'to clearly distinguish the two aspects of the self, the *I* (subject) and the *me* (object)'
(1987: 21). Logan argues that in the Romantic period, the reflected self
became an object of interest in its own right, in that people reflected
on their experience of reacting to the world and the world's effects on
them. This encouraged the development of methods of introspection,
psychoanalytic probing and, of course, psychology as an independent
field of study.

The view I have adopted throughout this book is that to reflect on a
self as an effect of the world is to reflect on a virtual object that has been
socially and individually constructed. If this self is taken to be 'real',
we can begin to comprehend some of the features of twentieth-century
attitudes to self, as Logan describes them. These include an effort to
'find a self' and 'to get in touch with an inner me'. Existentialist philosophers emphasised that this was an individual project 'with no major
help from others or the past' (Logan 1987: 23). Logan believes that
people now no longer feel whole by asserting the Renaissance person's
plain-spoken, 'I am', searching instead to find an inner (or lost) me. He
thinks this search underlies the idea of self as consumer, as victim of
the world, as an object of contemplation, as the recipient of the admir-
ation of others, etc. While there may be an element of truth in this, the
role of 'I' in constructing a self, rather than searching for it, is surely
underplayed in this analysis.

The concept of an inner self underlies Karl Weintraub's *The Value
of the Individual: Self and Circumstance in Autobiography,* a history
that begins in Ancient Greece and progresses through to the eighteenth century (Weintraub 1978). His definition of 'modern man's self-
conception' (circa 1978) was that a modern person holds 'the belief that
whatever else he is, he is a unique individuality, whose life is to be true
to his very own personality' (Weintraub 1978: xi). Paraphrasing from
the book, his conception of self can be summarised in the following
statements:

1. We feel a deep need to be true to the self.
2. Each person's life is special and each person has something of their
   own to give to the world.
3. The self is inviolable and ineffable.
4. The ineffable cannot be found in 'the general'; individual difference
   is of great value in itself.
5. It is extremely difficult to come to know one's own self.
6. A person must set out to search for it ('the inner law of one's
   being').

7. The self gives the person its own norms to follow.
8. A person is responsible to their self to fulfil their specific potential to the fullest.
9. To fail one's individuality is 'a crime against the cosmos'.

The influence of Romantic thinkers is evident in this picture of self. According to Weintraub, the historical parting of the ways in the development of self-conception occurred when people began to seek self autonomously rather than in models given 'externally' as it were. In his view, the individuality of pre-modern persons was found in the 'interstices' of their outward projects; they were not curious about their 'own reality'. Weintraub appears to be universalising his own conception of self when he assumes that pre-modern people were not curious about a 'real' aspect of themselves.

If an inner self is virtual rather than really there, it is odd to think of a person in thrall to it and obeying its commands. In any case, Weintraub feels obliged to hedge in this modern self with some of the old virtues. A person should not glorify this self (i.e. they should show modesty) or act arbitrarily (i.e. they should be faithful), and a person must not become morbidly introspective to the point of becoming unhinged (i.e. they should stay rational). It is true that people do not automatically know what hidden potential lies within them, but this potential may be a quality they are desperate to conceal for fear of being ostracised or prosecuted. Weintraub does not argue that individual uniqueness is an absolute value to be pursued regardless of its consequences. Moreover, if to be 'individually unique' becomes the norm, there are probably conventional ways of doing so and the model of self remains largely external.

John Lyons, a historian publishing in the same year, is not taken in by an inner self. 'My message is, put baldly, that the self which modern doomsayers accuse of being invisible, was a fiction in the first place' (Lyons 1978: 18). Lyons suggests that faith in a unique self was needed to break the hold of an animistic connection to the world and to nature. The scientist had to see himself as 'solitary and beginning, as it were, at the start of time if he was to see the isolatable fact in a manner that made it fit in a new way into the cosmos' (Lyons 1978: 219). Lyons thinks that the Romantic rejection of received doctrine was also rooted in personal experience but in a different manner – from 'the sensations of the heart' (1978: 220). Lyons main point, consistent with the thesis of this book, is that self has always been a fiction and that Romantic attempts to fill the void left by the loss of the soul have ended up as tragedy or comedy. If the 'void' is unavoidable, we cannot prognosticate with any confidence about the future trajectory of self.

A number of sociologists consider that reflexivity in the form of 'self-direction' has become increasingly important as a mechanism of social control in modern societies. For example, Anthony Giddens (1991) argues that people are subtly influenced and controlled in their choices by the options made available to them and the expert advice that is on tap to guide that choice. Nikolas Rose (1998: 79) goes further in suggesting that ours is a society in which people live their lives 'according to a norm of autonomy', implying that this is a pseudo-autonomy. In fact, Rose eradicates the agency of the person altogether when he says that: 'To account for the capacity to act one needs no theory of the subject prior to and resistant to that which would capture it – such capacities for action emerge out of the specific regimes and technologies that machinate human beings in diverse ways' (1998: 186–7). A sociologist would perhaps be inclined to argue that no theory of the subject (i.e. psychology) is needed, but a sociological theory without embodied persons whose biology is essential for their agency makes little sense.

History of self as a unity

The human body is a unitary entity, but I hope to have shown in earlier chapters that the same body may house several persons and an even larger number of selves. If concepts of person and self are constructed, we can look to the sources of a unitary identity, and its fragmentation, in social processes. I assume that a singular identity is established in a variety of ways – bureaucratically (e.g., through registration of births and deaths), legally (e.g., through the assignment of rights and responsibilities to unique persons) and, more loosely, by processes that bind the person to an existence as a singular moral being with a credible history. Historical and anthropological evidence suggest that these requirements are sometimes relaxed but chiefly in ways that are socially regulated; at special festivals people may invert social roles, change gender, indulge to excess or flout normal conventions. It seems unlikely that any society has ever enforced a strict adherence at all times to the conventions and norms regulating a singular social identity. In contemporary society, there are fewer ritual or communal sites/occasions for the relaxation of convention. People are now more likely to say that they express 'different sides of their personality' which they may 'discover' by engaging in different activities of their own choice.

Taylor (1989: 507) discusses the modern tendency to find fulfilment in different kinds of self-expression and to look for a technical fix to promote personal growth or to remove obstacles to happiness. He believes that the pursuit of self-fulfilment encourages a style of life that is shallow and empty, in part because it reduces the language of morals and politics to mere 'values'. Taylor is presumably right in thinking that strong moral and political commitments are conducive to a coherent and consistent (i.e. unitary) social identity. However, Taylor does not think that we can any longer embrace an all-encompassing cosmic view of the universe. He says that what we have to develop instead is allegiance to a package of competing goods; moral dilemmas are unavoidable, and the exclusive pursuit of one good might ultimately undermine itself as a moral project. Taylor argues that: 'we need languages of personal resonance to make crucial human goods alive for us again' (1989: 513). His notion of 'personal resonance' is developed to combat the view that we should rationally calculate what is good for us on the basis of utilitarian values and instrumental reasoning.

Taylor reflects a pervasive theme in twentieth-century writing on self which can be summed up as a syndrome of loosely related polarities: strong, unitary, integrated, committed, communal and traditional versus despairing, empty, fragmented, vulnerable, exposed and demoralised. For instance, Brewster Smith (2002: 239) thinks our present historical situation is 'pathological and cannot last'. At the other extreme, new freedoms and multiplicity in self-expression are welcomed. John Andrews (1989) construes visions of reality as personal styles and suggests that each individual is responsible for choosing their own 'reality'. Kenneth Gergen interprets postmodernism as a world in which: 'There is no false view of society from which people must be emancipated [...] all positions are discursive constructions' (1999: 209). Accordingly, we need not 'search for what is fundamentally true or real' but rather strive to 'add to the cultural resources for relating' (1999: 214).

It is tempting to interpret the polarisations unity versus disunity (good/bad) and established/traditional versus new/expansive (good/bad) as reflecting conservative and progressive responses to social change. However, this is too easy. On the one hand, it is not progressive to suggest that any old discourse or any old vision of reality is as good as any other. On the other hand, it is not necessarily reactionary to argue that a unitary self strongly committed to a single moral project is preferable to a fragmented self expressing itself in a variety of dispersed projects. Taylor is in the conservative camp that endorses strong commitments, but he acknowledges that people inevitably face moral dilemmas. This is likely to predispose them towards adopting multiple perspectives if moral dilemmas are not easy to resolve. I have argued that the default position in contemporary society is that people assign singular personhood to each other and that this is essential if they are to develop as moral agents with a capacity for rational choice. It is hard (in fact, almost impossible) to imagine a world in which singular personhood were forsaken for the kind of dissociated identities discussed in Chapter 4. There are simply a huge number of words in the English language that depend for their meaning on singular personhood and self-consistency. The following are just a few of the negative descriptors: false, inauthentic, cheat, bluff, imposture, deceit, pretence, double-dealing, cunning and insincere. However, inconsistent forms of self-expression are not condemned when they are socially regulated and expressed in clearly defined contexts, such as work and home. The playful expression of different selves is essential in the theatre, in humour, in games and in many other contexts. Many forms of social behaviour, like flirtation, can vary between high deceit and harmless fun depending on the context.

There certainly seems to have been a trend in the twentieth century towards greater tolerance or even encouragement of flexible self-expression. In mid-century, psychologists thought that a strong, unitary sense-of-self was healthy, and they devised questionnaire measures of 'ego-strength'. By 1989, Ellen Langer was able to write: 'A single-minded self-image leaves both individuals and corporations dangerously vulnerable' (1989: 44). People with chameleon qualities are now valued for their ability to adapt flexibly to different circumstances. While there must be moral limits to this tendency, it is not easy to define them. Kurt Back (1989) has illustrated changes in the direction of a 'fragmented and unclear' self in the past 100 years by commenting on themes within spy and murder mystery novels. He notes a decreasing emphasis on the individual personality (e.g., criminal type, master detective) and an increasing attention to the work of organisations (e.g., police department, intelligence agency, criminal gang) within which the identity of an individual is submerged, making it difficult to identify the truth of their perceptions or beliefs. It may be in response to a requirement to take on a variety of personas in such different circumstances that people have created the concept of a 'real me' as a hidden presence (e.g., 'You don't *really* know me'). This is a unitary entity that they value, esteem and protect despite presenting a variety of fragmented public selves that serve to maintain their social roles.

Tail end

It seems fitting to end by reflecting on being an author of a cross-disciplinary text who has had to cast aside the clan allegiance of one discipline. Indeed, many years ago, when I temporarily switched my

academic interest from psychology to anthropology, I found it curious
to be regarded as a traitor to the clan. Moreover, in order to fulfil my
new identity, there was a subtle pressure to undergo the initiation rites
of working in a remote and alien land. Clearly, there are advantages in a
strong and undivided commitment to one discipline, such as the depth
of knowledge it ensures and the benefits of the *Gemütlichkeit* of clan
meetings. Perhaps cross-disciplinary study will become, or has already
become, a new specialisation, in which case it will also inspire in-group
loyalty and out-group suspicion.

In my view, a new specialisation would undoubtedly lose some of the
advantages that an uncommitted and fragmented perspective can offer.
However much Descartes appeared to be committed to Catholicism,
he was on the right lines with his method of doubt. When the infant
begins to doubt that it is the centre of the world, it begins to dawn that
others have their own self-perspective. And for the adult to doubt the
reality of *their own* self – to view it not as natural and inevitable but as
constructed – leads to an expansion of ways of relating to the world,
including the possibility of being a thinker without a self.

Bibliography

Abbey, Ruth. 2000. *Charles Taylor*. Princeton, NJ: Princeton University Press.

Abelson, Raziel. 1977. *Persons: A study in philosophical psychology*. London: Macmillan.

Althusser, Louis. 1969. *For Marx*. Trans. Ben Brewster. London: Allen Lane.

Andrews, John D. W. 1989. Integrating visions of reality: Interpersonal diagnosis and the existential vision. *American Psychologist*, **44**: 803–17.

Andrews, Kristin. 2008. It's in your nature: A pluralistic folk psychology. *Synthese*, **165**: 13–29.

Arbib, Michael A. 2005. From monkey-like action recognition to human language: An evolutionary framework for neurolinguistics. *Behavioral and Brain Sciences*, **28**: 105–67.

Arendt, Hannah. 1978. *The life of the mind. Vol. II: Willing*. New York: Harcourt Brace Jovanovitch.

Astington, Janet. 1996. What is theoretical about the child's theory of mind? A Vygotskyan view of its development. In *Theories of theories of mind* (pp. 184–99). Eds. Peter Carruthers and Peter K. Smith. Cambridge: Cambridge University Press.

Austin, John L. 1964. *Sense and sensibilia*. Reconstructed from the manuscript notes by G. J. Warnock. Oxford: Oxford University Press.

Baars, Bernard J. 1997. *In the theater of consciousness: The workspace of the mind*. New York: Oxford University Press.

Back, Kurt. 1989. Thriller: The self in modern society. In *Texts of identity* (pp. 207–36). Eds. John Shotter and Kenneth Gergen. London: Sage.

Bargh, John A. and Katelyn Y. A. McKenna. 2004. The internet and social life. *Annual Review of Psychology*, **55**: 573–90.

Bayne, Timothy. 2006. Phenomenology and the feeling of doing: Wegner on the conscious will. In *Does consciousness cause behavior?* (pp. 169–85). Eds. Susan Pockett, William P. Banks and Shaun Gallagher. Cambridge, Mass.: MIT Press.

Benediktson, D. Thomas. 2006. The first silent reader of Latin literature. *Classical World*, **100**: 43–4.

Bennett, Max R. and Peter Hacker. 2003. *Philosophical foundations of neuroscience*. Oxford: Blackwell.

Bennett, Max R., Daniel Dennett, Peter Hacker and John Searle. 2007. *Neuroscience and philosophy: Brain, mind, and language*. New York: Columbia University Press.

314

Benton, Ted and Ian Craib. 2001. *Philosophy of social science: The philosophical foundations of social thought*. Basingstoke: Palgrave Macmillan.

Bermúdez, José L. 1998. *The paradox of self-consciousness*. Cambridge, Mass.: MIT Press.

    2003. The domain of folk psychology. In *Minds and persons: Royal Institute of Philosophy, Supplement 53* (pp. 25–49). Ed. Anthony O'Hear. Cambridge: Cambridge University Press.

Berrios, German E. and Ivana S. Marková. 2003. The self and psychiatry: A conceptual history. In *The self in neuroscience and psychiatry* (pp. 9–39). Eds. Tilo Kircher and Anthony David. Cambridge: Cambridge University Press.

Beyle, Henri. 1949. *Stendahl: Memoirs of an egotist*. Trans. T. W. Earp. London: Turnstile Press.

Bhaskar, Roy. 1979. *The Possibility of Naturalism: A Philosophical Critique of the Contemporary Human Sciences*. Brighton: Harvester Press.

Blackman, Derek E. 1991. B. F. Skinner and G. H. Mead: On biological science and social science. *Journal of the Experimental Analysis of Behavior*, **55**: 251–65.

Blasi, Augusto. 2004. Neither personality nor cognition: An alternative approach to the nature of the self. In *Changing conceptions of psychological life*. Eds. Michael Chandler, Chris Lalonde and Cynthia Lightfoot. Mahwah, NJ: Lawrence Erlbaum Associates.

Boesch, Christophe. 2005. Joint cooperative hunting among wild chimpanzees: Taking natural observations seriously. *Behavioural and Brain Sciences*, **28**: 692–3.

Bourdieu, Pierre. 1977. *Outline of a theory of practice*. Cambridge: Cambridge University Press.

Boyer, Pascal. 2000. Evolution of the modern mind and the origins of culture: Religious concepts as a limiting case. In *Evolution and the human mind: Modularity, language and meta-cognition* (pp. 93–112). Eds. Peter Carruthers and Andrew Chamberlain. Cambridge: Cambridge University Press.

Boyle, Mary. 2002. *Schizophrenia: A scientific delusion?* 2nd edn. London: Routledge.

Brand, Myles. 1984. *Intending and acting: Towards a naturalized action theory*. Cambridge, Mass: Bradford, MIT Press.

Bratman, Michael E. 2007. *Structures of agency: Essays*. Oxford: Oxford University Press.

Braude, Stephen E. 1995. *First person plural: Multiple personality and the philosophy of mind*. Lanham, Md.: Rowman & Littlefield.

Brockmeier, Jens. 2005. The text of the mind. In *Mind as a scientific object* (pp. 432–49). Eds. Christina E. Erneling and David M. Johnson. Oxford: Oxford University Press.

Bruner, Jerome. 1992. *Acts of meaning: Four lectures on mind and culture*. Cambridge, Mass.: Harvard University Press.

    1997. A narrative model of self-construction. In *The self across psychology: Self-recognition, self-awareness, and the self-concept* (pp. 145–61). Eds. Joan G. Snodgrass and Robert L. Thompson. New York: Annals of the New York Academy of Sciences.

Burkitt, Ian. 1991. *Social selves: Theories of the social formation of personality.* London: Sage.

Byrne, Richard W. 1999. Human cognitive evolution. In *The descent of mind: Psychological perspectives on hominid evolution* (pp. 71–87). Eds. Michael C. Corballis and Stephen E. G. Lea. New York: Oxford University Press.

Byrne, Richard W. and Andrew Whiten. 1988. Tactical deception of familiar individuals in baboons. In *Machiavellian intelligence: Social expertise and the evolution of intellect in monkeys, apes and humans* (pp. 205–10). Eds. Richard W. Byrne and Andrew Whiten. Oxford: Oxford University Press.

Calvert-Minor, Chris. 2008. The 'strong programme', normativity, and social causes. *Journal for the Theory of Social Behaviour,* **38**: 1–22.

Cannon, Betty. 2003. Sartre's contribution to psychoanalysis. In *Understanding experience: Psychotherapy and post-modernism* (pp. 27–51). Ed. Roger Frie. London: Routledge.

Carpendale, Jeremy and Charlie Lewis. 2004. Constructing an understanding of mind: The development of children's social understanding within social interaction. *Behavioral and Brain Sciences,* **27**: 79–96.

Carr, David. 1986. *Time, narrative and history.* Bloomington, Ind.: Indiana University Press

1997. Narrative and the real world: An argument for continuity. In *Memory, identity, community: The idea of narrative in the human sciences* (pp. 7–25). Eds. Lewis P. Hinchman and Sandras K. Hinchman. Albany, NY: SUNY Press.

Carruthers, Peter. 2004. *The nature of the mind: An introduction.* London: Routledge.

Cazeneuve, Jean. 1972. *Lucien Levy-Bruhl.* Trans. P. Riviere. Oxford: Blackwell.

Cheney, Dorothy L. and Robert M. Seyfarth. 1990. *How monkeys see the world.* Chicago, Ill.: University of Chicago Press.

Clark, Andy. 2008. Memento's revenge: The extended mind, re-visited. Available at http://consc.net/mindpapers/2.2i (accessed 28 December 2008).

Clark, Andy and David J. Chalmers. 1998. The extended mind. *Analysis,* **58**: 7–19.

Claxton, Guy. 2005. *The wayward mind: An intimate history of the unconscious.* London: Little, Brown.

Collingwood, Robin G. 1961a. Human nature and human history. In *The idea of history* (pp. 205–31). Oxford: Oxford University Press. First published in 1936.

1961b. *The idea of history.* Oxford: Oxford University Press. First published in 1946.

Cooney, Jeffrey W. and Michael S. Gazzaniga. 2003. Neurological disorders and the structure of human consciousness. *Trends in Cognitive Science,* 7: 161–5.

Cooper, Anthony Ashley, Third Earl of Shaftesbury. 1981. *Complete works, selected letters, and posthumous writings.* In English with parallel German translations. Ed. and trans. Gerd Hemmerich and Wolfram Benda. Stuttgart: Frommann-Holzboog.

Costall, Alan and Ivan Leudar. 2004. Where is the 'theory' in theory of mind. *Theory and Psychology*, **14**: 623–46.

Coulter, Jeff. 1983. *Rethinking cognitive theory*. New York: St Martin's Press.
1999. Discourse and mind. *Human Studies*, **22**: 163–81.

Coulter, Jeff and Wes Sharrock. 2007. *Brain, mind and human behavior in contemporary cognitive science*. New York: Edwin Mellen Press.

Crabbe, M. James C. 1999. *From soul to self*. London: Routledge.

Craik, Fergus I.M., Tara M. Moroz, Morris Moscovitch, Donald Stuss, Gordon Winocur, Endel Tulving and Shitij Kapur. 1999. In search of the self: A positron emission tomography study. *Psychological Science*, **10**: 26–34.

Cushman, Phillip. 1990. Why the self is empty: Toward a historically situated psychology. *American Psychologist*, **45**: 599–611.

Damasio, Antonio. 2000. *The feeling of what happens: Body and emotion in the making of consciousness*. London: Heinemann.

Danziger, Kurt. 1997. *Naming the mind: How psychology found its language*. London: Sage.

Davidson, Donald. 1994. Donald Davidson: Reply to Ralf Stoecker. In *Reflecting Davidson* (pp. 287–90). Ed. Ralph Stoecker. New York: de Gruyter.
2001. Actions, reasons, and causes. In *Essays on Actions and Events* (pp. 3–19). Oxford: Oxford University Press. First published 1963.

Davison, Kenneth. 1964. Episodic depersonalisation. *British Journal of Psychiatry*, **110**: 505–13.

Deacon, Terrence, W. 1997. *The symbolic species: The co-evolution of language and the brain*. New York: W. W. Norton.

Deikman, Arthur J. 1999. 'I' = awareness. In *Models of the self* (pp. 421–7). Eds. Shaun Gallagher and Jonathan Shear. Exeter: Imprint Academic.

Dennett Daniel C. 1987. *The intentional stance*. Cambridge, Mass.: MIT Press.
1991. *Consciousness explained*. Boston, Mass.: Little, Brown.
2003. *Freedom evolves*. New York: Penguin Viking.

Descartes, René. 1901. *The method, meditations and philosophy of Descartes*. Trans. John Veitch. New York: Tudor Publishing Co.
2005. *Descartes's meditations: A trilingual HTML edition*. Eds. David B. Manley and Charles S. Taylor. Available online at www.wright.edu/cola/descartes/mede.html (accessed 28 December 2008).

Donald, Merlin. 1991. *Origins of the modern mind: Three stages in the evolution of culture and cognition*. Cambridge, Mass.: Harvard University Press.
2001. *A mind so rare: The evolution of human consciousness*. New York: W. W. Norton.
2004. The virtues of rigorous interdisciplinarity. In *The development of the mediated mind: Sociocultural context and cognitive development* (Chapter 12). Eds. John Lacariello, Judith A. Hudson, Robyn Fivush and Patricia J. Bauer. Mahwah, NJ: Lawrence Erlbaum Associates.

Dreyfus, Hubert L. 1989. Alternative philosophical conceptualisation of psychopathology. In *Phenomenology and beyond: The self and its language* (pp. 41–50). Eds. Harald A. Durfee and Daid F. T. Rodier. Dordrecht: Kluwer.

Dror, Itiel E. and Robin D. Thomas. 2005. The cognitive neuroscience laboratory: A framework for the science of mind. In *The mind as a scientific object* (pp. 283–92). Eds. Christina Erneling and David M. Johnson. Oxford: Oxford University Press.

Dunbar, Robin. 2000. On the origin of the human mind. In *Evolution and the human mind: Modularity, language and meta-cognition* (pp. 238–53). Eds. Peter Carruthers and Andrew Chamberlain. Cambridge: Cambridge University Press.

Edwards, Derek and Jonathan Potter. 1992. *Discursive psychology*. London: Sage.

Elder-Vass, Dave. 2006. *A method for social ontology*. Paper presented to IACR Annual Conference, Toronto, August 2006.

   2007. For emergence: Refining Archer's account of social structure. *Journal for the Theory of Social Behaviour*, **37**: 25–44.

Elliot, Anthony. 2001. *Concepts of the self*. Cambridge, Mass.: Blackwell, Polity Press.

Emirbayer, Mustafa and Ann Mische. 1998. What is agency? *American Journal of Sociology*, **103**: 962–1023.

Epstein, Seymour. 1973. The self-concept revisited or a theory of a theory. *American Psychologist*, **28**: 404–16.

Erneling, Christina. 2005. Introduction: Is the 'mind' just another name for what the brain does? In *The mind as a scientific object* (pp. 247–50). Eds. Christina Erneling and David M. Johnson. Oxford: Oxford University Press.

Ey, Henri. 1978. *Consciousness: A phenomenological study of being conscious and becoming conscious*. Trans. John H. Flodsrom. Bloomington, Ind.: Indiana University Press. First published 1963.

Fajans, Jane. 1985. The person in social context: The social character of Baining 'psychology'. In *Person, self and experience: Exploring Pacific ethnopsychologies* (pp. 367–97). Eds. Geoffrey M. White and John Kirkpatrick. Berkeley, Calif.: University of California Press.

Feest, Uljana. 2003. Functional analysis and the autonomy of psychology. *Philosophy of Science*, **70**: 937–48.

Feinberg, Todd E. 2002. *Altered egos: How the brain creates the self*. Oxford: Oxford University Press.

Fernyough, Charles. 2004. More than a context for learning? The epistemic triangle and the dialogic mind. *Behavioral and Brain Sciences*, **27**: 104–5.

Flavell, John H., Frances L. Green, Eleanor R. Flavell and Nancy T. Lin. 1999. Development of children's knowledge about unconsciousness. *Child development*, **70**: 396–412.

Foster, Mary L. 1994. Symbolism: The foundation of culture. In *Companion encyclopedia of anthropology: Humanity, culture and social Life* (pp. 366–395). Ed. Tim Ingold. London: Routledge

Foucault, Michel. 1977. *Discipline and punish*. London: Allen Lane.

   1984. What is enlightenment? In *The Foucault reader*. Ed. Paul Rabinow. New York: Pantheon.

   2004. *The order of things*. London: Routledge. First published 1966.

Fragaszy, Dorothy and Susan Perry. 2003. Towards a biology of traditions. In *Traditions in nonhuman animals: Models and evidence* (pp. 1–32). Eds.

Dorothy Fragaszy and Susan Perry. Cambridge: Cambridge University Press.

Frankfurt, Harry G. 1988. Freedom of the will and the concept of the person. In *The importance of what we care about* (pp. 11–25). New York: Cambridge University Press.

Fraser, Ian. 2007. *Dialectics of the self: Transcending Charles Taylor.* Exeter: Imprint Academic.

Frith, Chris. 2007. *Making up the mind: How the brain creates our mental world.* Oxford: Blackwell.

Gallagher, Shaun. 2000. Philosophical conceptions of the self: Implications for cognitive science. *Trends in Cognitive Science,* 4: 14–21.

    2005. *How the body shapes the mind.* Oxford: Clarendon Press.

Gander, Eric M. 2003. *On our minds: How evolutionary psychology is reshaping the nature versus nurture debate.* Baltimore, Md.: Johns Hopkins.

Geertz, Clifford. 1983. 'From the native's point of view': On the nature of anthropological understanding. In *Local knowledge: Further essays in interpretive anthropology* (pp. 55–71). New York: Basic Books.

Gergely, György. 2004. The development of understanding self and agency. In *Blackwell handbook of childhood cognitive development* (pp. 26–46). Ed. Usha Goswami. Oxford: Blackwell.

Gergen, Kenneth J. 1988. If persons are texts. In *Hermeneutics and psychological theory* (pp. 28–51). Eds. Stanley B. Messer, Louis A. Sass and Robert L. Woolfolk. New Brunswick, NJ: Rutgers University Press.

    1999. *An invitation to social construction.* Thousand Oaks, Calif.: Sage.

Giddens, Anthony. 1979. *Central problems in social theory: Action, structure and contradiction in social analysis.* London: Macmillan.

    1991. *Modernity and self-identity: Self and society in the late modern age.* Palo Alto, Calif.: Stanford University Press.

Glas, Gerrit. 2004. Idem, ipse, and loss of the self. *Philosophy, Psychiatry and Psychology,* 10: 347–52.

Gordon, Robert M. 1998. The prior question: Do human primates have a theory of mind. *Behavioral and Brain Sciences,* 21: 120–1.

Gräslund, Bo. 2005. *Early humans and their world.* London: Routledge.

Gray, Jeffrey. 2004. Consciousness of self: The point of view. In *Consciousness: Creeping up on the hard problem* (pp. 261–6). Oxford: Oxford University Press.

Greenspan, Stanley I. and Stuart G. Shanker. 2006. *The first idea: How symbols, language, and intelligence evolved from our primate ancestors to modern humans.* Cambridge, Mass.: Da Capo Press.

Hacker, Peter M. S. 2001. Wittgenstein and the autonomy of humanistic understanding. In *Wittgenstein, theory and the arts* (pp. 39–74). Ed. Richard Allen and Malcolm Turvey. London: Routledge.

Hacking, Ian. 1995. *Rewriting the soul: Multiple personality and the science of memory.* Princeton, NJ: Princeton University Press.

    1999. *The social construction of what?* Cambridge, Mass: Harvard University Press.

Hall, Stuart. 2000. Who needs identity? In *Identity: A reader.* Eds. Paul du Gay, Jessica Evans and Peter Redman. London: Sage.

Hallam, Richard S. and Kieron O'Connor. 2002. A dialogical approach to obsessions. *Psychology and Psychotherapy: Theory, Research and Practice*, **75**: 333–48.

Hallowell, A. Irving. 1967. *Culture and experience*. New York: Schocken Books.

Harré, Rom. 1986. Emotion talk across times: Accidie and melancholy in the psychological context. In *The Social construction of emotions* (pp. 220–7). Ed. Rom Harré. Oxford: Blackwell.

1997a. Forward to Aristotle: The case for a hybrid ontology. *Journal for the Theory of Social Behaviour*, **27**: 173–91.

1997b. Pathological autobiographies. *Philosophy, Psychiatry, and Psychology*, **4**: 99–109.

1998. *The singular self*, London: Sage Publications.

2002. Public sources of the personal mind. *Theory and Psychology*, **12**: 611–23.

2005. Transcending the emergence/reduction distinction: The case of biology. *Royal Institute of Philosophy Supplements*, **80**: 1–20.

Harré, Rom and Luk van Langenhove. 1992. Varieties of positioning. *Journal for the Theory of Social Behaviour*, **20**: 393–407.

1999. *Positioning theory: Moral contexts of intentional action*. Malden, Mass.: Blackwell.

Harris, Grace G. 1989. Concepts of individual, self, and person in description and analysis. *American Anthropologist*, **91**: 599–612.

Haskell, Robert E. 1993. Vico and Jaynes: Neurocultural and cognitive operations in the origin of consciousness. *New Vico Studies*, **11**: 24–51.

Hawkes, Terence. 1972. *Metaphor*. London: Methuen.

Hayes, Steven C., Dermot Barnes-Holmes and Bryan Roche. 2001. *Relational frame theory*. New York: Kluwer/Plenum.

Heelas, Paul and Andrew Lock. 1981. *Indigenous psychologies: The anthropology of the self*. London: Academic Press.

Held, Barbara S. 2002. What follows? Mind dependence, fallibility and transcendence according to (strong) constructionism's realist and quasi-realist critics. *Theory and Psychology*, **12**: 651–69.

Hermans, Hubert. 2001. The dialogical self: Toward a theory of personal and cultural positioning. *Culture and Psychology*, **7**: 243–81.

Hermans, Hubert J. M. and Harry J. G. Kempen. 1993. *The dialogical self: Meaning as movement*. San Diego, Calif.: Academic Press.

Heyes, Celia M. 1998. Theory of mind in non-human primates. *Behavioral and Brain Sciences*, **21**: 101–48.

Hirst, Paul. 1979. *On law and ideology*. Basingstoke: Macmillan.

Hobson, R. Peter. 2000. The grounding of symbols: A social developmental account. In *Children's reasoning and the mind* (pp. 11–35). Eds. Peter Mitchell and Kevin Riggs. Hove: Psychology Press.

Holden, Constance. 2004. The origin of speech. *Science*, **303** (5662): 1316–19.

Holland, Dorothy. 1997. Selves as cultured: As told by an anthropologist who lacks a soul. In *Self and identity: Fundamental issues* (pp. 160–90). Eds. Richard D. Ashmore and Lee Jussim. Oxford: Oxford University Press.

Hood, Thomas. 1900. *The poetical works of Thomas Hood*. London: George Routledge.

Horner, Victoria and Andrew Whiten. 2005. Causal knowledge and imitation/ emulation switching in chimpanzees (Pan troglodytes) and children (Homo sapiens). *Animal Cognition*, **8**: 164–81.

Howie, Dorothy and Michael Peters. 1996. Positioning theory: Vygotsky, Wittgenstein and social construction psychology. *Journal for the Theory of Social Behaviour*, **26**: 51–64.

Humphrey, Nicholas. 1993. *The inner eye*. London: Vintage.

  2002. *The mind made flesh*. Oxford: Oxford University Press.

Hundert, Ed J. 1997. The European enlightenment and the history of the self. In *Rewriting the self: Histories from the Renaissance to the present* (pp. 72–83). Ed. Roy Porter. London: Routledge.

Hutto, Daniel D. 2008. *Folk psychological narratives: The sociocultural basis of understanding reasons*. Cambridge, Mass.: MIT Press.

Ingold, Tim. 1994. Introduction to humanity. In *Companion encyclopedia of anthropology: Humanity, culture and social life* (pp. 3–13). Ed. Tim Ingold. London: Routledge.

Jackendoff, Ray. 2002. *Foundations of language: Brain, meaning, grammar, evolution*. Oxford: Oxford University Press.

Jacob, Pierre. 2003. Intentionality. In *The Stanford encyclopedia of philosophy* (Fall 2003 Edition). Ed. Edward N. Zalta. Available online at http://plato.stanford.edu/archives/fall2003/entries/intentionality.

James, William. 1890. *The principles of psychology. Vol. I*. London: Macmillan.

  1961. *Psychology: Briefer course*. Ed. Gordon Allport. New York: Harper & Row. First published 1892.

Jaynes, Julian. 1976. *The origin of consciousness in the breakdown of the bicameral mind*. London: Allen Lane.

Johnson, David M. 2005. Mind, brain and the upper paleolithic. In *The mind as a scientific object* (pp. 499–510). Eds. Christina E. Erneling and David M. Johnson. Oxford: Oxford University Press.

Jones, Raya A. 1997. The presence of self in the person: Reflexive positioning and personal construct psychology. *Journal for the Theory of Social Behaviour*, **27**: 453–71.

Jopling, David A. 1997. A 'self of selves?' In *The conceptual self in context: Culture, experience, self-understanding* (pp. 249–67). Eds. Ulric Neisser and David A. Jopling. New York: Cambridge University Press.

  2000. *Self-knowledge and the self*. New York: Routledge.

Josephs, Ingrid E. 1998. Constructing one's self in the city of the silent: Dialogue, symbols, and the role of 'as-if' in self-development. *Human Development*, **41**: 180–95.

Kaye, Kenneth. 1982. *The mental and social life of babies: How parents create persons*. Chicago, Ill.: University of Chicago Press.

Kelly, George. 1955. *The psychology of personal constructs*. New York: Norton.

Kendall, Gavin and Gary Wickham. 1999. *Using Foucault's methods*. London: Sage.

Kihlstrom, John F., Lori A. Marchese-Foster, and Stanley B. Klein. 1997. Situating the self in interpersonal space. In *The conceptual self in context: Culture, experience, self-understanding* (pp. 154–75). Eds. Ulric Neisser and David A. Jopling. New York: Cambridge University Press.

Kinsbourne, Marcel. 2005. A continuum of self-consciousness that emerges in phylogeny and ontogeny. In *The missing link in cognition* (pp. 142–56). Eds. Herbert S. Terrace and Janet Metcalfe. Oxford: Oxford University Press.

Kirsch, Irving. 1998. Volition as a believed-in imagining. In *Believed-in imaginings: The narrative construction of reality* (pp. 157–68). Eds. Joseph H. De Rivera and Theodore R. Sarbin. Oxford: Blackwell.

Knight, Chris. 2000. Play as a precursor of phonology and syntax. In *The evolutionary emergence of language: social function and the origins of linguistic form* (pp. 99–129). Eds. Chris Knight, Michael Studdert-Kennedy and James Hurford. Cambridge: Cambridge University Press.

Kuhn, Deanna. 2000. Theory of mind, metacognition, and reasoning: A lifespan perspective. In *Children's reasoning and the mind* (pp. 301–26). Eds. Peter Mitchell and Kevin Riggs. Hove: Psychology Press.

Lakoff, George. 1997. The internal structure of the self. In *The conceptual self in context: Culture, experience, self-understanding* (pp. 92–113). Eds. Ulric Neisser and David A. Jopling. New York: Cambridge University Press.

Lakoff, George and Mark Johnson. 1980. *Metaphors we live by*. Chicago, Ill.: University of Chicago Press.

Landrine, Hope. 1992. Clinical implications of cultural differences: The referential versus the indexical self. *Clinical Psychology Review*, **12** (4): 401–15.

Langenhove, Luk van and Rom Harré. 1999. Reflexive positioning: autobiography. In *Positioning theory: Moral contexts of intentional action*. Eds. Rom Harré and Luk van Langenhove. Malden, Mass.: Blackwell.

Langer, Ellen J. 1989. *Mindfulness*. Reading, Mass.: Addison-Wesley.

Leahey, Thomas. 2003. Mind as a scientific object: A historical-philosophical exploration. In *Mind as a scientific object* (pp. 35–78). Eds. Christina E. Erneling and David M. Johnson. Oxford: Oxford University Press.

Leary, Mark R. 2007. *The curse of the self: Self-awareness, egotism, and the quality of human life*. Oxford: Oxford University Press.

LeDoux, Joseph. 2002. *Synaptic self: How our brains become who we are*. New York: Penguin, Viking.

LePan, Don. 1989. *The cognitive revolution in western culture*. London: Macmillan.

Leudar, Ivan and Philip Thomas. 2000. *Voices of reason, voices of insanity: Studies of verbal hallucinations*. London: Routledge.

Lévi-Strauss, Claude. 1963. *Structural anthropology*. Trans. Claire Jacobson and Brooke Grundfest Schoepf. New York: Basic Books.

Levy, Robert I. 1989. The quest for mind in different times and different places. In *Social history and issues in human consciousness* (pp. 3–28). Eds. Andrew E. Barnes and Peter N. Stearns. New York: New York University Press.

Lewis, C. S. 1960. *Studies in words*. Cambridge: Cambridge University Press.

Libet, Benjamin. 2000. Do we have free will? In *The volitional brain: Towards a neuroscience of free will* (pp. 47–58). Eds. Benjamin Libet, Anthony Freeman and Keith Sutherland. Exeter: Imprint Academic.

Lieberman, Phillip. 1994. The origins and evolution of language. In *Companion encyclopedia of anthropology: Humanity, culture and social life* (pp. 108–132). Ed. Tim Ingold. London: Routledge.

Little, Todd, Patricia H. Hawley, Christopher C. Henrich and Katherine W. Marsland. 2002. Three views of the agentic self: A developmental synthesis. In *Handbook of self-regulation research* (pp. 389–404). Eds. Edward L. Deci and Richard M. Ryan. Rochester, NY: University of Rochester Press.

Locke, John. 1959. *An essay concerning human understanding.* Ed. and Abr. Raymond Wilburn. London: Dent & Sons. First published 1700.

Lodge, David. 2003. *Consciousness and the novel.* London: Penguin Books.

Logan, Richard D. 1987. Historical change in prevailing sense of self. In *Self and identity: Psychosocial perspectives* (pp. 13–26). Eds. Krysia Yardley and Terry Honess. Chichester: John Wiley.

Loevinger, Jane. 1976. *Ego development.* San Francisco, Calif.: Jossey Bass.

Lukes, Steven. 1973. *Individualism.* Oxford: Blackwell.

  1985. Conclusion. In *The category of the person: Anthropology, philosophy, history* (pp. 282–301). Eds. Michael Carrithers, Steven Collins and Steven Lukes. Cambridge: Cambridge University Press.

Lyons, John O. 1978. *The invention of the self: The hinge of consciousness in the eighteenth century.* Carbondale, Ill.: Southern Illinois University Press.

Macdonald, Paul S. 2003. *History of the concept of mind.* Aldershot: Ashgate.

MacIntyre, Alasdair. 1981. *After virtue.* Notre Dame, Ind.: University of Notre Dame Press.

MacKinnon, Richard C. 1997. Punishing the persona: Correctional strategies for the virtual offender. In *Virtual culture: Identity and communication in cybersociety* (pp. 206–35). Ed. Steven Jones. Thousand Oaks, Calif.: Sage.

MacWhinney, Brian. 2004. Language evolution and human development. In *Origins of the social mind: Evolutionary psychology and child development* (pp. 383–410). Eds. Bruce J. Ellis and David F. Bjorklund. New York: Guilford Press.

Maddocks, Fiona. 2001. *Hildegard of Bingen.* London: Headline Publishing.

Malle, Bertram F. 2004. *How the mind explains behavior: Folk explanations, meaning, and social interaction.* Cambridge, Mass.: Bradford Books, MIT Press.

  2006. Of windmills and straw men: Folk assumptions of mind and action. In *Does consciousness cause behavior?* (pp. 207–31). Eds. Susan Pockett, William P. Banks and Shaun Gallagher. Cambridge, Mass.: MIT Press.

Mallon, Ronald and Stephen P. Stich. 2000. The odd couple: The compatibility of social construction and evolutionary psychology. *Philosophy of Science,* **67**: 133–54.

Mancuso, James C. and Theodore R. Sarbin. 1983. The self-narrative in the enactment of roles. In *Studies in social identity* (pp. 233–53). Eds. Theodore R. Sarbin and Karl E. Scheibe. Westport, Conn.: Praeger.

Manicas, Peter T. 2006. *A realist philosophy of science: Explanation and understanding.* Cambridge: Cambridge University Press.

Marková, Ivana. 1987. *Human awareness.* London: Hutchinson.

  2000. The individual and society in psychological theory. *Theory and psychology,* **10**: 107–16.

2003. *Dialogicality and social representations*. Cambridge: Cambridge University Press.

Marks, Isaac. 1987. *Fears and phobias*. Oxford: Oxford University Press.

Markus, Hazel. 1977. Self-schemata and processing information about the self. *Journal of Personality and Social Psychology*, **35**: 63–78.

1986. Possible selves. *American Psychologist*, **41**: 954–69.

Markus, Hazel R. and Shinobu Kitayama. 2002. Models of agency: Sociocultural diversity in the construction of action. In *The annual Nebraska symposium on motivation: Cross-cultural differences in perspectives on self* (V. 49) (pp. 1–57). Eds. Virginia Murphy-Berman and John J. Berman. Lincoln, Nebr.: University of Nebraska Press.

Martin, Jack and Jeff H. Sugarman. 2003. A theory of personhood for psychology. In *About psychology: Essays at the crossroads of history, theory, and philosophy* (pp. 73–87). Eds. Darryl B. Hill and Michael Kral. Albany, NY: SUNY Press.

Martin, Raymond, and John Barresi. 2000. *Naturalization of the soul: Self and personal identity in the eighteenth century*. London: Routledge.

2006. *The rise and fall of soul and self: An intellectual history of personal identity*. New York: Columbia University Press.

Martin, Rux. 1988. Truth, power, self: An interview with Michel Foucault, October 25 1982. In Michel Foucault, *Technologies of the self: A seminar with Michel Foucault* (pp. 9–15). Eds. Luther H. Martin, Huck Gutman and Patrick H. Hutton. Amherst, Mass.: University of Massachusetts Press.

Mascolo, Michael F. and Kurt W. Fischer. 1998. The development of self through the coordination of component systems. In *Self-awareness: Its nature and development* (pp. 332–83). Eds. Michael Ferrari and Robert J. Sternberg. New York: Guilford Press.

Maturana, Humberto and Francisco Varela. 1980. Autopoiesis and cognition: The realization of the living. In *Boston Studies in the Philosophy of Science* Vol. 42. Eds. Robert S. Cohen and Marx W. Wartofsky. Dordrecht: D. Reidel Publishing Co.

Mauss, Marcel. 1985. A category of the human mind: The notion of person: the notion of self. In *The category of the person* (pp. 1–25). Eds. Malcolm Carrithers, Steven Collins and Steven Lukes. Cambridge: Cambridge University Press. First published 1938.

McAdams, Dan P. 1996. Personality, modernity, and the storied self: A contemporary framework for studying persons. *Psychological Inquiry*, **7**: 295–321.

McCall, Catherine. 1990. *Concepts of person: An analysis of concepts of person, self, and human being*. Aldershot: Avebury.

Mead, George H. 1962. *Mind, self and society*. Chicago, Ill.: University of Chicago Press. First published 1934.

Melchior-Bonnet, Sabine. 2002. *The mirror: A history*. Trans. Katherine H. Jewett. London: Routledge.

Melser, Derek. 2004. *The act of thinking*. Cambridge, Mass.: MIT Press.

Merleau-Ponty, Maurice. 1966. *Phenomenology of perception*. London: Routledge Kegan Paul.

Messari, Sophia and Richard Hallam. 2003. CBT for psychosis: A qualitative analysis of client's accounts. *British Journal of Clinical Psychology*, **42**: 171–88.

Michel, A. Alexandra and Stanton E. F. Wortham. 2002. Clearing away the self. *Theory and Psychology*, **12**: 625–50.

Millikan, Ruth. 2004. Existence proof for a viable externalism. In *The externalist challenge: New studies on cognition and intentionality* (pp. 227–38). Ed. Richard Schantz. New York: Walter de Gruyter.

Mineka, Susan and Michael Cook. 1988. Social learning and the acquisition of snake fear. In *Social learning: Psychological and biological perspectives* (pp. 51–74). Eds. Thomas R. Zentall and Bennett G. Galef. Mahwah, NJ: Lawrence Erlbaum Associates.

Mitchell, Robert W. 1994. Multiplicities of self. In *Self-awareness in animals and humans: Developmental perspectives* (pp. 81–107). Eds. Sue Taylor Parker, Robert W. Mitchell and Maria L. Boccia. New York: Cambridge University Press.

Mithen, Steven. 2000. Mind, brain and material culture: an archaeological perspective. In *Evolution and the human mind: Modularity, language and meta-cognition*. Eds. Peter Carruthers and Andrew Chamberlain. Cambridge: Cambridge University Press.

Moeller, Hans-Georg. 2006. *Luhmann explained: From souls to systems*. Chicago, Ill.: Open Court.

Mühlhäusler, Peter and Rom Harré. 1993. *Pronouns and people*. Oxford: Blackwell.

Neisser, Ulric. 1997. Concepts and self-concepts. In *The conceptual self in context: Culture, experience, self-understanding* (pp. 3–12). Eds. Ulric Neisser and David A. Jopling. New York: Cambridge University Press.

Nelson, Katherine. 2001. From the experiencing I to the continuing me. In *The self in time: Developmental perspectives* (pp. 15–34). Eds. Chris Moore, Karen Lemon and Karen Skene. Mahwah, NJ: Lawrence Erlbaum Associates.

  2003. Self and social functions: Individual autobiographical memory and collective memory. *Memory*, **11**: 125–36.

  2004. Evolution and development of human memory systems. In *Origins of the social mind: Evolutionary psychology and child development* (pp. 354–82). Eds. Bruce J. Ellis and David F. Bjorklund. New York: Guilford Press.

  2005. Emerging levels of consciousness in early human development. In *The missing link in cognition: Origins of self-reflective consciousness* (pp. 116–41). Eds. Herbert S. Terrace and Janet Metcalfe. New York: Oxford University Press.

Nichols, Shaun. 2008. Folk psychology. In *Encylopedia of cognitive science*. London: Nature Publishing Group. Available online at www.dingo.sbs. arizona.edu/~snichols/Papers/FolkPsychologyECS.pdf (accessed 28 December 2008).

Nienkamp, Jean. 2001. *Internal rhetorics: Toward a history and theory of self-persuasion*. Carbondale, Ill.: Southern Illinois University Press.

Nightingale, David J. and John Cromby. 1999. Reconstructing social constructionism. In *Social constructionist psychology: A critical analysis of theory and practice* (pp. 207–24). Eds. David J. Nightingale and John Cromby. Buckingham: Open University Press.

Nisbett, Richard and Timothy D. Wilson. 1977. Telling more than we can know: Verbal reports on mental processes. *Psychological Review*, **84**: 231–59.

O'Connor, Kieron P. and Richard S. Hallam. 2000. Sorcery of the self: The magic of you. *Theory and Psychology*, **10**: 238–64.

O'Connor, Kieron, Frederick Aardema and Marie-Claude Pelissier. 2005. *Beyond reasonable doubt: Reasoning processes in obsessive-compulsive disorder and related disorders*. Chichester: John Wiley.

Oshima-Takane, Yuriko. 1999. The learning of first and second person pronouns in English. In *Language, logic, and concept: Essays in memory of John Macnamara* (pp. 373–409). Eds. Ray Jackendoff, Paul Bloom and Karen Wynn. Cambridge, Mass.: MIT Press.

Parfit, Derek. 1984. *Reasons and persons*. Oxford: Oxford University Press.

Parker, Ian. 1992. *Discourse dynamics: Critical analysis for social and individual psychology*. London: Routledge.

Parker, Sue T., Robert W. Mitchell and Maria L. Boccia, Eds. 2006. *Self-awareness in animals and humans: Developmental perspectives*. Cambridge: Cambridge University Press.

Pennisi, Elizabeth. 2004. The first language? *Science*, **303**: 1319–20.

Petitto, Laura A. 1987. On the autonomy of language and gesture: Evidence from the acquisition of personal pronouns in American Sign Language. *Cognition*, **27**: 1–52.

Petrarca, Francesco. 1992. *Secretum (Il mio segreto)*. Milan: Tursia.

Pico della Mirandola, Giovanni. 1960. *Oration on the dignity of man*. Washington, DC: H. Regnery.

Plotkin, Henry. 2002. *The imagined world made real: Towards a natural science of culture*. London: Allen Lane.

Polkinghorne, Donald. 2004. Ricoeur, narrative and personal identity. In *Changing conceptions of psychological life* (pp. 27–48). Eds. Michael Chandler, Chris Lalonde and Cynthia Lightfoot. Mahwah, NJ: Lawrence Erlbaum Associates.

Popper, Karl R. and John C. Eccles. 1977. *The self and its brain*. New York: Springer.

Potter, Jonathan and Margaret Wetherell. 1987. *Discourse and social psychology*. London: Sage.

Potter, Jonathan and Derek Edwards. 2003. Rethinking cognition: On Coulter on discourse and mind. *Human Studies*, **26**: 165–81.

Povinelli, Daniel J. and Jochen Barth. 2005. Reinterpreting behavior: A human specialization? *Behavioral and Brain Sciences*, **28**: 712–13.

Prinz, Wolfgang. 2006. Free will as a social institution. In *Does consciousness cause behavior?* (pp. 257–76). Eds. Susan Pockett, William P. Banks and Shaun Gallagher. Cambridge, Mass.: MIT Press.

Rabinow, Paul and Nikolas Rose. 2003. Introduction: Foucault today. In *The essential Foucault* (pp. vii–xxxxv). Eds. Paul Rabinow and Nikolas Rose. New York: The New Press.

Ramachandran, Vilayanur. 2006. *Mirror neurons and the brain in a vat*. Available online at www.edge.org/3rd_culture/ramachandran06/ramachandran06_index.html (accessed 28 December 2008).

Ratcliffe, Matthew. 2006. *Rethinking commonsense psychology: A critique of folk psychology, theory of mind, and simulation*. Basingstoke: Palgrave Macmillan.

Read, Kenneth E. 1955. Morality and the concept of the person among the Gahuku-Gama. *Oceania*, **25**: 233–82.

Reddy, Michael J. 1993. The conduit metaphor: A case of frame conflict in our language about language. In *Metaphor and thought* (pp. 164–201). Ed. Andrew Ortony. Cambridge: Cambridge University Press. First published 1979.

Reddy, Vasudevi and Paul Morris. 2004. Participants don't need theories: Knowing minds in engagement. *Theory and Psychology*, **14**: 647–66.

Revonsuo, Antti. 2005. *Inner presence: Consciousness as a biological phenomenon*. Cambridge, Mass.: MIT Press.

Richards, Graham. 1989. *On psychological language and the physiomorphic basis of human nature*. London: Routledge.

Ricoeur, Paul. 1991. Narrative identity. *Philosophy Today*, **35**: 73–81.

Rizzolatti, Giacomo, Luciano Fadiga, Vittorio Gallese and Leonardo Fogassi. 1996. Premotor cortex and the recognition of motor actions. *Cognitive Brain Research*, **3**: 131–41.

Roessler, Johannes. 2003. Intentional action and self-awareness. In *Agency and self-awareness: Issues in philosophy and psychology* (pp. 383–405). Eds. Johannes Roessler and Naomi Elan, New York: Oxford University Press.

Rorty, Amélie O. 1988. *Mind in action: Essays in the philosophy of mind*. Boston, Mass: Beacon Press.

Rose, Nikolas S. 1990. *Governing the soul: The shaping of the private self*. London: Routledge.

    1998. *Inventing our selves: Psychology, power, and personhood*. Cambridge: Cambridge University Press.

Ryle, Gilbert. 1949. *The concept of mind*. London: Hutchinson.

Sarbin, Theodore. 1968. Ontology recapitulates philology: The mythic nature of anxiety. *American Psychologist*, **23**: 411–18.

    1998. Believed in imaginings: A narrative approach. In *Believed-in imaginings: The narrative construction of reality* (pp. 15–30). Eds. Joseph de Rivera and Theodore R. Sarbin. Washington, DC: APA Publications.

Sarbin, Theodore R. and Karl E. Scheibe. 1983. A model of social identity. In *Studies in social identity* (pp. 5–28). Eds. Theodore R. Sarbin and Karl E. Scheibe. New York: Praeger.

Sartre, Jean-Paul. 1992. *The transcendence of the ego*. New York: Hill & Wang. First published 1936.

Sass, Louis A. 1997. The consciousness machine: Self and subjectivity in schizophrenia and modern culture. In *The conceptual self in context: Culture, experience, self-understanding* (pp. 203–32). Eds. Ulric Neisser and David A. Jopling. New York: Cambridge University Press.

Savage-Rumbaugh, Sue, Stuart Shanker and Talbot J. Taylor. 1998. *Apes, language and the human mind*. New York: Oxford University Press.

Sawyer, R. Keith. 2003a. Non-reductive individualism. Part II: Social causation. *Philosophy of the Social Sciences*, **33**: 202–24.

2003b. *Emergence and complexity: A new approach to social systems theory*. Paper presented at the annual meeting of the American Sociological Association. Atlanta, Ga. Available online at www.allacademic.com/meta/p106832_index.html (accessed 21 July 2008).

2004. The mechanisms of emergence. *Philosophy of the Social Sciences*, **34**: 260–82.

Scheibe, Karl E. 1998. *Self studies: The psychology of self and identity*. New York: Praeger.

Seale, Clive. 1999. *The quality of qualitative research*. London: Sage.

Sebanz, Natalie. 2007. The emergence of self: Sensing action through joint agency. *Journal of Consciousness Studies*, **14**: 234–51.

Sedikides, Constantine and John J. Skowronski. 2003. Evolution of the symbolic self. In *Handbook of self and identity* (pp. 595–609). Eds. Mark R. Leary, June P. Tangney. New York: Guilford Press.

Shear, Jonathan. 1999. Experiential clarification of the problem of self. In *Models of the self* (pp. 401–20). Eds. Shaun Gallagher and Jonathan Shear. Exeter: Imprint Academic.

Shotter, John. 1997. The social construction of our inner selves. *Journal of Constructivist Psychology*, **10**: 7–24.

2001. Towards a third revolution in psychology: From inner mental representations to dialogically structured social practices. In *Jerome Bruner: Language, culture and self* (pp. 167–83). Eds. David Bakhurst and Stuart G. Shanker. London: Sage.

Siegel, Jerrold. 2005. *The idea of the self*. Cambridge: Cambridge University Press.

Skinner, B. F. 1957. *Verbal learning*. New York: Appleton-Century-Crofts.

1976. *About behaviorism*. London: Vintage Books.

Smith, Brewster M. 2002. Self and identity in historical/sociocultural context: 'Perspectives on selfhood' revisited. In *Self and identity: Personal, social, and symbolic* (pp. 229–43). Eds. Yoshihisa Kashima, Margaret Foddy and Michael J. Platow. Mahwah, NJ: Lawrence Erlbaum Associates.

Sodian, Beate. 2006. Theory-of-mind: The case for conceptual development. In *Young children's cognitive development: Interrelationships among executive functioning, working memory, verbal ability, and theory of mind* (pp. 95–130). Eds. Wolfgang Schneider, Ruth Schumann-Hengsteler and Beate Sodian. Mahwah, NJ: Lawrence Erlbaum Associates.

Sperber, Dan. 1996. *Explaining culture: A naturalistic approach*. Oxford: Blackwell.

Spiro, Melford E. 1993. Is the Western conception of the person 'peculiar' within the context of world cultures? *Ethos*, **21**: 107–53.

Sprague, Elmer. 1999. *Persons and their minds*. Boulder, Col.: Westview Press.

Sterelny, Kim. 2004. Externalism, epistemic artefacts and the extended mind. In *The externalist challenge: New studies on cognition and intentionality* (pp. 239–54). Ed. Richard Schantz. New York: De Gruyter.

Stich, Stephen and Shaun Nichols. 2002. Folk psychology. In *The Blackwell guide to philosophy of mind* (pp. 235–55). Eds. Stephen P. Stich and Ted A. Warfield. Oxford: Blackwell.

Strawson, Peter F. 1959. *Individuals: An essay in descriptive metaphysics*. London: Methuen.

Studdert-Kennedy, Michael. 2000. Evolutionary implications of the particulate principle: Imitation and dissociation of phonetic forms from semantic function. In *The evolutionary emergence of language: social function and the origins of linguistic form* (pp. 161–76). Eds. Chris Knight, Michael Studdert-Kennedy and James Hurford. Cambridge: Cambridge University Press.

Suddendorf, Thomas and Andrew Whiten. 2003. Reinterpreting the mentality of apes. In *From mating to mentality: Evaluating evolutionary psychology* (pp. 173–96). Eds. Julie Fitness and Kim Sterelny. New York: Psychology Press.

Tauber, Alfred I. 2005. The reflexive project: Reconstructing the moral agent. *History of the Human Sciences*, **18**: 49–75.

Taylor, Charles. 1977. What is human agency? In *The self: Psychological and philosophical issues* (pp. 103–35). Ed. Theodore Mischel. Oxford: Blackwell.

　1988. Wittgenstein, empiricism, and the question of the 'inner': Commentary on Kenneth Gergen. In *Hermeneutics and psychological theory: Interpretive perspectives on personality, psychotherapy, and psychopathology* (pp. 52–61). Eds. Stanley B. Messer, Louis A. Sass and Robert L. Woolfolk. New Brunswick, NJ: Rutgers University Press.

　1989. *Sources of the self: The making of the modern identity*. Cambridge, Mass.: Harvard University Press.

Teichert, Dieter. 2004. Narrative, identity and the self. *Journal of Consciousness Studies*, **11**: 175–91.

Terrace, Herbert S. 2005. Metacognition and the evolution of language. In *The missing link in cognition: Origins of self-reflective consciousness* (pp. 84–115). Eds. Herbert S. Terrace and Janet Metcalfe. New York: Oxford University Press.

Tollefsen, Deborah P. 2002. Collective intentionality and the social sciences. *Philosophy of the social sciences*, **32**: 25–50.

Tomasello, Michael, Malinder Carpenter, Josep Call, Tanya Behne and Henrike Moll. 2005. Understanding and sharing intentions: The origins of cultural cognition. *Behavioral and Brain Sciences*, **28**: 675–735.

Tulving, Endel. 2005. Episodic memory and autonoesis: Uniquely human? In *The missing link in cognition: Origins of self-reflective consciousness* (pp. 3–56). Eds. Herbert S. Terrace and Janet Metcalfe. New York: Oxford University Press.

Velmans, Max. 2000. *Understanding consciousness*. London: Routledge.

Vico, Giambattista. 2000. *New science*. 3rd edn. Trans. David Marsh. Ed. Anthony Grafton. London: Penguin Classics. First published 1725.

Vovelle, Michel. 1990. *Ideologies and mentalities*. Trans. E. O'Flaherty. Cambridge: Polity Press.

Vygotsky, Lev S. 1962. *Thought and language*. New York: Wiley.

Warner, C. Terry. 1986. Anger and similar delusions. In *The social construction of emotions* (pp. 135–66). Ed. Rom Harré. Oxford: Blackwell.

Webb, Keith. 1995. *An Introduction to problems in the philosophy of social sciences*. London: Continuum/Pinter.

Wegner, Daniel M. 2002. *The illusion of conscious will*. Cambridge, Mass.: MIT Press.

Weintraub, Karl J. 1978. *The value of the individual: Self and circumstance in autobiography.* Chicago, Ill.: University of Chicago Press.

White, Hayden V. 1978. Foucault decoded. In *Tropics of discourse: Essays in cultural criticism* (pp. 230–60). Baltimore, Md: Johns Hopkins University Press.

Whiten, Andrew and Richard W. Byrne. 1997. *Machiavellian intelligence II: Extensions and evaluations.* New York: Cambridge University Press.

Williams, Malcolm. 1999. *Science and social science: An introduction.* London: Routledge.

Williams, Meredith. 1985. Wittgenstein's rejection of scientific psychology. *Journal for the Theory of Social Behaviour,* **15**: 203–23.

Williams, Richard. 1992. The human context of agency. *American Psychologist,* **47**: 752–60.

Wittgenstein, Ludwig. 1953. *Philosophical investigations.* Oxford: Blackwell.

   1980. *Remarks on the philosophy of psychology. Vol. I.* Eds. Gertrude E. M. Anscombe and Georg H. von Wright. Trans. G. E. M. Anscombe. Volume II. Eds Georg H. von Wright and Heikki Nyman. Trans. C. Grant Luckhardt and Maximilian A. E. Aue. Oxford: Blackwell.

Young, Jeff, Janet S. Klosko and Marjorie E. Weishaar. 2003. *Schema therapy: A practitioner's guide.* New York: Guilford Press.

Zahavi, Dan. 2005. *Subjectivity and selfhood: Investigating the first-person perspective.* Cambridge, Mass.: Bradford Books, MIT Press.

Zelazo, Philip and Jessica Sommerville. 2001. Levels of consciousness of the self in time. In *The Self in time: Developmental perspectives* (pp. 229–53). Eds. Chris Moore, Karen Lemmon and Karen Skene. New York: Lawrence Erlbaum Associates.

Index